Praise for BURY US UPSIDE DOWN

"With its great in-the-cockpit stories of the first jet-fighter combat forward air controllers, *Bury Us Upside Down* is an incredible account of how it all started. The reader will feel the G forces, the strain of avoiding ground fire, the satisfaction of a completed rescue, the black humor of combat-hardened pilots, and the effects on the families of those who didn't return. But most of all the reader will feel proud that America can produce such men."
—MARK BERENT,
combat pilot and author of the bestselling Rolling Thunder series

"Retired Maj. Gen. Don Shepperd . . . and writer Rick Newman paint a complete picture of one of the most harrowing assignments pilots undertook during the Vietnam War. . . . [*Bury Us Upside Down*] makes current-day battle watchers think twice about the risk and sacrifice pilots—and any soldier, airman, sailor, or marine—encounter when they put on the nation's uniform."
—*National Guard* magazine

"Rip that Nintendo out of your kid's hands and hand him *Bury Us Upside Down*! This outstanding book will give him insight into what real aerial combat, flown by real heroes, is like. Undoubtedly the best book of its type, . . . [*Bury Us Upside Down*] is the truth writ bold and simple—the story of the men who fought the war flying the toughest missions imaginable, and their families. It is a book of heroes, and just reading it gives you insight into what a true hero feels."
—WALTER J. BOYNE,
bestselling author of over fifty aviation books and former director of the National Air and Space Museum, Smithsonian Institution

"Journalist Rick Newman and former Misty pilot Don Shepperd bring the reader into the bases, bars, and jets where the pilots lived and worked, let off steam, and came to terms with a war against a foe that would not give up. . . . Readers with a sure grasp of the war will lap up every assault and acronym. At heart, though, this is a story of heroes, fliers, and families."
—*Milwaukee Journal Sentinel*

"*Bury Us Upside Down* is a superb book about pilots in a tough mission in a tough war. It is perhaps the best view of aerial combat ever written. You are put in the cockpit with the pilots who flew these missions as it happens. The result is mesmerizing. When you pick up this book, you'll have trouble putting it down, and you will never forget its powerful testimonies of combat aviators."
—Gen. Ronald Fogleman, USAF (Ret.), former Air Force chief of staff

BURY US UPSIDE DOWN

BURY US UPSIDE DOWN ★

The Misty Pilots and the Secret Battle for the Ho Chi Minh Trail

RICK NEWMAN and DON SHEPPERD

FOREWORD BY
Senator John McCain

BALLANTINE BOOKS / NEW YORK

2007 Presidio Press Trade Paperback Edition

Published in the United States by Presidio Press, an imprint of The Random House
Publishing Group, a division of Random House, Inc., New York.

PRESIDIO PRESS and colophon are trademarks of Random House, Inc.

Originally published in hardcover in the United States by Presidio Press, an imprint of
The Random House Publishing Group, a division of Random House, Inc., in 2006.

Insert photographs courtesy of The United States Air Force and John Haltigan.

LIBRARY OF CONGRESS CATALOGING-IN-PUBLICATION DATA
Newman, Rick
Bury us upside down : the Misty pilots and the secret battle for the Ho Chi Minh Trail /
Rick Newman and Don Shepperd.
p.   cm.
Includes bibliographical references and index.
ISBN 978-0-345-46538-2
1. Vietnamese Conflict, 1961–1975—Aerial operations, American.   2. Ho Chi Minh Trail.
3. Aerial observation (Military science).   4. Air pilots, military—United States.
I. Shepperd, Don.   II. Title.
DS558.8N49 2006
959.704'348—dc22   2005048175

Printed in the United States of America

www.presidiopress.com

4   6   8   9   7   5

Book design by Casey Hampton

FOREWORD

By Senator John McCain

Wars are painful experiences, not only for the soldiers, sailors, airmen, and Marines who take part, but also for their families and the countries that send them. It has become all too common to focus exclusively on combat and the stories of those who fight, so it is often easy to forget war's tragic effects—on the families of those involved and on the innocents—the citizens on both sides who also bear the burden. The Vietnam War, America's longest and arguably most painful war, was a tragedy for two countries, theirs and ours.

Bury Us Upside Down is a unique book because it covers the full gamut of warfare—not only the stories of those at war, but of their families, their countries, their governments, and their politicians. In short, it is a well-researched book about warriors and the effects war has on a country. I have seen these effects of war on my family, on my nation, and ultimately on myself. Several of the men in this book were my companions in prison. Through their eyes you also will experience these effects.

Though I entered the theater earlier, my Vietnam story truly begins on October 26, 1967. In a few moments my life and future were inexorably altered as my aircraft was hit by a Soviet-made surface-to-air missile. While ejecting from the stricken aircraft, I broke both arms and a leg, and soon found myself surviving for over five years in the infamous "Hanoi Hilton" prison in downtown Hanoi.

It was during my years as a prisoner of war that I first encountered the "Misty" warriors featured in the following pages. Solitary confinement, denial of medical attention, and torture became the standard treatment for American POWs. As I endured this new way of life, I met Maj. Bob Craner. While I was in solitary confinement, Bob occupied the cell next to mine. We became acquainted through the tap code described later in the book. This clandestine means of communication, performed by tapping on the walls of our cells, enabled us to become acquainted. Although I could not hear his voice or see his face, he gave me encouragement in times of despair, and strength in times of weakness. I only hope I was able to provide him with some comfort through those hellish days.

During my confinement I learned of Maj. Bud Day, the first "Misty" commander, who was subsequently awarded the Medal of Honor for his actions while a POW. His story of survival, escape, recapture, and torture during a two-week escape attempt is without compare in excitement and intrigue. I also encountered Guy Gruters, shot down twice, the second time with Bob Craner. Guy's story of desperately attempting to save the life of fellow warrior Lance Sijan—a Medal of Honor recipient and the namesake of Sijan Hall at the Air Force Academy—is heartbreaking. You will also read of P. K. Robinson. Although we met just before our return on the Freedom Flights, our short time together and shared experiences as fellow POWs will forever cause me to consider him a close brother and companion.

This wonderful book will introduce you to these and other "Misty" warriors—157 of them flying two-seat USAF F-100 fighters as "fast FACs," forward air controllers, seeking out targets for bomb-dropping fighters over North Vietnam. It was an impossibly dangerous mission for which they paid the ultimate price. This book goes beyond the normal war story. It proves to be engaging and accessible to fighter pilot and civilian alike. You will be able to understand their story and the story of so many others who never returned home.

An extraordinary book that adds a critical volume to the literature about the Vietnam experience, *Bury Us Upside Down* serves to remind us of why war is such a serious endeavor. We would do well as a nation to heed the lessons and messages it contains. I would like to personally thank Don and Rick for their efforts in bringing this story to light and celebrating all the heroes from America's longest war.

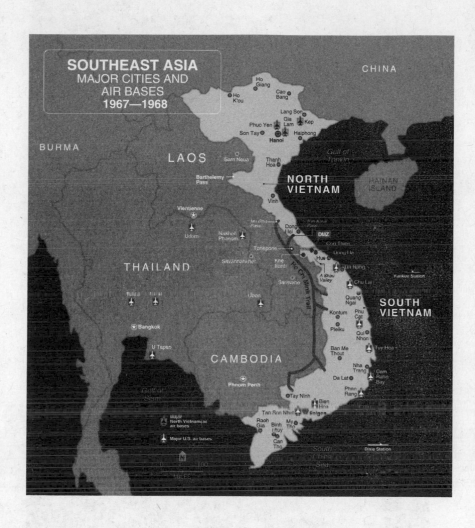

SOUTHEAST ASIA
MAJOR CITIES AND
AIR BASES
1967—1968

CHINA

Ho
Giang

Ho
K'ou

Cao
Bang

Lang Son

Gia
Lam · Kep

Phuc Yen

Son Tay

Hanoi

Haiphong

BURMA

LAOS

Sam Neua

Thanh
Hoa

**NORTH
VIETNAM**

Gulf of
Tonkin

Barthelemy
Pass

HAINAN
ISLAND

Vinh

Vientienne

Mu Ghia
Pass

Dong
Hoi

Ban Karai
Pass

Udorn

Nakhon
Phanom

Tchepone

DMZ

Con Thien

Dong Ha

Hue

Da Nang

THAILAND

Savannakhet

Khe
Sanh

A Shau
Valley

Chu Lai

Yankee Station

Saravane

Quang
Ngai

Ubon

Kontum

Phu
Cat

**SOUTH
VIETNAM**

Pleiku

Qui
Nhon

Takhli · Korat

Ban Me
Thout

Tuy Hoa

· Bangkok

Nha
Trang

Cam
Ranh
Bay

Da Lat

CAMBODIA

Phnom Penh

Phan
Rang

U Tapao

Tay Ninh

Bien
Hoa

Gulf of
Siam

Tan Son Nhut

Saigon

Rach
Gia

Binh
Thuy

My
Tho

Major
North Vietnamese
air bases

Can
Tho

Dixie Station

· Major U.S. air bases

South
China
Sea

N

100

MILES

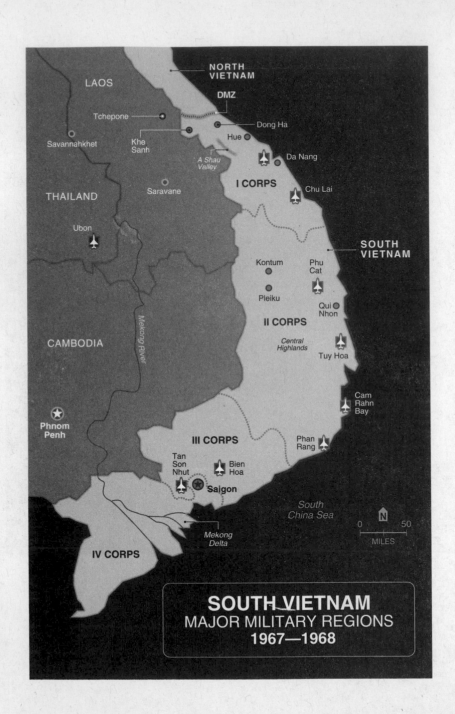

SOUTH VIETNAM
MAJOR MILITARY REGIONS
1967—1968

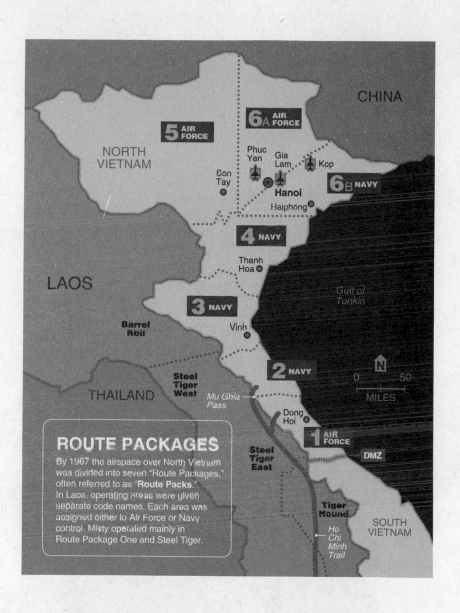

CHINA

NORTH VIETNAM

5 AIR FORCE

6A AIR FORCE

Phuc Yen

Gia Lam

Kop

6B NAVY

Son Tay

Hanoi

Haiphong

4 NAVY

Thanh Hoa

LAOS

Gulf of Tonkin

3 NAVY

Barrel Roll

Vinh

2 NAVY

Steel Tiger West

Mu Ghia Pass

THAILAND

N

0   50

MILES

Dong Hoi

1 AIR FORCE

ROUTE PACKAGES

By 1967 the airspace over North Vietnam was divided into seven "Route Packages," often referred to as "**Route Packs**." In Laos, operating areas were given separate code names. Each area was assigned either to Air Force or Navy control. Misty operated mainly in Route Package One and Steel Tiger.

Steel Tiger East

DMZ

Tiger Hound

Ho Chi Minh Trail

SOUTH VIETNAM

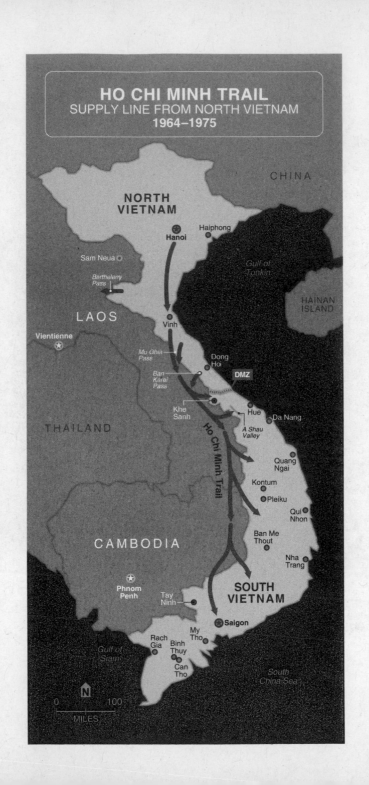

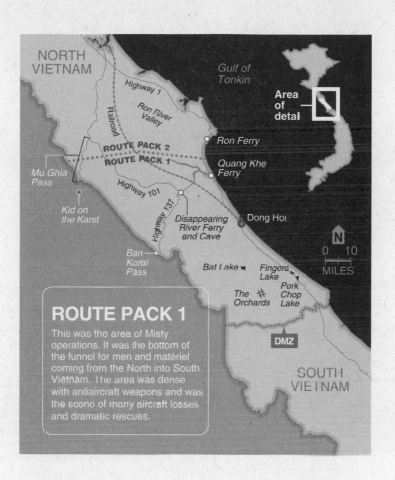

NORTH
VIETNAM

Gulf of
Tonkin

Highway 1

Ron River
Valley

Railroad

Area
of
detail

ROUTE PACK 2

ROUTE PACK 1

Ron Ferry

Mu Ghia
Pass

Highway 101

Quang Khe
Ferry

Kid on
the Karst

Highway 137

Disappearing
River Ferry
and Cave

Dong Hoi

N

0   10

MILES

Ban
Karai
Pass

Bat Lake

Fingers
Lake

Pork
Chop
Lake

The
Orchards

DMZ

SOUTH
VIETNAM

ROUTE PACK 1

This was the area of Misty
operations. It was the bottom of
the funnel for men and matériel
coming from the North into South
Vietnam. The area was dense
with antiaircraft weapons and was
the scene of many aircraft losses
and dramatic rescues.

CONTENTS

INTRODUCTION

The lights of Baghdad burned bright in the background as "Pepe," an A-10 Warthog pilot, peered through night-vision goggles into the desert below. It was the night of April 6, 2003. U.S. Army and Marine units had been tearing through the desert for a week in a race to capture the Iraqi capital and depose Saddam Hussein. They were finally approaching the outskirts of Baghdad and would attack into the city the next morning.

Pepe was an "A-FAC," an airborne forward air controller who scouted for surface targets that could be destroyed from the air before U.S. ground forces ever encountered them. His job was to scour a thirty-by-thirty-mile "kill box" south of Baghdad, searching for Iraqi Republican Guard tanks—a last line of defense, and a dangerous one, against the invading Americans.

He found one. It was nestled against what looked like an apartment building. Pepe zoomed in on the tank with his targeting pod and slewed the crosshairs of an aiming pointer over it. He punched a button on the A-10's throttle control and a narrow white infrared pointer hit the tank. The beam was invisible on the ground, but created a flashing marker to pilots wearing night-vision goggles.

Pepe called two Navy F-18 Hornets flying nearby, equipped with weapons able to take out such targets. He told them to look for the "sparkle" in their NVGs—the tank. When they found it, Pepe turned on his laser designator, a high-energy beam that would "illuminate" the tank for precision weapons and guide them in. The lead Hornet then fired an AGM-65 laser-guided Maverick missile, and they all watched as seconds later it blew the tank apart. Pepe and the two Hornets repeated the procedure several times, clearing Iraqi armor from the path of U.S. soldiers and Marines, who rolled into Baghdad the following day.

With weaponry as advanced as something from *The Matrix,* Pepe and the other pilots who flew over Iraq during the fighting there were the most modern warriors on earth. Yet their tactics for finding and destroying targets came directly from a conflict that now seems primitive and barbaric by comparison—the jungle war in Vietnam. In the turbulent and tragic aftermath of that war—thoroughly documented elsewhere—a few civilians recognized the military advancements that emerged from the conflict. But that grueling and bloody war was also a laboratory for military science that has helped Americans fight smarter, faster, and with less risk to troops ever since.

The Army pioneered airmobile tactics for rapidly moving troops through the battle zone by helicopter, a key element of ground operations in Iraq, Afghanistan, and elsewhere. The Vietnam War was a proving ground for special operations forces, which today are as vital as any conventional troops. Technical experts contrived electronic sensors and other gizmos that were prototypes for many of the tools in the military toolbox today. And the Air Force developed the concept of fast FACs—forward air controllers flying jets and looking for targets—that remains a staple of aerial warfare even in an era of smart bombs, night-vision goggles, and laser and infrared targeting.

The original forward air controllers in Vietnam were "slow FACs" who spotted targets by buzzing low over the countryside in prop planes dating to the Korean War or earlier. Fancy reconnaissance jets like the U-2 and the RF-101 could map vast amounts of terrain and photograph hundreds of targets, but it usually took days for the pictures to get developed and for attack planes to arrive on-scene with their bombs. Many enemy targets didn't wait around that long. The slow FACs could find enemy troops and weapons and trucks and storage areas in real time while fighters with bombs were flying nearby. Since they didn't have lasers, they'd "mark" their targets with rockets that spewed white smoke and showed the bomb-droppers where to aim. Then they'd invite the fighter jets, swooping in from much higher, to "hit my smoke." One by one the targets disappeared, though it often took many bombs for one to score a hit.

The North Vietnamese were a smart enemy, however. They rapidly built up a system of antiaircraft guns that could easily reach the lethargic prop planes the slow FACs flew. The Air Force knew it would need FACs flying more robust planes. Finally, when the slow FACs flying over the Ho Chi Minh Trail in North Vietnam and Laos started getting shot down at alarming rates, the Air Force formed a top secret outfit code-named Commando Sabre.

This experimental unit became the most innovative air operation of the war. "Misty," as it became known, on account of the call sign chosen by the first commander, borrowed many of its tactics from the slow FACs. But other techniques had to be developed on the fly. To see targets as small as a single truck camouflaged beneath trees, the Mistys flew low—often below the minimum allowed altitude of 4,500 feet. Anytime they buzzed over something valuable to the North Vietnamese, they attracted walls of antiaircraft fire. Every day was an asymmetric duel between men in the air and men on the ground. They had different guns and different advantages, yet the fight was as personal as if they were facing each other with bayonets.

It was a hush-hush mission. The mere formation of the fast FAC unit indicated how successful the North Vietnamese had been at defeating the slow FACs that were getting blown out of the sky. All the air defenses being sent down the Trail—including surface-to-air missiles—were working. If the slow FACs couldn't find the air defenses and help clear them out, that jeopardized all the other aerial missions near the Trail—including the B-52 bombing runs that were a key U.S. advantage. The Air Force wasn't about to telegraph that vulnerability to Hanoi.

The Mistys were a secret weapon of sorts: Like the spy satellites that were first able to photograph missiles on their launch pads in the Soviet Union, the Mistys provided an invaluable glimpse into the hub of enemy activity. There were several centers of gravity in North Vietnam—Hanoi, Haiphong Harbor, industrial and rail facilities—but the Ho Chi Minh Trail was a lone conduit that was essential to the North's war effort. Without the Trail, the North could not send men, weapons, or field commanders to the south. The Mistys spent every mission crisscrossing the skies over this vital lifeline, prying into North Vietnamese activity. And they worked diligently to disguise their mission, using irregular tactics and any other tricks they could think of to fool the communists. If the enemy knew what they were up to—and there were spies throughout South Vietnam, probably even cooking the food or doing the laundry on U.S. bases—air defenses along the Trail would get even thornier. The aim of the gunners would get better. The North might even send some of its treasured MiG-21s—purportedly flown by Soviet pilots—down the Trail to do battle with the Mistys.

To evade ground fire, the Mistys flew nauseating zigzag patterns that placed huge G-forces on the body and left fit, young fighter pilots exhausted after a mission. Lacking night-vision goggles or laser viewfinders, the Mistys used the naked eye to look for telltale signs of enemy activity beneath the jungle canopy—dust on the treetops, or tread marks that disappeared into the foliage. And, hampered by a war strategy that failed to interdict war matériel at its source—Haiphong Harbor, and the transportation routes that ran into North Vietnam from China—the Mistys fought a maddening battle to stop an endless flow of enemy traffic literally truck by truck.

Rarely have fighter pilots performed such exciting work. As with all wars, most of the bombing missions in Vietnam were tightly constrained. Pilots flew in two- and four-ship flights against preplanned targets or on close air support missions for Army troops. They returned once they had dropped their bombs or delivered their payload. But not the Mistys. They flew extended missions that could last four hours or more, trolling over enemy terrain as they saw fit. The Mistys had enormous freedom in the cockpit, and sometimes they paid the price. Planes came back with battle damage virtually every week, sometimes every day. Of 157 pilots who served with Misty from 1967 to 1970, 34 were shot down. Two of those were shot down twice. Three were captured and imprisoned in Hanoi. Seven were lost and declared missing. Eventually their status was changed to KIA: killed in action.

By the mid-1980s, most Americans were eager to forget about the scalding national experience the Vietnam War had become. But some couldn't. At the end of the war in 1975, more than twenty-five hundred American service members were missing and unaccounted for. Virtually nothing happened to resolve those mysteries for more than a decade. Finally American and Vietnamese negotiators struck a deal: U.S. teams began going quietly into Vietnam, escorted by local officials. They conducted interviews, researched documents, investigated areas where planes had crashed and ground battles had raged, and searched for evidence of missing Americans.

They started to find remains and bring them home. By then, most friends and family members of the missing had learned to expect no answers from the government, and to get on with their lives without any help from the military machine that had sent their people to Vietnam. But answers started to trickle back. Among the missing was Howard K. Williams, an F-100 pilot who had joined Misty in March 1968 as traffic was flooding down the Trail and Misty was approaching its glory days. When Howard was shot down that same month and never heard from again, he left a wife, a six-year-old son, and dozens of others close to him trying to live a week, a month, a year without knowing if he'd ever return. Eventually they figured that he wouldn't. It was a slow, agonizing recognition that the worst thing imaginable had happened.

They grieved, struggled, healed, and reconstructed their lives. Then, twenty-three years after Howard K. Williams had been shot down, astonishing news arrived: His remains had been recovered in a remote part of Vietnam. There was a formal burial ceremony at Arlington National Cemetery in Washington, D.C., along with write-ups in the local papers in Columbus, Ohio, where Howard and his family had lived. But by the early nineties the return of remains from Vietnam was a routine event that attracted little attention outside of family circles. Tying up the long-standing loose ends from a war nobody wanted to talk about was no longer news.

There are still more than eighteen hundred Americans who presumably died during the Vietnam War and remain unaccounted for. U.S. investigators still sift through the earth in Vietnam, Laos, and Cambodia seeking evidence relating to their countrymen from a generation ago. In little-noticed press releases, the Department of Defense announces the return of remains from Vietnam every week or two, on average. The announcements get little attention. Yet across America, families that have been lacerated with anguish live through an experience they came to believe would never happen: the return of their loved ones. This is the tale of one missing man, the family who went on without him, and the extraordinary unit he served with when he disappeared. There are many, many other stories like this one.

BURY US UPSIDE DOWN

ONE

"MISSING MAN"

The casket seemed like overkill. But it was too awkward for anybody to mention.

As seventy-five guests sat anxiously in the chapel at Arlington National Cemetery, the organist softly playing "Amazing Grace," a military caisson clanked to a stop outside the gates. Pallbearers from the Air Force Honor Guard, every thread of their uniforms neatly in place, lowered a flag-draped coffin from the horse drawn carriage. The men carried it up the steps and methodically marched it down the aisle, then set it before the small altar at the front of the chapel. The stiff, practiced precision of the pallbearers' movements, their reverential bearing, all of the military formality—it was impressive, to be sure. Yet it was starkly at odds with what was inside the casket: practically nothing.

In the second pew, Jean Kahoon grew uncomfortable as she listened to friends and colleagues eulogize Howard Keith Williams, her big brother. He had been shot down while flying an F-100 fighter jet over North Vietnam twenty-four years earlier and never heard from again. John Buckmelter, a childhood friend, described how Howard had fallen in love with flying when he was just a boy hanging out at the Jefferson County airfield near Steubenville, Ohio. Roger Williams, Howard's younger brother, described how pleased he had been to be able to go to Vietnam as an Army soldier at the same time Howard, his hero, had gone over to fly jets. Fellow pilots Roger Wise and Chuck O'Connor told stories of going to flight school and learning how to be fighter jocks with "Willy." "He was always a little more focused, a little more mature," O'Connor recalled.

But there was so much more to him, thought Jean, than his military career and his fascination with flying. There was the neighborhood sled-riding hill where she and her brother and dozens of other kids would go careening over rocks and bushes and have to jump off their sleds to avoid landing in the creek at the bottom. There were all the jobs Howard worked as a kid to pick up spending money and add to the family clothing fund: the paper routes, the lawns he mowed, the summer labor at their grandfather's farm in West Virginia where they'd bale hay and plow up potatoes and milk cows. Best of all was the three-man band Howard helped form. He played trumpet and was good enough to get paying gigs at local nightclubs on weekends. In her mind, Jean could still see the drum majorette her brother had dated for a while in high school, the one with the great legs who wore her skirt so short it barely covered her panties.

Then there were all the special things between Jean and Howard, born two years apart and the oldest of eight children. Jean helped Howard deliver the papers and took over the route when he moved on to bigger jobs. She was with Howard at the farm in West Virginia when he tried chewing tobacco for the first time—a short-lived habit. And all the nights they spent together hiding in the attic, talking and drawing, came cascading back. Their dad had been a carpenter for U.S. Steel, and he had been injured and out of work for a while. The family could afford just one upstairs bedroom for the girls, and one for the boys. But the setup had its charms. Each bedroom had a closet that led to a crawl space at the top of the house. That's where the family kept its supply of drawing paper—blank newsprint that occasionally came bundled with the morning news. Jean and Howard would sneak up there once the younger kids were asleep and spend hours drawing cartoons and planning out the future. They'd clamber back down to their beds once they heard their mom climbing the steps to check on the kids. Not once did they ever get caught—not surprising, since Mom knew what they were up to all along.

And there, in a box twenty feet in front of her, Jean's big brother Howard, who caused her profound heartache when he left home and giddy joy whenever he came back to visit, had been literally reduced to shards: a bone fragment, one tooth, a sliver from a signal mirror that was part of his survival gear, and a piece of a plastic Ace comb. The remains, recovered by American investigators a year earlier, in 1991, were so sparse that Jean wondered, what's the point of putting them in a casket? She even had her doubts about whether they were actually Howard's. There had been so much that didn't make sense, so many fishy explanations, that it was hard to believe anything the government said.

Was it just coincidence that Howard had told her, in the last letter she ever got from him in Vietnam, that he was flying reconnaissance missions up north, taking pictures and getting shot at, and that he feared he might not make it home? Or that he wanted her to listen to a song that he said was about siblings like them—"Bang Bang, My Baby Shot Me Down"? And how could the U.S. government not have known for twenty-three years what happened to Howard? That coffin, which contained her brother's so-called remains, was about as hollow as everything else the government had offered about her brother in the years since she had last heard from him.

Jean wasn't the only person in the chapel bothered by the contents of the casket. In the front row, Keith Williams—Howard's son, who was six when his dad disappeared over North Vietnam—had his own reservations. It was Keith who had flown to Travis Air Force Base near San Francisco when the remains were first returned to the United States, to "escort" them to the San Francisco airport. It seemed ridiculous to him that the Air Force had put a handful of body parts into a full-sized coffin. And he began wondering all over again how his father had died, and how much pain he had gone through. As Keith had gotten older, people who seemed to know such things had whispered to him horror stories about American pilots who had gone down in that part of North Vietnam, close to the border with Laos. Often they were murdered the moment they were discovered by local Vietnamese militias. Other times they were captured and tortured, only to die miserably before they ever made it to infamous prisons like the Hanoi Hilton. They were even shot at in their parachutes while descending.

Those who got tangled in trees could be wounded and left hanging until they bled to death.

On the flight out to Travis, Keith had begun writing a eulogy on three-by-five-inch note cards, a eulogy he stood to give in the chapel at Arlington. Most of his recollections were the vaguest of sketches, filled in over the years by the stories he heard from friends and relatives and colleagues who had flown with his dad. So Keith described his dad largely as others had to him. He was "a man whose love of life and family propelled him to excel in all of life's endeavors . . . As a self-taught artist, he shared with us his aesthetic ideal. . . . Music was another pastime my father pursued with dedication and single-mindedness. With a few songbooks, a tuning pipe, and hours of devotion, he brought laughter and joy to those who heard him play."

His true passion, however, had been flying: "Diving, turning, zooming, and rolling amid the clouds allowed my father to push himself and his aircraft to the limits. Covering a mile every six seconds, my father was privy to a view of the world reserved for very few individuals. A world with no lines or boundaries between people or nations, with a crisp blue sky surrounding him, just on the edge of heaven."

Of those who spoke at the chapel that day, Keith Williams had known the man represented by the empty casket least of all. Yet the mere appearance of the son did more to animate the memory of the father than any words could have. Keith's lanky six-foot-two frame, his mannerisms and voice, his gentle face and slightly crooked smile—almost everything about him, except the ponytail that hung over the collar of his dark suit—made it seem as if Howard himself were standing at the lectern delivering his own eulogy.

From the fourth row of the chapel, Dick Rutan was struck by the resemblance. Competitive, excitable, and unflinchingly self-confident, Rutan fit the stereotype of a fighter pilot much better than the calm and studious man he was there to honor. In Commando Sabre, the top secret unit he and Howard had belonged to when Howard was shot down, Rutan was considered one of the most aggressive pilots—and all of the pilots were aggressive. After Vietnam, Rutan had achieved aviation exploits that made him a legitimate celebrity, especially among the flight buffs in the pews around him. In December 1986 he and a female pilot, Jeana Yeager, had flown the Voyager aircraft completely around the world without ever stopping—the first time anyone had made such an unrefueled, nonstop flight. The Voyager hung for the world to see just a few miles away, across the Potomac River, in the Smithsonian Institution's National Air and Space Museum.

Now, the fearless flight pioneer was uncharacteristically reserved. Rutan had been to dozens of funerals for colleagues killed in combat, yet this one punctured his emotional armor. He had last seen the lean young man at the lectern as a four- or five-year-old, back when he and Howard were in training together. And now it was as if his old flying buddy were reincarnated and standing before him once again. If you have to leave the way Howie did, Rutan thought, it's good you can leave something like that behind.

But the vacant casket represented more to Rutan than just a lost flying buddy. It had been Rutan who had urged Howie, back in 1968, to join Commando Sabre, known informally by the radio call sign the unit used—"Misty." That came from the famous song by Johnny Mathis, which had been a favorite of the unit's first commander. Rutan and Howie had both been sent to Vietnam in 1967 to fly F-100 fighter-bombers on conventional missions in the South. Rutan had heard about Misty through back channels, and begged to join. The pilots would fly long missions over North Vietnam, looking for supply trucks and supplies and surface-to-air missiles (SAMs) and other matériel being shipped down the Ho Chi Minh Trail. The pilots couldn't say much about the mission, which was just as well, because in one respect Misty sounded like suicide. To be able to find and direct strikes on targets that were expertly camouflaged, in mountainous jungle, the pilots had to fly so low they were fat targets for the North's antiaircraft guns. It was dangerous and exhausting work—and probably the most exciting flying a fighter pilot could find in Vietnam.

Rutan got in and insisted that his friend Howie join the unit. Misty needed a hotshot like Howie, Rutan argued. His trademark calm in the cockpit was the perfect demeanor for the unit's stressful missions. And Howie's flight skills were unsurpassed. Howie had won the coveted "Top Gun" trophy in his F-100 class at Luke Air Force Base in Arizona, nailing the highest scores in gunnery and bombing.

The allure was irresistible, and Howie volunteerd. Misty was happy to have him. He and Rutan both loved the freedom of flying with the unit. Unlike the tightly regimented operations in conventional squadrons, the Misty pilots flew as they saw fit in order to complete their missions, often making up their own rules. The outfit had renegade status and ruffled a lot of brass feathers. But it was a favorite of Gen. William "Spike" Momyer, the top Air Force general in Saigon, and the pilots pretty much got what they wanted. To Rutan, Misty was what war was supposed to be about: courageous men taking extraordinary risks, and receiving a few extraordinary privileges in return.

Dick Rutan and Howard Williams never got to fly together. Howie was shot down on his ninth mission. When Howie didn't return and was declared missing in action, the Misty commander appointed Rutan as summary courts officer, responsible for packing up Howie's stuff, paying his accounts at the officers club, and getting his other affairs and records squared away. That was always a devastating responsibility, made even tougher when Rutan later got a letter from Howie's wife, Monalee, back in Columbus, complaining that somebody had stolen Howie's Leica camera. The Air Force had told him to expect an angry letter like that—"anger transference," they called it—but it was damned hard all the same.

Sitting in the chapel at Arlington, Rutan still felt guilty. But it had helped to see Monalee again, his first encounter with her since they had both been at Luke back in 1967. The hostility was long gone. She was now Monalee Meyers, and she sat in the front row of the chapel next to her husband Fritz, whom she had married in 1982. What she had gone through getting to that point, how tough it had been not knowing for years whether her husband was dead or alive while trying to explain to a growing boy what had happened to his dad, Rutan didn't know. He was simply relieved to see that she seemed stable and healthy and had everything under control.

Rutan also met Chuck O'Connor and Roger Wise and some of Howie's other friends and family members. Another Misty pilot was there, too—Brian Williams, known as "B. Willy." He had been Howard's crewmate on March 18, 1968, when their plane went down. They all talked about what had happened. For some of the people at the ceremony, it was the first time they had heard the story of Howie's disappearance firsthand.

B. Willy had been in the back of the two-seat F-100, with Howie in the front, flying the jet, on a typical Misty mission scouting for targets along the Trail. It was about 11:30 in the morning on a clear day. They had just spotted what they thought was a North Vietnamese supply area and were turning around to go back for another look when they heard a loud *thud* and felt something hit the belly of the aircraft. A moment later B. Willy saw flames in his rearview mirror. Fire was spreading rapidly throughout the back of the plane and the pilots knew they'd have to bail out. Howie aimed the plane toward high terrain, where there would be fewer enemy soldiers on the ground. Then they prepared to eject. "We better get out!" B. Willy had shouted. "I'm right behind you," Howie responded.

"I'm punching now," B. Willy called out. Then he jettisoned the canopy and pulled up on the ejection seat handles. He made a safe landing, and spent a couple of hours on the ground before a rescue helicopter picked him up. There was no sign of his copilot, however. Rescuers looked and listened until dark, and stayed alert for the next couple of days, too, but nobody ever heard from Howard Williams again. The Air Force declared him missing in action. B. Willy, meanwhile, got a clean bill of health a couple of days after the shootdown, and he climbed back into the cockpit.

Rutan had trouble accepting his friend's disappearance. He made surreptitious plans to catch a chopper ride into the jungle with some members of the secret special operations teams that went behind enemy lines. He'd hike to the crash site, see if Howard's body was inside the plane, and bury him if it was. Then he'd catch a ride back to base and put Howie's case to rest. It was the very least he could do for his friend and the members of his family back home.

The day before he planned to go, Rutan got an anonymous phone call. The voice sternly warned him to abandon the trip, and he obeyed. It was a puzzling episode, but Rutan figured that somebody had intelligence proving that Howard was either dead or imprisoned and was trying to save him from a futile and risky adventure. Years later, however, Rutan wished he had gone through with his original scheme. The Air Force hadn't said a single meaningful word about Howard's fate for twenty years. Whoever had placed the mysterious phone call was protecting something, but it wasn't Howard's family or his interests. How incredibly callous, Rutan thought for the thousandth time, as he sat in the pew. What bullshit.

Up on the altar, the encomiums for Howard continued. Chuck O'Connor concluded his remembrance by saying, "Over the years, I wondered where 'Willy' was. I hoped he'd come home. . . . Today, I know where he is. He's come home." A chaplain read from the Book of John: "In my Father's house are many rooms; if it were not so, would I have told you that I go to prepare a place for you? And when I go and prepare a place for you, I will come again and will take you to myself, that where I am you may be also."

As the ceremony concluded, the pallbearers wheeled the casket back out to the horse-drawn carriage. The people in the chapel filed outside silently. They boarded buses that followed the caisson as it wound its way toward Howard's grave site. Honor guards bearing the Stars and Stripes led the way while a military band played "We Will Be True To Thee Till Death" and "America, America." As the caisson drew close to the grave site, eight military pallbearers pulled the casket down and carried it across grass, trim and plush, toward the spot reserved for Howard.

There was a distant droning overhead. It became louder. The military men knew what it was—the Air Force's ultimate gesture of respect, the "missing man" flyover. The sky was thickly overcast, though, and the planes were hidden behind clouds. "They'll never break through," someone said as dozens of heads began searching the sky. "Yes they will," countered Rutan. "They'll do it." A moment later they did. Four F-15s, piloted by airmen who were toddlers in 1968, streaked over the assemblage in the classic diamond formation, flying well below allowable minimum altitudes—like Misty, bending the rules to accomplish their mission.

This was the best military aviators had to offer, the utmost gesture of final respect and deference for a fallen comrade. As the crowd slipped into plastic seats at the edge of the grave site, virtually everybody there was moved in some way: by the pallbearers' meticulous handling of the flag as they removed it from the coffin and folded it into a perfect triangle, by the mournful music the band played, by the stoic grandeur of the rows and rows of plain white gravestones that surrounded them.

But Howard K. Williams wasn't home. His son and his closest sister and the brother who worshiped him and his best friend and many others at Arlington that day felt it. There was a kind of transparency to the whole affair, as if there was a bureaucratic imperative to come up with something that could be labeled "remains," process them through the prism of heroism at Arlington, and stamp "closure" on one more Vietnam tragedy.

The tragedies didn't close that easily. Nobody could tell, but in the front row of seats next to the grave site, the disquiet was swelling beyond the bounds it had been allotted. Monalee Meyers had spent most of the day, most of the past month actually, worrying about other people being able to attend the ceremony. She had tracked down old friends and acquaintances to make sure they knew about it. She had arranged a luncheon for afterward at a nearby hotel. And she had decided not to eulogize Howard herself, since that might be awkward for Fritz, her second husband. Instead, she had offered her son Keith the opportunity, since she thought it might produce some needed closure for him.

She had had plenty of time and opportunity, after all, to grieve and come to terms with what had happened to Howard. There had been dozens of difficult thresholds, each crossed with a bit more strength than the last: saying good-bye to her husband when he left for Vietnam in 1967, hearing the terrible news in March 1968, hoping and praying Howard would be among the returning POWs in 1973 and then learning that he was not, having him declared officially deceased in 1978, several memorial services over the years, trying to explain it all to an aching, confused boy. With it all came monumental anger and pain. But she was not one of the agonized protesters who still, twenty-five years later, were chasing after politicians demanding answers that were never going to come. She had remarried and moved on, but still continued to honor the memory of her son's dad.

Arlington wasn't supposed to be for her, it was supposed to be for others and for Howard. But it was troubling, the virtually empty casket sitting in front of her. For someone to have been such a huge part of your life, she thought, and that's all that's left of him? A couple of bone fragments you could hold in your hands? When she and Keith had discussed how to handle the ceremony, Monalee had suggested putting the remains in an urn instead of a casket. But that seemed unsatisfying, too, like it would somehow trivialize the majesty of Arlington to have such an elaborate ceremony for a mere urn. So they had decided on a casket after all.

As the graveside rituals finished up, there were a few quiet sobs from the gallery behind Monalee, as Keith and his son Ian each placed a rose on the casket. The honor guard fired a twenty-one-gun salute. The pallbearers presented the folded flag to Keith. But there were no tears in the front row, where Keith loosely hugged his son Ian and Monalee sat placidly next to Fritz. There had been rivers of tears over the years, at moments both ceremonious and spontaneous. Emotions had surged and receded. And Howard K. Williams's wife and son had learned to live with the strange fate of the most important man in their lives, with or without a few shards the government declared to be remains. Yet, as a lone bugler began playing the mournful finale to the event, a squall of memories and frustrations stirred inside Monalee, as if she were back in 1968. Taps had become difficult to listen to over the years, and she finally thought, this is it. I can't listen to this melody again.

TWO

BURY US UPSIDE DOWN

The first time Lanny Lancaster stepped into the Stag Bar at Luke Air Force Base in Arizona, he got the warmest greeting he could imagine. "HELLLLLOOOO ASSHOLE!" shouted two dozen fighter pilots, laughing as they offered the standard salutation for a new guy. This was the "fuck, fight, or go for your gun" Air Force, and Lanny reveled in the bawdy bravado that was usually on display on Friday afternoons at the Stag Bar. This was where young fighter pilots gathered after work to trade stories about flying, fighting, fast cars, and women. Females were welcome, as long as they were single. But the unofficial rule was no wives—and anybody whose mate showed up was likely to end up buying drinks for the whole bar. Wives and dates would typically materialize later for a proper evening meal in the officers club next door, and maybe a little dancing.

Lanny had arrived at Luke in January 1967 to learn how to fly the F-100 fighter-bomber, the workhorse of the Air Force's tactical fleet. There was plenty for Lanny to learn. He was a graduate of the Air Force Academy but had barely made it, sweating the academics until the last day. Lanny's classmates had called him "the bartender," on account of his wild stories, Texas twang, and loud manner. The wiry, balding bachelor was fond of saying that any good-looking woman could ride in his Chevy convertible, but "don't plan on becoming a permanent passenger."

After getting his wings, Lanny had been assigned to fly lumbering C-130 transport planes, a bitter disappointment for an aspiring fighter pilot. But the Vietnam War was dragging on, and the rule in the Air Force was that every pilot would get one tour there before anybody got two. That drew lots of pilots out of cargo planes and other "heavies" and into the fighters and bombers that were most needed in the war. Pilots transferring into fighters from other types of planes were derided as "retreads," but most didn't care. Flying fighters was a dream come true. And as Lanny stood in the Stag Bar, he quickly began to realize that the whole world of fighter jocks was different from the slower moving world of transporters and logisticians. The "tactical" Air Force, it was said, ran on a combination of cigarettes, popcorn, whiskey, twenty-five-cent beer, jet fuel, and testosterone. As the odor of smoke and booze and the shouts of exuberant pilots enveloped him, Lanny believed it.

He was a true "green bean," eager and naïve. On his first day at Luke, Lanny had pulled into a parking lot adjacent to the flight line and noticed a crew chief, responsible for keeping the airplanes flying, working on an F-100. He boldly ambled toward the sweaty sergeant.

"Mind if I crawl in and have a look?" Lanny asked. "I've been flying those piece-of-shit C-130s and I'm ready for a real airplane."

The sergeant looked him over. He was unimpressed. "Guys like you have been doing their best all week to break my airplanes," he growled. "Now my guys have to work Saturdays to catch up." But the old sergeant gave in, and Lanny clambered up an eight-foot steel ladder into the cockpit. "I'll follow you up, Captain," said the chief, "so you don't fuck up my airplane any worse."

The bushy-tailed young pilot then got a stern lecture—the first of many—on the do's and don'ts of the F-100. "See those red flags? One's an ejection seat handgrip safety pin. The other is a canopy ejector handle safety pin. Make sure they're in before you climb into the seat. And this other red flag here is a trigger safety pin so the gun don't shoot. Make sure all the pins are in or your flying career could be real short. . . . Don't push any button with a red guard around it, or something will come off the aircraft and go *boom*. Also, don't pull this handle, or the drag chute will fall out. . . . Oh, one more thing. Here's the canopy switch. Don't close the canopy when no one's around. If the battery goes dead, you could be trapped and die in the heat before anyone notices. . . ."

Well, shit, thought Lanny. Don't touch this, don't pull that, don't lean back. Man, have I got lots to learn.

He quickly became one of the guys, though, and a regular at the Stag Bar, where there was an unusual amount of excitement one evening in late March. Howard Williams, one of the twenty-two pilots in Lanny's training class, had just survived a crash and was doing what fighter pilots do best—regaling his buddies with the war story. Howie had been flying solo in a flight of four F-100s practicing air-to-air combat. As the flight was climbing out into its assigned area, the instructor called for afterburner. Usually this quick dump of raw fuel into the engine exhaust produced a controlled explosion that rocketed the plane forward. But when Howie pushed the throttle, the jet, instead of surging ahead, suddenly shook as if it had collided with something. He heard two loud bangs, then fire shot out of both ends of the plane as the engine quit.

Howie was older and more seasoned than most pilots at Luke. He had already amassed more than 2,300 hours of flying time, making him a pro compared to classmates who had flown only a couple of hundred hours and were fresh out of initial pilot training. He had logged about 80 hours in the F-86 fighter and nearly 50 in the F-100. But most of Howie's time had been in B-47s under SAC, Strategic Air Command. He was a bomber pilot, and worse—a SAC-puke.

Yet he was lucky to be flying at all. Howie had been sent to Luke for F-100 training more than a year earlier and gone through most of the early classroom instruction, when it came time for the altitude chamber, a portion of training designed to teach pilots the dangers and symptoms of hypoxia—diminished oxygen supply to the brain. Hypoxia could be caused by malfunctioning equipment or by battle damage that disrupted cabin pressurization at high altitude, and pilots had to know how to respond.

Howie was mild-mannered, but he possessed one standard-issue fighter pilot trait—he was intensely competitive. So he made a bet with one of his classmates to see who could stay off oxygen the longest while the air pressure in the chamber dropped and the air thinned. Howie, who was tall and lean and as healthy as anybody in uniform, ended up passing out before he could get his oxygen mask on. A late round of drinking the night before probably had something to do with it, but foolish party antics didn't count as an excuse.

The ramifications were sobering. Flight surgeons at Luke, concerned that Howie might have an undiagnosed medical condition, grounded him indefinitely. The situation got worse when an electrocardiogram, ordered up after the incident, showed some kind of defect in Howie's heart. Howie's flying career looked finished. But the bad readings turned out to be an error due to a flaw in the EKG machine, discovered only after an unusual number of pilots were diagnosed with the same problem. Still, Howie stayed "on the beach," as pilots called the dreadful condition of being unable to fly. While his colleagues proceeded through training, he was given a staff job in the Luke Command Post. Devastated, he discussed leaving the Air Force with his wife, Monalee, and going to school to study aeronautical engineering— what he probably would have done earlier had his family had the money to send him to college. Monalee persuaded him to hang in there a little longer.

It took a year, but the Air Force bureaucracy finally decided it had done enough tests on Howard K. Williams to conclude that he was healthy enough to fly. By then, however, it was too late to rejoin his class. He had to cool his heels and start over with a new class, a full-year delay in getting qualified in the F-100.

Needless to say, the whole episode was humbling. Howie had never been a braggart or a loudmouth, but he had brimmed with confidence since the early days when he had washed planes in exchange for free rides at the local airfield in Steubenville, Ohio. He could down martinis on a pace with the strongest drinkers in the Air Force, and raise hell in the finest fighter-jock tradition. And truth be told, the altitude chamber incident—immature, foolish, and frightening as it was—made Howie something of a Big Man on Campus, a legend, whose story was passed down. "Don't do this," future students were told. Then they were regaled with the incident. Howie's classmates in fact, admired his persistence to get airborne again, no matter what the mindless bureaucrats at headquarters said. He wasn't a war hero—in fact, he had pulled a dumb-shit trick—but it was another way he stood out from the rest.

As Howie recounted the flameout to his colleagues at the Stag Bar, there was a detached coolness in his demeanor that impressed the greener guys in the crowd. In the custom of fighter jocks, who always honor a good flying story, free drinks began to stack up in front of Howie's barstool. As he sipped martinis, he explained what happened after the engine failed. He checked to make sure the ejection seat safety pins were removed. He pointed the jet toward an uninhabited area. Then, at about 8,500 feet, he sat up straight in the seat, raised the ejection seat handles, and pulled the triggers. There was a blast of air as the canopy blew off the cockpit. A second later the seat rocket fired and Howie was shot into the air. His parachute deployed another second later, and after drifting toward earth, he hit the ground hard—"like jumping off a fifteen-foot wall," he said.

The plane hit the desert floor and skidded for about twelve hundred feet, breaking into hundreds of pieces. But Howie, aside from a bruised toe, injured when he touched down and kicked a rock, was undamaged. A rescue helicopter picked him up in the desert at about 5:30 in the afternoon, about half an hour after he had ejected. It took him to nearby Davis-Monthan Air Force Base, where a flight surgeon looked him over and pronounced him fit to continue flying. Howie landed back at Luke at about 9:15 that night. He went to his locker to stow his gear, as if it were a routine day on the job.

The next evening at the Stag Bar, Howie held court, since a crash was a hell of a lot more interesting than most things that happened during training. "There was nothing to it," Howie insisted to his rapt audience. "I didn't get any cactus in my ass. And I didn't even lose my sunglasses," he pronounced proudly, pulling the shades out of his pocket as proof.

Even at home, Howie was nonchalant about the mishap. His wife, Monalee, a petite, pretty blonde who had been the daughter of the local Plymouth dealer back in Steubenville, had gotten a call that afternoon saying that her husband had bailed out and was out in the desert waiting to be picked up. She was a bit shaken, but these things happened, and in truth Monalee worried more about the way some of the pilots drove around after downing a few drinks at the Stag Bar than she did about the risks of flying. Howie had called her after he got back to base and told her the whole thing had been "a piece of cake." As they talked it over later, he worried more about the investigation that would follow. Would it somehow find that he had screwed up, risking his flight status yet again? Or would it conclude that the plane had malfunctioned—which, Howie was sure, was what had happened.

Howie was right. After three weeks of interviewing Howie and others, and testing recovered parts, the Air Force determined that aircraft 55-3729 had experienced a "catastrophic engine failure" accompanied by two "compressor stalls." The number four main engine bearing had failed. That reduced the oil pressure to zero. The engine disintegrated, making the plane unflyable. Howie was relieved. There'd be no more detours in his pilot's career—his flying status was secure.

That was fortunate, since Monalee and Howard were quite comfortable at Luke. For one thing, it was warm, unlike their previous posting at Pease Air Force Base in New Hampshire. And the camaraderie at Luke was fantastic. Howie was a self-taught musician, picking up the trumpet in high school and even earning a few bucks at local nightclubs, then buying a guitar in New Hampshire and staying up night after night learning how to play. By the time he got to Luke, Howie would invite other musicians over with their guitars or saxes or drum kits, usually on Sundays, and they'd spend the evening strumming "If I Had a Hammer" or "Puff the Magic Dragon" or whatever the latest folk or pop tunes were. The Williamses lived in a ranch-style house on base that had an L-shaped living room/dining room combo that was as big as a bowling alley. The guys would play music or talk about flying in the front of the house, the women would gossip or play cards in the middle, and in the back the kids would run around.

Their son, Howard Jr.—also known by his middle name, Keith—was five by then. There were lots of opportunities to travel and explore the marvelous surrounding desert, if Flagstaff and Tucson counted as adventures. They even went to Mexico. And when Howie was unable to get his thrills flying, he relied on his Lotus Mark VII for exhilaration. Howie had purchased the car as a kit when he was based in England on temporary duty a few years earlier. He called Monalee back in the States to tell her he wanted to build a car, and since he was a man who had never even changed the oil, she thought he meant a model car.

Why was he even bothering to tell her this? she wondered. Then he said, "It will be a little money," and explained his plan.

Howie and a couple of pals ended up building the car during downtime in one of the hangars at Brize Norton Air Base, about sixty miles northwest of London. Then they drove it to the Lotus factory in Hethel to have it checked out. The shock absorbers were upside down, but everything else was okay, and when Howie was posted back in the States, he had the car shipped to Baltimore and picked it up there. Then he drove it from New Hampshire to Arizona, where he casually competed in races set up in parking lots on the weekends.

Most important, after years of flying big, boring airplanes, Howie was finally living his dream and learning to be a fighter jock. That was one thing he shared with Lanny Lancaster. On the surface, he and Lanny had little in common. Lanny was outgoing and gregarious while Howie was usually quiet, withdrawn, and intense (except when he was strumming a guitar or sipping a martini). Beyond that, Howie was married with a son, while Lanny was single and looking to stay that way. And the married guys and the bachelors tended to form their own fraternities and stick with them. Yet Howie and Lanny formed a quick friendship, and they ended up in the same "flight," a group of students that would eventually fly most of their training missions together. Plus, they were both pretty good with the stick, which created a natural, competitive camaraderie between them.

Dick Rutan was another classmate built for competition. Thin, six-foot-two, serious, full of vinegar, with steely blue eyes that looked like they could pin a guy to a wall, Rutan was a fighter pilot right off a recruiting poster. And he already had the mannerisms down flat. Rutan was one of the prime orchestrators of Stag Bar antics such as "carrier landings," in which several tables would be pushed together and doused with beer. Pilots would then get a running start and go sliding headfirst across the tables, supposedly mimicking the way archrival pilots from the Navy would slide their planes across the slick, glossy flight deck of an aircraft carrier. And Rutan, in his hyperconfident, assertive way, was fond of saying he was right where he wanted to be in life: serving his country, flying a fighter plane, training for war. Even among two dozen fellow ball-busters, he stood out.

Lanny, Howie, and Dick had gotten to know one another over drinks

early on. They shared their flying experiences. Howie had washed airplanes at the local airport for rides as a kid, learned to fly, joined the
Civil Air Patrol, and then the Air Force. When he first got his wings he
was assigned to fly the F-86 fighter. He was elated—until that assignment was canceled and he was sent to Strategic Air Command. Lanny
had been equally disappointed when he was assigned to fly C-130s out
of pilot training. And Rutan was just finishing pilot training after four
years as a navigator, the guy who plots courses and reads maps in big
airplanes. All three of them craved the thrill of powering up into a lim-
itless sky, alone, with one of the finest pieces of machinery money
could buy.

That would take a while, though. The F-100 course began with a
flurry of paperwork and processing. Then came books and instruction
manuals, nearly forty pounds' worth. The pilots dragged the stuff
home and taped the cockpit layout diagrams to the wall, turned the air
conditioner to full cold, and lay down on their beds to study their
Dash-1s, the bibles of aircraft systems.

Soon after came "Aircraft, General" an introduction to the F-100,
known as the Super Sabre. Things started to liven up a bit when the instructor fired up a movie projector and said, "Heads up, guys. Pay attention."

This was the notorious *Sabre Dance* movie. The film showed an
F-100 pilot approaching a runway, when he decided to go around for
another try by pulling the nose of the plane up to an exaggerated angle
while adding power. But the power came in too late. Lacking enough
altitude to drop the nose and pick up speed while free-falling, the pilot
selected the afterburner, which sent a huge plume of flame out the
tailpipe as he tried to make up for his mistake with thrust. But that
only sent the F-100's nose dancing wildly from side to side. Finally the
plane skated off the side of the runway, crashing and exploding in a
huge ball of flame. "The pilot didn't survive," the instructor stated
flatly.

"No shit," class members echoed as they shook their heads.

"Anybody wanna quit?" the instructor asked. Occasionally, pilots
did bail out of training after seeing this film. The F-100 had a fearsome reputation and high accident rate. It was informally called "the
widow-maker" on account of the number of pilots killed in the plane.

But none of these guys could be intimidated that easily. No one took the bait.

By the end of the first week, Howie and his classmates were becoming well versed in aircraft systems. It didn't take an engineering degree to be a pilot, but a bit of brains helped. Flying—and especially flying the fast-movers—involved the interplay of electricity, hydraulics, mechanics, and human skills. It was a delicate balancing act. Although Howie lacked a college degree, he was intelligent and had been studying planes since he began building models of them as a boy. A friend had said that Howie was the only person he had ever met who was both right- and left-brained, and Howie was indeed one of the calmest, most studious, and inventive characters in his class of twenty-two.

With those gleaming F-100s sitting out on the flight line, waiting to be saddled, the preliminary classroom work seemed tedious. But there were fascinating interludes. Lanny, Dick, and Howie were all captivated by the tales of an instructor pilot, or IP, who had just returned from a year's tour in Vietnam. He had worked as a forward air controller—a FAC—flying a light O-1 propeller aircraft, the Cessna Bird Dog. The IP had been assigned to work with the Army during his tour, flying over combat areas and helping pick out targets. It sounded more harrowing than any flying job these three had ever thought about. He told stories about looking for enemy troops who seemed invisible beneath dense jungle foliage, except for sporadic, violent bursts of anti-aircraft fire. Sometimes he'd have to fly at night, pointing out targets under flares for fighters streaking in with bombs or napalm. The weather was often terrible, but you had to fly anyway—the boys on the ground needed you. They were fighting and dying. And even back at the base it was never calm. Rocket and mortar attacks would come out of nowhere, and even the Air Force guys had to get into the act and throw grenades occasionally when their compound was attacked at night. Gung ho as they were, Lanny, Dick, and Howie didn't think being a FAC was for them.

Finally, after three weeks of what seemed like endless academic instruction . . . redemption! It was time to fly. Howie was scheduled to go first, and it was everything he imagined. Howie sat in the front of an F-100F, a two-seat model, with an instructor pilot in the back. The F-100, which the pilots typically called the "Hun," short for "Hundred," was big and powerful for a fighter—not as lumbering as the monstrosities Howie had flown at SAC, but substantial enough to carry five thousand pounds of bombs and other armaments. It had been the first Air Force jet capable of going supersonic in level flight, with a top speed of Mach 1.3, or about 875 miles per hour—a sports car, indeed.

After some preliminary checks, Howie gave the windup sign to the crew chief and pushed the start button. As compressed air from a ground unit turned the engine, he advanced the throttle and the turbojet engine roared to life as a mixture of air and jet fuel erupted in a controlled explosion. The airplane shook even at idle; you could feel the tremendous power of the Pratt & Whitney J-57 engine. Howie signaled the crew chief to pull the wooden chocks blocking the wheels. He pushed the power up and guided the jet toward the end of the runway.

Howie was cleared onto the runway. He advanced the throttle, pressing his flying boots firmly against the brakes. The jet bucked like a Brahma bull in a rodeo chute. He was cleared for takeoff and released the brakes. Then he pushed the throttle into afterburner and felt a kick in the back as the engine jumped from 11,000 to 17,000 pounds of thrust. As the plane accelerated down the runway, the IP yelled at Howie to pull back on the stick and raise the nose at 155 knots. The rush was thrilling, but Howie was already "behind the airplane"—it was moving faster than he was thinking. The moment they were airborne the wings began to wobble, and it felt like Howie lacked control of the jet. The IP had told him to expect that, but it surprised him anyway.

As the Hun picked up speed, however, the wing wobble stopped. At 300 knots they came out of afterburner, and Howie's mind caught up with the speeding jet as they climbed toward the practice area. Now it was time for some fun. The IP directed Howie to perform some simple aerial maneuvers he had practiced on trainer aircraft when he first learned to fly. For starters, Howie flew some lazy-eights, large climbing and descending turns making half an eight in the sky. Then some chandelles, steep, climbing, 180-degree turns, feeling the handling characteristics change. Then some loops, half loops, three-quarter loops with a rollout at the bottom, and other maneuvers meant to instill confi-

dence whether the pilot was upside down, right side up, diving verti-
cally, or arcing lazily across the sky.

They climbed to 25,000 feet, pushed the nose over, and began to
descend, flying faster until they sped through the sound barrier. It was
the first time Howie had been supersonic, and the only thing he noticed
as the Mach meter slipped passed Mach 1 was a slight jump in the nee-
dles on the pressure-sensitive cockpit instruments. Then they climbed
back to 20,000 feet and pointed the nose straight up until the airspeed
indicator read "0." The airplane stopped in midair, then quickly
flipped itself around, the nose pointing straight down as it entered a
vertical dive from which they recovered gingerly. It was all meant to
show that the aircraft was forgiving and predictable—as long as you
didn't "horse it around," or mishandle it. Then the plane would go out
of control and bite you in the ass. They finished off the one-hour,
fifteen-minute mission with practice landing patterns and a few touch-
and-gos at a nearby airfield, and finally a full-stop landing back at
Luke.

What a day! Howie smiled and shook his head. He had never flown
anything like this before—nothing this powerful, this wild. He was
amazed, enthralled. Lanny and Dick performed just as well as Howie
on their first rides, and after their first flights, all twenty-two students
got their North American "Machbusters" pin, for going supersonic.
They were all "Hun-drivers" now, albeit novices with much to learn.

First rides were always humbling, but it didn't take long for
Howie's quiet confidence to kick back in. For starters, as much as he
loved the Hun, he hated the two-seat F-model. He was a single-seat
fighter pilot, goddamn it. He didn't want anyone else in the cockpit,
and he became vocal about it. "I had enough of that shit at SAC," he
complained. "If I never fly with anyone else again, it will be too soon.
I don't even like the sound of my own breathing."

As the training progressed, Howie began to emerge as one of the
best "sticks" in the class. He mastered the instrument-flying phase,
learning to rely on the Hun's primitive cockpit instruments when visibility was poor. Formation flying was a breeze for him. Aerial refueling
from KC-135 tankers and air-to-ground bombing seemed to come
naturally. He got the top scores in the class in low-level "skip bombing"—practice deliveries of napalm—and excelled at strafing and dive-

bombing. Instructors graded and tracked every pilot's performance and ranked their proficiency, and as training progressed, Howie and Lanny Lancaster were vying with a couple other students for the coveted "Top Gun" honors, awarded to the pilot with the best combined score in several bombing and gunnery categories.

Lanny and Howie were running behind a freckle-faced, red-haired young lieutenant named Bob Franke as the competition reached the air-to-air gunnery phase. The challenge was simple enough: fire the Hun's 20mm cannons at a fourteen-by-thirty-foot dart-shaped object towed on a steel cable fifteen hundred feet behind another F-100. The dart, which looked like an X from behind, was meant to simulate an airplane, and each pilot got six missions on the dart. It took only two hits to qualify, but each pilot aimed to get more as a matter of pride.

Franke, a relaxed guy who got quite serious when it came to flying, had aced most of the other gunnery exercises and was comfortably ahead in the running for Top Gun. Howie and Lanny both figured they'd be buying him drinks at the end of the course. But Franke lacked the knack for aerial combat, and he continually positioned himself poorly for his approaches on the dart. He hit on just one of six missions. It was much easier for Howie, who had been through this kind of training when he flew the F-86 for a brief time before being transferred into bombers. He hit on four out of six missions. Lanny was a natural, too. He missed on his first go-round, but hit on the next five in a row.

Some other students had to finish dart training, so the instructor called for one more mission, and nobody complained. Lanny and Howie got to fly an additional sortie. The dart was tethered out. Lanny nailed it on his pass. Then Howie went for it and scored a direct hit. That gave him five out of seven on air-to-air. Lanny had done better, nailing six out of seven, but his overall score in all bombing events came in a notch below Howie's. That gave Howie top honors in his class, earning him lifelong bragging rights. And there was the vaunted plaque with a molded gun glued to it that read BARRY GOLDWATER TOP GUN AWARD, LUKE AFB, ARIZONA, HOWARD K. WILLIAMS. Senator Goldwater himself presented it to Howie at a dinner near the end of the course.

As training wound down, the pilots and their families began to address the obvious—most of the pilots would be heading to Vietnam soon to serve the standard one-year tour. It was the summer of 1967, and in Southeast Asia both sides were clearly escalating the war effort. The Air Force was clamoring for more fighter pilots. In Washington, a fierce behind-the-scenes battle was unfolding between the politicians and the generals over whether to expand the campaign, or curtail it, or pull out altogether.[1] But none of that was in the air at Luke, and most of the pilots took their war duties in stride. Even their wives did. They still remembered the men of their fathers' generation who had been drafted into World War II indefinitely and left home for two or three years. It wasn't pleasant, but going into combat is part of the job when you are a military family. Few talked much about it.

Besides, bravado carried the day, at least when more than one fighter pilot was in the room. After completing training and receiving their graduating certificates, Howie, Dick, Lanny, and their classmates gathered for one final night at the Stag Bar. They got roaring drunk, performed the usual antics, and sang fighter pilot songs, such as "Sammy Small":

> *Oh my name is Sammy Small, fuck 'em all*
> *Oh my name is Sammy Small, fuck 'em all*
> *Oh my name is Sammy Small and I've only got one ball*
> *But that's better than none at all, so fuck 'em all.*

They finished with raucous laughter, backslapping, and a macho farewell toast:

> *When our flying days are over*
> *When our flying days are past*
> *We hope they'll bury us upside down*
> *So the world can kiss our ass.*

As their departure dates for Vietnam drew closer, however, a bit of introspection seeped through the outer armor. When Howie and Monalee left Luke, they returned to Columbus, Ohio, which was close to their families in Steubenville, and also near an air base where Howie had once been posted. One night they went to the movies to see *Dr.*

Strangelove. It was customary for theaters to play "The Star Spangled Banner" before the curtain went up, and most of the audience, including lots of students from nearby Ohio State, stood up. But a few college kids remained slouched in their seats. Howie became livid. At intermission, Monalee thought he might throttle them, but instead he told her, "Even though I don't agree with them, they do have that right. And that's why I'm leaving."

Lanny Lancaster packed his flight gear, one sport coat, and two bags' worth of other belongings into his white '65 Corvette convertible and headed east from Luke to Granbury, Texas, where he visited friends and relatives before heading for Travis Air Force Base, near San Francisco—one of the last American way stations for Air Force pilots before Vietnam. Dick Rutan moved his wife, Geri, and his two-year-old daughter, Holly, into an apartment in Rocklin, California, about eighty miles northeast of San Francisco, near Travis. They had no family there, but Geri liked the Bay area, and there was some vague comfort in being close to Travis.

Just before shipping off, Howie paid a visit to Steubenville to visit family and friends. He and his best friend, John Buckmelter, spent a night on the town, such as Steubenville was. Bucky picked him up at the Williams house, showing off his new Buick convertible. They went to a nearby restaurant and flirted with the waitress. There were plenty of old times to recall: Hustling rides down at the airfield. Picking up tips on how to fly. Sneaking a Piper Cub out on the runway—and then getting it airborne for two minutes—without the owner ever knowing. And all the nights Bucky spent at the Williams house, flirting with Howie's sister Jean and sleeping in the bathtub.

They hit a couple of gambling joints to play craps and blackjack. Howie won a few bucks. They began to tie one on. While driving home, Howie bestowed some Air Force wisdom on his friend. "Being drunk is psychosomatic," he told Bucky. "If you look in the rearview mirror and see blue-light fever, you get sober real fast."

Finally, Bucky dropped off his old friend and gave him a big hug. "Take care of yourself," he said.

"That's a big rodge," Howie replied, using the Air Force shorthand for "roger."

Back in Columbus, Howard Jr. was just starting first grade. The Williamses stayed in temporary quarters at the Air Force base until their apartment was ready nearby. Only a couple of days after moving in, it was time for Howie to leave. The family drove to Wright-Patterson Air Force Base in Dayton, where Howie was booked on a military flight. They spent the afternoon in the Air Force Museum on base, checking out the old airplanes and other aviation relics. After a nice lunch, they drove Howie to his airplane. He held Monalee tighter than he ever had held her before and planted a long, tender kiss on her. Then he kissed his son, said good-bye, and boarded the plane. After a few tears, Monalee and Howard Jr. got back in the car and headed back to their new home in Columbus. It would be a tough year, but maybe it would pass quickly.

THREE

"I DON'T THINK HE HAS A CHANCE..."

John Haltigan had never even been overseas, and here he was in the midst of one of the most exotic places he could have imagined. The first overwhelming sensation to greet the brand-new, twenty-two-year-old second lieutenant as he descended the stairs from a chartered Continental Airlines jetliner was the suffocating heat. It seemed to clamp onto his body, and after just a few seconds on the tarmac at Tan Son Nhut Air Base, on the outskirts of Saigon, he could already feel the damp, oppressive climate sapping his energy.

Then there was the commotion. Not just the buzz of a busy airport, but the frantic movements of people arriving at war and leaving war and prosecuting war. Youthful troops new to Vietnam scampered off airplanes while glassy-eyed combat veterans on their way elsewhere lounged around the terminal like vagabonds, awaiting word that their plane was ready. Jeeps and trucks and other military vehicles darted about like insects on a pond. The *whap whap whap* of helicopter rotors and the roar of airplane engines produced a throbbing sound track to the scene, with the dull thumping of distant artillery fire adding a macabre beat.

But the smell is what really got his attention. It came at him in waves. First was a noxious industrial aroma, the by-product of streets clogged with cars, trucks, motorcycles, and a stream of other jury-rigged contraptions. Then came the pungent odor of 5 million people crammed into a city that had housed one-fifth that number only a few years earlier. The rot of open sewers and polluted waterways mingled with the smoke from outdoor markets where fish and meat and noodles simmered over open fires. It made Haltigan's nose tingle. Making it worse, this miasma was occasionally laced with the unmistakable tang of cordite, acrid and bitter. When the wind blew a certain way, it was easy to imagine that half the countryside was on fire.

Just fifteen months earlier, Haltigan had graduated from Northeastern University in Boston with a history degree. For a kid from Middlebury, Vermont, going to school in Boston had seemed like an adventure in itself. Then he faced the usual options for a twenty-two-year-old in 1967: wait to get drafted into the Army, or take the initiative and join the service of his choice. So he decided to join the Air Force and put his degree to use as an intelligence officer. In August 1967 he graduated from Intelligence Officer School at Lowry Air Force Base in Denver. Once he graduated from Lowry, there was no time to waste—the Air Force immediately shipped him to Vietnam. No matter that he was totally inexperienced and bewildered with apprehension. When he got his orders, he had never even heard of Phu Cat, the base the Air Force had assigned him to. It hadn't entered the lexicon like Da Nang and Cam Ranh Bay, and Haltigan had to look it up to find out where it was.

From Saigon, it didn't take very long to get to Phu Cat, since it was only about 230 miles to the north, a journey Haltigan completed by plane and Army truck. But compared to the teeming capital, Phu Cat was a sleepy backwater. The war and the Americans who had come to fight it dominated the little village nearby, which gave the base its name. Most of the military-age Vietnamese men were off fighting for one side or the other, and the women left behind earned their living serving the Americans, doing laundry or washing dishes or performing other menial jobs on the base.

Yet Haltigan noticed many reminders of what life must have been like before the war. The ruins of a Buddhist pagoda sat on a knoll about half a mile east of the base. There were rice paddies in every direction, full of water, being plowed by old men wearing conical straw hats who drove water buffalo pulling wooden plows. The countryside was bucolic, with low, rolling hills covered with jungle vegetation, high trees, and elephant grass ten feet tall. To the west toward the border with Laos and Cambodia the mountains were more dramatic, steeper and more jagged. And as always in Vietnam, the wind bore odors, usually a faint salty smell from the South China Sea, about twenty miles to the east, suffused with wisps of burning wood from cooking fires, and occasionally incense. It was serene.

Like most of Vietnam, however, Phu Cat was a tableau of contrasts. Green and beautiful as it was, the surrounding countryside was routinely shredded by explosives. At night, red tracers and candle flares from mortars and artillery would constantly fill the sky, to illuminate any Viet Cong insurgents who might be thinking about sneaking up on the base. AC-47 "Spooky" gunships, converted from C-47s, the military version of the DC-3 airliner, would get into the act, too, dropping parachute flares and pouring machine-gun fire into the jungle to keep the VC at bay. There were plenty of VC out there, and machine-gun emplacements fortified with sandbags lined the base perimeter. But tough soldiers from the Republic of Korea—the "ROKs" of the 1st Tiger Division—guarded Phu Cat, and word was the Viet Cong didn't care to mess with the ROKs. So life inside the wire was fairly calm, marred only by occasional VC rocket and mortar attacks.

The base itself was a pleasant surprise. It wasn't exactly modern, but it was far more comfortable than Haltigan had expected. Most of the buildings were two-story prefabricated wooden structures with two crucial amenities: window air-conditioning units to fend off the debilitating heat, and hot water in the group showers. The officers slept two to a room, pretty grand living for a war. Haltigan's room was a square little abode at the end of the second-floor hallway in the officers' barracks, with a generator-powered A/C unit that kept it as cold as a meat locker. Haltigan didn't complain. The base also had a chapel and a rudimentary exchange where you could buy toiletries, magazines, and occasional souvenirs. Contractors prepared the food and it was tolerable with regular luxuries like ice cream and fresh salads. There was even seafood every now and then, delivered fresh from the South China Sea.

There were discomforts, to be sure, but for the most part they weren't life-threatening: With all the nighttime activity, it was nearly impossible for a newcomer, unaccustomed to the cacophony, to sleep. And the constant construction of runways and buildings churned the red clay dirt into fine dust and mud that got into everything—your clothes, your hair, your teeth. Grit was a part of everyday life at Phu Cat, but it didn't seem that bad as long as you stayed cool.

Haltigan checked in with his unit, the 37th Tactical Fighter Wing, which carried out the bulk of the operations at Phu Cat. He was to be a wing intelligence officer, responsible for briefing the pilots on all the things they needed to know to fly, survive, and carry out their assignments. The 37th had a straightforward mission: provide close air support—CAS—for the Army grunts fighting the ground war in the Central Highlands of South Vietnam. This was tedious life-or-death work, Haltigan quickly learned, choreographed with great complexity and often carried out under maddening conditions. The key links between the grunts doing the fighting on the ground and the pilots dropping bombs over their shoulders were air liaison officers, or ALOs, who lived and worked with the ground troops, and forward air controllers, or FACs, who would drone slowly over the combat zone in old propeller-driven O-1s and O-2s and pinpoint targets for the fighters and bombers to attack.

The ALOs knew everything the ground units were up to and would help plan operations. During an offensive they'd recommend enemy targets for the Air Force to attack, and in the midst of fighting they'd help call in bombs on targets that could be just a few yards in front of friendly troops. It was the job of the FACs overhead to physically locate the targets, a nifty trick in Vietnam since pilots could seldom see anything on the ground. Even brutally contested battlefields were often covered by double- and triple-canopy jungle, and the Americans, with technological advantages that made the Viet Cong seem prehistoric, learned to rely on smoke rockets, of all things, to tag the locations of troops and targets hidden beneath the foliage.

During a battle, FACs would establish radio contact with the ground troops and then have the grunts pop colored smoke grenades. The smoke would slowly waft up through the trees, and that told them where *not* to drop bombs. If there was no contact with enemy forces, the FACs would dive down and fire their own smoke rockets, 2.75-

inch white-phosphorous projectiles known as "Willie Petes," as close as they could to preplanned targets. Fighters would then come in behind them and aim for the smoke with their weapons—gravity bombs, rockets, napalm, cluster bombs that separated into dozens of smaller bomblets, 20mm cannons, whatever was most appropriate or on hand. "Hit my smoke," Haltigan learned, was a phrase he'd hear over and over.

Aiming at smoke, in fact, was an apt metaphor for the spotty results of much close air support. With an agile, smart, and fast-moving enemy beneath the trees, FACs often marked targets by guessing. Pilots dropped bombs on the smoke and nobody could tell what the results were. The notorious "bomb damage assessments," or BDA, the 37th was required to forward up the chain of command after bombing raids was much more of an estimate of damage than a tangible accounting, and many pilots knew it was generously padded. By the time Haltigan arrived at the 37th, pilots were deriding the missions as "tree-busting" and "monkey bombing," and they joked that most of their BDA consisted of "smoliage"—smoke and foliage.

Some of the pilots even seemed bored. Combat could be raging on the ground, but the Viet Cong had few antiaircraft weapons and no planes of their own, and they rarely fired at the armada above them. For some of the rowdy young cowboys who had gotten themselves pumped up for war, monkey bombing was dull—there was no real combat in the air.

There were exceptions to the tedium: night bombing, for instance, when the FACs and fighter jocks had to do their work under parachute flares. And then there were the brutal close fights on the ground, when pinpoint CAS could rescue American units from certain death at the hands of ferocious, practically suicidal, VC. In those battles, there was often so much confusion and smoke from explosions on the ground that ALOs, FACs, and the fighter jocks had to find other ways besides smoke signals to sort out friendly and enemy troops and identify targets. They'd use tree lines, ridges, or other terrain features to mark troop locations, and sometimes "walk" bombs in until they got closer and closer to the U.S. soldiers and the enemy troops they were entangled with. In desperation, sometimes the ground troops would shout, "Put it on top of us! We're being overrun!"

Haltigan heard many tales in his first days at Phu Cat of heroic, seat-of-the-pants CAS missions. But there were also far too many tragic situations when a pilot misunderstood instructions from the ground, or misinterpreted a landmark, or just screwed up and ended up bombing the good guys. Such "friendly fire" incidents often left dead GIs on the ground and ended too many pilots' careers.

Pilots at the 37th flew the F-100D, a sleek, powerful, single-seat supersonic fighter that could carry five thousand pounds of bombs and other weapons. It had four 20mm cannons on its nose, with rounds capable of chewing through a tractor-trailer. Haltigan's job was to brief the pilots before takeoff and debrief them after landing, passing information up and down the chain of command. Before the missions he would first deliver a routine recitation of takeoff times, call signs, radio frequencies, and other procedural data pilots jotted in their notebooks. Then came the meat of the briefing: the situation report—SITREP—describing what was happening on the ground. That's where the pilots would start to get a sense of the targets, the ferocity of the combat, if a big operation was going on, and the confusion they'd be facing on their mission. Once the pilots headed for the flight line, Haltigan could catch a few hours of sleep, since there would be work to do when they got back: debriefing the pilots, compiling after-action reports, digesting bits of intelligence they may have picked up, any signs of troop or equipment movements, weapon emplacements, or ground fire they had witnessed.

Haltigan was just getting used to this heady business when he got surprising news: After only a week with the 37th, he'd be getting a new job. He was told to report to "Misty," a special, top secret unit that worked out of a nondescript office in the back of the Wing Headquarters building. What in the world is Misty? Haltigan thought. He had heard vague rumors of a TS outfit operating from Phu Cat, but he didn't have access to the classified information. And, he was so busy trying to figure out his own job, he didn't have time to try to learn about somebody else's.

Suddenly he was assigned to Misty, and now Misty, whatever it was, would be his job, too. So one day in September 1967 he found his way to the Misty portion of headquarters and knocked softly on a wooden door that had a cardboard sign with the words NO ACCESS—

TOP SECRET scrawled across it in grease pencil. The door opened and John walked in on what seemed like a funeral—long faces, quiet voices, serious looks, a sullen, sad atmosphere. This didn't seem like a good start to the job he'd have for the next year.

A lieutenant colonel named Joe DeSalvatore, the senior intelligence officer, greeted him and asked him to come in. "Ray will be with you soon," he said. "He's debriefing the morning mission. Coffee?"

"No thanks," said John. He was eager to learn about his new job. "So, what's going on here? What's this Misty business all about?" he asked.

"North Vietnam," answered DeSalvatore stoically, without saying much more. Haltigan waited quietly for a fuller explanation, until a few minutes later a turbocharged young lieutenant hustled through the door, filling the room with energy. 1st Lt. Ray Bevivino looked like an Italian fireplug—short, with a dark complexion and flashing, mischievous eyes. Haltigan could tell right off the bat he was the kind of guy who was always on the move. He never stopped talking and seemed uncomfortable sitting down. "Glad to have you, John," Bevivino chirped. Then, faster than Haltigan could write it down, Bevivino began to explain what the unit was. "Misty is pure and simple about North Vietnam," Bevivino lectured. "The gooks are massing shit, serious shit, up north of the DMZ and moving it south. Our job is to find it and stop it. This is a pretty new mission. We've only been at it since June, July really. We've already lost our first commander, Bud Day." This much Haltigan knew—every time a pilot at Phu Cat got shot down, the base became electrified and everybody knew it. "That's why all the long faces," said Bevivino. "He was a good shit."

Bevivino launched into the tale with relish. It all began, he said, as the North Vietnamese Army units above the demilitarized zone, the DMZ, started shooting down American planes, particularly the slow-moving O-1 "Bird Dogs" that were doing the FAC mission in the North, scouting for NVA troops and equipment flowing down the Ho Chi Minh Trail into South Vietnam. The Air Force knew that this dated tactic, a staple of air operations in the Korean War, probably wouldn't survive the stiffening North Vietnamese defenses. It would take a high-performance jet to do the job. As more and more of the prop-driven "slow FACs" got shot down, 7th Air Force sent a staff officer up to investigate. He went out on a two-ship FAC mission, only to witness catastrophe with his own eyes. "A SAM blew one of the fuckers up right in front of the headquarters weenie," Bevivino recounted. "He shit his pants. Slow FACs came to an end and we started up."

The decision-makers at 7th Air Force had considered using the brand-new F-4 fighter for the "fast FAC" mission. But they decided it was too expensive and, with its two gas-gulping engines, that it would require too many tankers for midair refueling. Instead, they picked the aging F-100, and decided they'd need the two-seat F model, so one guy could fly the plane while the other scouted, navigated, and took pictures. The unit—known officially as "Commando Sabre"—started out as a small detachment of just sixteen pilots in July 1967. Because of the high risk, all would have to be volunteers. The top secret designation attracted a lot of interest, but some pilots came and went quickly, figuring monkey bombing wasn't so bad after all compared to flying back and forth over North Vietnam and getting shot at constantly.

The unit sputtered for a few weeks, learning the ropes through trial and error. Col. Ray Lee, vice commander of the 37th Wing, decided Commando Sabre was so complex that it needed its own staff and an operations area separate from the other units at Phu Cat. Then came the arrival of Maj. George "Bud" Day, the officer Lee chose to command the unit. The tempo picked up quickly once he arrived. Day was a natural combat leader, a hard-charging, pragmatic warrior who focused on the big picture and left others to argue over bureaucratic details. As one of the senior pilots at a base called Tuy Hoa, about fifty miles south of Phu Cat, he had already flown more than 70 combat missions in the South and 65 in the North. He had more than five thousand hours of flying time, making him one of the most experienced fighter pilots in Vietnam.[1] And he was a full-blooded jet-jock who loved being airborne and seemed indifferent to the nuances of checking the right blocks and tending to one's career.

Besides his solid reputation as a leader, Day had a peculiar claim to fame: He was perhaps the only pilot in the Air Force who had survived an ejection—without a parachute. While supervising another pilot during a training flight in England in 1957, Day's own F-84 jet flamed out, forcing him to eject just 400 feet off the ground. His chute deployed but then failed to open, flapping like a streamer as he sped toward the ground. The branches of a thirty-foot pine tree somehow broke his fall, and the risers from the chute got tangled in the tree and softened his landing. Day ended up bruised but safe, and after a brief recuperation he returned to flying.

Day looked as tough as his reputation suggested. He had a square jaw that Errol Flynn might have envied, and searing blue eyes that encouraged others to listen. His broad shoulders and lean waist gave him the torso of a middleweight boxer. It was Day who selected the unit's radio call sign—"Misty," after his favorite song—which is how just about everybody who knew about it came to refer to Commando Sabre.

Day was instantly popular with his pilots. But in a high-octane environment like the Air Force at war, every shit-hot leader had a nemesis, and Day's sat right above him. Col. Ed Schneider, commander of the 37th Wing and Day's boss, had disliked the idea of Misty from the start. General Momyer may have set Misty rolling, but the unit flew Schneider's planes and had to play by his rules. So Schneider "owned" Misty, and he made it clear he felt the Mistys were cowboys and renegades willing to break any of his rules for a little bit of wartime glory. He routinely tried to hamstring the unit and find reasons to cut back its missions.

Schneider's biggest gripe was what Misty did to his planes. They came back from missions in terrible shape, with holes in the wings from North Vietnamese AAA (antiaircraft artillery), and occasionally with entire chunks torn out of the fuselage. That damage counted against Schneider's safety record. Bud Day's shootdown caused another problem, since all commanders were held responsible for the losses in their units, even during wartime. Getting your pilots killed was no way for a colonel to earn his first star, and Day's downing had given Schneider a reason to tighten up on Misty, putting new restrictions on how low and how long they could fly and how aggressive they could be. And he reiterated his rule about the Hun's two 20mm cannons, which were devastating but effective only at low altitudes and close range—they were to be used only in extreme situations, such as pilot rescues. General Momyer, in Saigon, had stood up for the unit before, however, since Misty delivered results. He regularly forwarded photos taken by Misty pilots to the Pentagon, and he was known to brag that in Misty he finally had a unit that could find and hit targets. The good general, Bevivino hoped, would bail Misty out again.

Bevivino explained why Misty caused Schneider so much heartburn. "This is a pisser of a mission," he said. "The gooks got guns up the ass, thousands of them, and they all shoot." Misty missions, he continued, were assigned to work Route Package 1, one of the seven geographical zones 7th Air Force had divided North Vietnam into. Route Pack 1 included the portion of North Vietnam that was north of the DMZ and south of the eighteenth parallel. The "Pack" border ran all the way from Cape Ron on the eastern coast to the border with Laos—where the Ho Chi Minh Trail was the main attraction. It wasn't as dangerous as flying over Hanoi, where SAMs and AAA were as thick as weeds, and where planes were shot down almost daily. But the Trail was the lifeline that supplied troops, weapons, food, medicine, and just about everything else needed to sustain the insurgency in the South. And it was defended by the NVA in accordance with its value.

Well-manned antiaircraft guns lined the Trail, hidden beneath the dense foliage along the roads and beside the fords over the many waterways (no bridges were left after three years of sustained bombing). The men manning the guns yearned for targets, and the Misty FACs, flying low, made good ones. And the air defense troops who worked the Trail were evolving from a batch of undertrained amateurs into wily, experienced veterans increasingly familiar with American tactics. They were becoming adept at setting "flak traps," where they'd lure American planes down low by setting some curiosity out in the open, then start blasting away with AAA when they thought they had the airplane in their sights.

The war for the Trail, in fact, was becoming the seminal battle of the Vietnam War. Most of the attention, of course, had been focused on the ground fights in the South's Central Highlands, in places like the Ia Drang Valley and Pleiku and up in Con Thien, names that millions of Americans had become familiar with. But the Viet Cong that the Americans faced in those battles—along with increasing numbers of regulars from the North Vietnamese Army—would not even have been able to muster without the support that flowed down the Trail. The Pentagon knew this, and by 1967 had sent more bombs against Route Pack 1 than any other region of North Vietnam. That added up to as many as three thousand attack sorties per month, many of them cued by Misty pilots out hunting for targets.² But most people knew little about the war for the Trail. It wasn't a secret that the United States was bombing North Vietnam—but the details were kept very quiet.

The Mistys' procedure went like this, Bevivino explained: "We take off out of Phu Cat and go north. We look for SAMs, truck parks, fuel storage, supplies, gun sites, anything military that moves. When we find it, we act as FACs—fast FACs." The pilots would call in their finds to an airborne command-and-control center known as ABCCC, "AB-Triple C," and call for fighters loaded with bombs. On good days there would be as many as four Misty missions. The first mission would typically use the call sign Misty 11—that meant it was the first Misty sortie of the day, flying solo as a single ship. The next sortie would be Misty 21, and so on.

Once fighters were on station, a Misty pilot would "mark" the target with smoke rockets while the fighters rolled in behind and tried to hit the smoke, just like the missions in the South. Then the Mistys would refuel from an airborne tanker and do it all over again. What made the missions so dangerous was the hunt—flying low, to see targets as clearly as possible, and making repeated passes over hot areas, sometimes through continuous gunfire. "The missions are about four and a half hours, with two midair refuelings," Bevivino said with effect, since that was far longer than the more conventional missions in the South that Haltigan had just learned about in his one-week job at wing intelligence. As that was sinking in, Bevivino added, "Unless someone gets shot down." Then he described how Mistys would help coordinate rescues, doing anything necessary to help retrieve guys on the ground before the North Vietnamese got to them. "Then we refuel as many times as required."

Haltigan had been a good student during this extraordinary tutorial, listening quietly and doing little to interrupt Bevivino's oratorical flow. He was impressed. Jesus, he thought. Four and a half hours over the North, at low level through those guns. No wonder they lost their commander. How the hell does anyone survive?

Helping answer questions like that would soon be his job: Haltigan was there to replace Bevivino, who was due to rotate out of the wing. "Your job," Bevivino continued, "is to organize the intel for the Misty pilots so they can absorb it quickly. Always start with the previous day's losses—where airplanes went down. Rescuing our guys is the top priority. Next, show high-priority targets, IOIs, items of interest, from 7th Air Force—any other promising target areas for a pilot look-see. Then, tell them where we think the guns are, the defenses, so they don't get surprised and hit. Finally, put all the detailed crap, tanker call signs, base altitude, etcetera, on the card for them."

"Another thing," Bevivino warned. "Be careful how you brief at the 'stand-up.' " The stand-up was Colonel Schneider's afternoon staff meeting that covered the day's activities, bombing results, and plans for the next day. All the squadron commanders attended, and Misty had begun to steal the show, with far more compelling results to report than any of the other units. "We're up there reporting destruction of trucks, SAM sites, triple-A, pilot rescues, and we're showing photos to prove it, while the other units are reporting 'smoliage.' You'd think we'd be heroes," Bevivino complained, "but Schneider thinks we're out-of-control assholes, and he hates it that Momyer loves us. So fair warning."

The nervous young lieutenant, on his second week in Vietnam, nodded his head.

For the first few days Bevivino handled the intel briefings while Haltigan sat in and took notes. It was a new world with its own lexicon. He started to learn about landmarks in Route Pack 1 such as Bat Lake, Fingers Lake, and the Disappearing River, so labeled by the Mistys because of their shape or other distinct features.

The pilots constantly "jinked," turning, climbing, and diving, moving the airplane in three dimensions while in the air over the North, zigzagging aggressively to make it harder for gunners on the ground to get a bead on them. And there were way more guns in the North than anybody had to worry about in the South. Haltigan barely understood the mission, but he sensed quickly that there was something special about Misty, the enthusiasm the pilots had for their job, and the risks they were willing to take to accomplish it.

But most of all, Haltigan noticed the gloom that infected the unit as its members wondered what had happened to their commander, Bud Day. It was unusual. Even with his limited experience, Haltigan knew that the loss of a single pilot rarely produced such shock, especially in the middle of a war in which hundreds of pilots had been shot down. It was as if an aura of invincibility had been punctured, and the pilots took it personally. Missions continued, but there was none of the rowdy bar banter fighter jocks were famous for. Col. Ray Lee, the wing vice commander, met with the unit and urged all the men to be more careful, to fly higher, and not take so many risks. The pilots seemed to listen.

They talked over and over about what might have happened to Day and seemed to regard him as so invincible that he was likely to come walking through the gate at Phu Cat any minute. And they endlessly quizzed Corwin "Kipp" Kippenhan, who had been flying with Day when they were shot down, about any detail that might give a clue to Day's fate.

The day he was lost—August 26, 1967—had started expectantly. Day and Kippenhan, a former slow FAC who had flown close air support missions for the Army, were getting strapped in for Kipp's F-100 checkout flight, the first time he'd be in the front seat flying the plane instead of sitting in the back observing. As they were loading their gear in the Hun, Day noticed a small transport jet, a T-39, that had just landed—the "Scatback" that 7th Air Force sent up occasionally, with VIPs or hot intelligence, for high-priority targets they wanted Misty to find and hit. A vehicle drove straight from the Scatback to the Hun with some fascinating material: a picture of a surface-to-air missile, a Russian SA-2, in a fruit orchard up north in Route Pack 1.

The SAM photo had been snapped by a fast-moving reconnaissance jet, probably an RF-101, and it represented an urgent problem. The lumbering, eight-engined B-52 was the flagship of the U.S. bomber fleet, able to drop more than sixty thousand pounds of bombs on a single sortie. These Arc Light missions along the DMZ were brutalizing enemy troops and preventing them from massing for even bigger fights than they were already dragging the Americans into in the I Corps area. The NVA was beginning a big buildup near Khe Sanh, and the "Buff," the Big Ugly Fat Fellow, was one of the key weapons, helping disrupt it. But for all its muscle, the B-52 was no agile bantamweight. It depended upon "ECM," electronic countermeasures, and F-105 Wild Weasel SAM hunter-killer aircraft, not agility, to avoid SAMs. It could not dodge an SA-2 on its own. The SA-2 in the Scatback's picture would have to be found and destroyed before it claimed one of America's premier aircraft and its six-man crew. Day and Kippenhan had their marching orders—today it was up to Misty.

Day knew where the orchard was, near Fingers Lake just north of the DMZ that marked the line between North and South. The pilots took off, flew north along the coast for about thirty minutes, descended, then turned west for a high-speed run toward the target area. They started jinking as they crossed the coast and quickly found the orchard. But the SAM, like virtually all the North's important military targets, was expertly camouflaged and they couldn't make it out. What they were sure of, however, was that the swarm of AAA flak they encountered the moment they got near Fingers Lake would eat them alive if they were foolish enough to double back for another pass. So they flew over to Dong Hoi, along the coast, to mark for a series of fighter strikes against a truck park and a storage area that Mistys had pinpointed the day before. They shot some BDA photos of the aftermath, then gassed up on the KC-135 tanker out over the Gulf of Tonkin and headed back to look for the SAM, hoping the AAA gunners protecting it wouldn't be expecting them.

The gunners, unfortunately, were eager and alert. The two pilots approached Fingers Lake from a slightly different direction than before, hoping that another sun angle would bring out contrasts on the ground and help them spot the SAM. Day, who had taken control of the plane from the backseat, was jinking back and forth, trying to weave like a drunkard in order to present an unpredictable flight path. Still, the air was thick with AAA rounds, tracers, and flak. Finally Kippenhan, with the eyes of a hawk, spotted something. "I've got it in sight!" he shouted.

Day rolled out and pulled up, trying to gain altitude, eager to get out of the intense flak. But their luck ran out. A two-foot-long AAA shell from one of the 37mm guns struck somewhere in the tail of the Hun and exploded. Day pulled the nose of the jet around toward the coast and tried to climb, but the aircraft pitched over, nose down, and went into a steep dive. Both pilots were thrust upward into the top of the canopy, along with the cameras and other loose gear in the cockpit. The stick froze, indicating that the hydraulic system was shot—they had lost pitch and roll control. Other systems failed and warning lights came on. With the stick locked in place and the plane descending rapidly, Day considered turning the Hun upside down with the rudder so that the nose would move upward, not down. But the ground was getting too close and if it didn't work there'd be no time left to bail out. Only one thing to do—Day raised the ejection seat arms, firing the canopy. Then, according to procedure, he squeezed the triggers on his ejection seat handles. Since he was in the back he went first to avoid being fried by the blast from Kipp's rocket in the front seat. Kippenhan followed. The parachutes worked, but since they were so low to start with, both pilots drifted to earth in less than a minute.

Once a pilot bailed out in enemy territory, much was up to chance. Weather, wind, terrain, and the disposition of enemy forces all intervened. Would he come down in the jungle where he could easily hide and be hard to find? Or would he come down in the midst of the enemy? Getting captured was of course the nightmare scenario, but getting rescued—and leaving your buddy behind—wasn't so hot either. The guilt that came with leaving your crewmate behind—even if it wasn't your fault—could turn a guy inside out for years.

Even before they had bailed out, the ABCCC had picked up Bud and Kipp's Mayday call and ordered the rescue forces to launch. An HH-53 "Jolly Green," the giant Sikorsky rescue helicopter that had gained fame for making numerous Southeast Asia combat rescues, homed in on Kippenhan's parachute rescue beeper with little trouble, pinpointing his exact location by talking to him over his pilot survival radio. Kippenhan vectored the chopper above him by voice commands. The chopper hovered about one hundred feet off the ground while a pararescue jumper—a "PJ"—leaned out and lowered a fold-up rescue hoist on a steel cable from a door-mounted winch. Kippenhan let the hoist hit the ground to dissipate static electricity, lowered one arm of the hoist, straddled it, and quickly placed the safety strap around his body. The Jolly began to move off slowly with Kipp dangling below, being reeled up. As the hoist reached the helicopter door, the PJ reached out, grabbed Kipp, and dragged him abruptly backward into the chopper.

But finding Day was another matter. Kippenhan recalled seeing Day's parachute, but he also thought that Day was hanging limp—he may have been knocked unconscious during the ejection or even killed by ground fire. And Day had passed him going down, not a good sign. Kippenhan had lost a couple of panels from his own parachute, torn loose in the violent high-speed ejection, and was descending more rapidly than usual. Day was falling even faster, and a hard landing could have made any injuries worse. The Jolly Green hovered for several minutes looking for Day's chute and listening for a signal from his parachute rescue beacon or a radio message from his survival radio. But fire from the ground intensified and, with no sign of Day, the Jolly Green had pulled out. Kipp knew it would make no sense to orbit in heavy gunfire when there was no sign of the survivor, but he was crushed. His commander was being left behind, and Kipp could do nothing about it.

Back at Misty, hope wrestled with dread. Day was just about the toughest warrior most of the pilots had ever met, and he had always said he'd never allow the North Vietnamese to take him if he got shot down. If captured, he vowed he would escape. But the chances for a pilot on the ground in the North became grim if he wasn't picked up quickly. Still, on just about every Misty mission, for days, the pilots would scan the area near Fingers Lake, listening and looking for some sign of a parachute, a mirror flash, a beeper, or some hopeful crackle over the radio. But they saw and heard nothing. Hope slowly gave way to reality. Bud Day was gone.

Colonel Lee, the wing vice commander, wrote in his diary that Day was either captured or dead: "I don't think he has a chance to evade in the Fingers Lake area." The Misty pilots seem to have gotten the point, he wrote, and agreed to fly a little less aggressively. But with this group, Lee mused, you had to wonder how long the lesson would last. "They are still listening, and will probably continue to do so until the memory of Bud Day's loss fades."[3]

FOUR

THE PACK

It was time for John Haltigan to fly solo, and he was terrified. The bookish twenty-two-year-old had no real experience speaking in front of people, and now he had to face a batch of hardened, nononsense fighter pilots who got shot at every day and must have had little regard for a staff weenie like him. The pilots were often tired and impatient and didn't want to hear any extraneous banter. They wanted to get straight to the meat of the mission—targets, maps, photos of the terrain. It seemed strange to Haltigan for him to be briefing the Misty pilots, since they were some of the most experienced aviators in Vietnam and had probably forgotten more about Route Pack 1 than he would ever know.

But the Mistys put up with his nervousness and were even welcoming. Maj. Bill Douglass, Misty's operations officer, took Haltigan under his wing immediately. "Whiskey Bill" Douglass, so known not because of his drinking but because he had the deep, gravelly voice of a bluesman, was a former O-1 slow FAC whose plane—and body— had been badly shot up on a mission in the South during a previous tour. He had been with Misty since the beginning. Like Bud Day, the Misty commander, Douglass was an experienced fighter pilot. He and Day had devised many of the Misty tactics and procedures together.

While Day was the visionary who energized the unit and handled the colonels and generals, it was Douglass, the diplomat and driving force, who often quietly got things done without leaving broken glass in his path. He'd finagle whatever Misty needed from elsewhere on base and figure out the most effective way to match up the pilots.

Douglass was distraught at the loss of Day, who had become like a brother. But with only a week left in the unit before he was scheduled to rotate out of Vietnam, Douglass was eager to pass down every bit of knowledge he could. He tutored Haltigan like a father imparting his family's oral history to his son, fearful that anything left out might be lost forever.

Haltigan took a quick liking to other pilots in the unit, too. He discovered that Maj. Bob Craner, a quiet, laid-back officer from a town near Albany, was a Boston Red Sox fan, just as he was. Craner, in fact, had gotten to Misty via baseball. Growing up, Ted Williams had been his hero. When he learned that Williams had been a Marine jet fighter pilot in Korea, Craner decided it might be a good way to get out of Cohoes, the old, depressed mill town in upstate New York where he grew up. He first became a navigator, then a pilot flying F-86s and later F-100s.

Craner had been eligible to leave the Air Force in 1966 and had even lined up a job as an airline pilot. But with the war expanding, he figured it was his duty to stay in the Air Force a while longer, and when he heard about Misty he contacted Bud Day and asked if he could join. Craner had graduated from the Air Force's Fighter Weapons School at Nellis Air Force Base in Nevada, an elite training program reserved for the Air Force's best fighter pilots. Day was happy to have him, and Craner became the resident expert on the AAA guns and other weapons being employed up north. Craner had a reputation as a ferociously aggressive pilot, as tough as anybody in the unit. And he often dipped below altitudes considered safe, if that's what it took to get at a target. But he was as mellow on the ground as he was intense in the air, and he struck Haltigan as the antithesis of the stereotypical fighter jock. His thoughtful, philosophical musings were impressive. While few pilots questioned the war in 1967, Craner would often wonder aloud, "What are we doing here?" He and Haltigan got to be fast friends despite the differences in their jobs and ages.

Maj. Bob Blocher, muscular, handsome, and athletic, became another mentor. Like Craner, he was thoughtful and serious and seemed to make it his personal responsibility to make sure everybody in Misty was well taken care of. He had come from a stint flying F-100s in the South out of Phan Rang, a base along the coast about 150 miles northeast of Saigon. He and Bill Douglass had flown together in the same squadron in England, and Douglass tracked him down in Vietnam and recruited him for Misty. Douglass knew he was soon coming to the end of his own tour, and leaving Misty in good hands was a top priority, particularly after the loss of Bud Day. Blocher would be a steady, mature influence on the organization. He had the "right stuff" as a pilot, but also a good head on his shoulders.

Capts. Jere Wallace and Jim Mack were so smooth and debonair that they could have played themselves in the Hollywood version of Misty. Capt. Eben "Jonesy" Jones, an early version of stealth, was so quiet you had to pull every bit of information out of him. He probably never bragged a day in his life. Medium height, muscular, self-effacing, and fair-skinned, he always appeared sunburned. Perhaps it was the searing Southeast Asia sun, or maybe he was always blushing. Either way, he had a ready smile and always chuckled at himself.

Jonesy claimed to be the only guy who got into Misty by wrecking his commander's airplane. He had been flying the squadron commander's F-100 on a bombing mission out of Tuy Hoa, another beachside base 220 miles northeast of Saigon, when he got too close to the flight leader and picked up a fragment from one of the leader's bombs. Planes got "fragged" occasionally, usually because the pilot failed to keep enough distance from the airplane up ahead. "Pilot error" it was called. Repairing the damage would have been a minor matter for the maintenance guys, except that the plane caught fire in the hangar and ended up being demolished. Jonesy found himself with an enraged lieutenant colonel on his tail, and somehow he had to "get out of Dodge."

He pleaded with the personnel department at Tuy Hoa for any assignment that was available. The assignment officer said they had just gotten a request for something called Commando Sabre. "I'll take it," Jonesy volunteered, even though he knew nothing about the unit. "When can I leave?" The next day he was on a plane toward freedom.

He often compared joining Misty to signing up for the French Foreign Legion.

Making up for all these exceptions to the fighter pilot stereotype was Capt. Charlie Neel, a fearless, diminutive overachiever. Neel claimed to be five-foot-six, but exaggerated that by an inch. He had been a gymnast at the Air Force Academy, and he always had a cigar or cigarette in his mouth. And he talked endlessly about "kicking ass." He was one of those guys who seemed sure he could win the war all by himself if he tried hard enough.

Then there was Maj. P. J. White, newly recruited from the 612th Tactical Fighter Squadron at Phu Cat, where he had been the operations officer. He was to replace Bud Day as Misty commander. White was a towering and assertive six-foot-three farm boy from Missouri, yet he was as calm and friendly as a Saint Bernard. Like just about everybody else at Misty, he quickly put Haltigan at ease.

One thing all of the Mistys had in common: They worked like dogs, usually six or seven days a week, up to eighteen hours a day. Sometimes they flew several days in a row. Blocher and P. J. White had lobbied for a schedule that would put Mistys in the cockpit no more than three days in a row, because of the taxing, draining nature of the long missions. But it usually didn't work out that way. The unit was still small, with only sixteen pilots, and with R&R, temporary duty elsewhere, and other distractions, there was a constant need for aviators to carry out the day's mission. When they weren't flying, they were usually helping to keep things humming in Ops or updating the maps that lined every wall—probably the most precise, timely maps anybody had of Route Pack 1 or any other combat area. And most of the Mistys unwound as intensely as they flew. The one regular escape from the war was the Phu Cat Officers Club, where the small band of Misty pilots was often a rather vocal minority. Just about every evening a few of the Mistys could be found at the club, going over the day's missions or plotting new schemes for finding and attacking targets, and when that got old, figuring out new ways to antagonize one another or the other visitors and pilots at the bar.

The personable pilots helped Haltigan get comfortable with his new job quickly, and the routine started to become familiar. He was always amazed that the competitive, ego-assertive pilots got along so well and functioned as a team despite their dissimilarities. The first Misty mission typically took off before daybreak, so that they'd be in "the Pack" at dawn, when the light produced maximum contrast and it was easiest to see stuff on the ground. That meant the intel guy had to be up in the middle of the night, sorting through the daily Fragmentation Order, or "frag," that 7th Air Force sent listing all the day's flights and targets. There was also fresh intelligence from 7th to digest, although most of it was not news to Misty—the unit probably provided three-quarters of the intel on what was happening in Route Pack 1. Still, occasionally there were "hot items," like photos snapped by high-flying reconnaissance jets that showed the kinds of targets that got Misty fired up: new AAA guns, artillery pieces firing across the DMZ at friendly troops, storage areas for POL (petroleum, oil, and lubricants), hidden truck parks, or, in rare cases, a surface-to-air missile. SAMs, more than anything else, had to be taken care of immediately.

Preflight briefings started two and a half hours before takeoff. Haltigan would kick them off by going over the most recent Misty missions, since not every pilot picked up the word-of-mouth summaries from the O club the night before. Top priority was pointing out any new downed aircraft or AAA emplacements, the caliber of the guns, and anything else that might be a threat or valuable target. The general rule was, the farther north you went in the Pack, the more guns you'd encounter, and the bigger the caliber of the AAA. The smaller, more mobile 37mm gun sites were everywhere, but 57mm and 85mm sites guarded major transshipment points and river crossings and were a clue that other key targets were in the area. Unfortunately for Misty, discovering a concentration of guns often meant a rough day at the office: the more guns, the more important the target, and the more likely that the Mistys would be diving through the flak.

Every gun site or suspected site, along with any other items of interest, were noted on the detailed maps that covered the walls of the makeshift briefing room. Haltigan would also cover the precise times and coordinates of the B-52 Arc Light strikes, so that Mistys wouldn't get in the way. Finally, there were possible targets, many spotted on prior Misty flights, which the back-seaters plotted crudely on their maps or notebooks, and sometimes on the cockpit canopy with grease pencil.

Debriefings, after the Mistys returned from a mission, were longer. In three or four hours over North Vietnam, pilots sucked up a tremendous amount of information, and there was often quite a lot of activity to sort through. It was low-tech intelligence gathering. The pilots—usually the guy in back, or the GIB—jotted information on their cockpit knee pads, or wrote with grease pencil on the aircraft canopy, then transferred the information to a notebook for the debriefing. If the Mistys had directed air strikes, they'd describe the targets and their locations, and the call signs and types of aircraft that had dropped the bombs. And, most important, they would go over the BDA—how much they had actually managed to destroy. On some days, when the Mistys found a major truck park or storage depot or other "lucrative" targets, a single Misty flight might work five or ten flights of fighters with bombs, usually F-4 "Gunfighters" from Da Nang or Navy A-4s or A-7s from one of the carriers out in the Gulf of Tonkin. Sometimes they got F-105s and F-4s diverted from "Alpha Strike Packages" in the upper route packages around Hanoi, on account of bad weather or other problems up there.

Haltigan would compile all of that info into a daily intelligence summary—a DISUM—which the unit would forward promptly to 7th Air Force Intelligence. On days when there were big strikes, the DISUMs could be extensive, and the debrief might take an hour or two. Intel would also develop and analyze any photos the back-seater was able to snap with the 35mm Pentax and Nikon cameras scrounged especially for Misty. Haltigan would annotate and analyze those and send them on to higher headquarters, too. From 7th Air Force, the DISUMs would often ricochet throughout the military hierarchy: to other flying units, Pacific Command in Hawaii, the Pentagon in Washington, and even the White House, if the material was hot enough.

One of the first missions Haltigan briefed was an easy one. Bob Craner was scheduled to take P. J. White, the new commander, up for his "indoctrination" ride—an introduction to the Misty mission, the terrain it covered, and the tactics. Most of the new Misty pilots got five or ten indoctrination rides, to make sure they had enough experience to survive while scoping out heavily defended targets. But White was scheduled for only one, since he had already flown 210 combat missions in Southeast Asia, most of them over South Vietnam or Laos, but a few over the North. That was more combat flying than even Bud Day had done.

Since there were no specific targets for the flight, Haltigan's briefing was quick and concise. The North Vietnamese had been moving artillery farther south, close to the DMZ, and firing into American positions. That was a high priority for 7th Air Force—keeping North Vietnamese artillery from smacking the Marines just south of the DMZ. Otherwise, uncharacteristically, there were no new guns that anybody was aware of, just the usual stout defenses at the mountain passes, key intersections on the Trail, and other transshipment points.

There was a heated debate within Misty about whether they should try to kill every piece of AAA they could find—which might make the skies safer, but be exceedingly risky to do—or whether they should just locate the guns and stay as far away as they could. They could always go after them when they had to, on a particular strike or rescue mission. The strategy was shifting back and forth. The guns were getting so numerous—not to mention bigger and more accurate—that it was almost impossible to avoid tangling with them. Some felt it was better to seek them out deliberately rather than stir them up by surprise. Another approach was to attack the guns only if they fired at Mistys. Others felt it was best to suppress AAA only during strikes. So that gave Craner and White just about every option if they came upon any AAA. They were free to call for fighters and go after them, but there wasn't any definitive policy directing them to do that, so they could also fly around guns if they chose. Only one thing was sure—attacking gun sites meant high risk and, somewhere or other, more aircraft losses.

White was pleased to get his indoc flight from Craner. He had met the handsome, lanky, dark-haired pilot before and knew he was a Weapons School graduate, with an outstanding reputation as a pilot. He also knew him to be seasoned and mature, and was glad he wouldn't be flying with some wild-ass cowboy kid who would try to terrorize and impress him with reckless stunts. White anticipated the kind of smooth, uneventful flight he had flown dozens of times in the South.

That's just how it began. Craner, in the front seat, flew White north over the water, then turned west and headed for the coast. Shining white beaches gleamed up at them. These gave way to a narrow coastal plain studded with fields, rice paddies, and some orchards. It looked remarkably serene, White thought, just like North Carolina, the way the pristine coast merged into lush lowlands, with mountains off in the distance.

Except for the craters. As they skimmed over the DMZ, there were so many water-filled sinkholes left from B-52 and fighter strikes that it looked more like the surface of the moon than the verdant countryside it had been before the war. The massive gouges in the earth ran north, south, east, west, and crosswise without any apparent method to the strategy, except that the bombs appeared to have fallen in straight lines—the "sticks" that dropped out of B-52s as they emptied their bomb bays. Every place a road crossed a river or stream, the bridge and banks were blown away. There were towns and villages, but many of them had also been demolished. The only city of any size between the DMZ and the city of Vinh, two hundred miles to the north, was Dong Hoi. White thought it looked like Hiroshima, burned out and rubbled, only smaller. "Jesus, did we do all this?" he asked Craner, meaning the Mistys.

It wasn't the Mistys, Craner replied, but three years of continuous attacks, since 1964—well before Misty even started flying. There were scars from U.S. and Vietnamese air force bombers, Navy jets and ships, and American artillery shells.

After about half an hour of "visual recce," Craner scooted up toward Fingers Lake, where Bud Day had been shot down. He was showing White how the Mistys jinked, constantly changing his heading and altitude while moving fast. In the backseat, White also guessed that Craner was scouting for the bad guys who had nailed Day two weeks before. Craner was flying a little lower than the recommended 4,000 feet, but that seemed okay—for now, any guns below were silent. White was actually enjoying himself, as much as any fighter pilot could from the backseat, taking in the scenery and riding the ups and downs like an amusement park ride. What a great assignment Misty is going to be, he thought. Ought to be a piece of cake.

Without warning, out of nowhere, came a wall of high-caliber antiaircraft fire flying up out of the jungle. White first noticed the orange tracers erupting from the treetops below, then the tracers seemed to be headed right for the plane like bundles of darts. It was 37mm. He had never seen big AAA like that in the South, and he was terrified. They were sure to get hit. The new Misty commander flinched, bleated out a panicky protest, and awaited the impact of the shells. But nothing happened.

In the front seat, Craner remained completely silent. He calmly pulled the plane into a sharp, high-G-force turn, hit the afterburner, and executed a rapid 180. He didn't mention that on one of his own checkout rides with Bill Douglass they had flown through a similar crucible of AAA, a spectacular demonstration. To White it seemed like a miracle that they had survived. Instead, Craner asked White, "P. J., did you see where it came from?" The question implied that Craner would like to turn around and go after whoever had fired at them—perhaps avenging Day's shootdown.

White's eyes were watering. His heart was thumping. The last thing on his mind had been pinpointing the spot the firing had come from during those few seconds of terror. He was ready to scram. But Craner turned the plane around and they scanned the ground below. There was nothing but solid green forest. Evidently the gunners had taken their shot, and decided not to reveal their location any further. The guns had clammed up. White was relieved.

They went to gas up from an airborne KC-135 tanker orbiting over the Mekong River, the border between Laos and Thailand. P. J. hadn't handled a refueling for some time, since missions in the South didn't require it. Craner demonstrated how to stabilize the plane and put the ten-foot-long refueling probe that extended out from under the Hun's wing into the three-foot-wide metal basket at the end of the hose that trailed the tanker. "Just think that maybe the basket has some hair around it," Craner joked—an old riff. White needed some humor. He was still a bit shaken from the AAA and the mission wasn't yet half over.

They broke off from the tanker. Craner continued the tour farther north, showing White some of the most notorious landmarks in the Pack: Ban Karai Pass, a rugged slit through the jagged limestone mountains known as "karst." Also Ban Laboy Ford, a key river crossing near the mountains along North Vietnam's border with Laos. A two-lane dirt road snaked back and forth, a key link in the Ho Chi Minh Trail.

White couldn't believe the number of bombs that had been dropped to close the roads. Craner explained that all it took for the NVA to keep the road open was a lone bulldozer, to rearrange the dirt after the bombs did their damage. Even if a bomb hit in the middle of the road, it took little time to repair, and the steady stream of trucks that flowed south—during nighttime, at least—would continue on its way. "Dust to dust," Craner versified. "It's almost sheer folly. I guess it's worth it to slow them down, but it amounts to little more than harassment. We can't keep that road closed."

Mu Ghia Pass was another highlight on the tour. White saw a spectacular, high mountain pass running south out of North Vietnam into the lower, flatter valleys of Laos. The Mistys spent a lot of time up here, since it was one of the central choke points of the Trail. Another road snaked down the sides of steep mountain canyons on the Laos side, kept open by bulldozer drivers who rode in armored cabs. The pass, as seemed to be customary for all the busy thoroughfares in North Vietnam, was pockmarked with craters from top to bottom.

Farther north, a railroad ran next to Route 101, cutting across North Vietnam to the southeast, toward the coast. Near the spot where the railroad ended, Route 1A crossed the Ron River near a finger of land—Cape Ron, which jutted out into the Gulf just south of the eighteenth parallel. The bridge that crossed the river had been blown away for as long as anybody could remember, yet the NVA had devised innovative methods to move trucks across this waterway, and others. At night they'd pull out camouflaged ferries that were hidden beneath foliage that lined the banks and invisible from above during the day. The lack of a bridge barely slowed them down, Craner explained—although he didn't know where the ferry was hidden. They revisited Dong Hoi, farther south, and White wondered silently again about all the houses blown to smithereens—was this the result of his fellow fighter jocks vindictively off-loading excess bombs, or did someone really believe there were targets inside what appeared to be a peaceful little town?

The terrain was fascinating—but more important, nobody was shooting at them. White was starting to calm down from the earlier excitement and learning to track their progress on the customized Misty maps. In the backseat he fiddled with the Pentax 35mm camera—trying to figure out how he'd shoot pictures while in a three- or four-G turn. Suddenly Craner asked, "Did you see that?" White was too busy messing with his gear to have noticed anything, but Craner explained that he had spotted some AAA fire rising up from a nearby valley. This time, he thought he had a fix on where the guns were located. Craner called in to the ABCCC and asked if any fighters were available. It turned out there was a flight of four F-4s nearby, loaded with bombs and waiting for targets. Craner was pleased. White was not. "Oh great," he thought. "Here we go again."

Craner spotted the fighters, rocked his wings to signal that he had ID'd them, then told them to watch him roll in on the target. White gulped. Craner started at about 5,000 feet, began a pull-up, then rolled the plane over on its back, spinning upside down into a 30-degree dive angle. It was fancy flying, White had to admit. But he started breathing heavily as Craner flew below 2,500 feet—well inside AAA range, way too low. White could now see muzzle flashes on the ground and could tell from the tracers screaming past the windscreen that they were flying straight into a battery of 37mm AAA. He could even hear the shells zipping by. Finally Craner fired his Willie Pete smoke rocket and pulled back on the stick, turning the plane up and hard to the left. He called to the fighters: "Hit my smoke!"

"What smoke?" came the discouraging reply. White and Craner looked, and couldn't see any smoke, either. They had fired a dud, and would have to fly back into the hornet's nest and mark the target again. This time Craner started his dive lower and slower. White was desperate to intervene and suggest a more cautious approach, but he held his tongue and trusted the seasoned pilot. The muzzle flashes were brighter on the second pass, and the tracers more numerous, but they got the rocket off with a *swoosh* at around 2,000 feet. Craner quickly pulled up and away. Despite grunting heavily under the strain of the high Gs, White could distinctly hear the *bang, bang, bang* of supersonic shock waves beating against the fuselage as the AAA rounds came close. This time the marking rocket smoke was visible, and Craner cleared the F-4s in for the strike.

Instead of following the Misty flight path, however, the F-4s rolled in from above 10,000 feet and dropped their bombs from way too high—probably 6,000 feet or more. They weren't about to fly into the gauntlet of fire Craner and White had just survived. Predictably, the bombs plunged pell-mell into the countryside. The Misty pilots estimated that one or two may have done a little damage, but that they probably missed entirely. Still, Craner politely wished the F-4s a safe flight home instead of spewing curses, as White had in mind. They had risked their lives, White reasoned—twice, in fact!—so that a bunch of yo-yos could log another combat sortie without having to do much to earn it.

It was a troubling conundrum: What was the right trade-off between risk and reward? Did it make sense for pilots like Craner to be so aggressive going after a couple of AAA guns, when there were hundreds more to replace them? Or did the F-4s have the right idea?: Stay high, keep it safe, and come back another day? White's indoctrination ride gave him plenty to think about.

Back on the ground, White figured he now knew how to spot the blowhards in the group—anybody who said he wasn't tense during his first few flights up north was definitely lying. He also knew something else: If Craner was any indication, Misty was not like other units. White had known some eager pilots—and he was pretty aggressive himself. But as he began to take the measure of the men around him, there was a tangible kind of dedication that was missing from other combat squadrons in Vietnam. Part of it was the mission. Instead of being sent out to bomb dubious targets beneath the veil of the jungle, the Mistys were finding real weapons, and real supplies, and working on them until they were destroyed. Another part of it was the flying: Once you got above the DMZ, the rules were loosely obeyed, and when you were poking around in caves and bushes for three or four hours at a stretch, you had to let it hang out a little anyway. That attracted the best pilots and kept them motivated.

Then, there was the simple fact of the danger. Getting shot at on every mission scared off the wannabes, but it seemed to embolden the Mistys. It made the mission personal, a testosterone and adrenaline rush. Craner, for his accomplished smoothness, flew so aggressively that after his first flight, White suggested he back off a step or two. Craner's boldness worried him. It was almost as if the accomplished pilot were daring the North Vietnamese to shoot him down, just for the adventure. And, of course, losing their first boss had made the Mistys more committed than ever. Each one of them seemed to feel that he alone could make a difference in the war effort. That was doubtful, White knew. But it sure looked like these would be a fun bunch of guys to fly with.

FIVE

AIRBORNE DETECTIVES

Bud Day had done a bang-up job of starting Misty from scratch, but the unit needed some work. For one thing, there was a shortage of almost everything—including pilots. In just a couple of months Misty had grown from an obscure operation that flew just a few probing reconnaissance flights per week into a unit that garnered attention, some of it unwanted. On early missions there had been no aerial refueling slots allotted to Misty, and the pilots would have to beg gas from obliging tanker crews or leave the Pack after less than an hour. Now Misty had its own assigned tankers and got all the gas it needed. Other pilots operating in the Pack and the crews of the airborne command-and control plane, the ABCCC, usually perked up when Misty called out a target over the radio. There were demands from Saigon for more Misty intel and for near-continuous coverage of Route Pack 1 during daylight hours. That meant four Misty flights per day. But just as the mission was expanding, some of the original pilots were approaching the end of their one-year tours in Vietnam and starting to ship out one after the other.

The strain was becoming evident on those who remained. One Misty, Maj. Barney Dalton, had flown nine days in a row in mid-August and was grounded for the last week of the month by the wing's flight surgeon. The doc discovered that Dalton had flown eighty-five hours in three weeks, all of it on Misty combat missions. Dalton didn't feel exhausted, but armed with a set of bogus orders for a pilot "refresher" course in Japan, he headed out. His first stop on R&R was Okinawa, where he went straight to the O club—and experienced searing pain in his mouth when he started sipping his first drink. A puzzled dentist at the base clinic found nothing wrong, but asked Dalton if he had a habit of grinding his teeth. Dalton said no, and the pain gradually subsided. But on his first flight back with Misty, Dalton was marking a target along a river, battling through a beehive of AAA, when he peeled off and noticed that his teeth were tightly clenched and he was fiercely grinding his top jaw against the bottom. He made a mental note to try to relax a bit more in the cockpit.

P. J. White promptly discovered that, unlike the squadron he had just come from, the structure at Misty was very loose. Structure, in fact, might have been a grandiose word to apply to Misty. The unit was officially designated as Detachment One, 416th Tactical Fighter Squadron. But it was a bastard operation. In theory the whole outfit was the equivalent of a squadron, but was in effect run by just three men: the commander, the ops officer, and the intel guy. It was a shoestring enterprise, too, operating out of three dingy rooms on loan from the 416th.

For a high-tempo, top secret outfit, Misty had a shabby setup. There was no lounge where the pilots could relax before or after missions, like other units had—making the O club an even more important meeting point. White found that he had to fight for practically everything the unit needed, like space for the pilots to stash their helmets, parachutes, and other equipment. He had trouble getting communications gear that could handle sensitive classified intel. Many of the Misty planes lacked RHAW indicators, radar homing and warning gear, that could tell if a SAM was targeting an aircraft. Even the most mundane bits of equipment, such as typewriters and briefing boards, were in short supply around Misty.

The unit, White learned, was caught in the bureaucratic equivalent of a flak trap. It had been established at the direction of 7th Air Force and its four-star boss, Gen. Spike Momyer. But he was way down south in Saigon, more than two hundred miles away. For everyday support, Misty depended on the largesse of the 37th Wing commander at Phu Cat, Col. Ed Schneider. And he was not enthused about having the risky unit placed on his doorstep. When White would go to the daily stand-up briefings with the various commanders who reported to Schneider, he found that the "Wing King" was not very interested in bombing results—Misty's specialty—or in anything else that actually involved contact with the enemy. Schneider seemed to care more about sortie rates, abort rates, maintenance reports, and aircraft losses—and keeping these metrics up to par with the standards at other bases. He relentlessly discouraged "aborts," or scrubbed missions. Pulling Misty planes from the daily schedule because they had been shot up infuriated Schneider. An aircraft loss made him apoplectic. Misty was an irritation to him. The unit diminished his performance on all the statistical measures that higher headquarters graded him on. "The guy doesn't give a shit about our war up north," White would say in private. "We're a thorn in his side."

Even the appearance of Misty's little corner of the base bothered Schneider. The Wing King was fastidious about the condition of his facilities, and when White arrived at Misty, the southwest monsoon season was just ending. Mud covered the sandbags surrounding the Misty part of the building. Schneider informed White that General Momyer was planning to pay a visit soon and ordered him to clean up the "mudhole," as he called Misty's little area. White nodded, but figured that General Momyer would care more about the flow of troops and supplies that was intensifying along the Trail than he would about the tidiness of the office. He forgot about the encroaching mud and suited up for a mission. Momyer, when he showed up, said nothing about the mud.

Besides Momyer, there were other sympathetic people up the chain, to be sure. Maj. Jim Chestnut, director of combat tactics at 7th Air Force, was a huge fan of Misty—partly because he had helped set it up. Shortly after being assigned to Saigon earlier in 1967, Chestnut had studied BDA reports for all the units under the command of 7th Air Force. Results in Route Pack 1, he noticed, were particularly poor. Since so much matériel was coming down the Trail in that part of North Vietnam, Chestnut wrote a paper suggesting the fast FAC concept. It worked its way up to Momyer around the same time the slow

FACs were getting blown out of the sky, and Misty was hatched. Chestnut wasn't a supply officer, but when Misty needed support, he could bend the right ears and get the spigots opened just wide enough. Col. Ray Lee helped, too. As the wing vice commander—Schneider's number two—he helped spring free supplies and other gear, and he acted as a buffer between Misty and Schneider. Plus, he actually flew with Misty about once a week. That was something Schneider refused to do.

White had little time for Schneider's supercilious concerns. With most of his pilots either coming or going, White had to oversee an unorthodox transfer of institutional knowledge—while still learning the job himself. Misty had no formal training program for incoming pilots. Newcomers would get five to ten "checkout" rides—usually half in the front seat, flying the plane, and half in the back, scouting, handling the maps, and working the radios—and then be considered a fullfledged Misty FAC. Every Misty developed his own tricks for spotting targets, and on checkout rides the more experienced guys would share their secrets with the new arrivals.

But teaching a fighter pilot new tricks was not the most desirable job. Fighter jocks were about the most self-assured guys in the military, and it could be hard to convince them there was something they didn't already know. Besides, the work in Misty often ran contrary to procedures and techniques F-100 pilots learned throughout the course of their formal training. The Hun's primary mission was to deliver conventional—and even nuclear—bombs on preplanned targets. Pilots learned how to follow predesignated routes, find turn points, and stay on their course by using roads, railroads, mountains, lakes, towns, and other landmarks on the ground. Little of that mattered at Misty. They were on their own looking for small stuff—often tiny details that might offer a visual clue that a valuable target was nearby.

John Haltigan quickly realized, in fact, that for all the glory associated with flying the Hun through the crucible of combat, it was the back-seater—the GIB, or guy in back—who was the key person in the plane. The lowly GIB was the one who worked the maps and plotted out new sightings and did most of the scouting for targets. Still, like all fighter pilots, most Mistys hated being in the backseat of an airplane somebody else was flying.

Not all Mistys arrived qualified to fly the F-100. All FACs were fighter pilots of some sort, but in the first generation of Misty, four of the sixteen pilots who had been slow FACs flying the O-1 Bird Dog— Keith Heiniger, Barney Dalton, Kipp Kippenhan, and Dick Cunningham—were not current in the F-100. So when they showed up at Misty, they were consigned to the dreaded backseat. Day and Douglass decided to offer these FACs the opportunity to check out in the front seat with Misty. Kippenhan and Cunningham accepted, and were allowed to fly every other mission in the front seat, just like other Misty pilots—until Day and Kippenhan got shot down. Kippenhan had been in the front flying the plane, and Douglass and Lee, the wing vice commander, decided the Misty mission was dangerous enough without adding any other confusion. So the unfortunate slow FACs were reassigned to the rear seat for the duration of their tenure at Misty.

But the former slow FACs, the GIBs, were quite skilled, and their talents inevitably filtered down to the other Mistys. Heiniger, Dalton, Kippenhan, and Cunningham taught many a Misty how to see and find targets—skills that were hard to come by in the middle of a war. The former slow FACs were like airborne detectives, with an intuition for noticing something in the landscape below that didn't quite fit in, possibly indicating the hand of man. While a fighter jock might zoom right over a stand of trees at 4,000 feet and see nothing out of the ordinary, a guy like Heiniger could tell there were several trucks camouflaged under the canopy.

The Mistys rarely saw vehicles moving during daylight, so they had to look for other signs of activity. Sharp right angles in the terrain were more often than not the work of engineers, rather than nature, and could indicate a camouflaged road or bunker or an underground storage facility. Heiniger taught White and other newcomers to look for roads, paths, trails, or any other kind of traveled route that suddenly ended, or had no exit or return routes. SAMs, antiaircraft guns, field artillery, and any other kind of heavy metal had to get into place somehow, and as stealthy as the North Vietnamese were, it was hard to hide every trace of that kind of movement. Treadmarks that abruptly stopped in the middle of nowhere usually meant trucks or other vehicles were hidden nearby, or underneath foliage right where the tracks ended. Roads or trails that led into a river didn't usually just end—

there was probably a pontoon bridge or ferry somewhere along the riverbank. An unusual amount of dust on the treetops could suggest vigorous nighttime activity—trucks driving down the road, excavation for supply areas, even engineers building new roads.

Then there were the guns. At the time P. J. White took over, the Misty philosophy was, if they don't shoot at you, don't shoot at them. But AAA guns were intensely tracked, since their presence was usually a sure sign that there was something valuable nearby to protect. By the fall of 1967 the Mistys were well schooled in the characteristics of AAA guns—since they lived and died by them. A .50-caliber site, for instance, could be anywhere. These were portable single guns usually placed in a small round bunker that allowed the gun to be swung quickly around, through 360 degrees. Fifty cals were not much of a threat to Misty, since they were effective only up to about 1,500 feet. Pilots could often pick them out by the greenish tracers that helped tell the gunner where he was aiming—usually one tracer for every seven rounds.

A bigger worry was the 14.5mm AAA, which looked similar to a .50-cal but had two or four barrels that were both bigger. These weapons were known as ZPU-2s or ZPU-4s. They had to be moved by vehicle and were as big as the bed of a pickup truck—and could reach as high as 4,500 feet.

The real dangers, though, came from 37mm and 57mm guns. These were big. The 37s were as large as a big pickup truck and were usually towed on wheeled trailers. One site typically consisted of six guns placed in a circle with a diameter of two hundred feet or so, each gun in its own bunker, protected by sandbags. Foliage was often dangled over the top. There were several thousand 37mm sites in Route Pack 1, and they caused plenty of trouble. These guns could knock down a plane at up to 8,000 feet, and inflict damage at over 15,000 feet.

The 57s were bigger yet, and vicious. Each gun was the size of a semitrailer, and six of them would be spread across an area as big as a football field. They could be moved, but were so big that they usually stayed in place to protect major river crossings such as the Quang Khe ferry. Unlike the smaller guns, the 57s were often directed by Firecan radars, which made them more accurate. Part of the radar was usually situated in the middle of the guns, which were also identifiable by the fifteen-foot-long flashes that roared out of the muzzles when the shells were launched. These could destroy a plane as high as 12,000 feet, and even when they missed, they filled the sky with sinister dark flak bursts that formed the equivalent of an airborne minefield.

There were even bigger AAA pieces, such as 85mm and 100mm guns, but these were seldom seen in Route Pack 1—except occasionally as field artillery that was lowered and fired more horizontally across the DMZ into South Vietnam. The resourceful NVA learned to use all of its AAA guns as field artillery, in fact, converting them into ground assault weapons when necessary.

Dancing around the gun sites was one of the most delicate parts of the job, like trying to grab a rattlesnake by the neck with your bare hands. Sometimes the Mistys and their enemies on the ground would remain respectfully silent, neither wanting to provoke a bloodbath. But more often, somebody would fire a shot, and a fracas would ensue. Since the guns were usually well camouflaged, getting them to fire at you was often the only way to find out where they were. And sometimes the Mistys would aggressively buzz suspected "hot" areas, where they thought North Vietnamese equipment might be stashed. If AAA erupted—well, they were probably right. The smart pilots would carefully note the gun positions and get the hell out of there: One of the golden rules of experienced FACs was no second passes.

The Mistys had to be careful, however, about fixating on the guns. If Misty called in strike after strike on the guns instead of figuring out what the guns were protecting in the first place, they were letting the enemy divert their attention and playing right into their hands. White learned that he had to work on the pilots so they would keep their focus, and not turn it into a personal vendetta every time somebody got shot at. It was important to resist mano-a-mano engagements, tests of manhood, and White limited his pilots to three consecutive days of flying. After that they'd spend a mandatory day on the ground, unwinding and getting their head straightened out. And about every thirty days, he tried to get them a week of R&R, so they could regain a bit of perspective in "Rio Linda"—real life.

Still, the AAA in the Pack was starting to get so thick that 7th Air Force strategists began to doubt that their pilots could simply ignore it and operate around it. Some ferocious duels broke out. Shortly after

Schneider had admonished him to clean up the Misty "mudhole," White himself flew on a mission, with Keith Heiniger in the back, that turned into one of the classic brute-force battles of the air war. It was sloppy from the start. The previous night in the O club, White, his operations officer, Maj. Don Sibson, and a few other Mistys had decided to do a "MiG sweep," a fighter-jock lark in which they locked arms and plowed over everybody in their path, knocking over tables, bottles, and people. In the course of the adventure White tore the skin off both his shins. Then, climbing up the cockpit ladder for the first Misty mission the next morning at about 5:00 a.m., he missed a rung and banged one of the same shins, sending a trickle of blood down his leg.

The weather was lousy, and White doubted the mission would amount to much. Once airborne, he spent an hour flying up and down the coast looking for an opening in the murky overcast that would let them enter the Pack and take a look. They refueled, and finally White found a hole in the clouds near the DMZ. He turned inland at low altitude—about 1,000 feet—and began to trace the Ben Hai River, which ran smack through the center of the Demilitarized Zone. Just a couple of miles inland, Heiniger called out, "P. J., check two o'clock." White looked to his right, where he could see several large NVA field artillery pieces firing across the DMZ into friendly positions, probably one of the U.S. Marine bases in the Central Highlands. The artillery was well hidden beneath a copse of trees, but the muzzle flashes gave it away. The pilots were excited to have found something, but the thick clouds were likely to close in again before they could summon any of the fighters with bombs. Heiniger marked the location of the artillery on his map, noting the tree line and a small clearing nearby. Then they broke away, back toward the coast, to see about the weather.

It was marginal, but the clouds seemed to be breaking up a bit, and White decided to try calling in some strikes. He headed back for a closer look at the targets. White was a cautious flier and he tried to dip down unobtrusively, but the NVA had obviously picked up the plane. Orange and red AAA tracers suddenly streaked past the canopy. This caught White off guard and he flinched for a moment. He hit the afterburner and peeled off to the right in a four-G turn that hammered both pilots down into their seats. From the back Heiniger reported seeing "sheets" of tracers rising up from one of several antiaircraft guns protecting the big field artillery. They figured that there was probably one 37mm antiaircraft battery, and one 57mm battery—a total of twelve guns.

They raced back out over the water, and White frantically called the ABCCC for fighters. This was a hot target. It was unusual for NVA forces to give themselves away by doing something as brash as firing large-caliber weapons in the daytime. The NVA had probably figured the bad weather would keep the fighters grounded. White and Heiniger had caught them by surprise. Plus, the thick overcast had caused numerous aborts farther north, in Route Pack 6—where Hanoi was located. Dozens of fighters were on their way back loaded with bombs, looking for something to drop them on.

The first to arrive were a couple of Navy A-4s from the carrier *Kearsarge*. White radioed them, told them to expect lots of AAA, and to follow him in and watch his smoke. The artillery pieces had gone silent as he approached—now they were trying to conceal themselves—but the AAA was a hornet's nest. As White and Heiniger approached, one Navy pilot broke in over the radio to say the flak was as thick as anything he had seen over Hanoi—one of the most heavily defended places on earth.

White and Heiniger got through it and fired their rockets at the artillery, but the Navy fliers decided they needed to take care of the AAA guns before going after the main kill. And those guns, with their mouths spitting fire, didn't need to be marked. The first Navy pilot took a hit even before he got his bombs off. The bombs fell short, and the guns continued firing. The pilot reported that he thought he could limp back to the carrier. His wingman, coming in right behind him, got through the gauntlet unscathed. But his bombs missed, too.

Eight F-4s showed up. This time White told them to go straight for the antiaircraft guns. But with the tricky weather and the relentless ground fire, it was tough getting close enough to do any damage. The F-4s failed to get any direct hits. Then four F-105 Thunderchiefs arrived. The "Thuds," as they were known, had massive bomb loads, and this time results were better. The Thuds nailed two guns in the 57mm battery, along with the fire control radar that tracked the airplanes and directed the fire. White could see and feel the shock wave from the one-ton bombs—it was the first time he had seen two-thousand-pounders, and the explosions looked like small mushroom clouds from nuclear bombs.

Word was out now that a fight was on, and the bombing went on for another couple of hours. Fighters continued to arrive, and White and Heiniger directed nearly fifty strikes, until they had no more marking rockets left. By the end, the whole area was in flames. There had been several secondary explosions around the field artillery, probably stored rounds lighting off after bombs took out the barrels. Most of the AAA batteries were destroyed. Smoke poured into the sky. When White and Heiniger landed back at Phu Cat, they found two holes in their plane, one in the left wing flap and one in the vertical stabilizer— probably acquired on their first pass, White figured.

Those were the most satisfying days, when a Misty sortie ended with tangible results. But that was not always the case. Many Misty missions were frustrating and unproductive, as higher headquarters tried new, often ineffective tactics to get better results from the bombing campaign that had been going on for nearly three years. One such experiment was to use Misty pilots as spotters for naval gunfire coming from Navy cruisers out in the South China Sea. One of the huge shells from the 8-inch guns would come flying in, and the Mistys would mark its location, reporting back to the ship on how far from the target it landed and in what direction. Ten or fifteen minutes later another shell would come crashing down. It seemed like a senseless waste of Misty's time, especially since there were hundreds of live targets elsewhere in the Pack that Misty could do something about and fighters could hit better.

On many other days, the Mistys noticed telltale signs of something going on, but were unable to pinpoint anything specific. The North Vietnamese were experts at camouflage, and they often won the hide-and-seek. On one day, Bob Blocher and another Misty were flying through the Pack when they noticed an airstrip, three or four hundred feet long, that could easily handle light aircraft flying in critical supplies or key commanders. They marked it on their maps and went to refuel. But when they returned it had disappeared. For several days they came back to the area looking for the strip, but it was as if the North Vietnamese had folded it up and taken it away. Most likely, Blocher reasoned, the troops manning the strip had figured out their prize had been spotted, dragged brush across it, fuzzed up the edges, taken off the corners, and made it look just like the surrounding terrain. It was maddening.

Another time, an argument had broken out between Misty and the intelligence staff at 7th Air Force. The North had begun an artillery barrage across the DMZ into the South. To the Mistys, it seemed so staged that it must have been a deliberate diversion, or some kind of trap. And they started noticing that traffic and other kinds of activity elsewhere in the Pack seemed to be increasing. The intelligence experts at headquarters disagreed and were pressuring Momyer to recalibrate the entire air interdiction effort and take on the artillery. Momyer flew to Phu Cat and listened to what P. J. White and his pilots had to say. Momyer sided with Misty, but the "victory" earned them the temporary enmity of Momyer's intel staff.

And then there was the weather, which was even more unpredictable than in John Haltigan's native New England. Visibility was always a factor in flying, but particularly in the narrow coastal areas and higher mountains of Route Pack 1. Whether it was dry and hot or cold and wet, whether the monsoons were coming from the southwest or the northeast, there always seemed to be morning fog that would obscure the roads and valleys, preventing bombing. The monsoons tended to pick a side of the Truong Son Mountains that ran along the border between North Vietnam and Laos, and stick with it for six months or so. During fall and winter, the terrain east of the mountains, in Vietnam, tended to be socked in—but Laos, on the western side, was relatively clear. In spring and summer it was the reverse. So the Mistys worked when and where they could, roaming freely and making their own decisions about where to concentrate for the day.

When thick clouds broke suddenly, it was usually a "target-rich environment" with all manner of truck activity being caught in the open. The Mistys would have a field day helping blow things up. The most effective tactic was to strafe the first and last vehicles in truck convoys, trapping the rest and leaving a turkey shoot for the bomb-dropping fighters once they arrived. On productive days, dozens of trucks would be destroyed. But that never seemed to crimp the flow of traffic down the Trail, and the NVA kept coming.

In the Misty intel room, the maps lining the wall were getting thicker and thicker with markings representing key Misty finds. There had always been a lot of AAA sites in the northern part of the Pack, near the Mu Ghia Pass and other transportation bottlenecks. But now the maps of the southern part of the Pack were getting blotted with lots of annotations, too. Most were gun sites, but 7th Air Force had also been sending up more hot items from other intelligence sources. These were presumed truck parks and storage areas, and there were also persistent rumors of SAM sites being constructed near a rubber plantation not far from where Day and Kippenhan had been shot down. And there was probably a lot more stuff Misty didn't know about, since the northeast monsoon season had started and there were periods of days when the rain swept horizontally across the tarmac and Misty was grounded.

Still, to Bob Blocher and others who had been around Misty from the start, activity certainly seemed to be picking up. But there were few of the original Mistys left, and most of the new arrivals were still getting their feet wet. John Haltigan worked constantly to update the maps and keep up with the briefings, but Misty was short-staffed, and he had his hands full just with day-to-day matters. P. J. White, when he wasn't flying, was usually up at the wing fighting for gear and trying to keep Schneider from curtailing Misty in order to protect his precious "statistics." The maps seemed to reveal that something was afoot in the Pack, but nobody at Misty had started putting the pieces together.

SIX

SUCCESS OR STALEMATE?

The Mistys were getting better, but so were the North Vietnamese. At Phu Cat, Misty had access to much of the sensitive intelligence 7th Air Force and the United States possessed regarding North Vietnamese activities on the Ho Chi Minh Trail. Misty even gathered some of that intelligence. But Misty was merely looking through a "soda straw" at one aspect of the war. They had a pinpoint focus on what happened yesterday and today, and what might happen tomorrow. But that was a short-range view that blotted out larger concerns about whether the overall bombing strategy was working and whether the U.S. was winning the war—and whether Misty was making a difference. Some of the guys thought about that—and a couple even talked about it—but the demands of the job didn't leave much time for strategic soul-searching.

In Washington, however, second-guessing the war effort had become a blood sport, and President Johnson himself agonized over some of the decisions about how to defeat the North Vietnamese. Public anger over the war and the nearly fifteen thousand Americans who had died in combat in Southeast Asia was already thick in the streets by the fall of 1967. The vast majority of the dead had been ground troops, which cast American attention on the land battles in the "Iron

Triangle" and War Zone C north and west of Saigon, and in the Central Highlands where Americans intercepted North Vietnamese troops moving in from Cambodia. And in I Corps, the area just south of the DMZ, Gen. William Westmoreland, in command of U.S. forces in Vietnam, was beginning to build up Army and Marine strength around Khe Sanh in anticipation of a major enemy offensive there.[1]

For the first time, television cameras were bringing war into the homes of middle-class Americans. They were trained almost exclusively on American GIs and the plight they faced in a strange, faraway land. The air war, inaccessible to cameras and to journalists in general, was vague and intangible, something measured mainly by numbers. Yet there was considerable drama in the air. U.S. air attacks on North Vietnamese airfields had begun in April 1967, leading to numerous swirling dogfights between U.S. pilots and the small fleet of Russian-built MiG combat jets flown by the North Vietnamese. In May, U.S. fighters shot down twenty-six North Vietnamese jets, cutting the enemy's pilot strength in half.[2] And yet the air war reports filtering back to the States consisted mainly of monotonous, even meaningless statistics, such as the number of sorties flown: More than 176,000 fighter-bomber missions over South Vietnam in 1967, and 108,000 over the North. B-52s flew 9,700 missions in the war zone, dropping an average of twenty-four tons of bombs per mission.[3] The numbers sounded impressive—but it was impossible to tell whether they added up to success or stalemate.

The growing skepticism over the U.S. military command's facile use of figures extended to the air campaign. Westmoreland and his briefers had become notorious for their reliance on the "body count"—the number of U.S. dead versus the number of enemy dead—as an indication that the U.S. and its South Vietnamese allies were winning. Had they applied the same logic to the air war, the numbers would have favored the Americans by an even more lopsided margin—if anybody had been able to trek into North Vietnam and tally up all the NVA who got killed trying to shoot down a single U.S. airplane.

But like the ground war, the air war never was about a body count, and by the fall of 1967 doubts about the effectiveness of bombing North Vietnam gripped the bureaucracy, from Saigon to U.S. Pacific Command headquarters in Honolulu to Washington. The bombing campaign, which had officially been launched as Rolling Thunder in March 1965, had several purposes: first, to force the North Vietnamese to stop sending men and supplies into the South in support of the insurgency there. "Gradualism," a measured increase in the intensity of the campaign, was meant to signal Hanoi that U.S. airpower could devastate North Vietnam's economy and turn its people against the war, if Washington chose to do so. President Johnson and his civilian advisers also hoped that overwhelming U.S. airpower would limit the need to send even more ground troops to Southeast Asia and compel the North Vietnamese into signing a peace treaty that left South Vietnam intact.[4]

The Central Intelligence Agency and other parts of the U.S. government obsessively measured the extent to which any of this seemed to be happening. In 1966 the Defense Department had commissioned the Institute for Defense Analyses (IDA), a Virginia-based think tank, to analyze the effectiveness of Rolling Thunder, the sustained aerial bombardment campaign against North Vietnam. IDA's so-called Jason Group, an assemblage of leading scientists, reported that the campaign to date had had no measurable effect on the North's ability to wage war in the South. More military equipment was being sent to the North by China and the Soviet Union than Rolling Thunder had destroyed, and the North's communist allies could most likely increase those shipments at will. The populace of North Vietnam lived by such primitive means that bombing power plants and railroads and industrial facilities had little effect on them.[5] Worse, the Jason Group found that, with the exception of a nuclear attack, no amount of bombing in North Vietnam was likely to have much of an impact.[6] Since the bombing had started, in fact, the North Vietnamese had doubled the number of men sent down the Trail every year. In 1967, according to CIA estimates, more than 100,000 North Vietnamese would infiltrate into the South via the Trail, up from 58,000 in 1966.[7]

Those conclusions were counterintuitive to airpower advocates who had watched bombing get more and more accurate and believed that an air campaign could be decisive. But for the moment, they were not the ones making the final decisions. Frustration with restrictions placed on the bombing, set by Defense Secretary Robert McNamara and the White House, had been roiling since Rolling Thunder began.

Military leaders, including the Joint Chiefs of Staff along with a few senior government officials, wanted the freedom to attack every target that could be found in North Vietnam, including power plants, railroads, industrial factories, and shipping facilities in Haiphong Harbor—the entire infrastructure supporting the war. But that might also have caused severe hardship to the civilian population, and it risked drawing China into the war. So for two years, expertly crafted memos bounced between the Pentagon, the State Department, Pacific Command, and the White House, arguing either for or against intensifying the bombing. Bureaucrats honed their infighting skills. The Joint Chiefs made private appeals to the president, circumnavigating the defense secretary.[8] In his own private sessions with the president, which outnumbered those of the chiefs, McNamara—who had become a "dove" on the war by 1967, according to some of his colleagues—routinely told Johnson that the generals were overzealous and unimaginative.

Finally, by the spring of 1967, McNamara and Johnson were so dissatisfied with the results of Rolling Thunder that they approved the bombing of many of the once-restricted targets. U.S. jets let loose on North Vietnam's single cement plant, its only explosive factory, its principal steel mill, and most of its power plants.[9] By May, virtually all major fixed targets had been struck and restruck, with most of them being destroyed. Only a few military options were left. The Americans could mine Haiphong Harbor in an attempt to seal it off from Soviet and other cargo ships that were delivering thousands of tons of war matériel. But that risked drawing the USSR into the fracas. The U.S. could have bombed locks and dikes, to disrupt the economy, but that would have flooded thousands of civilians out of their homes. There was also the option of invading North Vietnam on the ground—but that would have vastly increased the need for ground troops and represented a major escalation of war aims. None of these options had much appeal.[10, 11]

Still, the bombing advocates trotted out their statistics to show that the campaign was succeeding. Some cited CIA figures showing that in May 1967, the bombing of electric power plants in the North had knocked out 165,000 kilowatts of power-generating capability, about 87 percent of the country's total.[12] In theory, that should have cut deeply into the North's ability to make the steel needed for fuel storage tanks, for the pontoons that supported the numerous floating bridges along the Trail, and for the metal that went into making weapons. Momyer, the 7th Air Force chief, told McNamara that new tactics and weapons—such as the use of Misty—had helped increase bombing accuracy by 400 percent.[13] Adm. U. S. Grant Sharp, commander in chief of Pacific Command, reported that bombing along the Trail had backed up the North's transportation system so much that Haiphong Harbor was clearing only about 2,700 short tons of cargo per day by October, down from 4,400 short tons earlier in the year. And the need to maintain, repair, and defend the Trail occupied more than half a million North Vietnamese full-time, he pointed out. Those were people who might otherwise be pointing rifles at American GIs in the South.[14]

The divisions inside the government over whether the bombing campaign was paying dividends or not—and whether it should be sustained, expanded, or halted—were put on formal display at an August hearing before the Senate Armed Services Committee. Key senators had learned earlier that summer that McNamara and Johnson had been refusing some of the requests of the top brass, and the hearing was a showcase meant to pressure the White House into opening up the bombing campaign.

The generals laid it bare. Almost in unison they proclaimed that the bombing had severely damaged the North and disrupted its war preparations. Without it, the North would have been able to double the number of enemy troops in the field in South Vietnam, they said. Yet restrictions imposed by civilian leaders had curtailed the effectiveness of the air campaign, and the "doctrine of gradualism"—the slow and steady escalation that was meant to increase pressure on the North in measurable increments—instead gave the North time to build up air defenses that had become rather stout.[15] Gen. Earle Wheeler, chairman of the Joint Chiefs, noted how critical it was to keep relentless pressure on the Trail. "Most important, in my view," he told the senators, "is the application of as much force as we possibly can in a given period against the lines of communication in order to destroy, hopefully, and at least disrupt and attrit the flow of supplies to the South."[16]

For the first time in public, McNamara's most senior military advisers, including the Joint Chiefs, were openly arrayed against him. The master of reason rallied. He explained why the enemy's military strength continued to grow, despite an aerial campaign that by most measures should have been succeeding. Bombing the Trail and other supply lines had not been effective, he told the senators, because North Vietnam had a highly diversified and resilient transportation system consisting of rails, roads, waterways, and footpaths. The North moved some of its supplies in conventional ways—by train, truck, and barge—but they were also enormously resourceful when conventional means weren't available. Trail workers operated small sampans to cross narrow streams when there was no bridge. Human porters carried 50 or 100 pounds' worth of supplies at a time. On specially rigged bicycles, they could transport a 500-pound load. It was an ingenious system—low-tech and easy to maintain. And even under constant attack it had a capacity much larger than was needed. The whole logistics pipeline, from North to South, could move about 200 tons of supplies per day. Except for food—which could often be foraged locally—the entire enemy force in the South required only 15 tons of supplies per day.[17]

At Phu Cat, the Misty pilots were doing their part of the job, honing their target-finding skills. They were deciphering some of the clever camouflage and concealment techniques the North Vietnamese used to sneak stuff down the Trail, becoming more familiar with the terrain on their beat. The pilots noticed if a new ford appeared in a stream or river. Almost always it represented yet another offshoot of the ever-expanding Trail network. New roads and paths emerged and were duly charted on the maps. The Mistys learned to pay close attention to dust, which often signaled that new road construction was under way. And they developed good instincts for finding truck parks and storage areas, which were often hidden just off the Trail at key junctures.

No aerial unit in Vietnam, in fact, had as clear a view of the Trail as Misty. Yet for all its efforts, Misty had little more than a pinhole perspective on how the North Vietnamese sustained and used the Trail. In fact, despite the strategic importance of the Trail—and the vast intelligence resources the U.S. government was tapping to learn more about it—the Trail remained a mysterious operation that was poorly understood by the Americans.

The first tendrils of the Trail had been cleared in 1959 by the 559th Transportation Group, so named because it was formed in the fifth month of 1959. To those who knew about it in the Democratic Republic of Vietnam, or DRV—North Vietnam, to Americans—it was called the Truong Son Strategic Supply Route, after one of the mountain ranges it cut through. The inaugural mission was to smuggle two thousand weapons and five hundred troops into the South, to aid the Viet Cong in their insurgency against the government. From the beginning the group's commander, Col. Vo Bam, was instructed to keep the Trail thoroughly camouflaged. "This route must be kept absolutely secret," ordered one of his superiors. "It must not be allowed to become a beaten path—that is, not a single footprint, cigarette butt, or broken twig may be left on it after the men's passage."[18]

Vo Bam and the *bo dois,* as the soldiers who marched down the Trail were called, were resourceful and tireless. Parts of the Trail consisted of paved roads that would support trucks and machinery, but in other areas the network was primitive and they relied on bicycles, horses, and even elephants to carry equipment.[19] As the insurgency in the South expanded, the *bo dois* funneled into the South increased in number from about 2,000 in 1961 to 4,000 by 1964.[20] Getting there was treacherous and risky. There was little cover along the Trail, and the jungle that it traversed teemed with dangers. Some troops lost their way and starved. Others were attacked and killed by tigers or bears.[21] Even before the Americans first started bombing the Trail in 1964,[22] cemeteries began to spring up at way stations along the Trail, simple testaments to those who died along the supply route.[23]

The troops and other people who manned the Trail lived roughly, too. Along the Trail in North Vietnam and Laos were numerous camps run by at least a dozen *binh trams,* localized units responsible for providing the porters, security forces, engineers, air defense troops, and other laborers who maintained and defended the spidery road network. Some of these were regular troops from the North Vietnamese Army, but most were the equivalent of draftees, peasants pressed into service for the good of the country—including thousands of women. Many were farmers from coastal areas who had never experienced the rigors of jungle life until they were assigned to one of the *binh trams.* Some worked on the Trail for a decade or more. And to escape the relentless bombing, many lived underground seven days a week, except when they were manning their posts on the Trail.

By 1967 the *binh trams* were large and well established, with clear duties. Each was responsible for the antiaircraft defenses in its region, for repairing and sustaining its portion of the Trail, and for guiding passing infantry troops on their journey south. Transportation specialists helped manage the flow of equipment, especially when the paved road ran out and matériel had to be off-loaded from trucks onto animals or bicycles. Near Mu Ghia Pass, which crossed over jagged mountains from North Vietnam into Laos, Binh Tram 1 and transportation units attached to it added at least two bypasses to the primary route, so that trucks would have a way around when bombs knocked out the principal road.[24]

The Trail network became extensive. From September 1965 to March 1966 the *binh tram* units built 60 miles of new roads each month. By mid-1966 the Ho Chi Minh Trail consisted of nearly 450 miles of roads and paths that branched off in every direction. Its tentacles reached into Laos, where Washington had been approving limited air strikes, but also Cambodia, which was a U.S. ally and thus off-limits to bombing. By 1967 the route system was pushing through Laos and into South Vietnam, mainly from Cambodia to the west. The CIA estimated that 7,000 porters and 23,000 construction workers had toiled on this lifeline from the North.

The U.S. had distinct glimpses into how the North Vietnamese operated the Trail. Misty and other aerial reconnaissance units kept tabs on developments that could be seen from above. American and South Vietnamese commandos, organized into "Spike Teams," had been sneaking into enemy country since at least 1964, charting activity on the Trail, calling in air strikes when they found critical targets, and sometimes laying mines or carrying out other acts of sabotage. Signals intelligence experts such as the Marines' 1st Radio Battalion, which operated from a hilltop near Khe Sanh, routinely picked up North Vietnamese radio transmissions describing activity up and down the Trail.

But all the missions, the risks, and the technology still failed to provide a clear picture of what the North Vietnamese were really up to. Medical facilities, logistics hubs, and construction capabilities along the Trail were more extensive and sophisticated than most intelligence experts guessed. The Americans paid so much attention to the Trail's main arteries that important new bypasses and many supporting major logistics areas were often overlooked. Nor was there much awareness that the North relied heavily on local villagers for the labor force that supported the Trail, giving it a deep manpower resource that was somewhat immune from the usual laws of attrition warfare.

Nor did the Americans know exactly what the leaders in the North had in mind for the Trail. By the fall of 1967, Gen. Vo Nguyen Giap, the North's military mastermind, had decided to shift the strategy in the South. Instead of merely supporting a guerrilla insurgency, the North would mount a more conventional assault across the South, using many of its own regular army units. In secret meetings in Hanoi that fall, the DRV's Politburo had approved Giap's new plan, including a widespread, coordinated attack across the South at the time of Tet, the Vietnamese New Year, at the end of January. By October, Giap had ordered that preparations for the campaign begin.[25]

The 559th Group, responsible for the Trail, began major construction on new roads that would cross the border from Cambodia and Laos into South Vietnam. They now worked with bulldozers and other heavy machinery. Even with attacks on the Trail intensifying, the North's engineers managed to oversee construction of dozens of miles of new roads each month starting in October 1967. Trail workers, meanwhile, were able to maintain most of the existing network.[26] Moving mostly at night, *bo dois* began to infiltrate South Vietnam all the way down into the Mekong Delta—the region around Saigon. U.S. intelligence noted some of the new activity, but didn't recognize Giap's bigger plan. At Phu Cat, P. J. White and John Haltigan and a crop of new pilots just arriving at Misty were still learning the job and the mission. The frenetic activity on the ground made the job more lively and challenging than ever, but no broader scheme was apparent.

Even at the highest levels, the U.S. bureaucracy was preoccupied with bigger problems, and many of its leaders were racked with doubt. In the States, anger over the war and the ballooning body count was becoming explosive. On October 21, 1967, McNamara watched from his spacious office on the Pentagon's E Ring, its outermost corridor, as several thousand protesters marched on the building—one of the biggest antiwar demonstrations to date. The man who had crafted the war strategy with scientific precision now wondered if America could win at all. In September, CIA Director Richard Helms had written a memo arguing that the U.S. could probably pull out of Vietnam without wrecking its status as a world power or endangering its innate security concerns.[27] Richard Greeley, a chemist with the Mitre Corporation, who was one of the key scientists working on McNamara's electronic barrier program, estimated that destroying the North's supply network would require so many discrete events to happen that he put the odds of success at just 20 percent.[28]

In a November 1967 meeting at the White House, McNamara presented a reasoned analysis of the predicament. Despite all the bombing, he told the president and other members of the Cabinet, nothing would break Hanoi's will except the belief that they could not succeed. And they wouldn't believe that unless they thought the Americans were prepared to stay in Vietnam for as long as it took to win. With anger over the war mushrooming and the president facing wrenching pressure to end the bloodshed, McNamara questioned whether it was even possible to commit to the effort necessary to beat Hanoi militarily.

But those private worries over the war didn't transmit to the field. At Misty, a few new staff officers arrived to help beef up the operation. Excitement built as targets proliferated. In the briefing room, the BDA recounted in mission reports seemed substantial, and the Mistys started to ferret out some big kills. They were excited and beginning to feel effective. At the same time, with the Trail becoming the umbilical cord for Giap's audacious new offensive in the South, the air over Route Pack 1 got more dangerous than ever. AAA was increasing and the Mistys were taking more and more hits. Fighter losses everywhere over North Vietnam were increasing. Organizing and controlling the fighter jets and helicopters and other aircraft during rescues of downed pilots—RESCAPs—became a staple of the Misty's duties. This was a sideshow, not part of the original mission, but when a pilot was down, rescuing him became priority number one. Some RESCAPs went on for hours, with multiple refuelings, dozens of aircraft, and vicious duels between the warriors in the sky and those on the ground.

There were some spectacular rescues, but also too many heartbreaking failures. The losses took their toll, even up the chain of command. During one of the daily briefings in Washington, the Air Force chief of staff, Gen. John McConnell, was listening to the latest tallies of targets destroyed and lives lost. The gains seemed minimal, the price exorbitant, the results a pittance. Finally, as the meeting wrapped up, McConnell's anguish boiled over. "I can't tell you how I feel," he said to those left in the room, his head in his hands. "I'm so sick of it. . . . I have never been so goddamned frustrated by it all."[29]

SEVEN

FEET WET

John Haltigan was about to get some help. Down in Saigon, a fresh new intel officer, Roger Van Dyken, was trying to get out of a staff assignment and find something more exciting to do in the field. Van Dyken had done well at intelligence school, and for a second lieutenant with no experience, his first job was enviable: He was one of General Momyer's briefers. It was a great opportunity for a young officer to make all the right connections and set up a future of choice promotions. But Van Dyken felt out of place in an office, shuffling papers and swimming in bureaucracy. The scene in Saigon was even worse than he had expected. One officer explained the best way to fit in: "Don't try to do too much, don't look for work, or everybody will hate you."

Van Dyken, earnest and eager, was looking to do more in Vietnam than mark time, so while he was waiting for his high-level security clearances to come through, he poked around for other jobs closer to the action.

Like Haltigan, Van Dyken had studied history, at Dordt College in Sioux Center, Iowa. He had planned to become a teacher after he graduated in 1966, and had at least half a dozen offers on the table. But the draft board back home, in Ripon, California, told him they'd yank him right out of the classroom for enlisted duty no matter which job he took. When Van Dyken was a kid, a neighbor boy had joined the Air Force, and when he came home on leave he reported back that it was a good outfit. So Van Dyken figured that instead of getting drafted, he'd catch a bus to Omaha to get information on the air force's officer training program and see if he could get a commission.

His father, Sam, meanwhile, who owned an appliance store with his brothers and ran the thirty-acre almond farm his family lived on, had decided to run for Congress. Roger became his campaign manager. Midway through the summer of '66, with the campaign gaining momentum, Van Dyken received his notice of physical, meaning his draft notice was about two weeks away. Since he hadn't heard from the Air Force—and he wanted to finish the campaign—Van Dyken volunteered for the Navy, because they had a ninety-day delay option that would get him through November. A week later a packet arrived in the mail—his acceptance into Air Force officer training school, which would begin at the end of November. Van Dyken hopped on his Honda 160 Scrambler motorcycle, raced to the Navy base in San Francisco, and persuaded an officer there to discharge him so he could join the blue-suiters as an officer.

His first two choices for Air Force duty were pilot and navigator, but allergies got in the way. His third choice, intelligence, entailed fewer physical demands, and that became his specialty. After graduating from intelligence school at Lowry in October 1967, Van Dyken volunteered for Vietnam, figuring a war was as good a place as any to apply his history degree. But he hardly had an academic temperament. One day at Tan Son Nhut in Saigon, while he was killing time waiting for his clearances, Van Dyken was chatting with some Army helicopter crews heading out on a mission into the Mekong Delta. He asked if he could come along. "Sure," they said. "Hop on." It was fascinating to see the checkerboard streets of Saigon from the air, packed with bikes and people and mopeds and lined with palm trees. The side doors of the Huey chopper were wide open and gusts of air washed over him.

They headed out over the rice paddies at 1,000 feet or so. One of the gunners fired into a hootch on the ground, for reasons Van Dyken wasn't privy to. When the gunner squeezed the trigger, the vibration of the gun popped a pack of Marlboro cigarettes out of his rolled-up sleeves. The small box vibrated forward on the metal floor, under the

seat where Van Dyken was strapped in, then toward the open doorway. Van Dyken tried to reach the packet but it inched away, out of
reach. He decided to unclip his seat belt for a moment to rescue the
smokes—and just as he did, the pilot jerked the Huey out of level flight
into a rollover dive. In a split second Van Dyken found himself floating
out the door, with the chopper beneath him. He grabbed for whatever
he could and managed to get a grip on some part of the helicopter and
haul himself back inside. He strapped himself in, but was haunted for
weeks by the terrifying vision of a rice paddy directly beneath his feet
as he hung in space for an interminable moment.

The helo crew, meanwhile, got new orders, and had to drop Van
Dyken at a Green Beret outstation in the bush, miles from the comforts
of Tan Son Nhut. They told him they had radioed an O-1 pilot, who'd
be passing by in a while and would land and pick him up. For the next
thirty minutes, Van Dyken was the only soul at the lonely little landing
zone, unarmed, and scared as a rabbit in the middle of the Mekong
Delta, which was infested with Viet Cong. Finally, Van Dyken heard
the insectlike buzz of the O-1 approaching, and his inadvertent introduction to life in the field neared its end.

Van Dyken wasn't intimidated, though. In fact, he was excited, and
when he heard of a unit upcountry that was looking for a temporary
intel officer, at a base called Phu Cat, he went for it. He had no idea
what Misty was, but he contacted P. J. White, who encouraged him to
come on up. In late October he hopped a flight that was bringing some
entertainers to Phu Cat—a small band and two strippers. On his first
night at his new assignment, Van Dyken watched a base full of men,
many who hadn't been around women in weeks, go wild as the two
girls gyrated and took off their clothes. They even brought an airman
up onstage and stripped him to his underwear. Then, in a surreal climax, the strippers ended their performance by singing "God Bless
America."

John Haltigan was overjoyed when his twenty-three-year-old assistant arrived. "Rodge!" he greeted Van Dyken, like an old friend. "Hey,
ma' man! How's it goin'!" Van Dyken let few people call him "Rodge,"
but this time the new arrival didn't care. He was happy enough to encounter a friendly face. Like Haltigan when he had first arrived, Van
Dyken felt like he was out of his league, a naïve farm boy who would

never fit in with the hard, sophisticated warriors at Misty. Yet Halti-gan's easygoing, optimistic demeanor was reassuring, and something about him seemed to indicate that at Misty, the mission was all that mattered. The pale Vermont native reminded Van Dyken of Ichabod Crane, his uniform draped awkwardly over his bony frame. Even in uniform Haltigan didn't look military, his creases never quite straight and his short hair somehow perpetually scraggly. But he focused on the job with energy and earnestness that was a refreshing antidote to the war-weary cynicism Van Dyken had encountered during his brief so-journ in Saigon.

Misty, Van Dyken found, was just the kind of action he was look-ing for. It was still a tiny outfit, only about eighteen pilots, but every day they returned from their missions with tales of getting shot at, and sometimes with real bullet holes in their jets to prove it. Misty pro-duced real results—guiding strikes onto targets nearly every day—in-stead of the kinds of vague, overstated BDA reports that the analysts in Saigon always had to downplay by half. Misty, by now, even had its own lore, from the loss of Bud Day to the many unique aspects of the mission and the territory they covered.

At the bar after missions, for instance, Van Dyken heard the Mistys joke about "the kid on the karst," a young NVA antiaircraft gunner whose job was to defend the Trail from atop one of the limestone rock formations just south of the Mu Ghia Pass. He was such a bad shot that the Mistys would take new pilots or visitors up there to give them a taste of ground fire—"AAA kindergarten," they called it, a primer for the big guns, with minimal chance of getting shot down. The Mistys imagined that the kid on the karst had terrible eyesight and the best he could do was fire toward the sound when he heard a plane approach-ing. They regularly tormented the kid by arriving at high speed just after sunrise, alternating their approach directions. They laughed as the kid's bullets arced behind them and fell harmlessly to the ground. Misty had an unofficial standing order: Don't attack the kid on the karst, lest he be replaced by a first-team gunner with good eyesight.

Some of the pilots who had first impressed John Haltigan were still around: the feisty, bombastic Charlie Neel; Jonesy Jones, laconic yet intense; Bob Craner, the steel-jawed tactics expert who seemed to know where every gun was in North Vietnam. There were some newcomers, too. Jim Fiorelli, who had just arrived, was an Air Force Academy graduate and the original "Pillsbury Doughboy," a slightly chubby Italian whose sense of humor was almost as refined as his taste buds. Mick Greene was a Naval Academy graduate and an engineer. He looked like a bantamweight boxer, taut and intense. Jim Mack, two years senior to Fiorelli at the Academy, was a muscular air defense pilot who had converted from F-102 air-to-air fighters to tactical fighter-bombers for the war. Van Dyken got to be particularly friendly with Guy Gruters, an Academy grad who had been a member of the judo club and looked fearsome: He was a hulking six-foot-three, weighing 205 pounds, all muscle. He was perhaps the most imposing Misty—and also the most religious, saying a private grace before every meal and attending mass daily at the base chapel. Gruters could be as gentle as a monk, but downright mean when he was in the cockpit— and as aggressive as any pilot flying over the North.

On November 8, when Van Dyken had been at Misty for about a week, Neel and Gruters paired up for a mission. They were a true odd couple. Gruters's hulking frame was a tight fit in the cockpit. Neel, on the other hand, was so short that when he applied for the Air Force Academy, as the story went, he had put clear tape on the bottom of his feet to boost his height by one-sixteenth of an inch in order to reach the minimum required height. The other pilots joked that Charlie was the only Misty who had to get a ten-yard running start to jump onto the first rung of the aircraft cockpit ladder. Yet Charlie always managed to leave an impression, even if it wasn't quite what you'd put on a recruiting poster. During one flight, with Jim Mack in the front seat, Charlie had decided to take a bathroom and cigarette break while the Hun gassed up on one of the tankers. Little did he know that while he "stood" in the backseat peeing into a bottle and puffing a smoke, an NBC camera crew led by a female correspondent was filming the Hun from the tanker, for a feature to be aired back home.

Charlie Neel gave cadets like Gruters merciless grief when they were at the Academy together. Neel belonged to the class of 1961 and was in his final year when Gruters had first arrived at Colorado Springs. The first year was hellish for "doolies," as freshmen were known. Neel and his classmates used to put the new doolies into hard military "braces," a rigid at-attention posture against the wall, and force them to recite passages from *Contrails,* the official guide to the Academy and its many mysterious ways. When the doolies inevitably failed the examination, they'd be ordered to do push-ups and sit-ups until their muscles gave out. Gruters, when he was a freshman, had sworn he would kill upperclassmen like Neel if he ever got the chance. He was probably joking, but no one could be sure.

Now the doolie and the upperclassman were flying together. As they climbed into the plane, Neel, in the front seat, pressed the electric seat control until he was sitting as high as he could get. In the back, Gruters did the opposite, adjusting the seat to its lowest position. Still, his helmet barely cleared the Plexiglas canopy. They had the first flight that day, and, as was often the case, the North Vietnamese jungle looked peaceful and serene from 4,500 feet. The morning fog lingered in a few valleys, but otherwise the view was unusually clear. With Neel flying from the front, the two pilots peered into the inscrutable foliage below, scanning for targets along the Trail.

Suddenly Gruters blurted out, "Did you see that?"

"What?" asked Neel.

"I don't know, but it was something different. A bunch of big, low humps covered with what looked like camouflage. Both sides of the road."

The unusual formation was a dead giveaway. Misty had taught them both that anything so odd-looking in the middle of the jungle had to have some connection to the men and weapons flowing down the Trail. But they also knew to play it cool. Instead of swinging around quickly for another look and setting off a swarm of antiaircraft gunners, the pilots decided to continue moving and come back later. Best to whistle past the graveyard nonchalantly, thought Neel. Maybe the "gomers"—the bad guys—will think you're just passing by.

They needed gas, and Neel turned the jet west toward the tanker tracks, which followed the Mekong River that divided Thailand from Laos. When they came off the tanker and reentered the Pack, Neel flew low—really low—and as fast as possible to get a good look at the humps and then scramble up and away. With the sun higher, the humps produced fewer shadows and less contrast and were harder to spot. But that first glimpse had helped them know what to look for, and sure enough, there they were—dozens of mounds in the earth that had to be fuel tanks, or bunkers, or huge storage containers of some type, almost completely buried on their sides. Grass and shrubs were thrown on top of them as camouflage. The humps lined both sides of the road, with trees swaying over them, providing more cover.

The intelligence honchos down in Saigon had been wondering for months where all the trucks coming from the North were being refueled on this section of the Trail, where it diverged into Laos and South Vietnam. This could be the place. Gruters called in the find to the ABCCC, flying in safer skies to the west, and asked them to scramble or divert whatever fighters they could muster for an impromptu, high-priority bombing run. If the target turned out to be what they thought it was, it was big enough to justify several hours' worth of bombing.

Then Neel and Gruters searched for the inevitable AAA. Before they had drawn a shot, they made out three batteries of six 37mm guns on one side of the target and two more batteries on the other. That was a formidable thirty guns. Other antiaircraft weapons, better hidden, would probably join the fight once the bomb-droppers came rolling in. These were tenacious defenses. No doubt, something very hot was down there.

The two pilots flew west over Laos and the Mekong River once again to gas up for the action. When they returned, four F-4 fighters out of Da Nang—the "Gunfighters"—were stacked up over the area, laden with bombs. Another four were on the way. Neel and Gruters would lead the strike, firing smoke rockets at the targets to mark them for the fighters.

Gruters contacted the fighters on the radio and briefed them. "Gunfighters, this is Misty one-one. We've got what appears to be a large fuel storage area on both sides of a north-south road. Lots of guns on both sides. Two sets of 37s on the east side, three on the west. Best bailout is to the east, 'feet wet' "—over the ocean.

Charlie Neel took over from the front seat. "I'm rolling in for a mark. Keep your eye on me," he instructed. "I'll put down two smokes. Anywhere between the smokes on both sides of the road is okay. Alternate the bombs on both sides. Expect secondary explosions."

As they prepared for their assault on the humps, Neel jinked left, then right, to throw off any AAA gunners who might be tracking the plane. He pulled the nose sharply down toward the target and fired two 2.75-inch white-phosphorous smoke rockets. They hit right where he aimed. Smoke gushed out. It was a perfect mark for the fighters.

Neel pulled out hard. The aircraft rotated into a steep climb. Both pilots groaned as high G-forces smashed them into their seats. They were gaining altitude when a sickening *thump!* echoed from the belly of the plane. The aircraft shuddered and several warning lights flared on the instrument panel. One warned FIRE, another ENGINE OVERHEAT. Acrid smoke and fumes filled the front and back cockpits. They had been hit, probably by an unseen 37mm gunner directly beneath them.

Urgent calls came over the radio from the F-4s. "Misty, you're on fire! Get out!"

"Don't listen to them, Guy," Neel advised. "Let's stay with it to the coast." The two pilots weren't about to bail out into a hostile nest of North Vietnamese gunners and other angry troops they had just attacked. There was a chance they could make it to the water and eject feet wet, where a rescue should be far easier.

Gruters said nothing, his silence signaling his agreement with Neel. "Stow your stuff. Put your glasses in your pocket," Neel advised hurriedly. Both pilots wore glasses and had to remove them to prevent their eyes from getting punctured during the ejection. They pushed their helmet visors down, preparing to punch out. Neel coaxed as much altitude as he could out of the damaged aircraft for the short ride east to the water. "Come on, baby, hold together for us," he urged. "Don't blow yet."

More warnings came over the radio. "Misty, you're really burning now. Big pieces are coming off. Eject! Eject! Before she blows!" A hundred-foot-long flame was trailing the crippled jet. Their problems multiplied. Every gunner in North Vietnam seemed to be shooting at them now, hungry to kill a crippled bird. Most of the flak fell harmlessly behind, but some tracers streaked past the canopy. Their shock waves beat against the fuselage. The rounds were coming close.

The water was five miles away. "Oh, baby, just give me a few more seconds," Neel prayed. As the coastline passed underneath, the plane's controls began to atrophy. Neel knew they would seize completely once enough hydraulic fluid had spilled out. As the jet started to roll uncontrollably to the left, Gruters, in the back, yanked his ejection seat handles upward.

The canopy flew off. Blowing dust and debris suddenly blinded Neel. He felt the heat and saw the flash as Gruters's seat rocket fired. Neel struggled to hold the plane level, so he wouldn't slam into the rolling wings or fuselage when the rocket motor beneath his seat shot him out of the cockpit. But the Hun had stopped responding. It was dead.

Gruters found himself drifting peacefully toward the ocean. He checked his parachute panels—they were all intact. His inflated life raft hung fifteen feet below on a cord. He activated his underarm "water wings," which would keep him afloat despite the ninety pounds of gear he carried on every combat mission, stuffed into every available pocket in his flying suit, G-suit, and survival vest.

Charlie Neel, meanwhile, was unconscious. He had managed to pull the ejection handle, but something, probably his three-hundred-pound seat, had hit him on the head during the bailout and broken his helmet into two pieces that hung on both sides of his head. While Gruters was methodically going through emergency procedures to prepare for his water landing, Charlie was out cold, descending blithely toward the relative safety of the South China Sea a few hundred yards offshore.

The pilots were still hot targets, though. North Vietnamese gunners shot at them from the shore as they drifted down. Bullets whipped past them—*zip! zip! zip!*—reverberating as they cut through the air. None hit.

Neel awoke about 1,000 feet above the water, his head pounding from a concussion. Holy shit! Where am I? he thought. He got oriented just as he hit the water at what seemed like fifty miles per hour. He plunged thirty feet below the surface, with no time to take a deep breath—he had forgotten to inflate his water wings. He now had a long swim up, with his gear weighing him down like an anchor. Goddamn, I'll never carry extra shit again, he thought as he struggled gasping, coughing, and spitting to the surface. He could breathe now, but he was tangled in a web of spaghetti-like nylon parachute shrouds.

The two pilots had splashed down about two hundred yards apart and clambered into their rafts once they untangled themselves from their parachute lines. But the water was choppy and they couldn't see each other above the wave tops. The warm tropical water was safer than land, but it was still full of sharks and deadly sea snakes. And they practically had to hug their rafts, since the air was full of lead.

Despite ejecting successfully from a crippled aircraft and getting into their life rafts, they were by no means home free. They weren't far from land, and shore gunners continued to shoot at them, adding mortar rounds to the onslaught. The shells arced in and exploded menacingly close to the rafts. Hot metal fragments flew in all directions.

Neel used his radio to contact the F-4s overhead. "Gunfighters, Misty one-one Alpha. They're shooting at us a lot," he fretted. "Do you have one-one Bravo in sight? Can you give us some help?"

"Misty, Gunfighter," one of the pilots assured Neel. "We have you both." The contact with the F-4s was a tremendous relief. It meant the Air Force knew they were down and that a rescue was under way. At Phu Cat, P. J. White got word from 7th Air Force's search-and-rescue directorate that a Misty jet had been shot down and that a rescue was in the works. He forwarded the news up to his bosses at the 37th Wing, letting them know it was Neel and Gruters who were in the drink. Charlie and Guy had a lot of friends in the other squadrons, and tension spread rapidly across the base as word got around that the two Mistys had been knocked out of the sky.

One of the F-4s quizzed Neel about the incoming fire. "Where are they shooting from?" he asked.

"Just put something on the beach about one hundred yards inland, right opposite us, and I'll talk you into where I think it's coming from," Neel replied. "Jesus," he muttered. "I never thought I'd be FACing from a goddamned raft."

The Gunfighters bombed the shore for twenty or thirty minutes. Smoke obscured the coastline and the firing began to subside. The first set of Gunfighters left to get gas and was quickly replaced by another flight of four, which continued bombing along the beach. Neel listened anxiously on his emergency radio for the rescue helicopters, as the waves and wind pushed both rafts rapidly toward land.

An F-4 rolled in on Neel. He thought it was just making a friendly "keep-up-the-morale" pass to signal that they saw him. The jet got closer. Uncomfortably close. The nose of the plane was pointing right at him, when it suddenly launched two pods of nineteen rockets each. The rockets screamed just over Neel's head, their black exhaust blocking his view of the F-4. The plane pulled out so low it almost hit the water, kicking up ocean spray that blinded Neel in his tiny raft. The jet's shock wave tossed the raft like a cork as Neel hung on for dear life.

Neel howled curses into his radio. "Hey, you dumb shit! That's me in the raft! You're supposed to rescue me, not shoot me, you sonofabitch!" His rant was interrupted by important news. A transmission came over the radio from one of two "Jolly Green" rescue helicopters: "Misty, this is Jolly. Two birds coming in toward your position now. Get ready!"

A Jolly Green splashed down right behind him in a high-speed water landing and taxied toward the raft. Neel slipped out of his parachute harness as the water spray kicked up by the helo's rotor wash stung his eyes.

A pararescue jumper reached out while the helicopter was still moving, grabbed Neel by the collar of his flight suit, and in one motion yanked him out of his raft and into the chopper. The other Jolly Green picked up Gruters, and the two were reunited in less than an hour at Dong Ha, an Army base that was the nearest safe landing spot. Medics checked them out and decided they didn't have any life-threatening injuries that needed immediate attention, so they were flown on to Da Nang, the nearest Air Force base.

On the ramp at Da Nang a flock of Gunfighter F-4 pilots met them with booze and dry flight suits to celebrate the rescue. When they first saw the two mismatched Mistys, one of the F-4 drivers joked, "We don't have any flight suits big enough or small enough for the two of you. But at least this underwear doesn't have shit in it." Neel's new skivvies were too big, Gruters's were too small. Nobody cared. As the backslapping subsided, Neel asked about the "imbecile" who had nearly killed him with rockets and almost pancaked into the water.

It turned out that an old friend, Jerry Nabors, had flown the plane and done the shooting. Right after Neel and Gruters had hit the water, the F-4s spotted about a dozen North Vietnamese sampans racing out of the mouth of a river to capture the downed pilots. Some of the bombs Neel saw being dropped on the beach were falling on the sampans. The F-4s sank about four of them near the shoreline and thought the others had turned around. But one had slipped through unnoticed until it was less than a hundred yards from Neel's raft. Neel couldn't see it because of the chop, but Nabors could. He blew the sampan out of the water at the last minute, firing from point-blank range, saving the doolie and the upperclassman from almost certain capture.

It was gratifying for Neel and Gruters, therapeutic even, to hash over the ordeal with the Gunfighters and retell their stories. But there were more urgent matters: Gruters was badly hurt, and despite being cleared by the Army medics—who were trained to deal with life-or-death combat injuries and left lesser problems for the docs back in the hospitals—he needed prompt attention. One of his arms was limp and useless and riven with pain. His neck ached. He was whisked to the Navy hospital on base in the "meat wagon," the flight line ambulance.

It wound up being an extended stay. Gruters had torn the tendons in his arm during the ejection, and the bones in his wrist had been crushed. The docs repaired the damage and ran a heavy cast most of the length of his arm. On top of that, the force of the ejection had compressed his neck, which needed to be held immobile. He spent several days on his back, barely moving. The doctors said it would probably be a couple of months before he could fly again.

Neel caught a flight back to Phu Cat the same day and got an even more enthusiastic welcome there than he had at Da Nang. Ray Lee and P. J. White met him on the tarmac with fervid handshakes. They conducted a quick debriefing. Although Neel had felt pretty good after getting picked up by the Jolly, he now had a whopping headache, no doubt from whatever he had banged his head against during the ejection. It was protocol for fighter jocks to brush off injuries, but White made sure Neel went to the base hospital for a thorough checkup before landing at the bar to relish in his war story. The hospital released Neel that evening. Needless to say, he couldn't buy himself a drink once he got to the O club.

The drinking had gone on for an hour or two when it occurred to Neel that he ought to call his wife, Linda, and tell her what had happened, just in case she'd heard about it through the grapevine somehow. Linda Neel was a short, shapely, and ravishing brunette who had met Charlie when he was a second lieutenant going through pilot training at Craig Air Force Base in Alabama and she was a student at Methodist College in nearby Huntington. In addition to being a fighter pilot's wife, she was also a fighter pilot's daughter. When Charlie got shot down, Linda happened to be visiting her parents in Colorado Springs, where her dad was in charge of the command post overseeing the air defense of the United States and Canada at North American Air Defense Command, NORAD. He had seen a classified report that very morning detailing the shootdown and successful recovery of a pilot named Capt. Charles B. Neel, over North Vietnam. He had called the 37th Wing Command Post over secure telephone lines to ensure that Charlie was okay. Then he told Linda.

By the time Charlie thought about calling his wife, he had drunk enough for three or four fighter pilots. But he still managed to reach Linda on the Military Affiliate Radio System, a patchwork communication line run by ham radio operators. The system was known as MARS, which was fitting since it seemed like every word got bounced off the Red Planet before it finally made its way back to the States. Because of the delay in sending sound across this far-ranging radio network, each speaker typically said "over," after each transmission, to indicate that they were finished speaking. It was awkward at best, especially for civilians unaccustomed to military formalities.

When the MARS call connected with Linda at her parents' home, Charlie greeted her. "You'll never guess what happened to me today! Over."

"You got shot down?" Linda answered.

"Say 'over,' honey," Charlie slurred.

"Over," she said.

"How did you know, over?"

"Daddy told me, over."

"Well, I'm okay, over."

"Well, it sounds like you're drunk, over."

"Well, a little bit, but I'll be okay tomorrow, over." And the line went dead.

Linda understood the flying game and the men who played in it. She knew Charlie wouldn't call unless he was okay, but she was glad to hear it directly from him, not just through her father. The details arrived in a letter two weeks later, after Charlie was flying Misty missions again.

Gruters's wife, Sandy, also got a call at home in Sarasota, Florida—but not from her husband. It was Air Force procedure at the time to send a telegram to the family whenever a pilot was shot down and rescued, explaining the unclassified details of the incident and relaying the status of the pilot. Gruters knew that if he didn't call first, the telegram would do little but cause worry. But he was bed-bound in the hospital, not to mention exhausted, hurting, and medicated. He didn't want to call right away. So he managed to get the telegram canceled, figuring he would call the next day.

When he got through to Sandy in Sarasota, however, she already knew. A reporter from the local paper had picked up news of the shootdown from the wire services and called her for comment—catching her completely off guard. He explained that her husband had been shot down in North Vietnam, but had been rescued and was not seriously injured. "It was a 'happy' rescue," he told her. Sandy was astonished, since she didn't know her husband was flying over North Vietnam, but also relieved. When Gruters finally called, he filled in some blanks: He was actually beat up pretty bad and would be in the hospital recuperating for a while, how long he wasn't quite sure.

Both pilots earned a Purple Heart for the mission—and a little time away from the war. Neel was granted a week's convalescent leave, which he decided to spend in Hong Kong. One of the squadron flight surgeons got a free trip by volunteering to make sure the buccaneering pilot was still stable after the ejection. The control tower chief, who supervised the air traffic controllers, had a break coming, too, and tagged along. Just before Charlie got on the C-47 "Gooneybird" for the ride to Hong Kong, he got a call from Wing Personnel, which handled assignments.

Charlie was due to leave Misty in January and eager to know where he was going next. "Sir, I have some news about your follow-on assignment," said the clerk. "And I think you are going to like it. You are going on pilot exchange duty with the Royal Air Force. You will be flying Lightnings with Number 5 Squadron at RAF Einbrooke in Lincolnshire in the United Kingdom."

Despite the roar from the flight line, almost the entire base could hear Charlie shout "Wahoo!" over the phone line. He was one happy pilot. Exchange duty with a foreign air force was considered a plum assignment. Charlie envisioned him and Linda punting on the Thames River, shopping in London, drinking in the pubs, and, oh yes, there would be flying jets during the week. Life couldn't get any better. "When we get to Hong Kong," he told his traveling companions, "just like the old farmer at Christmas time . . . we are going to 'kill the fat calf.' Get ready to celebrate!"

When they landed in Hong Kong, they were met on the ramp by the usual Chinese salesmen hawking suits and shoes. All three ordered new wardrobes. Charlie was quickly measured for three suits, a silk-and-wool tuxedo, and several pair of shoes. He would need all the finery, he laughed, "in my new role as an Air Force ambassador to the UK." The tab came to about $250, and the suits would be delivered to their hotel in about eight hours.

The three checked into their hotel and the salesmen returned for a final fitting. They made reservations for dinner and at 6:00 p.m. their new clothes arrived. They hailed a cab. Decked out in their new duds, looking like businessmen with short haircuts and suntans, they wound their way to the Peninsula Hotel, Hong Kong's most exclusive restaurant. They started with the maitre d's recommendation, "velvet soup," a Hong Kong delicacy composed of cheese and chicken frothing in aromatic spices. "Don't forget the fine wines," Charlie instructed. "And if it's on the menu and it's expensive, just bring it."

Three and a half hours later, the big spender was full of fine wine, and bluster, too. "War is hell," he laughed as he toasted the Mistys, the president, and the queen of England. The doc, feeling rather magnanimous himself, decided Charlie was still normal.

Guy Gruters wasn't quite as normal. He ended up spending three weeks in the hospital at Da Nang and was granted an additional three weeks of "military convalescent leave," which he planned to spend with his family. When he finally left Da Nang he was still stiff, and his cast was a burden, but he made a stop at Phu Cat before heading home. The Mistys were elated to see him. He was one of their favorites. Then he headed for Cam Ranh Bay, another base farther south along the coast, and presented his orders for a "space-A" flight—space available—on a C-141 cargo jet headed back toward the States. On the afternoon of Thanksgiving Day, 1967, Gruters knocked on the door of

his home in Sarasota. Sandy opened the door to one of the best sur-
prises of her life. She was hosting Thanksgiving dinner for their children, Dawn, three, and Sheri, two, along with Guy's parents, who also
lived in Sarasota. She had no idea Guy was coming home for the holiday, but needless to say she was delighted beyond words.

Two weeks later Gruters packed his bags, kissed Sandy and the kids
good-bye, and headed back to the war. The cast would come off on
January 1, he told Sandy, and he would start flying again right after
that. He had one week to make it back to Phu Cat, space-A. Sandy
didn't like it, but knew her husband had to go back. Gruters's father
was more forceful. He had never shown much emotion toward his son,
but now he grabbed him, hugged him, and said, "Hey—that's enough
of this stuff, son." Gruters was moved, but unpersuaded. Off he went,
to fulfill his duty to country, Misty, and self.

Up in North Vietnam, meanwhile, a huge stash of valuable fuel, or
ammunition, or whatever Neel and Gruters had originally seen buried
in the ground, was now being diligently guarded by AAA gunners—
someplace else. Once the two pilots had ejected on November 8, the
rescue effort had quickly overtaken the strike on the storage containers. The North Vietnamese always had alternate plans when storage
areas were discovered, and they promptly moved the containers to new
locations. By the next morning there was no sight of the humps that
Neel and Gruters had seen in the morning light that early November
day. It was as if they had never existed.

EIGHT

AWOL 01 BRAVO

L ife was busy at Misty, and often the dramas came one after the other. The day after Neel and Gruters were shot down and rescued, the 480th Tactical Fighter Squadron, which was part of the 366th Tactical Fighter Wing, based at Da Nang, had scheduled several bombing runs into heavily defended parts of North Vietnam and Laos, along the Trail. There were hundreds of such flights into enemy territory every day, from squadrons based at Da Nang, Cam Ranh Bay, Tuy Hoa, Phan Rang, and Phu Cat in South Vietnam, and from Ubon, Takhli, Korat, Utapao, Udorn, and Nakhon Phanom in Thailand. The air war had such a steady, predictable rhythm by the fall of 1967 that it took extraordinary events to get much attention. Five or six pilots were getting shot down every week, killed or captured and becoming POWs. Risky flights barely rated a mention, and nobody outside the 480th paid much attention to the flights the squadron had on the scheduling board for November 9.

The pilots of the 480th flew the F-4C Phantom, one of the Air Force's newest jets. It was getting a bad rap, though—mainly because it had begun life as a Navy aircraft and wasn't equipped the way the Air Force wanted it. The biggest shortcoming was that it had *no internal gun*—a fatal flaw to some Air Force pilots, especially those who flew up in Route Packs 5 and 6, over Hanoi, where MiGs came up to do battle from time to time. The new missiles were a nice bit of technology, but a machine gun or cannon mounted in the fuselage had been the fighter pilot's preferred weapon since Baron von Richthofen used his to shoot down eighty enemy planes in World War I. Worse, every F-4 had two seats, a bad setup that the Navy worsened by putting a RIO—a radar intercept officer who was not a full-fledged pilot—in the backseat. The Air Force, at least, filled the backseat with a second pilot, and even if he was a lowly "guy in back"—a GIB, who didn't get to do the flying—he'd be able to manage the aircraft in an emergency.

The F-4 was a modern and capable jet, however, and pilots who flew it quickly recognized its superior abilities. It had two engines instead of one, and was fast and nimble. It was equipped with the most modern air-to-air missiles, such as the Sparrow and the Sidewinder, which allowed pilots to take aim at enemy planes from farther away than ever before. And unlike the aging F-100s the Mistys flew, the F-4 had the latest air-to-air radar and other electronics.

The frag order that the 480th received from 7th Air Force that day had called for a series of nighttime raids against 57mm antiaircraft batteries near Ban Laboy Ford, a river on Route 137 in the mountainous karst region on the border between Laos and North Vietnam. Up until about a month earlier, the 480th had been focusing on NVA units just north of the DMZ, especially the field artillery that fired relentlessly into U.S. Marine positions across the border. Misty had controlled some of those attacks. But as American intelligence had detected the huge push of men and weapons to the South, blasting and disrupting the Trail had become a priority. It was becoming clear that operations along the Trail had become North Vietnam's center of gravity, the sine qua non of its war strategy.[1]

The commander of the 480th was Lt. Col. John Armstrong, a demanding West Pointer with impeccable military bearing. He was scheduled to take off at 8:00 p.m. The flight up to Ban Laboy Ford, about 145 miles to the northwest, would take about twenty-five minutes. Armstrong's back-seater, responsible for gathering the latest intel reports, plotting the tanker tracks, and handling the maps was a burly, handsome, twenty-five-year-old Air Force Academy graduate named Lance Sijan. Armstrong had his hands full running the squadron and delegated to Sijan a long list of duties to prep for the mission. It would be up to Sijan to prepare lineup cards with key information about the flight, compute takeoff data, and ferret out the frequencies and call signs they were to use from the frag order.

Shortly after 8:00 p.m., two F-4s, call signs AWOL 01 and AWOL 02, were wheels up. Sijan and Armstrong were in the first jet. The two planes streaked northwest across the DMZ at about 20,000 feet. In the backseat of AWOL 01, Sijan fiddled with a radar display that showed the rapidly changing topography of the terrain below. He also monitored the radar homing and warning gear that could warn of missile launches, an increasing possibility, since 7th Air Force intelligence believed the NVA was moving more missiles south to prevent B-52 strikes against the Trail. The flat coastal plain receded into a mountain range with peaks as high as 5,000 feet and deep gorges so narrow they were barely visible from above. Farther west the landscape became even more severe. Lance looked at the "radar shadows" on his backseat display produced by line after line of razor-sharp, limestone karst peaks. Somehow, the North Vietnamese managed to move supplies through this jagged, brutal terrain. Sijan thought it was amazing. Hidden somewhere inside this lunar maze were the guns protecting the ford—the guns the Phantoms were seeking to destroy.

It was a clear night, and as usual once the sun went down, there was lots of activity along the Trail. Nighttime FACs and the relatively new C-130 gunships were dropping flares on key target areas, to illuminate them for the fighters. Armstrong and Sijan could see other jets attacking truck convoys and key intersections, including one about thirty miles south of their position. It was a vivid fireworks display.

As they got close to the ford, Armstrong checked in with the command-and-control aircraft orbiting nearby. The ABCCC then contacted the FAC marking targets in the area, call sign Nail 11—a nighttime version of Misty, except that the Nail FACs flew O-2 prop planes that were essentially a military version of the "push-pull" Cessna Skymaster, which had both a front and back engine. These slow FACs could operate on the Trail and survive, but they needed the night for protection.

Everything seemed to be in order and the FAC started to prepare for his marking run. The two AWOL jets descended from their cruising altitude of about 20,000 feet down to 14,000, also getting ready for the attack. AWOL 02 split off, since the jets would come at the target from different directions. Flares drifted down and lit up the ford. Nail 11 dived in to mark the target, and then he cleared AWOL Lead—Armstrong and Sijan's jet—to move in for their attack.

Armstrong rolled off his perch toward the target and put the Phantom into an aggressive 50-degree dive. But when he was still a few thousand feet above "pickle altitude," the point where he should have released his bombs, Armstrong started to peel away from the target. He broke off the run and started to climb back into a high orbit. "Pass aborted," he called out to Nail 11. "I lost my target reference." The FAC asked if he wanted to have another go at it. "Roger," Armstrong replied. There was still plenty of light from the slow-falling parachute flares, and none of the pilots had noticed any tracers on the first run. Everything seemed to be lined up for a second shot.

Armstrong pointed the Phantom toward the target again. His dive angle was just as steep this time, but he approached from a different direction, to keep the gunners on the ground guessing. This time, however, tracers started to fill the sky. Orange 37mm shells and 14.5mm ZPU rounds, hundreds of them, screamed past the cockpit. Then the FAC, orbiting overhead, saw something unusual—a bright red spark near the Phantom. Suddenly, without warning, the jet erupted into a fireball that plummeted to earth two miles north of the target. For several seconds the wreckage lit up the jungle. But it quickly burned itself out, and the night was dark again.

The Nail FAC caught his breath, then immediately initiated rescue procedures. He called AWOL 02, AWOL 01's wingman, to ask if he had seen any parachutes or other signs of a bailout. Nobody had picked up any sign of the pilots. They discussed the way the massive fire had quickly burned itself out. The wreckage, they guessed, must have landed on a steep slope where the fuel rapidly·spilled away. AWOL 02 began listening intently for a survival radio beeper or radio call or any other sign of Armstrong and Sijan. A rescue package that had been on standby at Nakhon Phanom Air Base in Thailand—two Jolly Green choppers, two A-1E "Sandy" Skyraiders, and an HC-130 tanker—took off promptly and raced toward the scene. But the rescuers had no work that night. The jungle below was dark and silent, with no sign that either of the pilots had survived the crash.[2]

For the next day and a half 7th Air Force kept rescue crews on high alert, so they could get up to Ban Laboy Ford on less than half an hour's notice. A stream of aircraft flowed through the area continuously, to make sure somebody was there if one of the pilots came up on the radio. Several Mistys transited the area, including Jim Mack, Jere Wallace, P. J. White, and Don Sibson. It was a vigilant but unproductive watch: The jungle remained inscrutable, the airwaves silent.

At the 5:00 a.m. Misty briefing two mornings after the crash, Jim Mack and Jonesy Jones heard the usual: There might be some targets of opportunity up by Mu Ghia Pass. The weather would probably be bad, almost surely in the morning. SAMs were popping up farther and farther to the south, so watch your ass. Haltigan, the briefer, also reminded the groggy Mistys that two pilots were still missing up around Ban Laboy Ford. Keep a listening watch, he implored. "No need to mention it," thought Mack. The Mistys always watched and listened for downed pilots.

Mack had grown up in a small farming town near Rock Island, Illinois, and after graduating from the Air Force Academy in 1962 had been assigned to fly air-defense interceptors. His nickname, "Fuzz," had trailed after him since he was a child, but Mack developed a bawdier explanation: It was because he had so much hair on his ass, he liked to tell his colleagues. Fuzz Mack had volunteered for Vietnam and was selected for training in the F-104 Starfighter, which jet-jocks called the Zipper because it was "faster than a pilot zipping up his pants when her dad came home." Then the Air Force decided to pull its F-104s out of Vietnam, and Mack was rerouted to F-100 training— an agreeable trade-off that put him in one of the Air Force's most popular fighter-bombers. When training ended, however, Mack got devastating news: He was being sent on to FAC training and would fly the O-1 prop plane, a huge letdown for a fighter jock. "That's it," he had told friends. "When I get back from this war, I'm getting out." He even filed papers to leave the service after he returned from Vietnam.

The O-1 may have been a dull plane, but Mack's missions were not. He became a "Covey," flying out of Kontum, about 250 miles north of

Saigon in the war-ravaged Central Highlands. The Coveys flew secret missions helping to direct attacks against the Ho Chi Minh Trail in Laos, which was getting to be almost as dangerous for slow-movers as flying over North Vietnam. Mack even flew into Cambodia a few times. That was technically forbidden, since Cambodia was a U.S. ally that strenuously wished to stay out of the war. But clandestine "trail watch" teams, usually Army Green Berets or CIA operatives, operated in Cambodia, and sometimes they got into trouble and needed help. In the minds of the rescuers, restrictions didn't apply when American lives were at stake.

After one hundred missions as a Covey, the Air Force asked Mack if he wanted to be a mission planner at 7th Air Force headquarters. He had no interest in flying a desk and said no, so the Air Force made him a FAC working farther south in the Iron Triangle northwest of Saigon, mainly directing ground support strikes by pilots flying his beloved F-100. About six months through his yearlong tour, Mack got a call from Lt. Col. Ken Miles, an old buddy he had gone through F-100 training with. Miles now commanded the 614th Tactical Fighter Squadron, an F-100 outfit at Phan Rang, along the coast about 150 miles northeast of Saigon. He remembered Mack as being a "good stick" from training days and offered him an F-100 job, which Mack immediately accepted. Miles waived the usual checkout procedures and told Mack to go refine his bombing skills on an uninhabited island a few miles out to sea. "Get yourself loaded up with some bombs and go practice," the commander instructed. "Tell me when you're ready and we'll put you to work."

Mack was ecstatic. The opportunity got even more interesting a few days later when Miles told him that a unit called Misty was experimenting with "fast FAC" missions in the North and looking for volunteers. Miles explained what he knew of the mission, and Mack jumped on it. The next day he was saluting P. J. White at Phu Cat. By early November he had been at Misty for two months and was considered one of the more experienced guys.

Mack and Jones went to the "PE shop," where they zipped on their personal equipment—G-suits and survival vests with their emergency radios, .38-caliber revolvers, extra batteries, and other standard flying gear. They hoisted the twenty-five-pound parachutes onto their backs and headed for the Ops truck that would take them to the flight line. Mack and Jones were assigned an aging Hun affectionately known as "Leakin' Lena" because she burned through oil the way the fighter jocks pissed beer. The two pilots, flying as Misty 11, were airborne by about 6:15 a.m. They found most of Route Pack 1 clobbered with fog as advertised and decided to head farther north, where the weather might be better. Plus, that gave them a chance to make a quick pass through the area where Sijan and Armstrong had gone down.

As they approached Ban Laboy Ford, Mack cycled the throttle outboard and inboard, engaging the afterburner three times and igniting a series of roaring booms that would be immediately familiar to a pilot on the ground. It was a standard signal to downed airmen, indicating they had not been forgotten—in a code they were intimately familiar with.

Mack figured he'd accomplish little, besides waking up some sleepy North Vietnamese gunners and blowing some petrol out the ass of the airplane. Any pilot who hadn't come up on the net after a day and a half was either dead or captured. Yet to his astonishment, his UHF radio receiver crackled and began to emit a high-pitched wail that was the unmistakable signature of a handheld survival radio beeper. "I read your beeper!" Mack barked into his radio. The survival radio had a notoriously short range, which meant that Misty 11 was probably right on top of it. Now to determine who had the radio—Sijan, or enemy troops hoping to lure a vulnerable rescue force.

"This is AWOL 01 Bravo," came a sturdy reply. "Bravo" meant it was the back-seater—Sijan. "Alpha" would have been the front-seater—Armstrong. "How do you read?"

"Loud and clear, AWOL!" Mack answered. "Hold on for a sec!" he shouted as he called the ABCCC, call sign Cricket. The controllers aboard Cricket had overheard the exchange with Sijan and were as excited as Mack. They provided Mack with Sijan's "personal authenticator" information—questions supplied in advance by Sijan, that only he would know the answers to. If Sijan passed his own quiz, it would prove he was who he said he was and indicate that he was not calling with a gun to his head. Mack scribbled down the questions and called back down to Sijan.

"AWOL, authenticate the car you drove in high school."

"'57 Chevy!" Sijan answered eagerly.

"And who is the best team in the NFL?"

"The goddamned Green Bay Packers!" said the Wisconsin native. "Now get my ass outta here!"[3]

Mack relayed the replies to Cricket, which confirmed they were the right answers. Mack grinned inside his mask. Sijan seemed to be in good spirits, he thought. That would help in the rescue.

Cricket had already set the rescue effort in motion. Two Sandys were on the way. They'd scour the terrain surrounding Sijan and "suppress" any ground fire with an arsenal of ordnance they carried—standard bombs, cluster bomb units, rockets, and guns—and help locate Sijan. Then the Jolly Greens would descend, hover, and lower the jungle "penetrator," a crude seat on a cable that the downed airman would grab on to for a quick ride up into the Jolly. Cricket had also diverted some F-4s that were headed for a bombing run "downtown"—over Hanoi—to join the rescue instead. They'd provide extra firepower if the North Vietnamese put up a fight.

Misty 11 needed gas. "Don't move," Mack ordered Sijan. "I'll be right back." They flew to the tanker, a KC-135 over the Mekong, to fill up. Before they headed back for the action, one of the tanker crewmen who had been monitoring the voice traffic called over the radio to them. "We've been listening, Misty," he said. "Good luck. We'll hang around the south end of the track down here for you guys." This would minimize transit time to and from the tanker to the rescue site.

Nobody ever put it into words, exactly, but mostly everybody involved in the air campaign knew that rescues like this had become the epic duels of the air war over North Vietnam. Unlike momentous ground battles, in which hundreds or even thousands died, the objective was not territory or destruction or prestige or momentum. It was people—quite often, a single individual. A downed American pilot in North Vietnam was a vital prize for which both sides were willing to spill lots of blood, one to capture, one to rescue.

For the North Vietnamese, every captive U.S. service member added to the leverage they could exert in negotiations with the American government. A few might even provide useful intelligence, if the torture were persuasive enough. North Vietnamese field commanders had standing orders to go to great lengths to capture downed pilots, and casualties didn't seem to matter. Even if it cost 100, or 1,000, North Vietnamese lives to face down the air strikes, a single pilot was the equivalent of strategic military terrain and worth quite a fight.

To the Americans, numbers didn't matter, either. The ethos of the U.S. military was to leave no man behind. Even if that was impossible in practice—especially in the Air Force, where some planes disappeared without a trace—it was crucial to morale and to the esprit de corps of elite warriors like fighter jocks to know that their comrades would stick their necks out to save them.

The math wasn't always rational—sometimes the A-1s or the helicopters or the jets attempting a rescue got shot down themselves, multiplying the problem and costing more lives. The North Vietnamese quickly became familiar with the Americans' fanatical focus on saving their people and took full advantage of it. When the situation permitted, they'd set flak traps around a downed airman and use other clever tactics to see how high they could raise the toll.

The Sijan rescue was starting to take on the tenor of a dramatic battlefield event. Officials at 7th Air Force were fully aware of the situation and word filtered out to other units that a giant rescue effort was under way. More planes began to stack up overhead. It wasn't going to be an easy pickup, either. When Mack and Jonesy returned from the tanker, they tried to determine Sijan's exact location. They called down to him and asked if he knew where he was. He promptly fired a flare out of the trees, one of the precious few he had. Wow, thought Mack. This is going to be tougher than I had wanted. Sijan was stuck on the side of the karst beneath a high hilltop, near the point where tough scrub melded into triple-canopy jungle. It would be impossible to spot him visually, and the steep peaks surrounding him limited the routes in and out. If the NVA had guns up on those hills, it could be a murderous mission. The NVA in effect would be on the high ground looking down on the rescuers.

Down below, the situation was even worse than they thought. Sijan had been knocked cold when he ejected, his helmet having been torn off his head. He didn't remember landing on the karst. He had been unconscious for the better part of a day and a half, with only a few moments of awareness, when he gulped a ten-ounce bottle of water and gave himself a morphine shot to ease the riveting pain in his head and his left leg. When he came to, he tried to figure out what had happened. In his mind he envisioned a blinding white glare, and then a fireball just as Armstrong, flying the plane, released the six bombs. Then Sijan remembered the preflight briefing. The bombs had been equipped with a new type of radar fuse, so that they'd explode in an airburst above the target, expanding the radius of blast damage. The realization was horrifying: The fuses must have been defective and lit off way too soon, perhaps even "ringing in" on the airplane instead of the ground. They had been blown out of the sky by their own bombs.

Sijan had no idea what had happened to Armstrong. But he quickly ascertained that he himself was in rough shape. His hair was crusted with blood and his skull was bashed up behind his left ear. Three fingers on his right hand were bent backward. There were lacerations on one of his forearms. And his left leg was mangled beneath the knee, with two bones poking out of purple flesh. He did his best to bind up the wounds with scraps of his shredded flight suit. But by day two of this ordeal, the athletic and determined pilot found it hard to simply concentrate his mind on a task for more than a few minutes.[4]

After the first contact with Sijan, several fighters started making high-speed passes over the area where they thought the injured pilot lay, to see if they could pinpoint his location. The second Misty flight of the day, Misty 21—flown by Ray Lee, the wing vice commander, and Don Sibson—had arrived on scene. They swooped down to check for ground fire and promptly drew some from a hillside overlooking the river that ran through the ford. Several F-4s were doing the same thing, mapping out the defenses they'd have to pummel once the rescue got under way in earnest.

The first two rescue aircraft, call signs Sandy 7 and Sandy 8, arrived around the same time to suppress the air defenses. Two more were on the way. The Sandys were slow, low-flying A-1E Skyraider prop planes, but they were indispensable in rescues. They escorted the helicopters, located survivors, and blasted away at the ground gunners until it was safe for the Jolly Greens to hover and complete the rescue. Today it was also their job to pinpoint Sijan's exact location by homing in on his rescue beeper. Ordinarily the beeper would help get the rescue aircraft close. Then the downed pilot would fire a "pen gun" flare and finally pop one of his orange smoke canisters, sending a vibrant plume into the air to guide the rescue chopper directly to his lo-cation. But whether through oversight or exhaustion, Sijan had fired all of the pen-gun flares from his survival vest when Misty 11 was first trying to get a fix on him. Another set of flares and smoke canisters was tangled with his life raft somewhere up in the treetops he had fallen through. So the Sandys would have to find him, two hundred feet beneath the roof of the forest, by triangulation—three aircraft homing in on his beeper at once. And even then, if they didn't get shot down, they'd still be relying on the downed pilot to talk the rescue chopper in the final 150 to 200 yards.

Finally, two huge Jolly Green rescue choppers, call signs Jolly 27 and Jolly 52, rumbled onto the scene, orbiting several miles to the southeast, in relatively safe airspace away from the guns. Once the Sandys had found Sijan and knocked out any ground fire with their rockets, cluster bombs, and 20mm cannons, they'd lay down a smoke screen to shield the action and call in one of the Jollys to hover over the pilot, lower the rescue seat, and sweep him off to safety. The second Jolly would be a backup in case anything went wrong, as it often did.

The mini-armada flying over Sijan certainly seemed to represent enough firepower to pull one pilot out of the jungle. But the NVA had plenty of muscle, too. On one of his passes Sandy 8 got walloped with ground fire and began to lose control of his airplane. He made a May-day call and headed for the hills southeast of the ford, near where the Jolly Greens were orbiting. Lee and Sibson followed the Sandy. The pilot bailed out just in time for a parachute landing. The burning plane exploded into the ground.

The pilot hit the ground and called out that he was okay. Sandy 7 momentarily left the scene of the Sijan effort to help rescue his wing-man. He trolled through the valley where Jolly Green 27 had spotted the pilot's parachute, and found it clear of AAA. They called to the pilot, who shot off a parachute flare. The Jolly hustled in and lowered the rescue hoist, then pulled out with the pilot still dangling beneath the chopper. The whole area was swarming with NVA and it could be a matter of seconds before they opened up on the big bird. The Jolly started to take some small-arms fire, but hauled the pilot up before any major fireworks began. The pilot was bruised but okay, which allowed Jolly 27 to go back for Sijan.

Two more Sandys showed up, and the three that were left started over trying to locate Sijan. Misty 11 and Misty 21 led four F-4s on strikes against several gun sites they had found. Dust and debris mushroomed up off the jungle floor as numerous 750-pound bombs impacted. That bought a few minutes of time for the Sandys to work on finding their quarry. One of the new arrivals, Sandy 5, was now in charge of the rescue, and he was in a hurry to find Sijan and get the Jolly Green in there. By now, he was sure, the NVA knew exactly what was going on and were racing their own men into the area to find Sijan.

But just as they were homing in on Sijan's beeper, the NVA gunners came back to life. While flying in between the steep limestone formations, Sandy 8 took fire in his left wing. That was doubly bad news—in addition to the problems it caused the plane, it meant that NVA troops were moving rapidly up the hillsides and getting more guns into place. Sandy 8 tried to keep flying. Ray Lee, watching from above, marveled at the bravery of the pilot and the durability of his plane. But it wasn't enough—the Sandy continued taking fire, and the controls froze up. He had no choice but to pull out and RTB—return to base, which entailed making a ninety-mile flight over enemy terrain to Nakhon Phanom in Thailand. Misty 11, Mack and Jonesy, escorted him there, where they watched the pilot crash-land the crippled plane on the runway, then walk away from the hulk.

Meanwhile, Misty 21 and other FACs were putting in as many strikes on the surrounding—and seemingly multiplying—guns as they could. A steady flow of fighters was diverted from other missions farther north. The two remaining Sandys had continued trying to pinpoint Sijan's location, and they thought they were getting close enough to call in a Jolly Green. They told Sijan to let them know when he heard the bird and saw the rotor wash starting to agitate the treetops above him.

The Sandys flew tight, banking orbits above the spot where they thought Sijan was, firing at any guns they thought could threaten the Jolly. Finally, Jolly 52 moved in, its crew primed for the daring rescue. The PJ even planned to ride down on the jungle penetrator seat and hop onto the karst, if that was necessary to find the injured pilot. Sijan reported that he could hear the Jolly, but couldn't see any rotor wash. He switched his radio back and forth from voice to beeper, so they could keep homing in on him. The Jolly got louder, but still no rotor wash. Sijan advised the chopper pilot to move in one direction to get closer, but the chopper pilot's own homing indicator showed that that actually sent them farther from Sijan.

The Jolly pilot decided to get as close as he could to the trees and do a "box search," moving slowly in a rectangular pattern until Sijan saw the trees starting to sway. But the maneuver was taking too long, and machine-gun fire opened up on the Jolly from at least three different directions. The chopper took several direct hits and had to pull away. Inside the helicopter, a seriously wounded crewman was screaming. The bird was losing oil pressure in one of its two turbines and the pilots worked feverishly to get the engine shut down before it caught fire. Jolly 52 was out of the game. It flew quickly back to base. Jolly 27 and a Skyraider with the call sign Hobo escorted it, in case the damaged bird had to crash-land itself and the crew needed to be rescued.

Now there only two Sandys left. It was about 10:00 in the morning. Sijan had been talking with pilots for more than three hours. One rescue aircraft had been shot down, two others had been shredded and disabled. Despite more than two dozen air strikes on guns in the area, the NVA defenses were getting tougher. The FACs continued to scour the area for guns, but there were gaps when no fighters were available to drop the big bombs. Misty 21 and other FACs fired on the gunners with their 20mm cannons, but those rounds had nowhere near the power of a 500- or 750-pound bomb blowing a crater in the ground.

Lee and Sibson were low on gas and went off to refuel. Sandys 5 and 6 were the last planes on the scene with some idea where Sijan was. Cricket, the airborne control plane, announced that two more Jollys were on the way and should arrive within about thirty minutes. Jolly 53 and Jolly 15 showed up at about 10:30, and Cricket sent them to a safe orbit until Sijan could be located. Two more Skyraiders were inbound as well.

But the rescue armada was taking on water as fast as it was bailing. Mack and Jonesy had returned from their escort mission to Nakhon Phanom and were once again flying over the rescue site. Just when it seemed like it couldn't get any worse . . . it did. As Mack watched Sandy 5 prowl through one of the gullies, aiming his rockets at a gun site camouflaged in the trees, a big AAA round tore a three-foot hole through the A-1's left wing. "I'm hit!" shouted the pilot. "I'm going in!" The damage had come from a 37mm gun—the biggest they had encountered so far—and it had fired *down* on the Sandy from one of the surrounding hillsides. The NVA had definitely figured out what was going on and were getting more formidable firepower into place above the rescue.

"Keep it heading west!" Mack screamed at the Sandy pilot. "Misty one-one has you covered!"

Then, with the amazement of a child discovering a helium balloon for the first time, the Sandy pilot called out, "Hey! It's still flying!" The tough old bird managed to rise up out of the gully. But Sandy 5 needed an escort to get back to Nakhon Phanom safely, and his wingman, Sandy 6, was the only obvious choice.

Sandy 5 limped off with Sandy 6 at his side. There were no Skyraiders left, which meant there was nobody in the air who had even a general idea where Sijan was. The rescue effort approached a state of disarray. Misty 11 and Misty 21, along with other FACs, continued seeking out NVA guns, marking them, and when nothing else was available, strafing them with 20mm cannons. The FACs themselves had to fly extremely aggressively with lots of jinking and high-G maneuvers, using lots of afterburner and devouring gas. They broke off frequently to refuel. At one point even the tankers ran out of fuel and headed home. Ray Lee and Don Sibson had to divert to Ubon Air Base, Thailand, to fill up and rearm. While there, they gobbled a quick lunch. When they got back to the rescue site, they were the only pilots who had been there during the early rescue attempt and knew roughly where Sijan was.

Misty 11, meanwhile, had been flying for about six and a half hours when Mack remembered that "Leakin' Lena," the old steed they were riding, leaked oil like a sieve and was not supposed to be in the air that long. The standard mission, after all, was only about four and one-half hours long. Mack had no choice but to head for pavement—what use would it be adding another downed plane to the fiasco? Cricket told him to fly to Ubon, Thailand, where he could debrief senior commanders on the rescue attempt.

Once in the chocks at Ubon, Mack couldn't believe his condition. He was an athletic, twenty-seven-year-old fighter pilot, yet he could not even raise himself out of the airplane. The high Gs, the adrenaline drain, and six hours of being in and out of afterburner had temporarily turned his muscles into mush. For the moment he was as good as disabled. He had never felt such exhaustion.

His psyche was beaten, too. The highs and lows of locating Sijan, and then feeling him slip away, had left Mack feeling hollow and numb. He mumbled through the debriefing. One senior officer, sensing his disappointment, confided to Mack, "Don't worry, Captain. We're going to put a 'black team' in there tonight." Mack had only heard rumors of such super-secret ground units operating behind enemy lines, and he didn't ask any other questions. But he felt defeated all the same.

Meanwhile, the aerial rescue mission gained strength. It was inconceivable to give up the fight for Sijan, no matter how bad the odds seemed. More Sandys arrived around 1:00 p.m. They began anew the effort to locate the stranded pilot. A new pair of Jolly Greens was on the way. F-4s began to line up overhead once again. The word was out among the F-4 jocks: This was a life-or-death battle for one of their brethren.

The new Sandys decided to try something different. Instead of orchestrating a mano-a-mano confrontation between the Jolly and the NVA gunners, they planned to lay down a smoke screen with their cluster bombs. Then, with the NVA temporarily blinded, sixteen F-4s orbiting overhead would shriek down all at once and pummel the gun sites and much of the surrounding area with bombs and rockets. With luck, that would throw the air defenses on the ground into chaos long enough for the Jolly to swoop in and pull Sijan to safety.[5]

Misty 21 led the first round of strikes. As jet after jet unloaded its weapons, the bottom of the karst that Sijan was perched upon seemed to be heaving up so much debris that it might collapse. As the concussions multiplied, Jolly 53 moved into place over Sijan, with two Sandys flying "daisy chains" around the chopper, protecting it like a precious child. The Jolly crew prepared to send a PJ down on the penetrator, in case Sijan was too badly injured to get himself aboard. But before the winch started to lower, the front of the helicopter absorbed some rounds. The pilot noticed hydraulic fluid bleeding onto the flight deck under his feet. Then the back of the helicopter started taking hits in the tail rotor. While the Jolly crew was assessing its own damage, the pilots watched one of the Sandys get nailed by several antiaircraft rounds that cut through his tail section. The pilot of Jolly 53 started having trouble controlling the aircraft and announced that he would be forced to return to base. The Sandy had no choice but to peel off as well.

It was nearly 2:00 p.m., roughly eight hours since Sijan had first been raised on the radio. As the A-1s surveyed the ground, it became apparent that the NVA was taking a severe thrashing in this battle for a single Air Force lieutenant. Numerous antiaircraft guns, most of them 37mm sites, had been obliterated by U.S. bombs. The NVA body count was probably in the dozens or hundreds. But retreating was not an option, and the NVA commander, whoever he was, continued pushing troops up the karst and hauling in more and heavier AAA guns. Plus, the rescue experts reasoned that the NVA was probably keeping plenty of its guns in reserve, to use when the rescue seemed to be at a climax and the rescue birds were at their most vulnerable.

Ray Lee and Don Sibson continued flying and directing strikes, hitting the tanker four times in addition to the gas they had taken on at Ubon. They finally ran out of fuel—and tankers. By the time they got back to Phu Cat they had logged eight and a half hours airborne, one of the longest fighter rescues ever. And they were as frustrated as Jim Mack: They had directed strike after strike on the NVA defenses closing in on Lance Sijan, only to watch one rescue attempt after another get turned back. It didn't get any better when they landed back at Phu Cat. Col. Ed Schneider, the fastidious wing commander, had a few stern words about being away from base for so long and taking unnecessary risks. Ray Lee fired back, arguing that all else was meaningless when a comrade's life was on the line. It didn't seem to get through.

By about 3:00 p.m., two new Sandys were in place along with Jolly 15. More F-4s hacked away at the bottom of the karst while the Jolly moved in over Sijan. But before the chopper could even get in position for the rescue, light-arms fire punctured one of its fuel tanks, forcing it to pull off. The Sandys and several other A-1s, flying low and fast, tried to target enemy troops without jeopardizing Sijan. They strafed the karst repeatedly, then backed off to regroup and reconsider their strategy.

Another sixteen F-4s had arrived, meanwhile, armed specifically with external Vulcan 20mm cannon pods strapped to their bellies and rockets and CBU-24 cluster bombs, considered ideal for knocking out guns in a rescue situation. Another four A-1s, armed with smoke and CS riot control gas, were due in about twenty minutes. The rescuers were building up their bench strength for yet another effort to punch through the NVA's wall of defenses.[6] No doubt, on the ground, the NVA was doing the same thing.

Jolly 15, damaged and leaking gas, went through a delicate aerial refueling with an HC-130 orbiting to the west. Since Jollys were so much slower, the HC-130 had to put down flaps to slow to an airborne crawl to enable the helo to plug his probe into the tanker's basket. It was a risky maneuver over hostile terrain, but Jolly 15 took on fuel faster than it was leaking and tanked up without any more problems. Meanwhile, Jolly 27 had returned after dropping off the Sandy pilot they had picked up earlier in the day. With the Sandys and the F-4s going after some guns down in the nearby valley beneath the karst, the Jolly 27 pilot decided to see if he could sneak in over Sijan while the gunners on the ground were being distracted by the other flights. But the gunners weren't that easily fooled. Jolly 27 took several machine-gun rounds in its outboard fuel tanks and started leaking gas. Now it would have to refuel, too.

With the sun's rays starting to slant through the treetops, the rescue effort was reaching a do-or-die point—and everybody knew it. There might be time for one more concerted push before darkness would overwhelm their efforts. A new A-1, call sign Firefly 15, was now controlling the rescue. His commands had a tone of urgency. Firefly promptly called in Jolly 15, but the chopper took the wrong route and attracted more small-arms fire. The hits were superficial and Firefly vectored the Jolly into the correct spot. For the first time, Sijan reported that he could see the rotor wash blowing the treetops overhead. The rescue forces were finally close to AWOL 01 Bravo.

The Jolly pilot called down and said he was about to lower the penetrator, with a PJ aboard to help strap Sijan onto it. To the astonishment of the Jolly crew, Sijan radioed back, "Negative, Jolly. Negative!" He explained that he had heard NVA troops making their way toward him and thought it was too dangerous to send down another man. Just lower the penetrator, he told them, and he would crawl over to it and get himself aboard.

For once, the Jolly was able to hover without getting shredded by ground fire. Occasional tracers would streak through the darkening sky, but the Sandys would quickly plaster the area where they came from, and calm would return. The Jolly hovered, the crew waiting to hear from Sijan.

At about 5:15, Sijan came on the radio and pleaded for them to hold steady. "Hover, just hover. I'm going to crawl to you!" That was the same thing he had said twelve minutes earlier, when they had first lowered the penetrator into the treetops. Was Sijan becoming delirious? Was he a captive, being used as bait to lure down a PJ or to hold the helicopter in position until NVA gunners could get off a clean shot?

The Jolly crew called back down to Sijan twice more over the next twenty minutes. Now, there was no answer. The Jolly pilot called Firefly Lead and asked what he should do. Against his instincts, Firefly invoked the standard guidance for such a situation: Suspend the rescue and pull out. He could no longer justify putting more American lives on the line if the pilot below was not responding.

At about 5:40 p.m., the winch controlling the jungle penetrator spooled upward. As the Jolly and a flock of A-1s began to peel out, a torrent of high-caliber AAA came pouring from the hillsides. Two Sandys got hit but managed to escape. Somehow the Jolly evaded the AAA, and before long the air over Ban Laboy Ford was quiet, deadly quiet. In the entire rescue force, there wasn't a single light heart as the various aircraft retreated through the twilight toward their home bases.

All in all, 108 aircraft had been involved in trying to rescue Lance Sijan. Two Misty flights had directed at least thirty-four air strikes, and there had been dozens of others. The NVA had scored some hits, but at the end of the day they hadn't claimed any more U.S. lives. The toll on the North Vietnamese had been high, though how high nobody knew. The calculus didn't seem to matter much anyway. The North Vietnamese just kept on coming.

The next morning the Air Force assembled its most seasoned rescue experts, as if following a swashbuckling Hollywood script. At four bases in South Vietnam and Thailand, the crews of twenty-three aircraft prepared for the first daylight search-and-rescue sorties. Among them were several unit commanders and friends of Sijan's from the 480th Squadron at Da Nang, who might be able to tell from his tone of voice or other quirks whether he was speaking freely or under coercion.

By 6:30 a.m. they were on station above the Ban Laboy Ford. Cricket, the airborne command post, and others called repeatedly through the early-morning mist, "AWOL 01 Bravo. AWOL 01 Bravo." One of Sijan's best friends from the 480th, Glenn Nordin, told Sijan they were back to rescue him. The on-scene commander was one of the Sandy pilots from the day before. He and five other A-1s flitted above the karst where Sijan was last believed to have been, daring NVA gunners to reveal themselves. All was quiet until just after 7:00 a.m., when some small-arms fire erupted from one of the hillsides. That provocation unleashed a fury of aerial firepower as the fighter pilots poured their frustration into the jungle below. But that was all the satisfaction anybody could get. Lance Sijan would not come up on the radio.

By about 8:25 the two Jolly Greens orbiting nearby were running low on fuel. The rescue commanders had to decide whether to suspend the operation or begin air-refueling procedures. Since more than twelve hours had passed since the last transmission from Sijan, it was not a difficult decision. The order went out around 8:30 a.m.: All aircraft involved in the rescue were to RTB, return to base.

The Jollys and Sandys tried to disguise their exits, lest the NVA gunners catch on that they were bailing out and open up with maximum force. The aircraft departed one at a time, each in a different direction. The NVA eventually fired some rounds as they realized what was happening, but all the aircraft managed to escape without damage. The only planes that remained overhead were Glenn Nordin's flight of four F-4s, which flew a lonely watch for their squadron-mate for several hours. Nordin and his colleagues repeatedly called down to Sijan, assuring him they'd be there if he came up on the radio. But as the sun rose higher, their hopes sank. They never heard from Sijan again.

At Phu Cat, Jim Mack went through a kind of agony that gripped many of the pilots who had tried to save Lance Sijan. Like all troops who face intense combat, Mack had found ways to deal with tragedy and devastation. But this mission hurt more than others. It was the first time he had left an aviator behind, and the sensation was sickening. He and P. J. White, the Misty commander, talked about it for hours, the twenty-seven-year-old fighter jock agonizing about being so close yet coming away empty, and his commander stressing that Mack had made an extraordinary effort and done everything he could. Then they turned their attention back to the war.

NINE

"SOM COM PEES BUTT"

"Ready for duty, sir," Guy Gruters said officiously. He was standing in front of P. J. White, saluting with his left hand because his right was still in a cast. Gruters had just gotten back to Phu Cat from his trip to Florida to visit his family, and his first stop was the Misty commander's office. He was ready to start flying again.

White looked him over. "You may be ready for duty, but your arm isn't," he said. "Look, you've done your part, Guy. You've been shot down, you've been injured. When your arm heals, let's send you to a less risky job down south to finish your tour. I don't want to have to sign another message to your wife telling her you're dead this time. She's done her part, too."

Gruters wasn't interested in soft duty. He wanted to get on the schedule the next day, but it wasn't possible with the cast. The docs had told him his cast wouldn't come off until the first of January, so he had no choice but to to cool his heels before he could get back in the hunt.

Meanwhile, there had been a few new arrivals at Misty while Gruters had been out of action. One of them was Capt. Ed Risinger, a redheaded Texan who had come from the 531st Tactical Fighter Squadron at Bien Hoa Air Base northeast of Saigon, an F-100 outfit known as the Ramrods that flew ground support in the South. Like many of the Mistys, Risinger had drifted into Phu Cat, the war, and fighter jets along an unconventional flight path. For one thing, he was probably the only fighter pilot in the U.S. Air Force without a high school diploma.

Risinger had been born in McAllen, Texas, and grew up moving about the Rio Grande Valley, sun-scorched places like McAllen, Pharr, Harlingen, Brownsville, and Rockport. His father worked for newspapers and was a troubled man who quit and was fired often. Risinger struggled under his difficult father, dropped out of high school, and tried to join the Merchant Marine. A Baptist preacher he ran into realized that his potential far outstripped his performance to date and arranged for him to attend East Texas Baptist College in Marshall, Texas, at no cost. The college was willing to overlook the fact that he hadn't finished high school. Then a Disciple of Christ preacher, Mark Randal, arranged for him to attend Texas Christian University in Fort Worth. After three semesters, when he was still in his sophomore year at TCU, he needed a job and joined the Air Force as an enlisted man.

Since he was attending college, the Air Force assumed that Risinger had graduated from high school, a requirement for officers. They didn't ask, so Ed didn't tell. He applied for the Aviation Cadet program and graduated from pilot training at Bryan Air Force Base, near College Station. The Air Force assigned him to fly reconnaissance jets, RF-84s and RF-101s, in Japan and South Carolina, then sent him to its toughest school, AFIT, the Air Force Institute of Technology, to finish his degree. Finally, after his study at three universities, he earned a Bachelor of Science degree in electrical engineering. He marched across the stage and graduated with honors, but still without a high school diploma.

Risinger took a wayward course to Vietnam, too. In 1967 he had been stationed in England, flying the F-100, when he learned he would not be selected for promotion from captain to major—"passed over" they called it. "Fuck 'em," Risinger had declared. "If they don't want me, I've got other plans." He asked for permission to cut short the remaining two years of his tour in Europe and volunteer for Vietnam. As a fighter pilot he wanted to go to war—and then get out of the Air Force. Once he was out, Risinger hoped to go to medical school and become a doctor, something he had dreamed of since he was a kid. But the Air Force said no. He'd have to finish his obligation in Europe before going anywhere else.

Risinger took two weeks of leave and headed for MPC, the Military Personnel Center at Randolph Air Force Base in Texas. There he met with Col. Hal Shook, one of the personnel bosses, who was sympathetic to his request. Risinger explained his plans. "Let me get this straight," Shook queried. "You've been passed over and you could sit in the UK drinking ale in the pubs, but you want to volunteer for the war?"

"That's right, Colonel," Risinger replied.

"You're getting a little long in the tooth for medical school," observed Shook. "What if you don't get in?"

"Well, sir, I plan to try to get into a medical school in Mexico."

"I'll just be damned," the old colonel said as he shook his head. "I find most people coming through here are trying to get *out* of going to Vietnam." He considered the odd request, then said, "Son, your orders will be waiting for you when you get home." They were.

In the late spring of 1967, Risinger was scheduled to fly to Travis Air Force Base in California, where he'd board a 6:00 a.m. flight for Hawaii. From there, his itinerary would take him to the Philippines, for jungle survival training. Then he'd fly on to Vietnam.

When Risinger got to Travis, he went to the officers club for a meal and bumped into an old friend, Marvin Overton, who was an Air Force doctor at Travis. They hadn't seen each other in years. Overton insisted on a whiskey-filled reunion. Late in the evening the two went to Marvin's house for a little sleep. Marvin called the base hospital and instructed them to give him a wake-up call at 4:30 a.m., so Ed could catch his 6:00 a.m. flight the next morning.

The call never came. Risinger woke up at 5:35 and realized he was in trouble. Marvin was still asleep. Ed ran to wake him. They threw on some clothes and raced to Base Operations in Marv's car. As Risinger ran in, he saw a plane all set to taxi out. The chocks were pulled and the bird was starting to move. Risinger ran out onto the ramp and waved the plane to stop. The door opened and Ed rushed up the ladder, asking, "Is this the flight to Hawaii?"

"No sir," the crew chief said. "That flight left twenty minutes ago. We're heading for the East Coast."

Risinger stood forlornly in the dark, watching the plane taxi and take off. Overton stood silently beside him. Then a major with clipboard in hand walked up to Risinger and asked, "Are you Capt. James E. Risinger?" He answered yes, and the major promptly informed him, "You are AWOL."

Before Risinger could sputter a protest, Overton, who knew the major, jumped in. "Hi, Bill," he explained. "This captain is under my care. He's much too ill to fly anywhere. I tried to keep him in bed, but he is hell-bent on going to Vietnam, so I agreed to let him go. Unfortunately, I was a little late in releasing him. Is there any chance of getting him on another flight?"

They had a short, friendly conversation as Risinger tried to look like a man on death's door. Then the major said, "Yes, come to think of it, there's a C-141 medevac bird leaving in about twenty minutes. It's heading to Hawaii. Let's go." The three hopped in the major's car and raced to the new departure point. Ed asked if it was okay for him to open his window, in case he had to vomit.

When they arrived, the C-141 was revved up and ready to go. Rows of stretchers, stacked three high, were on each side of the plane. Several good-looking nurses in green military fatigues were on board. Dr. Overton explained to them that Risinger was a seriously ill man, but had insisted that he be released to fly to Vietnam for duty. He asked them to take good care of his patient. As Overton turned to leave the plane, he said loudly, so the nurses would hear, "That is one brave, determined pilot. We need more men like him."

Overton departed the plane with a hand salute and Risinger headed to war. Instead of the usual uncomfortable trip—troops crammed sardinelike into rigid charter-airline seats—Risinger slept comfortably most of the way to Hawaii on his own private stretcher. Occasionally one of the nurses would inquire whether there was anything he needed. With a sniff and a stiff upper lip, Risinger would answer meekly, "No, thank you. I think I can make it now." After landing in Hawaii, well rested and ready to go, he managed to catch up with the connecting flight he had been scheduled for in the first place.

Risinger had gathered considerable experience flying the F-100, and by the time he arrived at Misty he was considered an "old head," a fairly senior pilot. But the purists at Misty, the guys who had flown fighters their whole careers, loved to tease him about his reconnaissance background. He wasn't a real fighter pilot, they'd say, just a glorified "recce puke." Ed fired back, saying that's what made him such a good Misty, the only one among them who could see through trees. "Kind of like Superman," he said.

Even though he was a new guy, Risinger already claimed one of the most spectacular Misty successes. In mid-December, during a break in bad weather, he had been flying in the front seat, with another new Misty in the back, when he had ducked beneath the clouds and found more than seventy-five vehicles streaming south. From the plane the pilots could see a guy in a white shirt running like mad down the road, to get away from the bombs he knew would be incoming. Risinger strafed several trucks at the head of the column, then circled back and nailed those in the back, bottling up the convoy. Many trucks were hidden in the trees, but as the fighters arrived they had a field day with the sitting ducks Risinger had found.

Then he saw a locomotive pulling five boxcars steaming into a tunnel behind one of the karst mountains. Risinger, flying in the front seat, pulled up, made a 270-degree turn, and descended to 400 feet, flying head-on at the engine. As he opened up with his 20mm cannons, the engine crew started jumping off the train, which chugged to a stop. Several F-105s arrived just as Risinger had to leave for the tanker. He pointed out the train and when he returned from refueling, the boxcars were lying on their sides and the track was destroyed in several places. The Thuds had done good work. Colonel Schneider, the 37th Wing commander, had a fresh worry, however. Shortly after the train raid, he issued an edict that outlawed strafing. Getting that low was too dangerous. "Save your bullets in case someone gets shot down," Schneider had ordered.

Risinger had arrived at Misty about ten days after Gruters and Neel had bailed out of their jet in early November, and had heard the whole dramatic story. Risinger had now been at Misty for about three weeks, Gruters was back in town, and the new Misty was eager to meet him. He headed off to Guy Gruters's trailer to introduce himself. As Risinger got near the door, he heard a tapping noise inside. He walked in. "Hey, don't you knock?" Gruters said, looking up. He was in the process of chipping off his cast with a screwdriver.

"What the hell are you doing?" asked Risinger.

"Just leave me alone," replied Gruters, motioning for Ed to leave.

Ed closed the door and smiled, realizing what Gruters was up to. This is a guy with balls, he thought.

After Gruters had pried the cast off his arm, he exercised his atrophied muscles for a couple of days. Then he went back to see the commander. "Now I'm ready for duty, sir," he said to P. J. White. "Look, the cast is off." He opened and closed his hand and moved his arm about, hiding the pain. Of course, he didn't mention that he had removed the cast himself without the doctor's permission. "Charlie Neel's been back on the schedule for some time," Gruters pleaded. "Now it's my turn. I want back in the cockpit."

White gave in. He was coming to the end of his Vietnam tour and was worn out from managing a bunch of edgy pilots, massaging an irritable wing commander, and jinking through regular four-hour missions over North Vietnam. He was busy closing things out and wasn't in the mood to argue. Besides, Gruters was the kind of pilot every commander dreamed about—a warrior who motivated himself and needed no prodding from higher-ups. Since paperwork flowed slowly in a war zone, White didn't think about asking to see the medical forms allowing Gruters back on flight status. Risinger, meanwhile, kept his mouth shut.

White told Don Sibson, the Misty operations officer, to put Gruters back on the schedule in a couple of days when he could fit him in—but to put him in the backseat and let him spin-up again on an easy mission. "And just where would that easy mission be?" replied Sibson, laughing.

Capt. Don Shepperd arrived at Misty late one evening, about a week before Christmas, and headed straight for the bar, where he met Jim Mack, who had been a classmate at the Air Force Academy. Shepperd, a trim, affable twenty-seven-year-old from Wheat Ridge, Colorado, had come from the 90th "Dice" Squadron at Bien Hoa, another F-100 unit flying missions in the South. Before that he had flown F-100s in Germany. The Air Force had then offered him an Olmsted Scholarship to study in France, but fearing he would miss the war, he declined and volunteered for Vietnam. He had also spent a tour with the 24th Infantry Division, as a FAC and air liaison officer working on the ground. Better than most pilots, he knew the Army.

He also knew his wife, Rose, who was certain to come unglued when she found out he had volunteered for Misty. Her last words as he got on the airplane to leave for the war were, "You've got an eight-month-old son. Think of him! Don't do anything stupid and don't come back with any medals!"

The word was out through the F-100 community: Even though Misty was officially "top secret," that didn't stop news of the unit from filtering back to wives and family members. And once stories and rumors got passed around in the wives' "bitch sessions," as the pilots referred to them, there was no controlling the flow of information. Gary Tompkins, one of the first Mistys, had rotated back to the States, where the wives spoke of Misty as if it were some sort of suicide squad. "Avoid it like the plague," they'd whisper. "It's certain death." Shepperd wanted to tell his wife about Misty before she heard it from someone else, but on the other hand he didn't want to ruin her Christmas. So he took a chance and said nothing.

Guy Gruters had finally flown again by the time Shepperd got to Phu Cat. Shepperd had known him vaguely at the Air Force Academy, and like Risinger he had heard about Guy's shootdown and wanted to learn the details. But Gruters was sleeping when Shepperd went looking for him. Shepperd noted from the scheduling board that Gruters had an afternoon go the next day with Bob Craner. He'd catch him in the morning along with Charlie Neel and Jim Fiorelli, whom he had also known at "the Zoo," as they had called the Academy, because the tourists lined the walls to watch the cadets. Fiorelli had even gotten into trouble there for carrying a sign that read DON'T FEED THE CADETS. The squadron tactical officer found that unprofessional, but Fiorelli got a lot of laughs with the prank and didn't care.

The next morning Gruters was suiting up in PE, the personal equipment section, when Shepperd walked in. "Hi, Guy, long time no see," he said, putting out his hand.

"Let me pass on the handshake," said Gruters. "It's still a little tender."

Maj. Bob Craner, the handsome, strapping six-foot-two-inch Weapons School graduate, was also preparing to fly. He had become Misty's tactics officer and was known for being aggressive and fearless. He'd be flying from the front seat, with Gruters spotting from the back—Guy's second mission since he had been shot down six weeks earlier.

Gruters zipped up his G-suit, slipped on his survival vest, and patted the pockets, checking especially for his survival radio. His pistol was missing from the holster sewn on the vest. PE had loaned out the .38 revolver because the base was always short. "Where's my pistol?" Gruters asked.

"Sir, we didn't know you were coming back to fly this early. We thought you wouldn't be back until 1 January. We don't have one for you," said the PE technician.

Gruters brushed it off. "No sweat. The weather's lousy and I won't be needing it." He didn't want any questions about why no paperwork had flowed from the medics putting him back on flying status.

"See you guys when you get back," said Shepperd. "Fly safe." Gruters and Craner lugged their gear out to the flight line van, which would take them to their airplane. Even for big men like Gruters and Craner, the bulky equipment seemed to double their size. The ensemble weighed nearly fifty pounds, half of it the parachute alone. Then there was the bulging G-suit with leg pockets, usually filled with extra water bottles, survival radio batteries, or signal flares. Most pilots had a leather sheath sewn on the G-suit to hold a machete or heavy knife they could use to hack through the jungle. There was also a smaller knife attached to the inner thigh, mainly used to cut the risers on the parachute if they got tangled on descent. The green mesh survival vests had a shoulder holster for the .38 revolver, more signal flares, a survival radio, a signal mirror, and a first aid kit. And there were other pockets that pilots could fill as they wished. Some carried extra batteries, some extra signal flares or ammunition. Charlie Neel even carried three radios, since they were so crucial to getting rescued. The gear was awkward and uncomfortable and quickly became sweat-soaked, but flying daily, the pilots became used to it.

Gruters and Craner were scheduled to take off about 2:00 p.m. and would be the last Misty flight of the day over the Pack. They'd get back to Phu Cat just as the sun set. On the way to the airplane the van stopped to pick up Charlie Neel, who had just returned from a mission. Charlie threw his gear on the van bench. "The weather's dogshit," Charlie complained. "But Guy, gimme your map. We got a quick look at some of those new guns in the Ron Valley." He pointed to a wide area rimmed by mountains in the northern part of the Pack, inland from the coastal city of Ron. "If the weather breaks and you can get in there, take a look. They must be protecting something because there're lots of them."

For all of the packaged intel that came out of Saigon, this was often the best type of information—fresh material passed from a pilot who had just landed. Charlie marked the location of the gun sites in grease pencil on Guy's maps. After the van dropped off Gruters and Craner, he'd go inside for the debriefing with the intel officers, who would mark the new finds on the maps in Ops, for tomorrow's missions.

The two pilots had a plan for dealing with the lousy weather. They'd fly north for thirty minutes, cross the DMZ, go out to sea and let down over the water, descend beneath the clouds, then turn inland and come in on the deck at "warp speed"—as fast as they could go. They'd scan quickly for "movers," trucks and other vehicles; note their position, then punch up through the clouds and hope for the weather to break. If it did, they'd call in some fighters for an attack. And they'd also look for the guns Charlie Neel had drawn their attention to.

There were no breaks in the weather, however, so they flew west to Laos. Same thing there, a solid deck of clouds as thick as frosting, with only a few mountaintops peeking up near Mu Ghia Pass and Ban Laboy Ford. They went to the tanker over Thailand, then came back and managed to pop down through a hole in the clouds. Vehicles were everywhere, like cockroaches caught in the middle of the night when the kitchen light goes on. That much activity was unusual for daytime, but the NVA knew that fighters wouldn't be bombing under such low clouds.

It infuriated Craner to think that the NVA could operate with impunity just because the weather was bad. He took a chance and strafed a few vehicles with his 20mm cannons—even though strafing was now forbidden. It was risky, because he had to stay under the clouds to avoid the mountains. That put the aircraft within range of virtually anyone on the ground with a gun, whether a handheld pistol or high-caliber AAA. From the backseat, Gruters could see flashes and tracers coming from everywhere in the late afternoon light.

It was maddening to see so many targets when the weather was bad, and so few when it was good. But even though Gruters and Craner had managed to get under the clouds for a quick strafing run, the overcast was simply too low to bring in fighters. They discussed going home, but decided to cycle over to the tanker one more time and come back to take one last look for Neel's guns. Craner flew up the Ron Valley, along the river, in the northern part of the Pack. The weather was improving slightly and both pilots scoured the landscape, seeking out the guns—and whatever they were protecting. Craner thought he saw some gun sites up ahead and started to circle them, hoping to draw fire to confirm their locations.

He got more fire than he wanted. Gruters saw giant orange flames erupting from a 57mm gun site, the biggest guns Misty fliers usually encountered. The whole battery had opened up on them, six guns firing all at once. There was no way to avoid the shells.

Gruters felt the impact as one struck the bottom of the plane. There was an explosion as the aircraft immediately went out of control. Suddenly it was upside down and Gruters was hanging in his straps, looking out through the top of the aircraft canopy at the ground 1,500 feet below. There was little time to think. Gruters instinctively pulled the handles and was blown out into the afternoon sky at over 450 knots.

The word hit Misty Ops like a bomb. Cricket, the orbiting ABCCC, had heard a brief transmission from an emergency locator transmitter, an ELT beacon, at 5:45 p.m. Craner and Gruters were flying the only airplane in the Pack, so there was no doubt whom it was coming from. Cricket couldn't raise them on the radio, though, and called the 37th Wing command post. It looked like another Misty was down. Word spread quickly, and the Misty pilots and wing staffers gathered at the command post. Nightfall was approaching. Everybody knew that the chances of a rescue diminished the longer a pilot was down. The Mistys unanimously wanted to launch—NOW—to locate their buddies and provide cover.

The first problem was that no two-seat Huns, the F-100F models, were available. Two were down for normal maintenance and two had bullet holes that had to be fixed. Jim Mack and Charlie Neel asked Colonel Schneider, the wing commander, if they could take two single-seat D-models. Schneider said no.

"Colonel, I know right where they are," Mack argued. "Charlie drew gun locations on their map when they were going to the airplane. They have to be in the Ron Valley!"

"Look," said Schneider. "There's no sense in going up there tonight. Our F's are out of commission and there is nothing meaningful you can do. The weather is bad and there is no chance of pulling off a rescue in the dark. We'll go first thing in the morning. Besides, there was no 'Mayday' call," he added. "They probably flew into the trees."

Mack became incensed. "Colonel!" he shot back, red-faced. "Bob Craner doesn't fly into trees!"

"No is the answer!" Schneider repeated, fixing his eyes on Mack. Then Mack got up, kicked a chair, and stomped out of the command post.

The Mistys were enraged. Even though they knew helos wouldn't make pickups after dark, they wanted to offer their comrades moral support over the radio. Most of all they hoped to locate them for a pickup at first light. Schneider had sensed the anger, and he also knew the Mistys had an inclination to take matters into their own hands. He posted extra guards on the airplanes all night long to assure the Mistys wouldn't disobey his orders.

P. J. White had just handed over command of Misty that morning to Lt. Col. Don Jones, who had been the 37th Wing's plans officer under Schneider. Most of the Mistys had met him, but none of them really knew him well. And Jones now had to herd a bunch of pilots with whom he had little rapport through one of the hardest struggles a squadron can face: dealing with lost comrades. All this on his very first day on the job.

Schneider had thought hard about who should replace White—not because Misty was so important to him, but because he was uncomfortable with the unit. Misty had already lost three airplanes, and the others came back with regular battle damage, fouling Schneider's maintenance statistics and his reputation as a manager. He also hated Misty's independence, the fuck-you attitude they exhibited toward him and his staff, and especially the support they got from his own boss at 7th Air Force, General Momyer. At best it was an awkward command situation for all involved.

Jones, Schneider thought, was the solution. As a lieutenant colonel, he was the highest-ranking officer to command the unit and was old by

Misty standards, which was just fine with Schneider. He had noticed Jones's organizational skills as a plans officer and thought he would bring an extra degree of maturity and discipline to Misty. Jones had graduated from the Aviation Cadet Program, Class 48B, the second class after the end of World War II. Jones described himself as a fireman who had never been to a fire: He repeatedly volunteered for combat in Korea, but ended up spending the war based in Newfoundland. For a major part of his career he had been assigned to the Air Rescue Service, which handled rescues worldwide during peacetime. Vietnam was his first real chance to fly fighters in combat.

Jones knew that after dynamic, popular commanders like Bud Day and P. J. White, the fighter jocks in Misty would likely regard him as a "many-motor" back bencher who didn't have the right stuff to fly single-engine fighter jets. They'd regard him as a fighter novice—just as Schneider wished. Whatever the case, Jones now had troops to lead, and he led them. "Okay, look, guys, let's suck it up," he told the Mistys once Schneider had left the room. "The boss is probably right. The helos can't perform pickups at night. Let's get a good night's sleep, get the F's in commission, and go get them first thing tomorrow. Right now we don't even know for sure where to look."

"Even more reason to go tonight," Charlie Neel pressed. "Maybe we could hear a beeper and at least save time locating them tomorrow morning."

"We'll launch before daylight and be over the Pack at daybreak," said Jones a bit more firmly. "If they're there, we'll find them."

The Mistys went to the bar, except for those scheduled to fly. As the beer flowed there was lots of grumbling and loud debate. But the beer soothed some frayed nerves and a consensus emerged: Under the circumstances, there was probably no sense in launching that night. Charlie Neel, for one, was so fired up and emotional that he'd be prone to taking more risks than usual. It wasn't worth risking more lives. Since it was Don Shepperd's first day on the job, and he hadn't even flown a Misty mission yet, he mainly kept his mouth shut at the bar. But for all the excitement, he wondered apprehensively what the hell he had gotten himself into. Don Jones, for his part, let the men complain freely, without hanging around. He repaired to his hootch, since he'd be flying the next day, and went to bed thinking, Jesus, I've been commander less than twenty-four hours and I've already lost an airplane. *This* is really going well.

Since the Mistys didn't know exactly where Gruters and Craner were, they developed a search plan. Misty 11 would launch at 5:00 a.m. and head straight for the Ron Valley, where they figured the pilots would have been looking for the guns Charlie had drawn on their map. Misty 21 would take off at 7:00 and concentrate on the southern part of the Pack. If there was no contact, Jim Mack and Don Jones, launching as Misty 31 at 11:00 a.m., would repeat the process in the afternoon. It would be the new commander's "dollar ride," his first mission as a Misty, when it was Air Force tradition to give the "instructor" a dollar as a goodwill gesture. The jets would cycle on and off the tanker so that at a minimum, there'd always be one plane searching while another was refueling. The final Misty flight of the day, Misty 41, would take off at 1:00 p.m. with Jonesy Jones flying in the front and Jim Fiorelli in the back. If anybody made contact with the downed pilots, they'd call immediately for rescue forces and fighters that were on alert, F-4s at Da Nang and F-100s at Phu Cat. They could also get fighters diverted from the Alpha Strike Force going north to Hanoi. It was an all-star lineup, backed up by plenty of muscle. If the Mistys couldn't find their mates down in the jungle, nobody could.

The maintenance troops worked all night to get four two-seat F-models into commission. Everyone knew what was at stake. The two morning missions took off on schedule. At 9:00 a.m. Jim Mack, Don Jones, Jonesy Jones, and Jim Fiorelli showed up for the afternoon mission briefs together. The early Mistys had made no contact with the downed crew. As Mack and Jones were taxiing out a couple of hours later, it was the same story—the weather was bad and still there had been no contact. Things were starting to look grim.

Misty 31 engaged afterburner and broke ground on schedule at 11:00. As they flew north they made radio contact with Misty 21, just finishing in the Pack. There was no news. With the lousy weather, Mack decided to stay on top of the cloud deck to conserve gas. He headed directly for the Ron Valley. When he was overhead, he did the same thing he had done during the Sijan rescue, hitting the afterburner three times—a signal to survivors on the ground to come up "voice" on the radio. Then he transmitted on "Guard channel," 243.0 Mhz, the UHF emergency radio frequency, "Misty four-one, come up voice. Misty four-one, come up voice." Mack and Jones listened intently over the noise of the jet engine.

About fifteen seconds after his transmission, Mack heard a brief hissing noise. Then came words they had all been dying to hear: "Misty, this is Craner!" There was a moment of elation in the cabin. But it lasted only a second. "I've been captured," Craner continued. "Two guards are walking me up the road. I'm on 82 Golf. I'm okay. There's lots of guns down here and tons of trucks moving south. Gruters is captured, too, and he's okay. Tell my wife I love her and I'll see her after the war!"

In a matter of seconds Craner had put out some vital intelligence: He and Gruters were captives, they were alive and okay, and they were in the Ron Valley on route number 82G. That was essential information for a rescue. Mack thought fast and had an idea. "Bob, put the guard on the radio!" he demanded. "Does he speak English?"

"Go ahead," transmitted Craner excitedly. "He's listening!"

"We will give you much money if you give pilot back," Mack implored. He had no idea whether anybody would approve such a ransom, but it was a stalling tactic. Who knew, maybe they were just a couple of green NVA soldiers by themselves out in the jungle who might get taken in by such an outlandish promise—if they could even understand English. "Beaucoup money," Mack promised. "Bring him back. He not fly again. Beaucoup money. We give you safe passage. You bring pilot to us, we give you much gold!"

"Keep it up!" Craner shouted into the radio. "He's excited!"

Cricket, the ABCCC, was monitoring the transmissions and launched the Sandy rescue force from Nakhon Phanom. Mack continued to repeat his desperate offer. "You bring pilot Saigon. We make you rich. Give you much gold!"

"He doesn't understand," Craner interjected. "But keep talking."

Meanwhile, Don Jones in the backseat was watching the needle on the RMI, the radio magnetic indicator gauge, that was homing in on Craner's radio transmission. They seemed to be north of Craner, but since the clouds were so thick they couldn't see the valley below, or any activity along Route 82G. But the radio signal was strong and the needle danced back and forth rapidly, a sign they were close.

"Stay high so we don't lose contact," Jones suggested to Mack.

"Roger that," Mack replied.

The Vietnamese guard was saying something on Craner's radio in Vietnamese that Jim didn't understand. Mack called in to the ABCCC, with an update on Craner. "Cricket, Misty 41 Alpha is on 82G walking up the road with two guards. 41 Bravo is captured also," he said, referring to Gruters. "Can you get us the Vietnamese words for, 'We will give you much money'? Also, we're going to need a tanker as close as you can get him to us." It was a race for time. Night was fast approaching and Mack didn't want to leave the area, fearing he would lose contact.

Don Jones, on his "dollar ride," was in awe. Misty was more exciting than anything he had hoped for.

"He doesn't understand," Craner kept saying into his survival radio. "But he understood 'Saigon.' "

"Bob, hang on," Mack announced. "We're going off-freq to talk to Cricket. We're coming to get you, babe!"

Mack switched off Guard channel to talk to Cricket and Misty 41—Jonesy Jones and Fiorelli—who, as planned, were getting gas from the tanker over Thailand. They had been monitoring the conversations, too. They couldn't hear Craner, but they could hear Mack talking to him, and they had a good idea what was going on.

"We've made contact with Craner," Mack said. "He's in the Ron Valley on 82G. We're going out over the water to let down and come in under the weather."

"Rodge," said Jonesy in Misty 41. Then he called the ABCCC. "Are you monitoring all from Misty?" he asked. "They've located Misty 41 Alpha."

"Roger," replied the command-and-control aircraft. "We've launched rescue and want to get six-digit coordinates and a firm fix on the weather."

Mack and Don Jones found a hole in the clouds and let down under the weather. They turned up the Ron Valley—and promptly got hosed by intense AAA.

"Shit, this might be a trap," Mack said to Jones. For the first time it had occurred to him that maybe Craner was talking with a gun to his head, or worse.

Cricket called Misty 41. They had obtained the Vietnamese translation Mack had asked for. "Go ahead," said Fiorelli. "We'll relay."

"Okay," Cricket began. "This is supposed to be, 'We give you much money.' It sounds like this: *Som com pees butt.*' "

Fiorelli relayed the phrase to Mack, who then switched to the emergency frequency. *"Som com pees butt,"* he called out. *"Som com pees butt."*

But now there was no response. Mack called over and over into the radio, and the rescue forces were on their way. But as the adrenaline rush produced by the initial contact started to fade, the unhappy truth was starting to sink in. The Mistys realized that there was probably no way they were going to reach Craner or Gruters, that they were grasping at straws trying to interest a single, faceless North Vietnamese soldier into accepting a bribe so that they could rescue two American pilots. "What a goat fuck," Fiorelli finally said, his disgust and disappointment flowing out over the radio network.

Back at Phu Cat, the other Mistys were following the ordeal on the command-and-control radio net. They weren't getting every detail, but knew enough to follow the story. When the idea of paying a ransom to retrieve Craner and Gruters came up, Roger Van Dyken said that he would volunteer to be the intermediary to deliver the money on the ground in North Vietnam and execute the exchange. Most of the Mistys were ready to try anything to get their comrades back, but a few of the most experienced guys knew this was a lunatic idea that would never get anywhere. They shot Van Dyken a look that said, "Get real."

It took Fiorelli and Jonesy Jones about twenty minutes to fly from the tanker to the Ron Valley. While they were en route, Fiorelli in the backseat made contact with a Vietnamese interpreter who was riding in the backseat of an O-1 slow FAC south of the DMZ. Fiorelli carefully copied the Vietnamese phrases for "We will take you to Saigon and give you much gold." The phrase was *"Chung toi se dua bau den Saigon. Va cho ban Nhieu vang."* "Doesn't sound a fucking thing like, 'Som com pees butt,' " he grunted.

It was getting dark. Mack and Don Jones were running low on fuel and had to leave. Misty 41, with Jonesy Jones and Fiorelli, arrived over the Ron Valley after tanking up, and they orbited over the area for the next hour and a half. There was no more radio contact with anybody on the ground. But as they flew in circles, Fiorelli faithfully repeated the only Vietnamese phrase he knew: *"Chung toi se dua bau den Saigon. Va cho ban Nhieu vang,"* he called out continually. *"Chung toi se dua bau den Saigon. Va cho ban Nhieu vang."* If anybody was listening, they weren't interested in the offer. Nobody heard another word from Craner.

The next day, in Sarasota, Florida, Sandy Gruters was preparing for Christmas while the girls, Dawn and Sheri, ambled around the house. The sun was shining and it was a fresh, beautiful winter day, the kind that entices people to move to Florida. Sandy was relaxed. For the time being she didn't have to worry about her husband. His cast wouldn't come off until the first of January, and until then he'd be safely grounded. There'd probably be some recuperation time after the cast came off, which would eat up a bit more of the three months remaining on his Vietnam tour. If all went well he'd be home in the spring. Plus, she was still buzzing from Guy's surprise visit at Thanksgiving. The memory of opening the door and seeing his smiling face still made her flush.

Through the living room window, Sandy saw a blue Air Force sedan pull up in front of the house and stop. She grimaced, but then she remembered that when Guy had been shot down in November, he had stopped the customary telegram the Air Force sent to family members telling them what had happened. Obviously the Air Force was just now catching up with the news. Typical. The military bureaucracy was creaky in ordinary times, and during a war nothing seemed to go smoothly. And here they were, coming to tell her that her husband had been shot down six weeks ago.

A young captain in a blue uniform stepped dutifully out of the car, carrying a stack of papers. Sandy met him at the front door. "I suppose you're here to tell me my husband has been shot down?" she smiled.

The officer was stunned. This was not the reaction he had expected. His jaw dropped as he stammered, "Well, yes ma'am. Are you Mrs. Sandy Gruters, wife of Captain Guy Gruters?"

"Yes I am, and I know all about it," Sandy replied. "He was just home and has just gone back. You're late."

"Well, ma'am," the captain continued, "I'm sorry to tell you we have a report that a Captain Guy Gruters was shot down two days ago in North Vietnam, the twentieth, and is officially MIA, missing in action."

Sandy swooned. "No, no," she muttered. "You see, he was badly injured when he was shot down last month. He was just home on leave. He can't fly. He has a cast on his arm that won't come off until January first. It couldn't be him. There's some mistake."

But she had begun to realize something was wrong. She invited the messenger in.

He was a lawyer from the judge advocate general's office at MacDill Air Force Base in Tampa, who had volunteered for the thankless job of holiday duty, bringing bad news to families over Christmas and New Year's. He had never run into this kind of situation before. Pilots virtually never got shot down twice. But he had confidence in his facts. "Well, ma'am," he told Sandy calmly, "the Air Force works hard not to make mistakes on matters such as these. We are extremely careful. I'm sure this information and the date are correct."

Sandy began to shake. Could it be? Was it possible that her husband could be down again—and missing this time?

The captain pledged to double-check the information, but he continued to carry out his duties. "Here is the official message, which I will leave with you," he said. Then he began to explain Sandy's legal options regarding pay and benefits. The words bounced off her consciousness, not making any sense. How could this have happened again? She barely heard the officer as he said, "I won't be back to bother you. The only reason I will come back is to tell you his status if we learn it. Your husband is now officially MIA. I will only be back to confirm that we know your husband is dead or a POW."

Sandy numbly signed some papers acknowledging she had received the official notice. Once the captain left, she reached for the phone to call Guy's parents. His father answered. He listened quietly, then told Guy's mother and younger brother, Terry, who was a cadet at the Air Force Academy and home on Christmas leave. Sandy drifted back to the last words she remembered the JAG officer saying. "Dead or a POW. Dead or a POW . . ."

The next morning the blue car pulled up in front of the house again.

Sandy's heart raced as the same young captain came up the walk. She opened the door. The captain smiled and gave her the latest information: "He's a POW." Sandy burst into tears. "Thank God," she sobbed. A day earlier that would have been dreadful news. But now her world had changed. It meant her husband was still alive.

Bob Craner's wife, Audrey, got a visit from a blue car, too. Audrey was British, and had met Craner while he was on a tour in the UK flying F-100s. But she liked to say she felt "almost" American, on account of moving from base to base with Bob as he took different assignments. She was waiting out the war in Hampton, Virginia, near Langley Air Force Base, with their son Lorne, eight, and daughter Charys, five. Her family was back in England, and being near the base gave her access to the commissary, medical facilities, and other military resources.

But she wasn't prepared for the isolation that set in after the two officers told her that her husband was a POW. She thought of Bob's decision a couple of years earlier to forgo a job he had lined up as an airline pilot and extend his Air Force tenure so he could help with the war. It seemed admirable then. It seemed stupid now. She was angry.

Audrey had many, many questions, but the Air Force representatives who came to notify her had no answers. That was intentional. The Air Force didn't want casualty notification officers providing any operational details about pilot losses. Much of the material was classified, and even a little information could lead to wild speculation and false hope. The officers' job was simply to present the basic facts of the loss and leave phone numbers for information on survivor benefits. The officer standing in Audrey's doorway said he would be back only if Bob's "status" changed. When she asked what that meant, he said, "Only if his status is changed from POW to dead, ma'am."

Eventually, Audrey got a letter from Mick Greene, one of the newer Mistys. He had been appointed "summary courts officer," responsible for handling Craner's belongings and shipping his things home. Greene explained to Audrey what he could about the shootdown, including the fact that Jim Mack had talked to Craner after he was a captive and Bob sounded like he was okay. Greene told the story of the North Vietnamese guard talking to them on his radio, and their effort to buy Bob's freedom. It made Audrey smile for a moment—her husband sounded as feisty and courageous as ever. There was a degree of relief in knowing that he was probably okay. But the information also unleashed a rush of other questions. Where was he now? How were the North Vietnamese treating him? How long would he be a prisoner? When would she see him? What should she do in the meantime? Nobody knew.

TEN

ORIENTATION

Jim Fiorelli had a favor to ask. It was the day before Christmas Eve, he wasn't on the Misty flying schedule for the next two days, and he had an errand to run . . . elsewhere in Vietnam. "Fio," as the jovial, self-effacing pilot was known, had been at Misty about six weeks and was well liked by just about everybody. Plus, he had played a historic role in the effort to rescue Craner and Gruters by relaying unintelligible Vietnamese to Jim Mack, who then passed the gobbledy-gook on to the NVA guard who had captured Craner. The Mistys, seeking solace in gallows humor, accused Fiorelli of getting Craner captured because he spoke Vietnamese with a dago accent.

If anybody could risk an unauthorized absence, it was Fio. He asked Don Shepperd, who had been at Misty less than a week, to cover for him if anybody noticed he was gone. The two pilots had known each other at the Air Force Academy, where Fio was two years junior to Shepperd. Fiorelli argued that he wouldn't be AWOL exactly, though he'd be "pretty AWOL." He didn't have permission to leave Misty, but then no one said he couldn't be gone, either—and he didn't intend to ask. Finally, Shepperd figured Fiorelli knew his way around Misty and its unspoken rules, and said sure, he'd do his best to cover if anybody came looking for Fio.

"Where you going?" Shepperd asked.

"Bien Hoa," said Fio, referring to an air base northeast of Saigon that was the home of his former unit, the 531st Fighter Squadron. Shepperd had heard Fio talk about a nurse he had supposedly fallen in love with and quickly surmised that Fiorelli's final destination wasn't Bien Hoa at all, but the huge Long Binh Army supply base about three miles down the road from it. Among other things, Long Binh was home to the 24th Evacuation Hospital. There were nurses there. Including Fio's nurse.

Shepperd playfully probed his flying mate. "How you getting there?" he grinned.

"Beats the shit outta me," Fio replied.

"How you getting back?"

"Beats the shit outta me." Both pilots laughed.

Fio had brought a homespun heartiness to Misty. He was a momma's boy right out of the Italian section of Wilmington, Delaware, and boy, did momma know how to cook. She'd send care packages—"boodle" packages, he called them—that became so popular around Misty that Fio had to hide them. They'd contain sausages, cookies, and spices with an aroma that filled the room. The goodies were rare reminders of the simple pleasures back home.

Fio had often said if it weren't for the Air Force he would have been "running numbers" for his Uncle Jimmie back in Delaware. His mother had steered him away from a life of petty crime and listlessness, urging him to find a nice, safe profession—a barber maybe, or a baker. Being a fighter pilot, during a war of all things, was not what she had in mind. Little did she know, however, that beneath her son's dark mane and boyish grin resided a true, naturally gifted fighter pilot.

Fiorelli had spent a year at the University of Virginia before receiving an appointment to the U.S. Air Force Academy, Class of 1964. He was a tough kid, and at the Academy he glided through the demanding physical challenges, and his one year of college helped him breeze through the first two years of academics. By that time Fio had found his calling as an original slacker. He always said he simply "endured" his junior and senior years, putting forth just barely enough effort to graduate so that he could become a pilot.

After the Academy, he finished high enough in pilot training at

Webb Air Force Base in Texas to be assigned to fighters. He chose the F-100. His instructors at Webb told him he would be "top graduate" if he tried harder at the academics. Fio laughed. He liked to say he had a knack for figuring out exactly how much effort it took to get exactly what he wanted and no more. The rest of the time he slept or ate Italian food. It had worked well so far, he figured, so why change anything?

Fio's F-100 training meant he was destined for Vietnam. He began his combat tour with the 531st Fighter Squadron, "the Ramrods," based at Bien Hoa. In addition to flying ground support missions in the South, Fio made his mark by virtue of taking on some extracurricular duties. Since he was a junior officer when he arrived, the Ramrods made him the squadron "snakekeeper." The 531st had an eight-foot "pet" python they found slithering through the sleeping quarters one day. They named it "Ramrod" after the squadron nickname and allowed it to roam freely throughout their operations building. Ramrod had an unpleasant disposition and a penchant for lunging at passing humans, which terrified visitors and the Vietnamese janitors who cleaned the building. Fiorelli's job was to remove the snake when it became a nuisance and capture rats to feed the mascot. "It's a lot more dangerous than flying," he would explain, "but it passes the time."

Then there was his cooking. The Ramrods had discovered that Fiorelli had acquired some culinary skills from his mother and begged him to cook for squadron parties. Flying duties kept Fio out of the kitchen most days, but when there was a special event he'd roll up his sleeves and work magic with the limited stores available at Bien Hoa, and of course his mother's spices. That April, shortly after Fiorelli arrived in Vietnam, the 531st had cooked up a party with some Special Forces. The ground troops wanted to say thanks for the air support that had saved their asses many a time when they were in tight spots in the jungle. And Fio was to be the chef.

A bunch of men eating and drinking alone was not much fun—no matter how vivid the war stories—so the Ramrods had rounded up the nearest "round-eyes," or Caucasian girls, they could find. The guests happened to be Army nurses from the 24th Evacuation Hospital at Long Binh, just a few miles from Bien Hoa. Several "bread trucks," as they called them—large flight line vans—arrived and shuttled them up to the party. The nurses knew they were the intended prey, but were thankful for the diversion from the grueling routine in the hospital.

Fio had spent the afternoon putting together a fresh salad and cooking up spaghetti and meatballs, then headed off for the flight line to fly a mission. By the time he got back it was nearly 10:00 p.m., and many of the nurses were starting to head back to Long Binh. Fiorelli had rustled up what was left of the food and was sitting alone, eating, when a bubbly, black-haired beauty walked up to him. The meal was the first taste of anything resembling home cooking she had eaten in a long time, she told him. "Glad you liked it," Fio had blurted out. He marveled at her beauty but never asked her name, and she disappeared aboard one of the bread trucks.

A couple of weeks later a new invitation came from the 531st. This time a pilot with an artistic flair had actually designed a flyer, beckoning the nurses of the 24th Evac to attend an "orientation." There would be opportunities to view "gun camera film"—an opportunity to turn out the lights—and the scintillating promise of a "ride" in an F-100. "Yeah, right," glowered one of the more senior nurses, who was approaching the end of her tour. "Many nurses may have gotten laid over at that squadron, but NO ONE has ever gotten a ride," she warned.

The nurses all laughed. Everybody knew the "orientation" was a ploy to hustle round-eyes and ply them with "blabbermouth," a devastating concoction of grain alcohol, wine, and vodka diced with oranges and lemons, served ceremoniously from a large vat. This witch's brew had lubricated many a romantic liaison, helping shut out the gunfire and chaos for a few fleeting moments. But many of the nurses had a real hankering for a little blabbermouth. The party sounded like a great idea.

Lt. Mary O'Neill, one of the nurses, thought about food and the Italian fighter-pilot cook with the sparkling brown eyes she had met ever so briefly a couple of weeks earlier. She had barely stopped thinking about him and his meatballs.

O'Neill, a San Francisco native, had joined the Army because she needed a way to pay for college and get her nursing degree. After training, she volunteered for Vietnam, not out of an overwhelming sense of patriotism but simply because it seemed like something interesting for a young single girl to do.

She arrived in Vietnam at Bien Hoa Air Base late in the evening in early 1967 and promptly experienced her first "Oh shit, what am I doing here?" moment. The taxiways were lined with armed soldiers. She boarded a heavily armored bus that made its way along dusty, traffic-filled roads to Long Binh, the giant Army support base about three miles away. Shortly after she arrived, hot and sweaty and smelling like a goat, a huge explosion ripped the night air. Viet Cong sappers were attacking the Long Binh ammunition dump right behind them, about a half mile away. Fires were burning. Secondary explosions erupted as mortars and rockets impacted the compound. Shrapnel flew in all directions. A sergeant appeared and addressed the group in a monotone as if nothing were happening. "Welcome to Long Binh." He smiled.

"Jesus, Mary, and Joseph," the young nurse said under her breath.

She was assigned to the 24th Evacuation Hospital, another half mile down the road. The 24th was a M.A.S.H.-like facility meant to stabilize patients who had been medevaced from the field, before they were moved to larger, more modern hospitals. It seemed like a makeshift outfit—supplies were short, surgical conditions were primitive, and the medical staff relied on innovation and duct tape as much as their formal training. It didn't take long for O'Neill to get a full, bitter taste of war's brutality. She helped treat the head injuries caused by bombs, bullets, and shrapnel, and tended to soldiers suffering from malaria, tropical funguses, and gastrointestinal diseases. Then there was the "VC ward," where she took care of Viet Cong and North Vietnamese prisoners who had to be convinced that the nurses were there to save them, not kill them. Now she was in the "post-op" surgical ward, and the daily pace was a gauge of the war's increasing intensity. Wave after wave of helicopters arrived every day bringing in wounded GIs. O'Neill and the other nurses and medics would rush out to the helos to drag off blood-covered soldiers, insert IVs, inject morphine, and pick up body parts. Then they'd tend to the survivors in post-op. There was no time to get to know the soldiers who shuffled through, since the conveyor belt of war rapidly pushed out the old patients and delivered new ones.

On the night of the "orientation" at the 531st, O'Neill had a rare night off. For once she didn't have to be back by 11:00 p.m. When she arrived at the base, she scanned the crowd and spotted Fiorelli in the corner with a beer in hand. She walked right up to him, and this time the two learned each other's names, and then some. By the time she arrived back at the surgical ward the next day, Mary O'Neill was smitten with a fighter pilot, and Fio with a nurse.

It wasn't easy working their budding relationship into the schedule the war demanded. Their days off never seemed to mesh. Occasionally Fio would come over on a motorcycle, sometimes at night, which was always a risky maneuver with Viet Cong lurking in unpredictable places. They'd visit for a few minutes in the hospital ward hallway when Mary was between shifts, but these meetings were so rushed that Mary wouldn't even clean the blood off her surgical gown. Every now and then Mary would catch a truck to Bien Hoa and see him between flights. One night they managed to escape together to Saigon, for the kind of date you could have only in a war zone: They drank beer atop one of the hotels and watched B-52 and C-47 air strikes light up the night off in the distance. But there was limited privacy in the war zone and it was difficult to be close.

One night Mary came off shift at 11:30 and went to the mess hall with Vickie, a nurse friend. It had been a rough day in the OR. They wearily wondered aloud about the war, which seemed mindless to both of them. Fio had called. He was on night alert, so there was no chance of a surprise liaison. Suddenly, roaring engines and loud booms split the night air from the direction of the Bien Hoa runway. Mary and Vickie rushed outside to see two aircraft, trailing bright flames from their afterburners, climbing into the night sky. "Arrivederci . . . fly safe, my love," waved Mary, and the two nurses went back inside to resume their late-night conversation.

They were still talking when, just before 3:00 a.m., a huge explosion shook the quarters. "Jesus, what was that?" asked Mary as the two rushed outside, expecting to see another attack in progress, maybe the ammo dump going up in flames again. But there was nothing: no flares, no lights, no secondary explosions, and no return fire. So the girls went to bed. Tomorrow would be another long day, literally full of blood and guts.

On her shift the next day Mary answered the phone. "Post-op, Lieutenant O'Neill." It was Fio.

"Hey, did you hear a big explosion last night?" he asked.

"Yes, Vickie and I were up talking. What was it?"

"It was me. I got shot down," Fio explained.

Fiorelli had been working with a FAC providing air support south of Long Binh in the swamps. When his aircraft was hit by small-arms fire, he turned it away from the Army base and the surrounding town, toward the black abyss that was the Mekong Delta. He could see the bright lights of Saigon farther to the southwest. He ejected at about 5,000 feet, which left plenty of time to watch his aircraft erupt into a gigantic fireball below him as it impacted the ground. He also had plenty of time to think and, needless to say, he was worried. Getting captured by the Viet Cong and spending the rest of his life in a cage was not appealing.

As Fio neared the ground, he recalled the emergency procedures for night and tree landings: feet together, arms crossed over the chest to protect the neck and vital organs. Also have to protect my nuts for future generations, he thought. The first contact was with high tree branches. His chute got caught and he started to tumble downward, headfirst. Crashing through the vegetation, he anticipated smashing into the ground and thought, This is really going to hurt bad. But suddenly he was jerked upright. His tumble had stopped. Now my troubles are just beginning, he worried as he hung in the tree, listening for the approach of Viet Cong.

He took out his pistol and decided to be totally still and make not a sound. He hung as still as he could for about an hour, not moving, barely breathing, listening intently for any sound. He heard nothing. Then he realized he still had his helmet on. He took it off and resumed his statuesque pose for another hour. In the impenetrable black night he feared he was hanging seventy-five feet above the ground, so he decided to drop his helmet to see how far he had to go to lower himself from the tree. The helmet fell about three inches. He had been hanging a footstep above the ground for more than two hours.

Mary's heart raced as she heard the story. But Fio acted nonchalant. "No big deal," he told her boldly. "I'll be flying again tomorrow." Somehow it didn't make Mary feel any better.

Their first real chance to get away together came several months later, when they both got time off and scheduled a trip to Bangkok in October. Finally they would have some time to get to know each other. But as always, there was a snafu. This time it wasn't combat . . . but crabs. "Not crotch crabs," Fio was quick to point out. "Real crabs." He and a friend had obtained some soft-shelled crabs from a street-side vendor, and Fio, of course, knew just how to sauté them with Momma Fio's spices. Unfortunately, he didn't know how to tell if they were contaminated, and the crabs gave him severe food poisoning. "VC crabs," he quipped. Still, it was a serious illness and he was evacuated to the hospital at Clark Air Force Base in the Philippines, a precaution against hepatitis developing.

Screwed again, thought Mary bitterly as she headed for Bangkok, alone.

Once there, she took a taxi to "Tommy's Gems," the in place for GIs—"Honest and with a military discount," the sign read. There she met an Air Force C-130 crew that happened to be heading to Clark. Throwing her long dark hair back over her shoulders, flashing her eyes, and shedding tears when required, she related her plight. "My one true love is wounded and in the hospital at Clark," she said with crossed fingers. Could these men, these gallant Air Force warriors, help her out? And oh, by the way, since she didn't have any orders, could they smuggle her into the Philippines?

Before long she was sitting in the hallway of the Clark hospital. Fiorelli almost had a heart attack when she entered the room. Mary knew the medical system lingo and managed to forge a pass that allowed Fio to depart the hospital on "convalescent leave" with "base friends." It wasn't Bangkok, but it was pretty good.

A few days later the temporarily happy couple was making their way back to Bien Hoa on a C-47. Fio at least had orders. Mary was on her own to talk her way back into the country, although getting back into Vietnam was easier than getting out. They had "borrowed" some pillows from the base hospital and Fio, still weak, slept with his head in Mary's lap as the webbed seat straps cut into her back. They bounced through the warm, turbulent Southeast Asian air, winging their way back to war.

A couple of weeks after that Mary got another phone call in post-op. "I'm going to Misty," Fio said plainly. The 531st had asked for volunteers to help fill out the fast FAC unit, and Fio had raised his hand—why, he wasn't quite sure. But he was excited. "Real flying," he told Mary. "Not monkey bombing."

Mary had heard vague stories about Misty at the Ramrod parties, where the F-100 pilots sometimes talked about the missions. Fio might be excited, but she was crestfallen. Was this the end of their relationship? It had probably been too good to be true, the dream of two lovers caught up in war, meeting, surviving, getting married, and going home together. She thought wistfully about watching the "gun camera film" and their unusual dates atop the hotel in Saigon. Fio must love Misty and flying more than he loved her, she figured. She wouldn't see him again. Mary hung up the phone and cried.

Mary hadn't heard from Fio once in the six weeks after he arrived at Misty. The flying schedule was demanding, Fio was learning a new job, and communication between their two bases was difficult. Fio had decided to make up for the radio silence by surprising her on Christmas Eve.

The 24th Evac, where Mary worked, was a depressing place on the warmest and sunniest of days. On Christmas Eve, it was one of the saddest scenes Mary could have imagined. As she stepped off duty in the post-op ward, she figured she would stop by the mess hall, where there would undoubtedly be a makeshift "feast," by Army standards. She'd go to mass at the post chapel and probably sing carols and participate in the candlelight service. But she had no desire to spend Christmas Eve with her fellow nurses, or with anybody, for that matter.

Then out of nowhere, Fio appeared. He was beaming. He took her in his arms, kissed her, and held her tight. As surely as he had vanished into the mysterious world of Misty, like thousands of other casualties of the war, he had reappeared as if from a fairy tale. It was the best Christmas Eve either of them ever had.

Nobody noticed Fio's absence from Phu Cat on Christmas Eve, and Shepperd kept his mouth shut. Spirits were subdued and voices were low, and once the customary Christmas truce went into effect that night, everybody seemed to be seduced by the quiet. There was no artillery, no mortar fire, no runway clamor, just silence. It was strange and captivating and sad, and suddenly nobody was interested in anybody else's business anyway.

In the squadron buildings there were the obligatory fake Christmas trees. A few tinfoil icicles hung limply in the humidity, and here and there a lonely Christmas ornament dangled, having survived the military mail system intact. At the mess hall there was turkey and trimmings. Handbills had announced midnight caroling and a candle-light service at the base chapel. But most of the Mistys found a convenient excuse to skip the services: There was lots of important flying coming up, and they had to work. In the Misty shack, someone had rigged up a turntable with an old Perry Como Christmas album that spun while the pilots rifled through reconnaissance photos. The Mistys were supposed to be stoics, and they tried to act like it was just another day on the job. The holiday season, after all, might be light on action, somebody suggested. "Yeah, right," said Don Jones. "Don't bet your ass on it."

"KILL FOR PEACE"

Northand South Vietnam agreed to a truce f⸺
1967. It was a tradition that went back severa⃞
a tradition that the North Vietnamese would selecti⸺
iday gesture and that both sides would bitterly a⸺
cheating. And while the deal prohibited all bombi⸺
nam, FACs didn't drop bombs—they only helped fin⸺
could. So the Mistys flew.

The Mistys usually found the roads and other m⸺
fares that formed the Trail to be as lifeless as a r⸺
thousands of truck crews and other troops remaine⸺
tunnels, and camouflaged bunkers a stone's thro⸺
ready to roll once daylight descended or clouds m⸺
were no such precautions during the bombing halt⸺
looked like the Ventura Highway at rush hour, with⸺
for miles.

In one of the Huns, Charlie Neel was taking D⸺
Misty commander, for one of his checkout rides. Jon⸺
even dapper man with a dark moustache he contin⸺
had worried many of the Mistys when he took ove⸺
been the Wing King's selection, somebody sent ove⸺

military mail system intact. At the mess hall there was turkey and trimmings. Handbills had announced midnight caroling and a candle-light service at the base chapel. But most of the Mistys found a convenient excuse to skip the services: There was lots of important flying coming up, and they had to work. In the Misty shack, someone had rigged up a turntable with an old Perry Como Christmas album that spun while the pilots rifled through reconnaissance photos. The Mistys were supposed to be stoics, and they tried to act like it was just another day on the job. The holiday season, after all, might be light on action, somebody suggested. "Yeah, right," said Don Jones. "Don't bet your ass on it."

"KILL FOR PEACE"

North and South Vietnam agreed to a truce for Christmas Day, 1967. It was a tradition that went back several years. It was also a tradition that the North Vietnamese would selectively ignore the holiday gesture and that both sides would bitterly accuse the other of cheating. And while the deal prohibited all bombing of North Vietnam, FACs didn't drop bombs—they only helped find targets so others could. So the Mistys flew.

The Mistys usually found the roads and other makeshift thoroughfares that formed the Trail to be as lifeless as a remote desert. The thousands of truck crews and other troops remained huddled in caves, tunnels, and camouflaged bunkers a stone's throw from the Trail, ready to roll once daylight descended or clouds moved in. But there were no such precautions during the bombing halt. Parts of the Trail looked like the Ventura Highway at rush hour, with trucks backed up for miles.

In one of the Huns, Charlie Neel was taking Don Jones, the new Misty commander, for one of his checkout rides. Jones was a slight, fit, even dapper man with a dark moustache he continually twirled, who had worried many of the Mistys when he took over the unit. He had been the Wing King's selection, somebody sent over to tame the unit.

As it turned out, however, Jones was no "seagull" who sat around Ops waiting for somebody to throw a rock at him to get him to fly. He had over seven thousand hours in B-17s, C-82s, C-47s, L-5s, and other aircraft, and he was one smooth pilot. There was no bombast when he spoke. He didn't seem to be out for rank or glory. Above all, Jones loved to fly. The guys saw it and respected it, and in the Misty spirit he promptly scheduled himself on tough and important missions. As sorry as the Mistys were to lose P. J. White, the new boss seemed to be a pretty good guy.

The weather had cleared by the afternoon, giving Jones an opportunity to get a good look at the Trail—and to start counting. The roads below were so thick with trucks that Jones had to estimate his count in twenties, making marks on a card to represent each score. The two pilots ground their teeth in frustration as they fecklessly watched the trucks stream down the road, many of them carrying ammo that would probably be fired at them tomorrow.

Jones's card was getting so full there was barely any space left to write on. The Misty commander finally gave up trying to get a precise count and estimated that there were fifteen hundred trucks heading south, and those were only the vehicles they could see. Since there was no bombing, the North's antiaircraft gunners were less aggressive than usual, and the Mistys were able to get down as low as 1,500 feet. That allowed them to snap images so detailed that in a few, the pith helmets of NVA soldiers were visible as they rode in the back of open-air trucks, on their way south to fight.

There might just be a small bit of consolation, however. On Christmas afternoon, while Neel and Jones were airborne, planners at 7th Air Force started wondering if they might be able to squeeze in a few strikes once the bombing halt officially ended at 6:00 p.m. The sun would be setting by then, but there still might be enough daylight to make a few runs. Neel was elated by the prospect when a controller from the ABCCC gave him a heads-up. Those dumb-shit truck drivers down there would think they were still in the clear, yet the invisible shield of political posturing that was protecting them would suddenly disappear.

Neel thought it over for a moment, then called back to the ABCCC, which had a colonel on board directing the air traffic flow. "Goddamn it!" Neel barked, as if he were in charge. "We need all the air-to-ground assets you can muster. We have targets out the wazoo. Get them lined up in flights of four, feet wet off Dong Hoi."

There was confusion, however, about what time actually constituted the end of the truce. What if the truce hours were in military Zulu time—based on the time in Greenwich, England? Or Washington time, for that matter? Then it would extend for several more hours. On the radio net, somebody asked if it would be "fair" to drop bombs on the North Vietnamese just seconds after a truce expired. Neel was appalled. Here was the enemy, blatantly exploiting a bombing halt to rush men and weapons down the Trail, so they'd be more effective at killing American GIs. And it might be unfair to try to stop them? He could have strangled the hand-wringers in the ABCCC, if they had been in the cockpit next to him. Yet they were responding like trained pups to the vagaries of their masters in Washington: If they made a mistake and bombed when they shouldn't have, if Hanoi received a "signal" other than Washington intended, somebody was sure to get thumped.

Frustration mounted. Most of the aircraft on alert that day had been sent over the Trail in Laos—where there was no truce—chasing a couple of trucks bold enough to make a daylight run. Only a few F-4s were within range of the biggest turkey shoot most of them would ever see. Neel couldn't stand it any longer. While waiting for the F-4s to arrive, Neel dived toward the head of one convoy and strafed the lead truck. That was against wing rules, but what the hell, he had the boss in the backseat. Besides, the NVA gunners had let down their guard, and this was an unprecedented chance to take out an entire fleet of trucks—not just the usual one or two. Then Neel promptly came back around for another pass and fired a smoke rocket into the second truck. Stopping the two vehicles in their tracks bottled up the whole parade, sending hundreds of drivers fleeing into the woods to escape the coming onslaught. Their vehicles remained on the road, motionless, a fantastic target.

The F-4s finally zoomed onto the scene, and the target was so obvious there was no need to mark it with smoke rockets. But to Neel's dismay, the big attack fizzled. The F-4s, armed with cluster bombs, missed the convoy. They were "nose dippers," as some of the Mistys derided the F-4 jocks: pilots who dropped their bombs from high altitudes because they didn't want to fly lower and risk getting shot down. From the height the F-4s had dropped their bombs, accuracy was always questionable, and sure enough, the CBUs strayed into the surrounding woods. Maybe they killed some of the truck drivers out in the trees, but the only trucks that ended up taking any fire were the two that Neel had nailed on his low-level passes. The F-4 pilots sailed on home, seemingly oblivious to their errant shooting. "Useless bastards," Neel cursed. "Makes you wonder why we hang our asses out, marking for them."

The shooting done with the cameras was more fruitful. The 35mm photos snapped by Misty and by some of the RF-101 reconnaissance jets flying that day produced bulletproof evidence that the North Vietnamese had exploited the so-called truce to maximum advantage. That in itself was no surprise: The North had always tried to strengthen its hand during U.S.-initiated halts in the action, especially when they coincided with Western holidays that the Vietnamese didn't recognize. What was more troubling was the way the North Vietnamese were thumbing their noses at the United States. They simply were not playing the game by Washington's rules.

The Christmas bombing halt, along with various announcements that Washington planned to escalate or relax the intensity of its war effort, was supposed to send a clear signal to Hanoi: If they reduced the infiltration of men and weapons into the South and engaged in sincere peace negotiations, the American military juggernaut would go gently on them. But if they persisted in their warmaking, the pain would be relentless and unbearable. It was an increasingly desperate effort by the Johnson administration to find a way out of the war without withdrawing from South Vietnam altogether or conceding defeat, or harming U.S. prestige. Yet North Vietnam's dismissal of the cease-fire demonstrated one thing above all: The leaders in Hanoi knew President Johnson was losing his leverage, probably even before he did.

In fact, deep divisions within the Johnson administration over whether to escalate the war or find a way to cut U.S. losses and simply get out were getting harder to conceal. At the end of November, Johnson announced that Defense Secretary Robert McNamara would be leaving the Pentagon to become president of the World Bank, a post

McNamara had shown interest in for several years. Newspapers speculated that McNamara was ill or overstressed by the war—perhaps even suicidal—but in reality he had come to oppose Johnson's own beliefs on the war. For at least six months McNamara had been questioning whether there was any military solution to the war, and in early November he had sent Johnson a memo with bleak conclusions. The only thing that would persuade North Vietnam to accept a peace settlement, he insisted, would be their belief that the United States would do anything necessary to prevail in Vietnam. But with public opposition to the war snowballing, there were obvious limits to U.S. involvement. Thus, McNamara believed, "there is . . . a very real question whether under these circumstances it will be possible to maintain our efforts in South Vietnam for the time necessary to accomplish our objectives there."[1] Shortly after receiving the memo, Johnson arranged for McNamara to be offered a job he couldn't refuse.

Getting rid of McNamara didn't resolve dissension over the war, which was being aired more frequently inside the Pentagon. A week before Christmas, the recently retired Marine Corps commandant, Gen. David Shoup, had publicly attacked the entire political basis for the U.S. role in the war, saying that it was "pure unadulterated poppycock" to claim that fighting in Vietnam was necessary to prevent communism from spreading closer to the United States. The Johnson administration, he charged, was using propaganda "to keep the people worried about the communists crawling up the banks of Pearl Harbor or crawling up the Palisades or crawling up the beaches of Los Angeles."[2]

Maybe they weren't creeping up on New York or L.A., but the communists were sure hauling ass for South Vietnam. At Misty, word went around that their startling Christmas pictures had rocketed up the chain of command to 7th Air Force, to the commander of Pacific Command, and even to the president himself. Rumors trickled back down to Phu Cat that "the Big Guy" had looked at the pictures, shaken his head, and muttered, "Sorry bastards."

The schizophrenia in Washington spilled directly into the air war. The 7th Air Force was notorious for giving guidance that made it sound like they wanted their aircrews to try hard, but not too hard. Napalm, for instance, was supposed to be "dive-bombed" from 3,000 feet rather than being delivered from low level. As a result it often ended up producing an intense but narrow fireball instead of blanketing a broad enemy position, the most effective tactic. Some commanders were also fond of saying that "no target in Vietnam was worth the loss of an airplane or pilot," an attitude that prevented losses—and also kept their own records clean.

Practically every Misty experienced the phenomenon after a couple weeks of flying: They'd be dodging AAA and maybe even flying below minimums to accurately mark a target for a fighter, who'd drift overhead, lazily pickle his bombs from a hopelessly high altitude, then cruise on home to rack up another "counter"—one more combat mission to add to his total. On one hand, who could blame them—higher-ups in Saigon and Washington were practically telling pilots not to risk any scratches while they fought the war. But cautious war fighting wasn't getting the job done. Mick Greene, an experienced pilot who had been the 37th Wing's safety officer before joining Misty and was in line to replace Don Sibson as the unit's Ops officer, was losing patience. He didn't mean to bad-mouth anybody, but "bad bombers" made Misty's job harder and more dangerous. They'd have to make multiple passes to mark some targets because the bomb-droppers couldn't hit them. They got shot at more and picked up more battle damage. It was only a matter of time before a Misty got shot down because other pilots were slacking off. And charades like the Christmas truce only allowed the North Vietnamese to aim more guns at the Americans. If we're not going to fight to win, Greene wondered, why not just go home?

Frustration penetrated the whole unit. Roger Van Dyken, after just two months in-theater, was already struggling to see the logic of the way Washington and Saigon were running the war. "It was downright painful for Misty to fly two missions and see 600 to 800 trucks headed south," he wrote in his diary on Christmas day, "loaded with supplies that will kill our men and prolong the war—and be able to do nothing. We watch them break the truce 39 times; mortaring, attacking, kidnapping, shelling—and we, the good guys with white hats, do nothing. Nothing, nothing, nothing." Van Dyken recalled a hand-scrawled poster a couple of the Mistys, in a cynical moment, had hung in the Operations office: "Like Misty says, KILL for PEACE!!"[3]

Bob Hope and Raquel Welch came to Phu Cat the next day. The Mistys who weren't flying along with other wing pilots and legions of Army troops based nearby crammed the makeshift open-air theater, desperate for a visit from ambassadors of the outside world, especially ones with short skirts.

Don Shepperd and Jim "Hog" Piner were returning from a morning Misty mission up north as the crowd was beginning to assemble before the show. The weather had been bad everywhere, and the two were coming home early. Piner, an acerbic, strapping Air Force brat born at Barksdale Air Force Base in Louisiana, was an experienced F-100 jock. He had had tours in Japan and Clovis, New Mexico, and had been an instructor pilot at Luke just before coming to Vietnam. He had been assigned to the 612th at Phu Cat and had been at Misty a little more than a month. Shepperd, in the backseat, was still getting checked out, but was eager for any kind of action—including tomfoolery. "Hog," he remarked, looking down at the crowd, "that's the best target we've seen all day. Whaddya think about giving them a low-level afterburner pass?" The roar would certainly warm them up for Hope.

Piner was always up for a stunt—but had been at Phu Cat long enough to learn the wing commander's peccadilloes. "You gotta be kidding," he replied. "The Wing King would shit his pants over that one. You and I would spend the rest of the war in Leavenworth." Piner put the landing gear down and made an uneventful descent, leaving Hope to get the crowd fired up on his own.

That was easy. Always racy but never bawdy, Hope joked about the name Phu Cat and was an instant hit. Many in the crowd had heard about Hope's troop visits from fathers who had served in previous wars. He was the military's favorite Hollywood celebrity—especially when he paraded a cast of long-legged lovelies across the stage, delighting the hundreds of men in the crowd. When Welch joined Hope at the microphone, John Haltigan maneuvered his lean frame into the front row and snapped a few souvenir photos with his 35mm camera. The keeper was a periscope shot of Welch, her shapely legs stretching from a pair of white go-go boots up into the miniest of minidresses.

Hope's visit was an opportunity for the troops at Phu Cat to blow off steam, but there was never a true day of rest in Vietnam. With so many GIs on the base for the show, the Korean forces protecting the base were on high alert. The gathering was a juicy target for an artillery or mortar attack, even a concealed grenade. That never materialized, but as often seemed to be the case, tragedy struck in an unforeseen manner that day. A CH-47 Chinook helicopter ferrying troops in for the show from one of the outlying combat zones crashed, killing all onboard. Word of the crash circulated in whispers through the crowd, but most people shrugged it off. More death, more senselessness. It was out of sync with the escapism up onstage.

Fuzz Mack had missed the Bob Hope show, as well as all the theatrics in the Pack on Christmas Day. In six weeks he had been involved in two failed rescue attempts, leaving Lance Sijan, Bob Craner, and Guy Gruters behind in the jungle. He was drained and needed a break. Don Jones realized it before Mack did. He could see the glazed, empty look in his pilot's eyes, and he knew that Mack had been flying in Vietnam for ten straight months. "Fuzz," he told Mack, "why don't you get the hell out of Dodge? Better yet—go to Australia!"

Now that was Rio Linda, as Charlie Neel liked to say—the real life, back in civilization. It had taken no persuading for Mack to book a flight to Sydney. He knew he'd miss the Bob Hope show, but he had heard there was another one scheduled on Christmas Eve at Phan Rang Air Base about 150 miles northeast of Saigon, along the South China Sea. That was a day before he was scheduled to leave for Sydney out of Cam Ranh Bay, which was a short hop up the coast. Besides, his old unit, the 614th Tactical Fighter Squadron, was based at Phan Rang and had just built a new hootch that it planned to christen with a bash on December 23. Mack had arrived just in time and discovered that, except for Hope himself, the whole Hope entourage—Raquel Welch, Jerry Colonna, Miss World, a Brazilian beauty with the most enticing cleavage Mack had ever seen—had shown up. His old squadron mates were pouring generous drinks, and he started to unwind immediately.

The next morning Mack had woken up facedown on the floor. His first thought was that he had been shot down and taken captive. Then he realized the men stepping over him were wearing U.S. Air Force flight suits.

"Help me," he said weakly. "I have to get to Cam Ranh for an R&R flight to Sydney."

"Pal, you're in Cam Ranh," said a reassuring voice.

Mack, head aching terribly, looked down at his boots where a tag read, "Deliver this body to any fighter ops squadron in Cam Ranh for a 1500 departure for R&R in Sydney." Eventually he pieced together the story: His buddies from the 614th had thrown him over the hood of a jeep, taken him to the flight line, flagged down a C-130 headed for Cam Ranh, and piled him onboard.

The rest of the Mistys remained in residence at Phu Cat, however, gearing up for action. Another bombing halt was expected to be announced for New Year's Day, and the Mistys were determined to find a way to rain on the parade of trucks going down the Trail. The truce, they had learned, would be over by 5:00 p.m. local time on New Year's Day, leaving at least an hour of good daylight to attack the endless convoys they expected to see. Of course, the weather would have to cooperate, and then there was that other minor factor—the bomb droppers would have to be able to hit their targets.

Two days after Christmas, Jim Fiorelli sauntered into Misty Ops from his AWOL party with Mary O'Neill. "You missed a good Bob Hope show," Don Shepperd teased him. Fiorelli just smiled. "Wipe that shit-eating grin off your face," Shepperd hooted. "Get down here and help us."

"Where the hell have you been?" asked Don Sibson, the burly Ops officer, suddenly realizing he hadn't seen Fio in three days.

"You don't want to know," said Shepperd. "The man is a warrior using his own free time to hunt the enemy in an undercover operation." He winked. Sibson took the cue and begged off. No point in asking questions you didn't want the answers to.

The entire Misty staff was working hard on plans to make a big strike at 5:00 p.m. on New Year's Day in several of the most popular gathering spots in Route Pack 1: Ron ferry, Quang Khe ferry, Mu Ghia Pass, and the Disappearing River, one of the most intriguing and exasperating targets in North Vietnam. Routes 101 and 137, key elements of the Trail, intersected at a river, the Song Troc. There was no bridge, however. Instead, the river seemed to "disappear" into a giant karst cave, which the Mistys were convinced housed a motorized ferry that was used to transport trucks across the river at night, in bad weather, and during truces.

Maps were being shuffled around like playing cards and pencils were flying. There was a great deal to coordinate in order for 7th Air Force to issue the frag order: fighter call signs, specific bomb loads, takeoff times, tankers, and refueling tracks. The Mistys were putting together a great surprise for the North Vietnamese, if only the weather would cooperate.

"Probably be another goat fuck." Fiorelli smirked.

"Don't be so cheerful," Shepperd quipped back.

"You are listening to the voice of experience," replied Fio importantly as he sat down to help.

As 1967 wound down, the Mistys focused on developing intelligence that would produce a historic series of bombing raids once the clock struck 5:00 p.m. on New Year's Day. The scheduling board showed that the last mission of the day on December 30 would be flown by Maj. Don Sibson, Misty's burly, handsome operations officer, and Capt. Jere Wallace, a tall, dashing Air Force brat who resembled Jimmy Stewart. Like Sibson, Wallace had been with the unit since September and his tour was due to wrap up soon.

It was an old fighter jock superstition that a pilot should not know when he was on his last scheduled mission. In Vietnam, in fact, many pilots had been lost on their final flights because they pressed too hard and took needless risks during their one last chance to kill enemy troops. So when Wallace returned to Phu Cat from his fifty-first mission on December 29, he was met by the fire trucks for the ritual "hose down," the ceremony marking the final mission. His Misty brethren met him on the tarmac with champagne, and the fire hoses opened up and gave him a thorough soaking. His Misty tour was over.

Wallace was replaced on the scheduling board by Capt. Don Snyder, who formally belonged to the 416th, the F-100 unit that operated next door to Misty. Snyder was one of the squadron's most experienced pilots, a flight commander who led two- and four-ship missions and had more than two thousand hours in the Hun. He had been a FAC himself in South Vietnam, flying O-1s back in 1965 out of Quang Tri, a base just south of the DMZ. But back then, the area had been pretty calm. Don Jones had already invited him to fly with Misty several times, thinking his experience would be an asset.

John Haltigan had become seasoned and knowledgeable in four

months of immersion at Misty. He began the preflight briefing on the thirtieth with an air of authority. "It's the usual story this time of year," he said. "Same as the last couple of days. The weather is bad and solid over the Pack, two- to three-thousand-foot ceilings. You should be able to get down okay and the visibility is good underneath, but I doubt you'll be able to work fighters." Then he highlighted the intelligence-gathering priorities. "We are particularly interested in refueling areas for the increased vehicle traffic we see coming south. Please report all areas of heavy traffic backups. We want to hit them hard on the first."

Adding to their motivation, North Vietnamese leader Ho Chi Minh, astutely grasping the mounting turmoil back in the States, had issued a proclamation bidding Happy New Year to Americans who were opposed to their nation's involvement in Vietnam.[4] His words could have hung in the Misty Ops shack like the disparaging trash talk from opponents that coaches sometimes post in the locker room before a big game, to get their players fired up.

Since he wasn't checked out as a Misty, Snyder would be flying in the backseat—which, like most fighter pilots, he hated. And he had particular reason to hope for an uneventful ride: As soon as he landed, he was due to leave for R&R with his wife in Hawaii. Snyder was relieved when he learned that Sibson would be flying up front. Sibson was known as a capable, mature pilot who didn't take foolish risks. The crusty New Hampsherite had flown B-47 bombers under Strategic Air Command before switching to fighters, but was unamused by the jet-jocks who derided him as a "SAC puke." Sibson was built like a middleweight boxer and perfectly capable of punching out taunters who pushed too hard. Like Wallace, he was approaching the end of his tour and would be heading home soon. Unlike some of the brash young Turks flying in fighters, that was likely to make him more cautious in the cockpit, not more reckless.

The weather was good as Sibson stroked the afterburner for takeoff at Phu Cat. But as they approached the Pack, Haltigan's prediction proved correct. There was solid overcast. Even Laos was pretty much clobbered, so Sibson went out to sea and let down over the water. That way he could get under the cloud layer without the risk of smashing into a mountain. Once he got beneath the weather, he turned the Hun back toward the coast and accelerated for a run inland. They flew west and weren't the slightest bit surprised to see heavy truck traffic on virtually every road. Snyder, in the back, marked locations on the map. As they approached the top of Mu Ghia Pass, they decided to fly south along the Trail network. Again, it was as crowded as a roadhouse parking lot on Friday night. And they were simply on a sightseeing tour taking notes—the weather was still unworkable for fighters.

They cycled through the tanker twice, and finally Sibson said, "Let's take one more look around Dong Hoi and go home." Snyder was in no mood to linger, either. He was eager to see his wife, Thelma, in Honolulu.

They let down one last time over the water and turned inland north of Dong Hoi, the bombed-out coastal city forty miles north of the DMZ. Sibson planned to follow Route 1 south and avoid some well-known gun sites where the road crossed a river just north of the city—or what remained of it. "We'll have to be careful south of town," he said to Snyder—just as the whole ground seemed to erupt in flame beneath them. They felt a heavy *thump* and Snyder looked out to see a gash in the left wing. Fuel was spewing out, smoking, bubbling, catching fire, then going out and catching fire again. They were in serious trouble.

Sibson wanted to turn toward the water, but the position of the AAA guns blocked that route. Then more ground fire broke out on the other side of the plane—37mm guns, and some big-time 57mm. They were bracketed by the guns. The only safe route seemed to be to the west, toward the mountains and jungle. The normal thing would have been to get above the clouds, out of sight of the gunners. But they were burning, and Sibson worried that they'd lose control of the airplane, that the instruments might fail if he went into the clouds. So he stayed beneath the overcast, jinking with all his might to stay clear of the gunfire. He fought hard to maintain control of the airplane as the hydraulic systems degraded.

Smoke was beginning to fill the cockpit. Snyder, in the back, bent over and looked down at the UHF radio panel to make sure he had selected the proper switch position to make a Mayday call to the ABCCC. While he was looking through the smoke at the panel, another 37mm round crashed into the jet, plowing right up the tailpipe. Several warning lights flared. The ENGINE FIRE and AFT ENGINE OVERHEAT lights flashed on. Snyder felt the airplane reel out of control.

There was no choice but to eject, even though Snyder, in the back, had been thrown into an improper ejection position as the airplane snapped. He popped the canopy and bailed out. Sibson followed. Since they had stayed low under the clouds, they both had a short descent into the jungle. That offered one advantage: They were only briefly suspended as targets for any locals firing small arms. Sibson landed safely in a clearing. Snyder descended into triple-canopy jungle. His parachute hung up on the second layer of foliage, about fifteen to twenty feet above the ground.

When the ABCCC had heard the Mayday call, they immediately launched rescue forces from Nakhon Phanom in Thailand. The timely alert allowed the Sandys and Jollys to arrive just before dark. They quickly found Sibson in the clearing and picked him up. Locating Snyder was more of a problem. His chute was hidden beneath the top layer of trees, and as he tried to fire pen-gun flares up through the brush, they kept getting derailed by branches and leaves. Worse, he was hurt. He was bleeding from numerous cuts the tree limbs had dished out as he crashed down through the jungle. And he had trouble moving his neck and looking up. Plus, he could hear voices, which sounded like they were coming from the top of an adjacent hill. This would not be a comfortable place to spend the night. Finally, Snyder aimed his last flare at a hole between the trees and let fly. The lead Sandy caught sight of the flare emerging from the treetops and quickly directed the Jolly into position for the pickup. Snyder hauled himself onto the hoist and rose, gasping, to safety.

The Jolly managed to evade the AAA with help from the two 20mm wing-mounted cannons on the Sandys. On its way south the Jolly stopped for gas at Dong Ha, just south of the DMZ, then headed for Da Nang, the huge air base along the coast in South Vietnam. Don Sibson was feeling pretty good, and he jumped on a C-130 headed for Phu Cat. When he arrived, the Mistys escorted him to the bar, where they proposed endless toasts to him, to the Sandys and Jollys who rescued him, to fighter pilots in general, and to their waiting wives. When someone jokingly asked if they should propose a toast to Secretary McNamara, he was quickly booed down. But Sibson had a serious concern. From the bar he called the base command post to ask them to not send the customary telegram to his wife, informing her that he had been shot down. He was fine, he assured them, and there was no point in worrying her.

A single pilot in Vietnam, however, couldn't always control the flow of information. Every pilot shot down in the North gained temporary notoriety, as the wire services dutifully reported every significant casualty. It was often impossible to mention every one of the 200 or 300 grunts killed in a primal episode of ground combat, but Air Force pilots were officers, not enlisted men, and when they landed in the North they suddenly became political pawns in the cynical POW sweepstakes that Hanoi and Washington gambled at. So it should have come as little surprise that back near Pease Air Force Base in New Hampshire, where Don Sibson's wife, Lee, lived, word of a local boy nearly captured in North Vietnam hit the news quickly. Bob and Sheila Weeks, who were close friends of the Sibsons, were listening to the radio when they heard the gripping report: A hometown hero, Don Sibson, had been shot down over North Vietnam. No further details were available. It was late at night, and Bob and Sheila slipped on their coats and went straight to their friend Lee Sibson's house and knocked on the door. As Lee opened the door, she wondered what her friends were doing there so late. As they explained what they had heard, her breath left her. Lee immediately phoned the Red Cross, using the number the international humanitarian organization had made available to all family members who had a loved one in the war. The news was good. They confirmed that Don had been shot down, but that he had been recovered and was okay. Her emotions overflowed. Panic mingled with relief as she grasped the worst possible scenario, then realized she had been spared. Above all else, she wished he would call.

Back at Da Nang, Don Snyder had been transferred to the big Navy hospital. He was in terrible pain, with serious injuries he had absorbed when he ejected from the out-of-control Hun. He managed to get a call through to a squadron-mate who was on duty in the Phu Cat command post. "Call my wife," he said. "Tell her I'm beat up but okay, and that I'll be in the hospital for a while. Oh, yes," he grimaced, "tell her to cancel her tickets for Hawaii. I won't be coming."

Needless to say, Snyder's wife, Thelma, back in Carnegie, Pennsylvania, was disturbed to hear that her husband had been shot down and that they wouldn't be seeing each other in Hawaii. Thelma had been a fighter pilot's wife for almost eight years and had seen her share of tragedy, as various friends from the fighter community had absorbed the news that their husbands had become casualties of accidents or of the war in Southeast Asia. She was relieved to hear that her husband was back in safe hands, but she didn't know the worst of it: He had a broken neck.

Snyder finally got a call through to Thelma at home. She was over-joyed to hear his voice, but dismayed when he told her about his neck injury. If there was any good news, it was that it would get him home from the war alive. He was likely to heal completely, but it would be a long time before he could fly again.

When New Year's Day finally arrived, Misty was ready. The thrust of the big attack would be on trucks streaming toward the DMZ on Route 1, the principal north-south road in North Vietnam. The patch-work highway began in Hanoi and ran parallel to the coast for about 150 miles before veering off to the west and hugging the base of the karst mountains near Vietnam's border with Laos for seventy-five miles, then turning back down the coast north of Dong Hoi. Fighters at several bases had been fragged for strikes along this portion of the Trail, and several extra F-100s had even been deployed to Phu Cat for the occasion, ready to chip in.

Misty flew all day long, with the usual four sorties. Traffic along the Trail was thick, just as it had been under the protective umbrella of the Christmas truce. This time, however, the NVA was going to get clob-bered once the bell tolled signaling the end of the holiday. And then, al-most as if on orders from the North Vietnamese high command, a fog bank rolled in from the sea shortly before the truce was scheduled to end. It settled over Route Pack 1 like a fluffy blanket, protecting every-thing huddled beneath. Don Jones and Hog Piner, flying the last Misty sortie of the day, didn't even bother to call for fighters. There was no way they'd be able drop bombs through the overcast. The elements, once again, had sided with the bad guys.

Jim Mack may have been the only Misty who wasn't choking on frustration at the bad luck. In fact, as he returned from his week of R&R in Australia, Mack was practically oblivious to the entire war. It had been seven days of irreverent escapism a world apart from the dreary life at Phu Cat, just the refreshment he needed. There had been such an abundance of music, dancing, free meals, and liquor that it all started to blur into one weeklong fiesta. The usual tourist stuff in Sydney provided an occasional break from the revelry, but there always seemed to be another party right around the corner. Mack had especially enjoyed the GI Auction, where he had fetched a high price when he was "sold" to the highest-bidding women watching the show in a hotel ballroom.

There had been one final fete the night before he left. Mack boarded the plane straight from the last party and promptly passed out. Shortly after the plane had taken off from Sydney, D. K. Johnson, an old upperclassman friend from the Air Force Academy, shook Mack awake. "Hey, aren't you from Ohio?" Johnson asked.

"What?"

"Aren't you from Ohio?"

"Deke, you asshole," Mack sneered, his head spinning. "You woke me up to ask if I'm from Ohio?"

"Look," Johnson said. "There's a dynamite stewardess up front, nice hooters, who says she's also from Ohio."

"Yeah right," Mack groaned, dropping back into his foggy stupor. It seemed like only a minute later when somebody was waking him up once more.

"What? You shithead, leave me alone!" Mack roared. He wiped at his bloodshot eyes and looked up at a surprising vision. It wasn't his buddy Deke leaning over him this time, but a ravishing platinum blonde in a Pan Am uniform. Her name was Penny, and she was from Akron, Ohio. Mack concentrated as hard as he could on her story. She had grown up in the Indonesian provinces of Java and Sumatra, speaking Indonesian and Dutch. Her father worked for Goodyear Tire Company. Later the family moved back to Ohio. She had become a stewardess—a "stew"—who regularly flew the Vietnam and Australia runs, ferrying GIs back and forth between the war and R&R.

"I hear you're from Ohio?" Penny laughed.

"Yeah," Mack grunted.

"When are you going home?"

"Soon," replied Mack. His one-year Vietnam tour was due to end in a couple of months, and he'd be leaving Misty for good. "Would you like to get married?" he teased. Penny laughed again. "Okay, then how about a phone number?" he asked. She smiled but bounced away without offering it. Mack stared at her lovely back, figuring he'd have a chance to talk to her some more after he got some more sleep and was a little more coherent.

The Pan Am flight landed for refueling in Darwin, Australia. Mack slept right through it. He woke up after takeoff and looked for his newfound love. But it turned out there had been a crew change. She was no longer on the plane. What a letdown, he thought. Then an old pal from pilot training, Bob Parker, stepped out of the cockpit. Bob was now a Pan Am pilot.

They caught up, then Mack asked a favor. "Hey, buddy," he implored his old friend, "you need to help me. I met a blond bombshell of a stew on the last leg. 'Penny' was the name on her name tag. She was based in San Fran. I need you to get me an address and phone number. I'll be going back to the States in about a month and I think she's someone I want to marry."

Mack hardly looked the marrying type. He reeked of liquor, and his breath smelled like the bottom of a birdcage. Parker chuckled but promised to try.

Mack said a quick good-bye when the jet landed at Cam Ranh Bay, and reminded Parker to send him Penny's address. The more sober he got, the more stunning she became in his mind.

About two weeks later at Phu Cat, Mack received a terse letter from Bob Parker. It read:

> Penny Boyle
> 646 Corbett St, SFO
>
> You owe me a beer, asshole.
>
> Love,
> Bob

Mack sat down and mailed Penny a note asking her for a date in San Francisco on March 1, when he expected to be passing through on his way back home. If he made it till then.

TWELVE

I HAVE A MISTRESS

Young Army enlisted men rarely enjoyed the privileges of officers, but for once Roger Williams was getting a bit of VIP treatment. Williams was a records clerk at U.S. military headquarters in Saigon, a REMF, or "rear-echelon motherfucker" to the troops living and bleeding out in the field. But Williams hadn't chosen soft duty. Six months earlier he had been serving out his tour with the Army as an infantryman in South Korea, when he decided to volunteer for Vietnam. When he got there, the Army realized he had some useful skills—he could read and write, for one thing, and knew how to run a small office—so they assigned him to a headquarters job handling personnel records. He carried a weapon to work, but in three months of duty he had never fired it.

Roger's older brother Howard was a fighter pilot with the 416th Tactical Fighter Squadron, which flew ground support missions in the south out of Phu Cat, where Misty was based. Roger was eight years younger than his fighter-jock brother, who was the oldest of eight Williams siblings. Like most of his brothers and sisters, Roger idolized Howard. Roger had been nine years old when Howard left for the Air Force, and every time his brother came home it was like Christmas—the excitement overwhelmed all the kids. Mrs. Williams had practically built Howard into a legend, telling all the other kids how he had gotten his first paper route when he was seven and never asked for a dime for clothes or candy or anything else from the time he was nine. He paid for his own expenses by working at the local hardware store, buying a tractor and cutting all the grass in town, even playing trumpet in a polka band to earn extra cash when he was in high school.

Roger had followed Howard into the military, enlisting in the Army out of high school in 1965. He took the test for officer candidate school, but Howard talked him out of following through—with Vietnam heating up, it didn't seem like a good time to be a junior officer in the Army, leading an infantry platoon. Still, Howard couldn't completely control his little brother. Since Howard was being assigned to Vietnam, Roger could easily have avoided the war—Pentagon policy stated that no more than one member of any given family would be forced to serve in a war zone. But Roger hoped that if he went to Vietnam, his brother would invoke the escape clause and serve someplace where it was safer. He didn't. So Roger had arrived in Vietnam about a month before his brother, and when Howard first got to Saigon and was processed through Tan Son Nhut, he stayed with Roger. It made the enlisted man as proud as a new father to host his fighter-pilot brother.

They had written lots of letters to each other and talked on the phone occasionally, and Howard had invited Roger up to Phu Cat for New Year's Eve. Howard knew the ropes by then and had given his brother precise instructions on how to hop rides on various aircraft. First, Roger found some transport pilots at Tan Son Nhut who let him fly up to Da Nang in the cockpit of their C-130, which was delivering a bellyful of aircraft engines. They arrived around daybreak. Then Roger, following his brother's itinerary, went to the operations hut for the O-1 FACs who flew out of Da Nang and asked if they could help him get to Phu Cat. At first they blew him off and told him not to bother them. Then Staff Sergeant Williams said he was on his way to visit his brother, Captain Williams, at the 416th. The FACs perked up. Which Williams, they wanted to know, as they ticked off nicknames for three of them: H. Willy, B. Willy, or C. Willy? H. Willy, Roger figured. Their demeanor suddenly changed. "He's always taken care of us," one of the FACs said. They huddled to figure out a plan. Roger was handed off a couple times from one pilot to another, and finally they put him in the backseat of one of their O-1 Bird Dog prop planes. The fragile little aircraft flew so low, tracking a road through the jungle, that Roger thought they must have looked awfully tempting to any Viet Cong below. The only weapons they had were two smoke rockets, a .38-caliber pistol, and an M-16 rifle.

As they got close to Phu Cat, the pilot called in to the tower air traffic controllers and transmitted a "VIP code," indicating that a senior officer was on board. That brought a van racing out to the runway to meet the plane. Roger was escorted to the Phu Cat officers club, where his brother Howard introduced him to the wing commander, the base commander, and several of his fellow pilots. Roger swelled with pride—heady stuff for an enlisted guy. He noticed that over dinner, the motormouthed fighter pilots who jabbered continually tended to pipe down when Howard had something to say. They seemed to defer to his brother with special respect. Those courtesies extended to Roger, who was favored at Phu Cat for another reason, too: The O club was well stocked with liquor but was always short of mixers, and Roger, with a finger or two on the supply pipeline down in Saigon, would regularly ship boxes of fruit juice and soft drinks up to Phu Cat.

There were no fancy plans for the visit. The brothers spent a lot of time hanging out in Howard's air-conditioned room in a wooden barracks, which he shared with Carl Jefcoat, another pilot in the 416th. The two aviators had scattered a few pictures of their families around, but otherwise it was pretty spartan. The only real items of interest were the two huge alarm clocks Howard kept right near the head of his bed, six inches from his ears while he slept. Howard was a profound sleeper who had trouble waking up, and sometimes he needed the added encouragement of an extra alarm.

There was also a table in the room that held a big TEAC reel-to-reel tape recorder. In addition to sending frequent letters, Howard exchanged tapes with Roger and with his wife, Monalee, and son, Howard Jr., back in Columbus, Ohio, a popular way to communicate for troops who could get a recorder. Howard had also picked up a guitar in Vietnam and liked to blow off steam by recording himself playing the repertoire of hundreds of songs he had learned.

Like other things he set his mind to, Howard had become proficient on the guitar. Even though he had taught himself how to play, his fingers skimmed over the strings with the ease of a professional. He changed keys seamlessly and rarely botched a chord or forgot a line. Howard was a baritone, but he sang with the delicacy of a nanny cooing a lullaby to a baby. Other pilots often stopped by for his impromptu performances, which offered a strange kind of comfort—like the special taste of cookies or other treats sent over by a wife or mother back home.

Howard's playing, in fact, was one of the few things that could get fighter pilots to shut their yappers. Sometimes they sang along, but Howard usually had a much better voice, and inevitably he'd end up entertaining the crowd. He sang a lot of ballads and had an ethereal quality to his voice that would often leave his guests silent when he finished a song.

With Roger there, the two brothers crooned a few tunes together, the TEAC recorder running the whole time. Brian Williams—the "B. Willy" whom the FACs at Da Nang had been referring to—was another pilot with the 416th, and he stopped by. Jefcoat was away on R&R, and they got a good jam session going, with all three of them singing along on songs like "Puff the Magic Dragon" and "Leaving on a Jet Plane." But Howard got the floor to himself when he started picking "Blowin' in the Wind." In a voice that was strong yet soft, he sang words that had already silenced thousands of listeners: "Yes, and how many deaths must there be till they know / That too many people have died?" There was no clapping when he finished, no commentary, no fighter-pilot irreverence—just quiet, as the three men spent a few seconds thinking of better things.

Howie and Roger also talked. Their mom back in Steubenville, needless to say, was rather concerned about having two sons away in a war zone, and she wrote letters to both of them with worry so tangible that it practically jumped off the pages and paced around the room. Howard called worry "nonproductive thought circles," but as the oldest child he also had a protective instinct and in his own letters home tried to make his job sound as routine as possible.

But Howard wasn't as blasé about risk as some of the other fighter jocks, the ones who cultivated a façade of fearlessness. He knew the dangers of his job and admitted it when he felt scared. He told Roger about one mission he had flown in the South as wingman for another pilot. As the two planes were returning and descending for a practice formation landing, the lead pilot drifted too far onto Howie's side of the runway. Howie, who was behind him, suddenly encountered turbulence from the lead aircraft. His wing dropped and scraped the pavement. Howard managed to muscle the jet under control and come to a stop without wrecking the airplane, which brought congratulations from other pilots who had watched the recovery—especially since the plane belonged to one of the wing's senior officers. But the incident shook Howard. "It scared the crap out of me," he told his brother.

Howard also recounted the gripping and awful story of Lance Sijan, the pilot who had been shot down over North Vietnam and survived for two days, only to be lost when the rescue aircraft were unable to penetrate relentless North Vietnamese ground fire to pull him out. Howard had not been involved in the rescue attempt, but he knew some of the pilots who had, and besides, by this time the story of Sijan was a legendary—and cautionary—tale. "They left that poor bastard in there," Howard told Roger heavily, as if he had been personally responsible for Sijan's capture.

As a grunt—albeit one based in the rear—Roger recognized his brother's pang as the weight carried by those who went on to live freely while their comrades died or suffered. And he realized that his brother worried more about leaving a colleague behind than meeting that fate himself. It was a subject that two brothers, two warriors, could talk about without really having to say much, but that would be pointless to try to explain to any of their family or friends back home.

The risks, at any rate, were obviously worthwhile to Howard, worth the distance from his wife and six-year-old son, and even worth the possibility that he might not come home. Unlike some of the pilots who derided the "monkey bombing" missions in the South, Howard felt committed, devout even, about doing anything he could to help the boys fighting on the ground. His kid brother was a grunt, for one thing, and for the moment was simply lucky not to be out in the bush fighting for his survival. But someday it might be Roger he was trying to save out there. Howard didn't say so, but he ran an occasional nonproductive thought circle himself, especially when it came to Roger.

Doing everything he could for the guys in the field was a surrogate way of protecting his little brother. Beyond that, it just seemed to be a matter of duty and decency to hang it out for the grunts. "I have it easy," he'd say, gesturing to the air conditioner fighting off the sticky Vietnamese air. "Those guys have it bad."

Howard described the tedious difficulty of the "close work," the close air support or CAS missions for the Army that would often leave him drained after just an hour or so in the cockpit. When friendly troops were entangled with the Viet Cong in a hand-to-hand infantry battle—which happened more and more frequently as the VC tried to "hug" their enemy, to negate the value of American airpower and artillery—it was excruciatingly difficult to drop bombs on the bad guys while sparing the friendlies. Howard would work intently with the O-1 FACs who'd control the strikes, who in turn took their guidance from fire controllers on the ground with the grunts. Sometimes they'd call for strikes within fifty feet of the friendly positions. Pinpoint accuracy was crucial, or the strikes could backfire, killing Americans.

Howard took great pride in the care he put into this work. In a letter he had written just before Christmas to his old flying buddy back in Steubenville, John Buckmelter, Howie described the difficulty of his latest mission, and the satisfaction it brought him. "This last sortie was a good one," he wrote, "better than anything for a week. Friendlies surrounded by two companies of NVA (North Viet regulars) within 150 meters. That's a challenge. . . . I flew a 2 hr. mission landed with minimum fuel and killed many NVA and it is now many Johnny Walkers later. . . . I saved many lives tonight!!! And for that reason (rationalization), I also enjoy killing VC. My kid brother is in Saigon (Sp. 5 in the Army) and he and his fellow 'grunts' are worth it."

Howard was anything but bloodthirsty, however, and he puzzled over the strange sense of fulfillment he gained from war. "Tiger," he continued in the letter, in writing that had become progressively illegible as the Johnny Walkers kicked in, "I've been trying to evaluate myself (as always). A Chicken Col. at Luke with WWII and Korea experience in fighters pulled me aside and said, 'Willy, you'll really enjoy combat.' I don't remember what I said, but thought, 'He's got to be s——— me.' He was right! I miss my lover and my son, but I have

Howard Williams with his wife Monalee and son Howard, Jr., in 1967, shortly before he left for Vietnam.

Maj. George "Bud" Day, who formed Commando Sabre and was its first commander. Day was shot down on August 26, 1967, and held as a prisoner of war for five and a half years. He was awarded the Medal of Honor for his resistance and courage.

Phu Cat air base, about two hundred miles northeast of Saigon, looking east toward the Gulf of Tonkin and the South China Sea. Construction vehicles constantly churned the red dirt into dust that permeated barracks and offices.

Col. Ray Lee, vice commander of the 37th Tactical Fighter Wing, Misty's parent unit. Unlike other wing officials, Lee flew missions over North Vietnam with the Mistys.

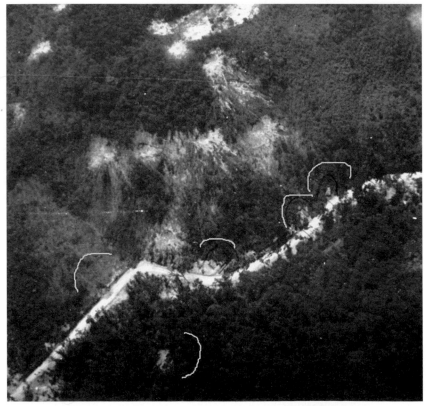

It took trained eyes to spot targets traversing the Ho Chi Minh Trail—such as the camouflaged trucks bracketed in this photo, from the fall of 1967.

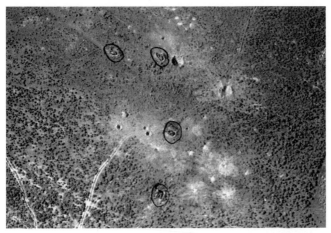

Four 14.5mm ZPU antiaircraft guns lodged in sandbagged revetments protect the Trail southeast of Tchepone, in Laos.

The spidery Trail network had an endless number of offshoots, and was often blanketed by clouds.

A Misty F-100F gulps gas from a KC-135 tanker over the Gulf of Tonkin. The Mistys typically refueled two or three times on missions that could last four hours or more.

P. J. White (right), who replaced Bud Day as Misty commander, and Jim Mack on the Phu Cat F-100 parking ramp, in early December 1967.

The troops pose for a picture while relaxing over a beer in Misty Ops in December 1967. Top row: John Haltigan, Hog Piner, Jim Fiorelli, P. J. White, Bob Craner, Jere Wallace, Ed Risinger, Cal Kunz. Bottom row: Roger Van Dyken, Charlie Neel, Mick Greene, Guy Gruters, Jim Mack, Jonesy Jones.

TOP: The Phu Cat Officer's Club, where some of the Mistys could be found virtually every night. RIGHT: John Haltigan snapped this picture of Bob Hope and Raquel Welch, on stage at Phu Cat during the Christmas Day show, 1967.

During Misty's early days, it was usually hard to find vehicles on the Trail during daytime. One exception: The 1967 Christmas "truce," when North Vietnamese trucks, spared American bombs, lined up bumper-to-bumper on their way south.

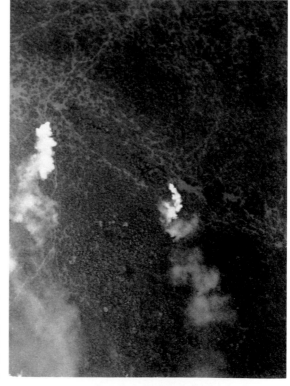

"Hit my smoke." Antiaircraft guns "marked" with white phosphorous ("Willie Pete") smoke rockets.

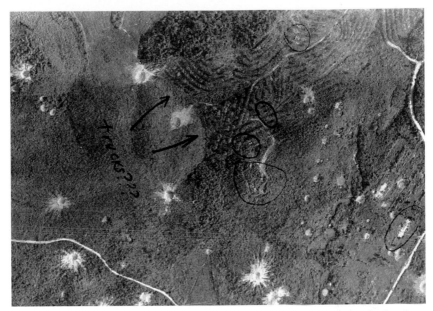

Vehicles may be camouflaged beneath trees in an area known as the Orchards, a few miles north of the demilitarized zone. One giveaway: The road in the upper right-hand corner of the picture abruptly ends.

Got one! A truck hulk next to the crater produced by the bomb that destroyed it, early 1968.

Don Jones, the third Misty commander, standing next to his F-100 after a mission with Jonesy Jones. A shell from a 37mm antiaircraft gun tore a hole in the right wing, which forced them to make an emergency landing at Ubon, Thailand.

Partially camouflaged railroad cars on a siding up the Ron River Valley, toward Mu Ghia Pass.

Railroad cars being struck by 750-pound bombs. This is a "shack," close enough to the smoke to qualify as a direct hit.

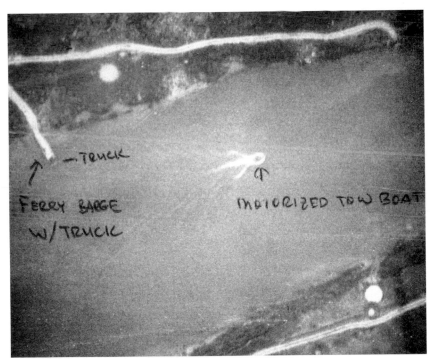

With most bridges blown up, the North Vietnamese used ferries that they usually hid during the day and took out at night. This is an unusual daytime sighting of a ferry in action, from the spring of 1968.

Another North Vietnamese logistical trick was to construct bridges just beneath the surface of the water, such as this one crossing a stream in Laos south of Mu Ghia Pass.

Trucks discovered by Lanny Lancaster and Don Shepperd north of Mu Ghia Pass during a break in bad weather, March 1968. The attacks that followed destroyed at least sixty vehicles, one of the Misty's biggest successes till then.

Charlie Summers, left, known for having the best eyes in Misty, with Roger Van Dyken.

Capt. Ed Risinger standing by a hole produced by a 14.5mm ZPU round that hit his F-100 just behind the storage compartment for the 20mm cannon rounds.

The Mistys in March 1968. Front row: P. K. Robinson, Don Jones, Jonesy Jones, Mick Greene, Howard "H. Willy" Williams (sitting), Lanny Lancaster, Elmer Slavey, Brian "B. Willy" Williams. Back row: Don Shepperd, Jim Fiorelli, Ed Risinger, Charlie "Whispering" Smith, Dick Rutan, Carroll "C. Willy" Williams, Hog Piner, Charlie Summers.

Misty commander Don Jones, left, shares a farewell glass of champagne after Brian Williams's last flight, late March 1968, one month after Brian and Howie Williams were shot down.

Jonesy Jones and Col. Ed Schneider, the wing commander who caused Misty much grief by reining in their tactics—and trying to keep the pilots alive.

Dr. Dean Echenberg, the Misty flight surgeon, after his back-seat ride over North Vietnam with Lanny Lancaster. A few days later, flight surgeons were banned from flying over the North, after one was shot down.

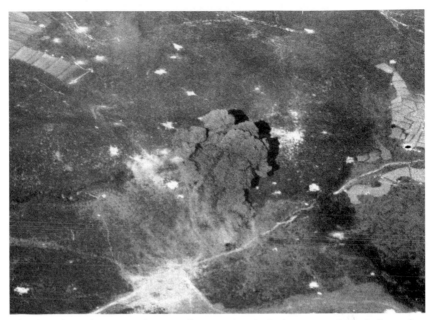

This is a direct hit on an SA-2 surface-to-air missile just west of Bat Lake, a few miles above the DMZ. Moments later the same pilot, call sign Master 01, was shot down while going after another target.

A storage tunnel at the base of Mu Ghia Pass, where the road drops down from North Vietnam into Laos. There were hundreds of such hideouts in the karst that ran along the western half of North Vietnam.

P. K. Robinson, left, and Stanley Mamlock, the fourth Misty commander, inspect a AAA hole in their plane's engine intake.

Charlie Summers, left, enjoys champagne after his last flight. Mike McElhanon flew in his back seat.

Bud Bacon, the fifth Misty commander. He ran the unit during the intense summer of 1968—Misty's most productive and dangerous period.

From left to right: P. K. Robinson, Chuck Shaheen, and John Overlock at a going-away party in August 1968. They're wearing the "party suits" that Shaheen picked up on a junket to Hong Kong. The day after the party, Overlock was shot down with Mike McElhanon. Both disappeared. Shaheen was shot down the day after that with Dick Rutan. Both were rescued.

P. K. Robinson, left, swigs champagne after his last Misty flight. Dick Rutan, who had been shot down and rescued from the ocean the previous day, looks on.

The "Disappearing River" cave, which the Mistys couldn't destroy. This photo was taken in April 2000, when six of the Misty pilots returned to Vietnam. The cliff atop the cave opening still bears scars from bombs that didn't quite make it in.

a mistress—it's called an F-100! Makes me wonder if I'm a case for the couch, but I really feel that it's true."

Like many of the pilots in Vietnam, life for Howie revolved around flying. The rest of the time he spent trying to dull the pain of being away from home. In his tapes and letters he yearned for his woman, like just about all the other troops thrust into the misery of prolonged combat. "I love you darling," he wrote in early January. "As you can see I've lost my fervor again. It happens occasionally. You and that boy are all that matter. Three cheers for us!" A week later the pangs were greater yet. "It's 11:15 now," he wrote one morning, "and I could use a nooner or sooner. Can you make it? I WOULD like to kiss your soft body and love you and love you ad infinitum. . . . God bless you my Darling & my handsome son."

Monalee's burden may have been even heavier as she struggled to comprehend the surreal and dangerous world her husband was living in. Howard had expected some R&R leave in April, and they were planning to meet in Hawaii, the first time they would have seen each other in eight months. Monalee hung her hopes on every detail of the trip, and agonized when there was no word. "Honey, I know you are busy and I am not mad or anything like that," she fretted in one letter, "but this is the longest time without mail—five days. . . . I must admit I am a little uneasy because you have been so great about letters and tapes." She wasn't as ribald as her husband, but Monalee's desires were tangible, too: "You know I love you so much and need you so— more and more. I feel that need. Love, love, and more love—good night honey." As she always did, Monalee ended her letter with a plea: "God keep you safe for us, Monalee & Howard."

Howie's morale revolved around the flying. His mood would be up when the missions were plentiful, and down when weather or other factors kept him grounded. "Flew today!" he had written in early December. "Tis a much better day for all of it." Unlike the Mistys, however, which ran four long scheduled missions per day, with two or three midair refuelings, the 416th flew many shorter missions, mostly in South Vietnam.

Each CAS squadron had pilots on alert around the clock, but sometimes there was nothing to do and the pilots just hung around the "alert pad," right off the tarmac. "On day alert," Howie had written to Monalee on December 13, "and have had only one sortie (#48). Haven't flown for two days (till today). Gets boring fast when not flying. I do need this flying badly to keep the spirits up." Then his letter got interrupted: There was a scramble and he had to rush out to the flight line for a mission. "It was a good one!!" he continued, after returning. "I saved lives tonight. Friendlies were surrounded, but no more. Worked in the dark with no flares and put the stuff exactly on target. That's a morale boost, honey. . . . Love you."

In mid-December, wing officials asked Howie if he would volunteer for a staff job in one of the command posts, or at TACC, the Tactical Air Control Center in Saigon. He said no, even though that would obviously be safer and perhaps give his career a boost. "Could be bad honey if I'm stashed away in a CP," he explained to Monalee. "My spirits do soar when I fly so let me fly."

Howie was a talented aviator—he had been Top Gun during F-100 training at Luke—and he monitored the development of his own skills with enthused detachment more akin to that of a teacher than a student. "My bombs have been excellent, not outstanding as yet, but that's coming," he had written Monalee. Yet he wasn't above a little stroking. After one mission he described the compliments he had earned, after pickling his two bombs, from the FACs who had directed the strike. "The FAC said, 'Beautiful 2,' 'Nice 2,' 'Outstanding 2.' This is not uncommon any more." Howie had also caught the attention of one of the more senior FACs: "I flew a mission directed by Joe Madden (Lt. Col.) the other day. I talked to him on radio and he said 'nice bombs Howie,' 'good shot Howie.' "

As Roger Williams listened to his brother's stories, he understood the diligence Howie put into his work. Roger figured that the FACs at Da Nang were so fond of "H. Willy" because he worked hard to do a tough job right, and in the process made their jobs easier. Even then, Howard fretted over the danger to the troops on the ground. "Sometimes the strikes are so close," he told Roger, "I can't imagine how they could survive."

There was a New Year's truce scheduled in the South, just as in the North, but Howie closed out 1967 with three sorties—one just before the truce went into effect. "There is no way of checking," he wrote to

Monalee the next day, "but I think that I dropped the last Cong killing bombs in 1967. Maj. Follis and I scrambled 20 minutes before the truce started (6 p.m. truce) yesterday. A FAC had been fired at just 8 miles west of Pleiku. We flew to the area found the target at 5:55 and salvoed two bombs, had two minutes left so we made two strafe runs. Would you believe at 1800 Guard Channel comes on and says 'Cease fire.' We did silence the fire and got 5 confirmed KBA [killed by air]. Happy New Year Charlie."

After Howard returned from his December 31 mission, he and Roger went to the New Year's Eve party the 416th was throwing at its squadron building, which went much like hundreds of other make-do parties across Vietnam that night. In place of real women there were dirty movies, and with nobody to impress with their gallant behavior, the pilots drank everything in sight and flung lewd remarks at the unresponsive actresses flickering on the wall. Roger got a glimpse of the other "Willys," Brian and Carroll, with their guard down—they were as rowdy as any of the grunts he had known. At midnight a couple of the more boisterous pilots went outside and fired their pen gun flares into the air, a ritual the security police promptly halted because flares were a signal the base was under attack. At some point Howie told Roger about the mission and his cynical greeting to the Viet Cong. "I can't believe you're killing people and saying 'Happy New Year, Charlie,' " Roger noted.

Howie thought for a moment. "I can't, either," he answered. "But I do."

Not surprisingly, most of the pilots were more subdued than usual the next day. Howard was on alert status—he had to be ready to hop into one of the planes if a call for close air support came in—and Roger hung out in the alert shack with him. All was quiet until there was an urgent request to scramble a couple of jets. Howard leaped into the van heading out to the flight line and Roger joined him. He shadowed his brother while he got a quick briefing en route to the jet and climbed into the Hun. Then Howard took off and Roger went back to the alert shack to wait out the mission. The pilots usually returned in an hour or two.

Howard was back much sooner than that. The strike had been called on a target that was barely off the end of the Phu Cat runway, and Howard had flown around for fifteen minutes before dropping a couple of bombs into the jungle shadows. A quick reconnaissance of the area revealed they had blown up a storehouse of clothing—but there were no signs of enemy troops, or even human beings for that matter. Howard was disgusted. "I guess we hit a Vietnamese laundromat," he scowled, complaining about wasting $10,000 or $20,000 worth of fuel only to produce "smoliage."

Roger Williams returned to Saigon much the way he had come, via the unofficial pilots' network. Howard continued to focus on his job and the mission, to keep all of the other doubts and hardships at bay. But sometimes they were unavoidable. "I strongly disagree with these truces," he complained to Monalee in his New Year's Day letter. The next day he was still pondering the vagaries of the war: "I seldom understand the war effort here. The flying sometimes allows me to forget stupid truces, graft, and medals for Colonels."

In fact, for the thousands of tons of U.S. bombs dropped during the war in 1967, it was the communists—not the Americans—who were most effectively intensifying the pain on their enemy. The death toll in 1967 had been 9,378 Americans killed in combat in Vietnam, more than all prior years combined. Another 56,013 had been wounded.[1] The jets flown by Bud Day and Kipp Kippenhan and Charlie Neel and Guy Gruters and Bob Craner, and, remarkably, Guy Gruters again were only three of 328 fixed-wing U.S. airplanes shot down over North and South Vietnam in 1967. In dollar terms the war had cost an astounding $21 billion that year, forcing President Johnson to ask for a 10 percent surcharge on federal income taxes. The proposal jolted public opinion. Shortly after Johnson floated the idea, polls for the first time showed that more Americans thought the war was a mistake than thought it was not.[2]

Still, there were plenty of optimists, both military and civilian, who insisted that if only the military pressure on the North were increased by some margin, the communists would surely collapse. The Joint Chiefs continued to argue that intensifying the bombing and expanding the ground war would quickly grind down North Vietnam and bring the war to a tidy end.[3] Admiral Sharp, commander in chief of Pacific Command, ticked off a host of successes in his 1967 year-end report to Congress, with a degree of precision that anybody flying combat missions would have pegged as a red flag.

The bombing of infrastructure targets in the North, Sharp claimed, had cut the country's ability to produce electric power by 85 percent. Economic losses in the North totaled more than $130 million. Strikes along the Trail and other transportation nodes had destroyed 5,261 motor vehicles, 2,475 railcars, and 11,425 watercraft, an amazing level of detail that good pilots would have scoffed at, since they knew how some targets were double- and triple-counted when pilots submitted their bomb damage assessments. Some vehicles were "destroyed" three or four times as pilots dropped bombs on truck carcasses that had simply been left alongside the road. Often it was impossible to ascertain the effect of bombing, with bombs pickled from 6,000 feet or higher. At best, BDA was a shoddy guess. Sharp himself seemed to hint at the incongruity when he acknowledged that rapid repair or replacement of destroyed items had left transport inventories roughly unchanged for the year. But not to worry, he assured Washington: Overall the bombing had diverted more than half a million people from other jobs to simply repairing and maintaining the damage done by American warplanes. "The cost and difficulties of the war to Hanoi have sharply increased," he wrote, "and only through the willingness of other communist countries to provide maximum replacement of goods and matériel has NVN managed to sustain its war effort."[4]

Despite Sharp's optimism, the trucks kept coming down the Trail, the troops kept flooding into the South, the battles kept getting bigger, and the grip on the South kept getting shakier. "What a farce this war," Howard Williams wrote to Monalee in early January The ink in his pen was running out, and in a wry moment Howie scratched his frustration onto the paper. "The war is about like my pen," he wrote as his handwriting disappeared.

THIRTEEN

McNAMARA'S FENCE

By the time Don Jones took over Misty, the unit was maturing into a smooth-running operation. In place of the frantic, go-go, hair-on-fire atmosphere of the first few months, a routine was taking hold. Misty finally had enough intel officers, three, to fully prepare the pilots for missions and process all the incoming data. More two-seat F-100Fs were arriving at Phu Cat, and for once the Mistys didn't have to beg for aircraft. KC-135 tankers were available and reliable. The pilots themselves had begun to institutionalize some of the tactics. There was a sensible rotation policy so that everyone didn't leave at once. Even the quarters had become sturdier and semipermanent. Their plywood barracks had been replaced by private two-man trailers that included showers and air-conditioning—luxury living, by wartime standards, that added to Misty's reputation elsewhere in the wing as a haven for prima donnas.

Though small, Misty was becoming a sophisticated unit. The pilots had figured out that much of the intel that came up from 7th Air Force was stale. Reconnaissance photos and other info gathered by the RF-101s and RF-4s that 7th sent streaking over the main roads in North Vietnam took two to three days to make it into the daily "frag" order calling for air strikes on the targets. Photos from the high-flying U-2s, which circled as high as 70,000 feet and were still extremely secret, took even longer. Sometimes Misty could glean the location of truck parks or storage depots from the reconnaissance photos. But a lot of the material was history, describing where NVA troops had been, not where they were at the moment. It was a predicament as old as warfare itself: Misty lacked credible, timely intel.

In fact, for a war that tapped virtually every intelligence resource the United States commanded, there was remarkably little teamwork. The CIA received invaluable "Spotlight" reports—live sightings of NVA activity by Montagnard natives sitting on hilltops overlooking the Mu Ghia Pass and other key transit areas. And there were whispers about new electronic sensors said to provide remarkable intelligence. But Misty rarely got any such information. The unit never even communicated with the Navy, which was assigned Route Pack 2, immediately north of Misty's turf. The best information available was "continuity intel"—a database of Misty's own intelligence, constantly tracked, updated, and checked against whatever other sources were available.

The tiny intel shop, in fact, was beginning to resemble a command center for a much larger organization—or maybe even a small laboratory. Since the beginning, the Misty pilots had worked from a set of maps carried by the "guy in back"—the GIB—and the package had become consistently more user-friendly. By December, several of the pilots and the three intel officers had come up with the idea of compiling all the maps into a laminated chart book that covered all of Route Pack 1, bound so that the GIBs could flip through them easily. The slick surface would allow pilots to write on the maps with grease pencil, then erase their markings when they were finished. That way, they could plot fresh targets on their maps during the intel briefing before each mission, and make notations on the same maps when they were over the Pack and noticed new details down below. That would make it easier to document new intelligence and pass it on to the next Misty mission.

Problem was, the Misty cupboard was bare. The Air Force didn't produce chart books like this, and there were no materials handy for making them. So the intel shop started scrounging. The maps were easy enough to come by, but finding a way to laminate them was an-

other matter. The intel officers gave it some thought and started thinking about the clear film that went into the big canisters for the camera
apparatus on the RF-101s. Could they get some of that film and cut it
to suit their purposes? Roger Van Dyken called a couple of his buddies
from intel school who had been shipped over to Vietnam and were
working in the intel shop at 7th Air Force. Sure, they could supply
some film, and it sounded like it would work just fine. But everybody
agreed that filling out a requisition and going through regular supply
channels would raise too many questions and get held up forever as
sergeants and majors with little else to do tried to figure out what was
going on. It would be much easier if Van Dyken simply flew down to
Saigon, took what he needed, and brought it back to Phu Cat himself.

Van Dyken went to base operations with a new intel officer, Lt. Cal
Kunz, to see about catching a ride on one of the frequent transports
down to Saigon. No sweat, the officer at base operations told them—
as long as you have a VOCO. "What's that?" Van Dyken asked.

"Verbal orders of the commanding officer," the attendant explained.

"By telephone?" Van Dyken answered.

"No, just a handwritten note signed by the commander."

"THE commander?"

"No, any commander." So the two lieutenants stepped around the
corner, wrote each other notes ordering themselves to Tan Son Nhut
Air Base in Saigon, and signed their names to the "orders." They
handed them to the clerk and were on the next flight to Saigon—
beneficiaries of bureaucracy run amok.

In Saigon they picked up several big rolls of clear film and some
other supplies Misty badly needed. After Van Dyken briefly caught up
with his intel pals, the two got on a plane back to Phu Cat, where the
intel shop started up the Air Force equivalent of a high school art project. They adjusted the size of the maps to fit the width of the film, got
out some Scotch tape, and began to assemble the chart books. They
worked the maps into a set that covered all of the Pack, from the DMZ
in the south to the edge of Route Pack Two, which was the Navy's area
of responsibility, and also "Steel Tiger," a separate area of operations
in Laos that was contiguous with Route Pack 1. They bound each
package in a cardboard cover. The intel shop hand-produced about a
dozen of the little masterpieces, enough for the eight pilots who flew in

four airplanes on a typical day, plus a few spares for the pilots back at the base to study. The extras would also be used to replace maps that went up in smoke during the inevitable aircraft losses.

The new map books pushed Misty's effectiveness up another notch. When the pilots spotted a target, they'd plot it as precisely as possible in their map books. During debriefings, they'd be able to say exactly where the target had been. That didn't necessarily help other pilots attack the target, but it greatly improved the ability to track important intelligence information and make better guesses about where NVA equipment and supplies were located. It became easier for the intel officers to designate areas of highest interest and narrow the areas for pilots to search. And more accurate plotting of antiaircraft defenses helped all pilots in the North fly more safely.

But there were still a few gaps in the intel operation. When the Mistys would come back with 35mm black-and-white photos of targets, it was sometimes hard to figure out exactly where the targets had been. The photos were usually clear enough—and occasionally spectacular—but matching the features in the photographs to the broader outlines of a map was often a guessing game. And while the pilots may have made notations on their chart books, a circle on a map didn't necessarily reveal what ridgeline a gun was mounted on, or what stand of trees may have been hiding a fleet of trucks. Misty needed more accuracy.

So the intel shop went back to the drawing board. If they could supplement their collection of maps with a montage of reconnaissance photos—in fact, if they could re-create all the key parts of Route Pack 1 and Steel Tiger in picture form—they'd have a far better tool for targeting. In debriefings, the pilots would be able to locate their targets on a photo, rather than a map, looking at essentially the same picture they had just seen from the cockpit. They'd be able to highlight reference points and terrain features that would make it easier to find the targets they had just scouted. That in turn would make it easier for the next set of pilots. There would be more guideposts helping them find something they may never have seen before, meaning they'd spend less time attracting lead over hot areas, getting their bearings.

It was a great-sounding idea. But was it possible to create such a photo montage? After all, Route Pack 1 encompassed about four thousand square miles of terrain. There wasn't enough space on the walls in the intel shop for all the pictures it would take to represent the entire region. Once again Van Dyken plugged into the back-channel second lieutenant network. Getting the pictures was no problem, his buddies in Saigon assured him. Over several years the RF-101s had shot thousands of reconnaissance photos of Route Pack 1, surely enough to patch together an aerial overview. Some of the photos were old, and probably wouldn't show new roads or bridges or other recent construction. They were at various levels of magnification that wouldn't necessarily match up. And as for figuring out how to assemble such a huge collection of pictures—well, that was Misty's problem. But if you want 'em, the helpful junior officers in Saigon said, just let us know and come down and get 'em.

By now, Van Dyken was figuring out the system. He knew not to fill out a formal request for the photos, as that would just attract unwanted attention, so once again he wrote up his own VOCO orders. He promptly returned from Saigon loaded down with half a dozen cardboard boxes full of photos, covering hundreds of square miles.

Now what? The intel shop had the pictures, but it was too cumbersome to go sorting through boxes every time they needed to plot something against the maps. The intel guys and a few of the pilots brainstormed and came up with the idea of mounting the pictures on a series of four-by-eight-foot boards affixed to roller wheels, like a bunch of mobile chalkboards. When they were interested in a certain area, they'd just wheel out the panel containing that part of the montage.

The Mistys were a resourceful lot. The project began to take on the flavor of a scavenger hunt, and the Mistys got competitive about who could come up with the most stuff. Don Sibson, the low-key operations officer, was the chief scrounger. He had been part of the brain trust that hatched the idea of the sliding panels, and now he became the foreman who was going to get the job done. Sibson took Van Dyken around to some of the "Red Horse" construction units that had built Phu Cat from scratch in the middle of the jungle. The civil engineers were notoriously stingy with their supplies, yet Sibson had a technique that Milo Minderbinder, the scheming logistics genius from *Catch-22*, would have been proud of. In a soft-spoken voice as gentle as any in the entire U.S. military, Sibson would meekly introduce himself to the young enlisted men manning the supply shops. "Hey, Airman," he'd begin, as the young troop strained to hear what he was saying. "We've got a little project going on down at Misty."

Then the soft sell would begin. "We're trying to put together a special display for a classified project and we could really use anything you might be able to spare," Sibson would mumble. "Do you think we might be able to steal a few two-by-fours, maybe a little plywood?" When Sibson—a major, after all—treated them like real people, they responded as if he were a general barking orders: "Well sure, Major, I think we may have a few spares lying around. How many were you thinking of?" Sibson was ready. He'd scratch his chin and fumble in his pocket for a moment, and finally produce a long, detailed list of exactly what he wanted.

If that didn't work, Sibson would return with a requisition he had filled saying that the Misty building had been damaged in a mortar attack, which was perfectly plausible in a war zone. When he said he needed the materials for a "self-help" project to repair the damage, the civil engineers would conclude that if they provided the supplies for Misty to do the repair, that was one less job they'd have to do. Within a couple of days Misty had all the materials it needed.

Suddenly the intel shop looked like a handyman's basement, filled with plywood, paint, two-by-fours, wheel rollers, saws, hammers, and other tools. Sibson had done some carpentry work back home in New Hampshire, and he mounted the wood panels on the rollers. Then came the painstaking work of assembling the photos. It took several days, but the intel officers and a few industrious enlisted men who worked in the shop glued every one of the hundreds of photos onto the wood panels, one overlapping the other where the terrain matched up. It took more than a dozen eight-foot panels, laminated on both sides, to accommodate the whole collection. The panels took up so much space that the enlisted guys built a new closet to house them.

The end result was one of the most sophisticated intel tools anywhere in the entire air operation. Not even 7th Air Force or Pacific Command had such an elaborate display. Every significant road or trail was re-created, as if you were floating above it, looking down. The montage let the pilots "walk" up main thoroughfares like Route 1 or 15 or 37 or 101 and examine the many offshoots. When they came back with fresh pictures, they could plot them against the same terrain they had just seen—and update the photomosaics with new information.

Pilots spent hours studying the photos before and after missions. They now had a tool for mentally rehearsing missions beforehand, which saved time, made them safer, and increased kills. The Mistys were finding targets faster and spending less time loitering over danger zones. They killed more targets and made better use of the intelligence they came back with. The intel weenies, it turned out, weren't such weenies after all. They had proven themselves as dedicated and re-sourceful as the best of the Misty pilots.

There was one other important change at Misty, compared to the early months: "Target frustration" was vanishing. Whenever the weather was good, it was a "target-rich" environment in Route Pack 1. In fact, it was a damn good thing Misty's intel was improving: The Americans needed every edge they could get to battle the tidal wave of vehicles streaming down the Trail by early January 1968. It was great shooting for the Mistys, since there had never been so many targets. But the pilots could tell something big was in the air. Down at 7th Air Force, strategists had once again been working on new ways to inter-dict the road traffic flowing down the Trail. This time they had decided to focus more on choke points and to send even more bombers into the already thoroughly ravaged Route Pack 1. More bombs: That would do the trick.

Had anybody asked Jim Mack or Don Sibson or Roger Van Dyken, they would have offered cautionary words. Yes, U.S. aerial tactics were getting more effective, and there were some spectacular successes. But no matter what the statistics said, the waves of matériel coming south were getting bigger and bigger. More was getting through. The same paradox that pertained to the overall war effort held true on the Trail most of all: As the United States added troops and intensified its war-fare, the North Vietnamese only seemed to gain strength. On top of that, the weather was getting worse over Route Pack 1 as the monsoon season picked up. Virtually every time the Mistys got a peek beneath the clouds, vehicles were roaring down the Trail.

The same persistent rain that shut down U.S. aerial missions seemed to have no impact on the NVA's ability to repair the damage inflicted on the Trail network. Misty reconnaissance and other intelligence indicated that Trail workers were rebuilding bridges, fords, roads, and rail lines as quickly as the Americans could take them out. New heavy engineering equipment was appearing every day, including armored bulldozers that would often keep pushing dirt even when fighters were buzzing overhead. The condition of the roads was improving, and the drivers ferrying war goods to the South were getting bolder.[1] Instead of pulling off the road and leaping into the woods when the bombers attacked, sometimes they'd just speed up—producing rumors that the drivers were chained to the steering wheel. The Mistys still helped nail some of them, but often there were no fighters nearby, since the air planners figured bombing missions would get weathered out. All Misty could do—short of violating orders and dipping down to strafe the trucks—was watch in frustration and document the torrent of traffic with their Pentaxes.[2] It was starting to feel like a losing battle.

In early January, Don Jones, Mick Greene, John Haltigan, and Roger Van Dyken quietly boarded a C-47 "Gooneybird" transport plane at Phu Cat and flew over to Nakhon Phanom, the air base in eastern Thailand. NKP, or "Naked Fanny," as it was known in the obligatory shorthand, sat on the western side of the Mekong River, the same river that flowed all the way down to the southern tip of South Vietnam. Up here the Mekong formed the border between Thailand and Laos. NKP was situated about due west of the Vietnamese Demilitarized Zone, less than fifteen minutes' flying time from the western tendrils of the Ho Chi Minh Trail and 250 miles southwest of Hanoi.

But NKP was a world apart from the tumultuous world of Vietnam. The Mistys had gotten more or less comfortable at Phu Cat and considered its modest amenities—air-conditioning, decent food—to be princely entitlements compared to the privations the grunts in the bush endured. NKP, however, was a real wonderland. The construction was new and sturdy, the buildings spacious. Troops based there played softball and other sports on lush green fields. The gyms were as good as any in the States, and the officers club was huge. Buildings were made of material resembling mountain redwood and bordered by white picket fences. Most noticeably to the Mistys, NKP was blissfully quiet. Unlike Phu Cat, the base was safely removed from the war zone.

There were no bombs or mortar or artillery shells thudding in the background, continually disturbing the peace. "It was so American," Roger Van Dyken wrote in his diary, "I felt homesick."

These were curiously lavish facilities for a wartime air base. But then the base hosted curious tenants. NKP was home to the 56th Special Operations Wing, a weird amalgam of helicopters, A-1 Skyraiders, and several World War II–vintage planes used for ambiguous missions in Laos, some prop-driven FAC airplanes such as O-2s and OV-10s, and AC-130 gunships. In addition to U.S. Air Force and Royal Thai Air Force operations, there were a number of "nonmilitary" organizations operating out of NKP, generally believed to be fronts for CIA operations: Air America, Continental Air Services, Air Asia, and Trans Asia. These "airlines" flew in and out with everything from old C-123s and DC-6s to Cessnas, Beechcraft Bonanzas, and Pilatus Porter aircraft—which could take off and land on much shorter runways than conventional planes.[3]

The Mistys soon discovered another reason the base occupied such a favored place in the Pentagon budget. NKP was home to an ambiguous-sounding facility called the Communications Data Management Center, manned by a unit informally known as "Dutch Mill." The data managed at NKP, however, was anything but run-of-the-mill communications. It was some of the most high-priority and supersecret intelligence of the war.

A year earlier, Defense Secretary McNamara had persuaded President Johnson to authorize the highest possible budget priority for a system of electronic sensors that would, in theory, be able to monitor NVA traffic going down the Ho Chi Minh Trail without the need for U.S. ground troops or human spies. The sensors would be air-dropped by Navy P-2s into place near key choke points, or placed there by commando teams infiltrating at night by helicopter. "McNamara's Fence," as the project came to be known, might just represent a solution to one of the most vexing problems of the war—locating and stopping the flow of men and supplies into South Vietnam. Johnson was dubious, but eager to support any measure that seemed like an alternative to pumping more troops into the meat grinder.[4]

By mid-1967 a small coterie of scientists and other technical experts—code-named "Task Force Alpha"—had begun a crash program to develop a ground-sensor network using modified undersea listening devices borrowed from the submarine community, along with a variety of other surveillance gizmos. That summer they tested the devices by dropping them from planes into the tough, red clay at Eglin Air Force Base in Florida. Then they moved on to more advanced evaluations at a jungle warfare training center in Panama. Results were mixed, but there was no time to waste on perfection, and the sensors were ordered over to Southeast Asia.

By December a range of devices that could detect noise, seismic disturbances, radio transmissions, and even human odors were being seeded along portions of the Trail, by ground and by air. At NKP, an IBM model 1401 computer whirred away behind a phalanx of locked doors, processing the data. Dozens of Air Force technicians and civilian specialists—who became known as the "pinball wizards"—droned away in secrecy, trying to decipher the unusual readings that filtered in.[5]

The Mistys had been invited over to learn about "Igloo White," as the overall effort was known, by the one-star Air Force general who ran the operation. The Mistys hadn't yet been officially informed about McNamara's Fence, but their status in the intelligence world— and their own top secret designation—evidently qualified them for an inside peek. The general ushered the Misty delegation into a briefing room, then unveiled some plastic jungle shrubs growing out of metal "pots" that were pointy on the bottom, like the tip of an artillery shell. "These," the general announced, "are not plants at all, but antennae and transmitters that will be our ears along the Ho Chi Minh Trail." He explained the scheme that the scientists had been dreaming up for well over a year. The bush-sensors, once implanted in the ground, would pick up the sounds of trucks going by, along with the voices of the drivers and any other troops marching along. The real mother lode would be data revealing where the truck motors stopped—the dearly sought truck parks. If the Air Force knew where the trucks hid during the daytime—instead of relying on old intel, risky low-altitude reconnaissance flights, and guesswork—it would mark the kind of breakthrough that might actually justify some of those overoptimistic BDA reports going back to Washington.

Haltigan and Van Dyken, the intel officers, were impressed. The biggest hole in the intelligence net was the lack of real-time information, and the "ears" on display in front of them might help stitch that hole. The triple-layered jungle canopy that covered much of the Trail provided immense visual camouflage for the truck parks and storage depots that were the way stations for ton after ton of Russian- and Chinese-supplied matériel on its way to the South. Misty's entire job was to pry beneath that canopy, and the pilots were very effective at catching any vehicles that ventured into the open during daylight hours. But that was the tip of the iceberg, and for every truck killed there were probably a hundred others that pressed on, bearing the troops and weaponry that would sooner or later make their way into battle against American GIs. If a bunch of phony shrubs laced with sensors could help overcome the blindness the pilots struggled with from above, that could be a huge advantage—perhaps even a turning point in the war.

The general had a request. Some of the shrubs had already been "planted" along portions of the Ho Chi Minh Trail in Laos, and the technicians listening for NVA activity needed to run a critical test. They wanted the Mistys to fly a very precise route over the sensors, at an exact time and a precise altitude, and light their afterburners. If the jets flew to the exact coordinates, Dutch Mill would be able to capture the sound of the engines and then calibrate how far away from the Trail the sensors had landed. There were other FACs who worked Laos—the supersecret "Ravens," who worked with the CIA and didn't officially exist, and the "Nail" FACs of the 23rd Tactical Air Support Squadron, based in Thailand—but they flew old, slow prop planes that didn't make enough noise to test the sensors. The Mistys, in their F-100s, could kick up quite a stir by comparison. In fact, the poor bastards listening to the input over their headsets would probably be knocked out of their chairs by the roar of the jet fuel exploding inside the afterburners—a rather jolting contrast to the squawk and buzz of ordinary jungle life.

The general escorted the four-person Misty contingent into his office and shook everybody's hand, a gesture that wowed the young intel officers more than the seasoned, suspicious pilots. He launched into a little pep talk, stressing the accuracy required for the test. "Gentlemen," he began solemnly, "your altitude must be exact. Your timing must be precise. There is no room for the smallest error. We are depending upon you to execute this critical test with the best you have to offer." The general's throaty delivery got the Mistys' attention. "There is so much riding on this, gentlemen," he intoned heavily, as if he were Eisenhower addressing the troops on the eve of D-Day, "that if we don't do this precisely and exactly correct"—now he paused for effect—"the Navy will get the project!"

Van Dyken reeled at the parochialism. He wanted to puke. The other Mistys wore sterile expressions, icy masks that hid their own cynicism and contempt for this bureaucratic bullshit. The group saluted and left, promising to uphold their end of the bargain. Mick Greene thought, Your fucking problem, General, will not be calibrating your phony plants, but getting your fighter pilots to drop their fucking bombs on the fucking targets.

For several days after the encounter the Misty pilots dutifully flew to the preassigned spots and hit their afterburners, though these were strange, mystifying missions on which Misty was generally kept in the dark. They guessed that they were being sent to areas where there was important ground activity, but nobody would ever say what exactly, and they often trolled around trying to figure it out themselves.

Misty heard little from Dutch Mill after that, although occasionally ABCCC did direct them to "go investigate movers"—the language typically used to refer to intelligence picked up by the sensors. These targets were always in Laos, and they were almost always losers—the pilots rarely saw any activity that was evident from the air.

During one sensor chase, in mid-January, Don Jones and his favorite flying partner, Jonesy Jones, got a call from the ABCCC to head for a "Delta" point in Laos—a shorthand reference to a predetermined spot on the ground—where one of the airdrop bushes had picked up some kind of activity. They were flying a Hun that was fresh out of a maintenance upgrade, with new paint and a finely tuned engine, and it handled like a brand-new plane. Don Jones, flying in the front seat, swooped over the target area—a bombed-out intersection—at 450 knots, and neither Misty saw anything. They came back around for another pass. This time they saw a single truck, cleverly camouflaged. But they couldn't tell what kind.

So they came around a third time to snap a picture with the Pentax. They flew too close, however, and Jonesy in the back couldn't get the camera into place. Their fuel was starting to run low and it was time to head home. But they'd have to go back over the intersection on the way to the tanker anyway, so they decided to dip down one more time to get that critical picture. This time a gunner in the trees evidently decided he couldn't hold off any longer, and he started to unload 37mm AAA rounds at them. One slammed into the plane's right wing, jolting it like a lightning strike. A utility light flashed on in the cockpit. Don Jones jinked abruptly, then looked out at the wing and started a careful climb, not wishing to put undue stress on the crumpled metal.

They headed straight for the air base at Ubon, Thailand, the closest landing point. The Hun was holding steady, but in the front seat Don Jones was nervously eyeing the instrument panel, waiting for more problems to surface. Contemplating a bailout, he thought, boy, are we lucky that we're over Laos instead of North Vietnam. The word had not yet filtered out that pilots captured in Laos were almost always killed on the spot.

As they approached Ubon, Don Jones in the front told Jonesy in the back that he thought he'd try to use the wing flaps as they came in to land, the conventional procedure for slowing the plane to a safe landing speed. "Nah, I wouldn't bother," Jonesy replied, without elaborating. So they made a fast, risky, no-flap landing, skidding off the concrete onto the tarmac at the very end of the runway. When they got out, Don Jones gasped at what he saw: A huge portion of the right wing near the fuselage was missing. Jonesy, sitting in the back near the damage, had been able to see the mangled wing all along and in his typical way had soft-pedaled the damage to his commander up front.

The two pilots caught a ride back to Phu Cat, where they had to report yet another badly damaged plane—and a freshly refurbished one, at that—to Colonel Schneider, the wing commander. Schneider had selected Don Jones as Misty commander because he saw the colonel as somebody who could reel in the hotshots in the unit. Yet after a month of Jones's command, more than half of Misty's planes had either been lost or severely damaged.

The teeming new pipeline of real-time intelligence that Van Dyken and Haltigan had yearned for never materialized. Misty never received any meaningful data from the array of ground sensors. One perennial problem was that such sensitive intelligence always got hung up in the various compartments of the classified bureaucracy: It was too sensitive to distribute through normal channels, but useless if it never reached the tactical units able to do something with the information. The North Vietnamese, with their uncanny resourcefulness, had also come up with some low-tech countermeasures. Once they figured out what the phony bushes really were, they would run wild animals past them, move them into vacant parts of the jungle, and even hang bags of urine over the chemical sniffers to generate bogus intelligence.[6]

Other pilots insisted that as the "pinball-wizards" improved their wizardry, the sensors paid off. Word got around that McNamara's exotic fence helped locate enemy units that were targeted by B-52 Arc Light strikes, which were devastating when the intel was good—particularly in Laos, where the approval of local chieftains, who often reported back to the North Vietnamese, wasn't required, as it was in South Vietnam. And the Raven and Nail FACs working in Laos were beginning to rely on sensor data to lead them to a treasure trove of targets. But for Misty in early 1968, such prospects turned out to be as fanciful as a North Vietnamese surrender. Their own intel remained the most reliable.

FOURTEEN

THE LONE RANGER

Unlike his friend Howie Williams, Dick Rutan was bored with the close air support missions being flown by his unit, the 612th Squadron at Phu Cat. Rutan was doing what he had long dreamed of doing—flying fighter jets in a war—and he knew as well as Howie that the bombs he delivered often helped tip battles in favor of the good guys. But the thrill of "the posse coming to the rescue" had worn off for Rutan. The out-and-back missions began to seem dull and unfulfilling, dropping ordnance into remote, impenetrable jungle where it was hard to tell whether there were enemy troops or not. Bombing missions in the South usually required the permission of local authorities, who everybody knew were often in cahoots with the Viet Cong. By the time bombs arrived, the bad guys had often been tipped off and moved along. Plus, there was no air-to-air combat in the South. There were no SAMs and not much in the way of enemy AAA, either. Most pilots who flew in the South were grateful for that. Rutan thought it made things too easy.

Rutan was a maverick. He had always been dissatisfied with the routine—and obsessed with airplanes. Back home in Dinuba, California, a farming town about thirty miles southeast of Fresno, Dick and his younger brother, Burt, would constantly nag their parents to take them to air shows at the half dozen airports within a day's driving distance. Rutan's father had gone to dental school on the GI Bill after a short stint in the Navy during World War II, and he had fixed up an old woodshed behind the garage where Dick and Burt slept. As the boys grew older, the bedroom became more of a laboratory, with tools and glue and balsa wood and model airplanes scattered everywhere. Soon, Dick and Burt began to scheme about building real planes.

Dick started taking flying lessons when he was fifteen, with money he earned working on local farms. On his sixteenth birthday, Rutan's mom drove him to a local airfield, where the adolescent aviator put his hours of training to use and flew solo for the first time. He got his private pilot's license before his driver's license.

When Rutan graduated from high school, he headed straight for the nearest Air Force recruiter. He had never been a strong student, however, and when he took the Air Force entrance exam he didn't score high enough to qualify for flight school. The Air Force needed navigators, though, since the big transport jets required them to plot flight paths and monitor charts on long ocean crossings. And many of the air defense fighters relied on navigators to operate missile systems and assist with radar intercepts. Besides, the recruiter told Rutan, he could always try again for pilot training once he had earned his nav wings. So in the summer of 1958, Rutan ended up at Lackland Air Force Base in San Antonio for the three-month preflight navigator course.

It was touch-and-go from the start. Rutan arrived at Lackland with sideburns and long hair groomed into a DA—"a duck's ass"—in the back. During roll call on the first day he was chewing gum, and a bulldog instructor walked up and stood nose-to-nose with him. "Hey Elvis!" he screamed. "Are you chewing gum?" Rutan, trembling and wishing he were back in Dinuba, was paralyzed and mute. "Okay, mister," the instructor ordered. "Swallow it!" Rutan did as he was told and got through the initiation. But as the Air Force weeded out the undesirables, the ax repeatedly fell right behind Rutan as he struggled with the academics.

Once in the air, however, Rutan soared to the top of the class. Near the end of the course, when it came time for the cadets to demonstrate their abilities in flight, Rutan got the highest check-ride score of any cadet. He moved on to advanced training and nine months later earned his navigator's wings and a commission as a second lieutenant. He spent seven years flying in the backseat of F-89 and F-101 fighter interceptors and in the nav's chair on the giant C-124 Globemaster cargo jet, called "Old Shaky." He got so good that when he was flying transports, he'd regularly turn off the LORAN electronic mapping aid and navigate by the stars just for fun.

He still yearned to be the guy in front, however, and in 1966 he made it into pilot training at Laughlin Air Force Base in Del Rio, Texas. Showing up with senior navigator's wings and seven years' experience as a navigator, the rangy, intense Californian now had plenty of seasoning to be a fighter jock. He had also flown more than a thousand hours as a commercial pilot before joining the Air Force and had an FAA commercial pilot's license. But he didn't bring that up at Laughlin. Rutan was so eager to succeed in Air Force pilot training that he resisted doing anything that would be perceived as "shining his ass." The only shining he wanted to do was in the cockpit.

Pilot training, unlike navigator school, turned out to be a breeze. Rutan, a natural flier with 20-12 vision, graduated first out of the 360 students from all six pilot training bases who got their pilot's wings in the spring of 1967. The next step was to select which type of jet he wanted to fly. A lot of pilots had to live with whatever the Air Force assigned them to. But Rutan, at the top of the class, got his first choice. He picked the F-100, the plane he had been dying to fly since he first saw one as a sophomore in high school, on display in front of the Fresno air terminal. It had been brand-new then, but had since become the aging workhorse of the Air Force's fighter-bomber fleet in South Vietnam. Rutan was fully aware that in choosing the F-100, he had picked a path that led directly to the war. He was ecstatic.

Rutan went through F-100 training at Luke Air Force Base along with Howie Williams and Lanny Lancaster. In August 1967 he said good-bye to his wife, Geri, and his two-year-old daughter, Holly, and boarded a plane for the Philippines and the "gentleman's course" in jungle survival. Finally, all training complete, he strapped into one last charter flight for the trip to Saigon, where he found a five-day wait for transport to his final destination, the 612th Squadron at Phu Cat.

Dick bellied up to the O club bar and ordered a "Bah Mee Bah . . . 33," the brand name that became the American term for "beer" in Vietnam. It wasn't bad, even cold. "This war shit isn't so bad," Rutan mused, "except for the waiting." Dick looked across the circular bar and saw another pilot he knew, Ed Hallern, whom he had been stationed with when he was a nav based in California. Hallern was now a "trash hauler" flying C-130 Hercules resupply missions in the Mekong River Delta south of Saigon.

Rutan's friend offered him a sightseeing tour. "We got some grunts to pick up," Hallern said. "Why don't you get your feet wet on a couple of missions with us while you're waiting for your upcountry transport?" Southwest of Saigon—known as the IV Corps area, or "Four Corps"—the Viet Cong owned all the roads and most of the countryside. When Army units needed to be moved, they called on the C-130s, the "Herks," to carry their men and equipment. Flying the Herks wasn't glamorous. In fact, it was hard, dirty work, and dangerous. Dick eagerly accepted the invitation.

Rutan rode in the cockpit with the crew. It was a short flight from Tan Son Nhut, the huge airfield at Saigon, to the assigned pickup point. The aircraft commander throttled back and aimed the four-engine transport into a short landing strip lined with rubber tress and covered with perforated steel plates, which formed the surface of the runway. Dick gulped. The C-130 was empty and light on landing, but he realized they would have to come out heavy and loaded. "I was wrong," he concluded, "This war shit *is* bad."

The C-130 landed with a jolt. Dick was thrown forward into his seat belt and shoulder straps as the pilot slammed on the brakes and pulled the engines into full reverse. The rear ramp went down. The grunts quickly drove a couple of jeeps and an armored personnel carrier into the back of the aircraft, then piled themselves in. Nobody thought of using a seat belt. Dick saw no loadmaster making weight and balance calculations, nor was there any real attempt to tie anything down. Speed was critical, since big aircraft often drew mortar fire from the VC. Everyone was eager to load fast and get the hell out of Dodge. Dick thought the floor would surely collapse, then he had another alarming revelation: They were actually going to try taking off from this tiny strip, weighted down like a barge. He rushed to the cockpit.

"No fucking way we're going to take off," he shouted to Hallern over the engine noise. "This thing won't even taxi."

The pilot removed his headset and shouted back, "Well, you can stay overnight and get mortared by the VC if you want. We'll be back tomorrow for the rest of the troops."

Grumbling, Dick strapped back in for takeoff and resigned himself. Hallern taxied to the end of the strip and turned around. He put the engines in reverse and backed up slowly, extending the tail over the end of the runway to use every available inch of space. Then he stomped on the brake pedals, held them down firmly, and ran the engines to full power. The airplane shook violently. There was a lurch as the pilot released the brakes. Dick began to sweat as the aircraft lumbered down the short, narrow strip. The runway was about to disappear beneath them as the pilot pulled the control wheel back into his lap. The transport staggered above the trees. They were alive! Rutan let out a big sigh.

Back at Tan Son Nhut, Rutan went back to the bar. "I'm going to die before I get to combat," he fretted. He decided not to wait for his assigned transport and bummed a ride on a C-7 Caribou that was headed for Qui Nhon, about a fifteen-mile drive from Phu Cat. At Qui Nhon he hitched a ride in the back of an open truck hauling some Korean troops to Phu Cat for guard duty. He knew he was a sitting duck, with no weapon, no helmet, no flak jacket. But it beat the hell out of dying in a goddamned C-130.

He arrived at Phu Cat just before dusk and was restless from the moment he arrived. Rutan had heard about Misty during his first few days on the base and went to ask Bud Day about joining. But Day had been shot down the day before, Rutan found out. That only intensified his interest—it must be some mission if the commander gets shot down, Rutan thought.

The Mistys rebuffed him, however. They told Rutan he wasn't quite qualified. All Mistys had to be "flight leads," a status bestowed on the more experienced pilots who were qualified to lead two- or four-ship formations on combat missions. So Rutan went back to his squadron, pestered his commander, and eventually became a flight lead.

He also learned a few other things about the war. During a short leave, he visited a U.S. Army helicopter unit at an exposed forward base in the Central Highlands and was startled at how brutal the war seemed on the ground. He saw suspected Viet Cong soldiers being held in primitive cages and watched a young American lieutenant beat one of them bloody. He talked with a helicopter gunner who, when he wasn't flying missions, removed his M-60 machine gun from the chopper so he could conduct his own perimeter defense. His body was laced with scars he had received from incoming fire, and the gunner talked as if he would never survive his tour. Rutan wondered where the Army found such rough, hardened troops.[1]

Meanwhile, he continued to gather the experience needed for Misty, and finally Don Jones accepted the aggressive pilot. Rutan flew his first Misty mission in January 1968, in the backseat with Mick Greene in the front. With so many ground gunners shooting at them, there was a lot more excitement than Rutan had experienced in several months of flying over the South. He was hooked immediately. Instead of flying out on a milk run, dropping a few bombs and coming home while a battle on the ground was still raging, Misty *was* the battle. The FACs were in the middle of everything. Even the debriefings were dramatic. Holy shit, thought Rutan. Misty's accomplishments made most other units seem insignificant. He had found his niche.

Plus, the flying was spectacular. Instead of boring and predictable thirty-minute round-trips to radar-controlled "sky spots" where intelligence guessed a few targets might be, the Mistys ranged all over their area of operations in Route Pack 1, doing whatever it took to sniff out valid targets. The nature of such work called for minimal restrictions and maximum autonomy—you couldn't very well find targets in the haystack of the Ho Chi Minh Trail if you had to check with the boss back at headquarters on every little detail. It was a rare opportunity to let it all hang out, with nobody looking over your shoulder.

Mick Greene, who had been with Misty since October and had become the unit's Operations officer, took Rutan up to Mu Ghia Pass for one of his checkout rides. Greene was looking for trucks and guns, and showing Rutan how to jink and weave to prevent the NVA gunners from getting a clear shot. They spotted a small bulldozer in the bushes, on the side of a road that passed through the canyon between two mountains. There were no strike fighters in the area, so Greene decided to strafe the bulldozer with the Hun's two 20mm cannons. He knew the hilltops were thick with gunners, and if he flew straight down the road every gomer up there would open fire on them. So Greene decided to approach the bulldozer at a 90-degree angle to the road, which would limit their exposure.

There was one challenge, however: The side of a mountain loomed in their pull-up path. Greene dived in on the bulldozer, pressing in until he knew the mountain was becoming a factor. He squeezed off about one hundred rounds of 20-mike mike as the pilots called the rounds that flew from their guns, and immediately started a grueling 6-G pull-out, which smashed Rutan down in the seat. Greene could hear Rutan struggling to breathe as the treetops whizzed by and they climbed up the side of the mountain. It was a dirty trick to do that to the guy in back, but it would be a good learning experience.

What Greene didn't anticipate was the payback. On another mission a few weeks later, Rutan was in the front seat with Greene in the back. The weather was terrible, with the cloud deck hovering at just 1,500 feet. They raced out of the bottom of Mu Ghia Pass heading east at 500 knots. Rutan locked onto a single truck bolting down a dirt road that circumnavigated a karst peak that was sticking up into the clouds. Rutan pulled up sharply into the overcast, timed a turn to the right, and then dived out of the clouds to get a good position on the truck. The acrobatics left Greene panting in the back. They rounded the karst peak and were suddenly roaring toward the truck, head-on. The driver was desperately trying to find cover in a stand of trees up ahead, trailing a huge cloud of dust. He didn't make it. Rutan fired about fifty rounds right through the windshield, and the truck burst into flames. Greene nicknamed Rutan "Killer" after that, partly because of the truck—but partly because Greene was feeling close to death himself after the harrowing ride.

Rutan was so enthused about Misty that he began to work diligently to persuade his buddy Howie Williams to join. Dick and Howie had first met at gunnery school back at Luke Air Force Base, where Howie had been held back for several months after passing out in the altitude chamber. By the time Rutan's group arrived at Luke, Howie was an old head whom most of the other students looked up to. Plus, Howie ended up being Top Gun, and he was affable and smart—an easy guy to be friends with. The two pilots had kept in touch. Rutan had left for Vietnam first. While Howie was passing through San Francisco on his way to the war, Rutan's wife, Geri, who lived nearby, spent a day showing him around, and they had lunch together with a couple of other wives of pilots who had recently shipped out for Southeast Asia. Then Dick and Howie encountered each other at Phu Cat, where they had been assigned to sister squadrons flying CAS missions in the South.

The two pilots shared an insatiable love of flying, yet they were quite different. Rutan was boisterous and impulsive, precisely the kind of guy to seek out the hardest, most glorious mission the war had to offer. His competitive personality made him fun to be around. Howie enjoyed Rutan's company. As a former navigator, Rutan was a certain target for the barbs of career jet-jocks, and Howie wasn't about to spare him. In one letter home to his wife, Monalee, Howie described his upcoming missions and said, "Dick R. is spare pilot so Dick and I could conceivably fly together. I told Dick that if we fly together I'm lead—I won't follow an ex-navigator into combat."

Though he could mix it up with the pranksters, Howie was much more studious and deliberate than Rutan. He got frustrated with the mundane missions in the South, as many of the pilots did, yet Howie felt duty-bound to do everything he could to help the poor bastards fighting the war on the ground. While he knew about Misty and had several friends who had joined the unit, he was content to stick it out in the South.

Dick Rutan, however, was the kind of insistent character who rarely doubted his own wisdom. In spite of Howie's apparent satisfaction with swatting NVA troops in the South, Rutan foresaw a different future for the former Top Gun. Howie was such a talented aviator, for one thing, that he seemed ideal for Misty. He was unflappable in the cockpit, he looked like a Hollywood version of a fighter pilot, and he could put a bomb in a guy's back pocket. After Rutan joined Misty, he and Howie would meet for drinks occasionally and Rutan would pour it on, cajoling his friend to offer his talents where the real action was. His friend's eagerness for war made Howie wonder about his own attitudes. "Honey," he wrote Monalee in one letter, "Dick R. is really wrapped up with this war. He's enjoying it. I enjoy the flying too, but the worth of the war sometimes leaves a bad taste in my mouth. Wish I were a non-thinker. He has a big moustache and looks more like the Lone Ranger every day. Ha. Oh, well. Maybe I'll get the killer instinct later."

Rutan's evangelizing began to get through, and Howie started thinking about Misty. He made a visit to Saigon in January 1968 and saw Roger Wise, an old friend he had first met during pilot training. Wise had been flying F-100s out of Tuy Hoa, a base on the coast south of Phu Cat, when he heard they were looking for somebody of his rank at the Tactical Air Control Center in Saigon to help coordinate air support missions in the South. Howie told Wise about Misty and said some of his friends from the 416th and the 612th had been transferring over. What did his old pal think?

Wise hadn't heard of Misty. The guys working up north were hard to get information out of no matter what, and since Wise mainly worked with units flying in the South, he had no direct access to Misty's top secret operational details. But as a TACC controller, he did work with a lot of FACs in the South, mainly the old-style slow FACs flying O-1 or O-2 propeller-driven airplanes. FACing was dangerous work, he told Howie. A lot of those guys get shot down even in the South. They fly lower and slower than most of the other pilots. Flying up north as a FAC would be even worse—not the safest line of work for a guy with a wife and kid at home. Think about it, he warned his old friend. Howie shrugged off the admonition. He liked adventure, he told Wise, Dick Rutan's fabulous war stories no doubt buzzing in his brain.

Shortly after Howie's trip to Saigon, his little brother Roger, the Army HQ records sergeant, called Roger Wise and the two Rogers got together in Saigon. They had met when Howie had married Monalee in Steubenville in 1958, and Howie and Roger Wise and Chuck O'Connor—the Three Musketeers at aviation cadet training near San Antonio—had done a favor for a fellow from Ohio and driven his yellow Cadillac convertible all the way from Texas back to the Buckeye State. Wise and O'Connor had taken Howie's steelworker dad out and gotten him soused, eager to impress the old man with a taste of the dashing aviator lifestyle. The brash airmen—with freshly minted pilots' wings—made quite an impression on Howie's twelve-year-old brother. He admired them almost as much as he did his brother.

Roger Williams and Roger Wise went out for a few drinks in downtown Saigon. Both of them were worried about Howard. The younger brother asked the experienced pilot what would happen if Howie got shot down. Wise offered brave talk: "We'll go rescue him, that's what we'll do," he assured the soldier. The brother wondered: Can we do that? Sure, Wise told him.

But it was bullshit banter. Wise knew the risks. He knew that being a FAC was dangerous even in the South, where U.S. and South Vietnamese troops ostensibly controlled much of the terrain. Up north it was hostile territory no matter where you went down. The simple fact was that a lot of the guys who were shot down were gone for good once their plane disappeared.

Despite his own worries, however, Wise didn't want to puncture the intuitive confidence Roger Williams had in his brother. Before long the two men had drifted into the uneasy comfort that a bit of liquor and whiff of camaraderie bring to strangers in wartime. They met a guy at the bar who was a pilot for Air America, one of the weird, open secrets in Vietnam—everybody knew the so-called "airline" was really the air arm of the CIA, flying into who-knew-what forbidden zones. In accordance with his shady prestige, the Air America pilot had a limousine at his disposal, and the two Rogers ended up driving around Saigon with him, bar-hopping and enjoying the temporary luxury of the big car.

Rutan, meanwhile, quickly became one of the dominant personalities at Misty. Both in the air and in his attitude, he was as aggressive as Charlie Neel, the flamethrower whose zeal for hunting down the enemy was inversely proportional to his subliminal height. When Neel rotated out of Misty in late January, Rutan, with his piercing blue eyes, became the unit's benchmark for adrenaline and machismo. That did not exactly make him a role model, however, since a few in the unit felt Rutan's agressiveness could get him, and them, killed.

But he was a strong aviator, and popular, and he flew well with the other Mistys. Rutan was cooperative and respectful when he was the unenviable guy in back, a GIB once more, just like his old days as a navigator. On one sortie with Don Jones, the Misty commander, the mission began with an assignment to inspect the aftermath of an AC-130 Spectre gunship attack from the night before. Using its new night-vision devices, the fearsome warplane had supposedly unloaded its 20mm Gatling gun on several trucks rattling south through the darkness. Rutan and Jones, flying as Misty 41, were supposed to see if they could find any debris that might verify the effectiveness of the attack.

The airborne command center radioed some grid coordinates to them, and Rutan, flying in the back, quickly plotted them on the map. "It's well north of Bat Lake and a little ways south of the 'Y' in the river up there," he grunted into Jones's earpiece, the G forces from the constant jinking making it strenuous just to talk.

Before they got to the target site, however, a 37mm AAA shell suddenly came blazing past the cockpit. "Holy Christ!" Rutan shouted. "Break left!" The instruction was unnecessary—Jones already had put the plane into a tight turn.

"Where the hell was that guy?" Jones asked.

"God, I don't know," Rutan replied. Then he saw something. "There's some smoke down there by the hook in the road. It must have come from there." Rutan marked the spot carefully on his plastic map, so they could deal with the gun site later and report it to intel.

They arrived at the spot where the Spectre had supposedly taken out the trucks and found nothing. It was the usual mystery: The gunship pilots were sure they had hit *something,* but either they had overestimated their success or the North Vietnamese had hustled out and cleared the wreckage before accurate BDA could be accomplished. Jones called back to the airborne command post. Nice try, he reported, but no cigar. Still, the phantom trucks were likely to end up in somebody's BDA count.

Misty 41 headed back toward the nettlesome AAA gun they had encountered. The pilots flying up north had developed an unusual rapport with the guys on the ground manning the AAA sites. They were enemies to be sure, but there were also times when they could do each other a favor. Misty of course wanted to know where all the guns were—every single one—but it wasn't possible to blow them all up. A gun that didn't fire was the same as no gun at all, as far as they were concerned. So when they located a AAA nest that remained silent, they looked for what it was protecting. If it didn't fire, they monitored it, but most often just left it alone. "Fuck with the bull and you get the horn," was the saying.

The Mistys reasoned that some of the gunners down below were just as happy to let the F-100s fly on by, as long as they weren't attacking something the gunners were assigned to protect. When the gunners fired, they gave away the positions they had gone to great effort to conceal. Then they'd have to spend the night breaking down their equipment and setting it up in some other place instead of sleeping. So both sides occasionally saw virtue in looking the other way, a dangerous cat-and-cat game.

But not this guy. He had opened up on them in the middle of nowhere, when they hadn't even been screwing around in his neighborhood. This violated the unwritten rules. That kind of aggression had to be dealt with. Jones and Rutan figured they'd swing back to see if they could pinpoint his location a bit more precisely and maybe even bring a few bombs ringing down on the overeager gunner.

As they were getting close to their trigger-happy nemesis, a bright flame appeared out of nowhere, on the left side of the plane. Jones and Rutan both had the same immediate thought: Holy shit, a SAM! Jones could even feel Rutan grab the rear-seat controls, preparing to execute a hard evasive maneuver himself if Jones hesitated.

But the flash wasn't a SAM. It was an F-105 that they hadn't even seen—and the back half of it was completely ablaze. Must have gotten nailed by the same gun they were after, the two pilots reasoned. A couple of seconds after they spotted the burning Thud, the canopy flew off and a parachute came streaming out. The radio suddenly came alive with the blare of a parachute beeper, triggered once the chute opened up.

Rutan was instantly on the net. "Mayday! Mayday!" he barked, alerting all the rescue forces monitoring the emergency frequency. "Cricket, this is Misty four-one. We've got a 105 bailout and we need some help up here in a hurry." Cricket acknowledged the transmission, and Rutan pumped them as much additional information as he could. "The pilot is in his chute and his position is"—Rutan calculated the coordinates—"XE483523." Jones was amazed at Rutan's skill with maps. The pilot was still in the air, and Rutan had already estimated his location on the ground. "The area is remote," Rutan continued, "and we've got plenty of daylight. I believe we can get this guy out if we get moving."

Help started to show up: First, a Navy helicopter that volunteered to go in and try to pick up the downed pilot. Then the pilot's squadronmate, call sign Poncho 2, who said all he knew was that he looked over at his lead at one point and the plane had erupted in flame. While they awaited the all-important Sandys that would locate the survivor and provide cover for the helicopter, Misty 41 and Poncho 2 began flying a CAP, combat air patrol, over the area. They looked for any other defenses that might interfere with a rescue. By now the pilot had landed and the parachute was clearly visible from far away. That was good news—it would be an easy target for the rescuers to home in on.

Rutan plotted the pilot's actual position. It was only two hundred meters off his original estimate—amazing precision under such stressful circumstances. He called the new info into Cricket. Rutan and Jones also noticed that there were no villages nearby, which was reassuring—it was often local villagers who rushed to the scene of a shootdown and were the first to reach a pilot on the ground.

Other signs, however, were more worrisome. The parachute beeper continued to wail, when the usual procedure was to turn it off once you had hit the ground, so that it wouldn't interfere with other radio transmissions between aircraft trying to accomplish the rescue. Once the pilot turned the beeper off, it was also a sign that he was still alive. Besides, he needed to turn off the beeper to be able to talk on the radio, usually the only way to vector in the rescuers. A continual stream of noise, on the other hand, meant the pilot was either too busy—or too incapacitated—to turn off the beeper.

Repeated calls to the pilot to shut off his beeper drew no response. While flying CAP, Rutan and Jones noted several places that looked like they could be camouflaged AAA sites that might be a problem during the rescue. In fact, there were signs of AAA all over the landscape—literally hundreds of round pits or bunkers that at one time or another had housed deadly guns. Most were abandoned, and were visible because the dead vegetation used for camouflage had been thrown outside the pits. The active sites, of course, were filled with live greenery and carefully camouflaged. It wasn't always easy to ferret out the live sites, but Rutan had a knack for gun-hunting and noted several possible trouble spots, plotting them on his maps. If gunfire came from those areas once the rescue started, the Sandys would jump all over them. Misty 41 would be standing by, ready to join the fray if needed.

Misty 41 had to head off to the tanker for gas, and Poncho 2 was right behind. For thirty minutes nobody was overhead keeping an eye on the parachute nestled in the trees. When Jones and Rutan arrived back on station, the chute was gone. They flew back and forth over the spot Rutan had carefully noted on his charts, searching and making radio calls. Nothing. And the downed pilot had never established voice contact. Misty 41 stayed overhead long enough to burn through the better part of another tank of gas, but finally they had to call it a day— there was now nobody to rescue. That produced a sick feeling for every aviator, heading home knowing you had left a guy down there. But Rutan definitely was not bored.

FIFTEEN

TORCHED

Something was up. Nobody knew what exactly, but there were signals from many directions that the North Vietnamese were planning something big. At Misty, John Haltigan and Roger Van Dyken had been fitting various pieces of information together into a worrisome puzzle. First, Misty was taking more hits and was losing more airplanes. The sheer volume of North Vietnamese traffic on the Trail during the Christmas and New Year's truces had been greater than anything they had ever seen. Then there were the few words Bob Craner had managed to utter over the radio after his capture: ". . . tons of trucks moving south." Finally, every time the weather broke, it was a shooting gallery for Misty. Haltigan and Van Dyken and other intel experts within the U.S. command reasoned that the amount of stuff the North Vietnamese were sending south was far more than required to merely resupply and assist the Viet Cong. It wasn't business as usual. The NVA was clearly preparing for major action somewhere, as Haltigan and Van Dyken surmised in their daily intelligence summaries, the DISUMs sent to 7th Air Force.

Misty's job, of course, was to stop the movement of men and equipment south. But the weather, for the moment, was allied against them. The winter monsoons brought cold air sweeping in from the northeast, causing a sudden decrease in air and water temperatures. When that happened, the weather became totally unpredictable, especially along the narrow coastal plain.[1] And if the Misty mission had a particular vulnerability, it was bad weather. The Misty flights could almost always get under the clouds, but bomb-dropping fighters needed big breaks in the overcast to deliver accurate bombs—and there were precious few breaks in January 1968. Frustrations mounted as Misty pilots trolled beneath the cloud deck and ducked between rainstorms, watching trucks speeding south virtually at will. Occasionally the Mistys lost patience and broke the rules, dipping down low enough to strafe the vehicles with their 20mm cannon. They'd knock out a truck here and there—but often pick up some AAA holes in return. Most Mistys began to realize the marginal satisfaction wasn't worth the risk—or the wrath of Colonel Schneider, who would inevitably be pissed about the risks and the damage to his planes.

At U.S. military headquarters in Saigon, General Westmoreland was intensely interested in the North Vietnamese activity on the Trail. As far as his staff could tell, the NVA had recently pushed three divisions into South Vietnam, underneath the weather, and begun moving them into positions around the Marine base at Khe Sanh. North Vietnamese regulars had been caught scouting the area. Intelligence reported that the North had established a new command post just over the border in Laos, possibly to direct a Khe Sanh battle. A North Vietnamese defector claimed that his comrades were planning another Dien Bien Phu—a repeat of the 1954 siege and capture of a remote French outpost, which had driven the French out of Vietnam.[2]

That certainly seemed like a plausible scheme. The village of Khe Sanh was way up in the northwest corner of South Vietnam, just below the DMZ and close to the border with Laos—so close to the Trail network that it could almost function as a way station on the way south. There was only one land supply route into the U.S. base at Khe Sanh—Route 9, which ran through a hot Viet Cong area and could be cut off easily. The Marines had moved into Khe Sanh in late 1967 as part of Westmoreland's plan to put more pressure on the Trail and prevent what he thought would be an attempt by Hanoi to occupy the northern provinces of South Vietnam. By late January over six thousand Marines occupied the base and surrounding hills. Several thousand other forces moved north out of Hue to the east, on the Perfume River near the coast. There was also a new Special Forces camp at Lang Vei, a Montagnard village on the Laotian border. From these redoubts Westmoreland planned to pummel the Trail with attacks by CIA and Meo raiding parties, Marine artillery dispersed on firebase hilltops, and ubiquitous airpower.

Westmoreland had guessed right about the North's plans. Gen. Vo Nguyen Giap, the North Vietnamese defense minister and architect of Dien Bien Phu back in '54, was preparing to take big risks. He was an adherent of Mao's theory of a three-stage revolution: first, guerrilla warfare, then military parity with the enemy, and finally an overwhelming onslaught driven by superior force and numbers. The North had mastered the first stage and embarked on the second, but Giap was impatient to reach the third phase. His divisions got battered whenever they met U.S. forces head-on, which was allowing the Saigon government time to gain strength and establish legitimacy.[3] What Giap needed was a body blow that would stoke growing antiwar fervor in America and break Washington's will to carry on. That would weaken the Saigon government and bring the people over to his side, or so he reasoned.[4]

Khe Sanh was a linchpin of his strategy. As Westmoreland had deduced, Giap had moved the equivalent of three NVA divisions, about twenty thousand men, into the hills surrounding the base. Another unit got into position along Route 9, aiming to use troops and artillery to prevent ground reinforcement from the east.[5] The pieces were all being moved into place for an epic battle.

Westmoreland saw it unfolding, too. He told his staff to study Dien Bien Phu and prepare for a similar siege. But he also knew the Americans had advantages the French had not. U.S. forces were strong throughout South Vietnam, not just in a few fortified areas, as the French had been. And they had massive airpower available. Westmoreland was confident his troops would not be reliving a tragic historical episode. "We are not, repeat not, going to be defeated at Khe Sanh," he told his staff. "I will tolerate no talking or even thinking to the contrary."[6]

President Johnson wasn't so sure. In fact, he became unnerved by the prospect of a defeat such as the French had suffered. He had detailed aerial photos of the area around Khe Sanh plastered on the walls of the White House situation room, and a terrain model built. In one of the oddest orders ever issued to military commanders, Johnson demanded that the Joint Chiefs of Staff sign a formal declaration of their faith in Westmoreland's ability to hold Khe Sanh. "I don't want any damned Dinbinphoo," the Texan drawled to Gen. Earle Wheeler, chairman of the Joint Chiefs.[7]

Ed Risinger didn't want any "Dinbinphoo," either, and his job was to help shut off the Trail so that if there was a battle at Khe Sanh, it would not be a fair fight. In the first week of January, Risinger was assigned to ride in the backseat with a new guy, Charlie "Whispering" Smith. Charlie was a popular pilot who had just completed his ten checkout rides and was "front seat qualified," ready for his first mission as the lead pilot. Charlie was a Southern boy from Weinert, Texas, with a booming voice—thus the ironic sobriquet—and a loud, piercing laugh. He claimed that as a child he had been "saved" by the Lord and called to preach God's word. Since Charlie wanted to be a fighter pilot, and since David in the Old Testament had been a mighty warrior who had pleased God, Charlie figured that if he joined the Air Force that might fulfill his obligation.

So he got an ROTC commission while he was in college, got trained in the F-100, and landed at Phan Rang, flying close air support in the South before volunteering for Misty. Even in a unit of colorful characters like the Misty pilots, Charlie's eccentricities stood out. Unlike most pilots, who simply walked from place to place on the base, Charlie rode a bicycle. He was fastidious, and every time he parked his bike, he took out his handkerchief and carefully wiped the red Phu Cat dust from the metal. In addition to the nickname "Whispering," he became known to the Mistys as "Charlie the Clean Bike Rider."

The mission briefing started with the usual discouraging meteorological news. "The weather is Delta Sierra"—dog shit—"just like all month," Haltigan said, as practiced groans filled the room. Then he got to the targets. "The big thing we are looking for is anything coming south toward Khe Sanh. 7th Air Force tells us there is a big buildup, and clearly the NVA will be trying to move AAA and SAMs into the area to prevent helos, fighters, and B-52s from supporting the Marines. We even have reports that SA-2 Guideline SAM transporters have been seen moving south." Haltigan pulled out a reference book with photos and diagrams to show what a Guideline transport trailer looked like. "Look for something that looks like an eighteen-wheeler," he advised, "but with an SA-2 Guideline SAM on it, covered by a tarp. It will also likely have camouflage on top." Risinger and Smith studied the photos.

The pilots "stepped" to their aircraft. As they took off and ventured north into the Pack, it was clear that Haltigan had been right. The weather was dog shit indeed. "Looks like it will be a waste of time," said Risinger from the backseat. "Too bad. There's lots going on under those clouds. You can almost hear it." Then suddenly, as if by command, the clouds began to break. They were flying slightly above the western end of the DMZ and dipped down through a perforation in the overcast. Patchy fog covered low areas—but for the most part they could see the ground. And just seconds after breaking through the clouds, they flew right over a group of vehicles parked in a tight circle. "Tanks!" Risinger shouted as he noticed the ground nearby had been torn up by tread tracks. He could also clearly see cannons sticking out the front of the poorly camouflaged vehicles. "They're refueling!"

Risinger called the ABCCC as he directed Charlie to stay in a tight circle so he could get a picture. "Cricket, believe it or not, we've got tanks. I estimate eight of them just north of the DMZ."

"Tanks?" replied Cricket. "Tanks? Are you sure?" Intel knew that the NVA had moved some mechanized equipment down the Trail, but no tanks had ever been seen this far south. If the report was true, tanks would clearly be a significant threat to the Marines at Khe Sanh.

Ed asked Charlie to fly directly over the tanks and bank 90 degrees so he could take a close-up photo. But clouds were getting in the way once again and Charlie had trouble keeping the vehicles in sight. Ed caught a glimpse of the tanks out the right side of the canopy and quickly swung the 35mm Pentax into position. He snapped several pictures as the lousy weather closed over the vehicles like a cloak. "Damn, Charlie," Ed complained. "Wish we could have gotten closer."

At the debriefing after the mission, Haltigan, Risinger, and Smith examined the photos. They were clear enough, but taken from such a low angle and from so far away that they weren't very useful. It was impossible to tell if they were tanks, trucks, or just RVs on vacation. "Damn," said Ed. "I know they were tanks and I'll bet they were headed for Khe Sanh. Charlie, if you hadn't lost sight of the tanks, we'd be heroes," Risinger gibed his crewmate. "For punishment, go wash your bike."

Haltigan dutifully included the report in the DISUM, without documentation, but they never heard back from 7th Air Force. Not even a curious phone call. Without pictures it was deemed just one more exaggerated pilot report. No one believed them.

About two weeks later, just before dawn on January 21, the major NVA attack on Khe Sanh kicked off. The following day, helicopters, C-130s, and C-7 Caribous were ferrying ammunition, food, fresh troops, and vital supplies into the base's airstrip every few minutes as the NVA attacked the base from several directions, testing the Marine defenses. Then the weather turned bad. With thick clouds protecting them from air attack, the NVA dug trenches almost all the way up to the base's defensive perimeter,[8] almost overrunning it. The Marines beat them back, however, and when the weather cleared for a few hours, aerial resupply resumed.

The Mistys weren't directly involved in the support missions, although many other pilots at Phu Cat were. But from all the way up in the Pack the Mistys could see the drama unfolding as fighters from the Air Force, Navy, and Marines plastered the surrounding hills. B-52s flew around the clock, dumping tons of bombs on NVA positions that had been identified by reconnaissance photos and electronic sensors. From the Mistys' perch, it was almost like watching an enormous construction site from a distance—clouds of dust kept mushrooming into the air from all over the place. Then there were explosions on the hills and in the Marine compound as NVA rockets and mortars hit ammunition stockpiles and ignited into giant fireballs. If any Misty needed a reminder about the importance of interdicting the Trail, he needed only to look south.

As dramatic as Khe Sanh was, however, it wasn't the main attraction. The battle got Westmoreland's attention, sure enough, as the siege dragged on and he worked furiously to find ways to relieve the pressure on the Marines who were surrounded. But Giap and his comrades in Hanoi had an even grander plan in the works. So, while the world fixated on the saga unfolding at Khe Sanh, Viet Cong guerrillas and North Vietnamese regulars were also drifting into Saigon, Hue, and most of the other cities in South Vietnam. They came in twos and threes, disguised as refugees, peasants, workers, and South Vietnamese soldiers on leave for "Tet," the upcoming Vietnamese New Year. In Saigon, roughly the equivalent of five battalions of NVA and VC gradually infiltrated the city without any notice by the countless security police working there. Guns came separately in flower carts, jury-rigged coffins, and trucks apparently filled with vegetables and rice. Still more weapons were stashed helter-skelter, thanks to a Viet Cong network in Saigon and the other major cities that had stockpiled stores of arms and ammunition snatched during hit-and-run raids or bought on the black market.[9]

The Tet holiday was to be marked by yet another stand-down, this one a customary agreement between the North and South in honor of one of the most important events on the Vietnamese calendar. Westmoreland thought the truce was a bad idea, especially since the North Vietnamese had exploited all the other recent truces. And now it was clear that they had begun flooding the South with troops and weapons. Westmoreland asked the South Vietnamese government to cancel the truce, or at least pare it back from forty-eight hours to something less, and to permit bombing of the Trail over the North. They agreed in principle, but no cancellation notice ever went out to the troops in the field. So the U.S. command sent out its own notice canceling the truce—but only to U.S. troops stationed in I Corps, the area south of the DMZ where North Vietnamese infiltration seemed to be the heaviest. Troops there were told to continue with combat operations.[10]

The truce was canceled for good the next day, after the NVA and Viet Cong together launched the massive Tet Offensive. Enemy troops drove deep into South Vietnam's seven largest cities and attacked thirty provincial capitals throughout the country. Within the first day major cities such as Hue and Kontum were on the verge of falling to forces from the North. In a spectacular bit of daring, a nineteen-person Viet Cong suicide squad had overrun the U.S. embassy in Saigon and held it for six hours. Even U.S. military headquarters in Saigon was under attack, and Viet Cong troops held parts of the adjacent Tan Son Nhut airfield.

It was an astonishing turn of events. Nobody had foreseen the magnitude of Hanoi's plan—not Westmoreland or any of his planners, not

President Johnson or any of his senior advisers, not the combat troops who faced the North Vietnamese day after day.

When Jim Fiorelli and Don Shepperd came in to brief for their mid-morning mission on January 31, South Vietnam was suddenly a nation plunged into complete chaos. In addition to the cities, several bases were under attack. Nobody seemed to know where the next thrust might come from. Since Tet was a big holiday, many South Vietnamese troops were home on leave, their posts vacant—yet another advantage the crafty North Vietnamese had exploited.

Fiorelli's sense of humor had survived the first wave of Tet attacks. As he and Shepperd sat down to brief, Jim noted he was in the front seat, "as it should be." But the quip failed to soften the tense mood in the room. "This is big shit," Roger Van Dyken interrupted. "The entire country is under attack, even the U.S. embassy in Saigon, the Presidential Palace, and Westmoreland's headquarters at Tan Són Nhut. Bien Hoa, too," he added. "Reportedly the VC overran part of the airfield and are attacking aircraft on the ramps." Shepperd and Fiorelli looked at each other. While they knew that a major offensive was under way, they hadn't been aware how serious it was. "The embassy?" they both wondered. They also thought about their F-100 buddies at Bien Hoa and wondered how they were faring.

As they flew toward the Pack, Fio and Shep saw the aftermath of the first day's fighting everywhere they looked on the horizon. A huge black column of smoke rose from the Hue Citadel, the magnificent walled fortress along the Perfume River that had housed emperors and their minions from the early 1800s until the French arrived in 1947. The plume was visible for miles. Virtually every other town and village on the landscape was burning, as if some giant, ethereal torch had ignited the whole country at once. And to the west, bombs from B-52 strikes were still mashing the hillsides around Khe Sanh, tossing more dirt and flame into the surreal tableau. "Looks like a good day to be over North Vietnam," Shepperd deadpanned as they gazed at the carnage in the South.

For once, Fio didn't have a smart-assed comeback. Both he and Shepperd wondered if Phu Cat would be under attack when they got back. "At least the weather's decent," Fiorelli finally replied. "Maybe we'll have good hunting in the Pack."

SIXTEEN

"TANKS IN OUR WIRE!"

Fiorelli and Shepperd were distracted during their mission up North, wondering more about what kind of inferno they'd be returning to than about what was going on beneath them on the Trail. Besides, the mission was a waste of time—bad weather as usual. When they headed back toward Phu Cat and South Vietnam, flames seemed to engulf even more of the country than when they had come north only four hours before. In fact, almost every major city they could see was on fire.

To the west they watched as long strings of bombs fell around Khe Sanh, dropped from three B-52s whose contrails they could see receding to the west toward Laos and Thailand. To the east they looked down once again on the devastation in Hue. Explosions were going off all over the town and the plume of black smoke rising from the Citadel at Hue looked even fatter.

The cockpit had been pretty quiet. "Kind of reminds you of Revelation in the Bible," Shepperd reflected, for once without sarcasm. "Wonder if this is the apocalypse, or Armageddon?"

Fiorelli was not feeling philosophical. "We probably ought to put some thought into where we will divert if Phu Cat is under attack," he suggested.

"Looks like *everything* is under attack," Shepperd answered. The cockpit returned to silence.

As they got closer to Phu Cat, Fiorelli called the tower for landing directions. The controller said everything was okay. The ROKs, the army troops from the Republic of Korea who provided security for the area, were notoriously brutal. It appeared that their methods were working. Nor was any smoke coming from Qui Nhon, the coastal city to the east.

They landed uneventfully and taxied in. As they shut down the engine, Fiorelli raised the canopy. "Have we been under attack?" he yelled.

"Not yet," replied the crew chief. "But we hear everywhere else has."

An anxious calm carried the base through the day, and at the bar that evening the pilots talked about nothing but the massive, country-wide offensive. Everybody wondered whether Phu Cat would be next. Someone had called Bien Hoa, where there were three F-100 squadrons and where several of the Mistys had come from. The VC had captured part of the runway, including the aircraft "arming area" where bombs underwent a final check before takeoff, armament safety pins were pulled, and the 20mm guns were charged. More than twenty aircraft had been damaged. The pilots had been sent to bunkers while the grunts with helicopters and tanks tried to blast out the VC so aircraft could get to the runway. One pilot had been shot in the arm while taxiing for takeoff.

"Yeah, but there's light at the end of the tunnel," snickered Fiorelli, mocking General Westmoreland's famous utterance from the year before about the "progress" in Vietnam.

As Maj. Mick Greene listened to all the talk, he knew there was trouble brewing for Misty. Greene was the detachment's irascible Ops officer, a perfect foil to the easygoing command style of Don Jones. A 1956 Naval Academy graduate from the San Joaquin Valley in California, Greene was a small, muscular fireplug who had wrestled and played football in school. He had a high-and-tight Marine-style crew cut and a moustache that hid a scar and made him look somewhat sinister—like someone you wanted on your side in a bar fight. Greene had credentials to match his perpetual seriousness: a couple of thousand hours in both the F-100 and the F-86, tours in France and Germany, and a master's degree in mechanical engineering, which he had put to use helping with nuclear weapons tests. Greene had first flown out of Bien Hoa himself, and moved over to Phu Cat around the time Misty was being formed.

Like many of the other pilots, however, he had been a combat virgin when he first arrived in Vietnam. On his first night in the barracks at Bien Hoa, a huge *boom!* had erupted in the darkness. "What the hell was that?" Greene squeaked. It was an Army howitzer that had fired just a few feet from his hootch. A few days later he tasted incoming fire, too, as VC rockets and mortars exploded around the base, wounding eleven people. On the way to the flight line the next morning, Greene gaped at several revetments full of ashen metal—which had been F-100s the night before.

Greene got his first in-country checkout from Capt. Duane Baker in a two-seat F-100F. They bombed a "suspected VC area" in the South, under FAC control. As they rolled in on the target area for the first time, Greene wondered if he really had what it took for combat. Then several weeks later, Baker was strafing a suspected VC location west of the Marine base at Chu Lai when the wings came off his airplane during pullout from a' bombing run. The plane dived straight into the ground, taking Baker with it. Because of his engineering background, Greene was sent to the crash site with an accident investigation team led by Colonel Lee, the wing vice commander. They boarded an Army Huey chopper, along with a security detail armed with M-16 rifles. Greene didn't even know how to load an M-16.

Simply taking off was a trial. The chopper was jammed with people—the more security men the better, since they were going into a hot VC area—and the pilots weren't sure the chopper would be able to clear a fence and some power lines at the far end of the base. On their first try the pilot taxied to the downwind corner of the base, opposite the fence, then turned around and applied full power as he tried to build enough speed and energy to get over the hurdles. Just before they got to the fence the helicopter shuddered to a halt. "We're overweight! One person—out!" the pilot ordered. Then they turned around for another run. They off-loaded two more soldiers before the chopper finally vibrated into the air, up over the power lines. As they buzzed off toward the crash site, Greene glanced into the cockpit where the two pilots were slapping each other on the back, apparently amazed that they had made it. This was not the kind of careful, by-the-book flying the engineer was used to.

The team found Baker's remains and the cockpit section of the airplane in a shallow creek. The rest of the plane was somewhere else. Greene dug around in the wreckage to find instruments that might help explain what had happened. The flight surgeon who had come with them recovered Baker's body and the remains of his flight suit. After about fifteen minutes an Army lieutenant who was in charge of a couple of squads of soldiers flown in for extra security said the VC were approaching and they needed to get out of there. Greene said he needed a few more minutes. "Major, you can have all the time you want," the lieutenant answered. "But the choppers are leaving now!" Greene decided to go with the lieutenant. They flew back to Chu Lai and the wreckage became VC loot.

Greene's analysis helped identify a problem on one of the F-100's wing spars. The Air Force devised a reinforcement that was fitted to all the Huns in the fleet. Greene's expertise got him appointed the 37th Wing's safety officer. He was also the chief of standardization and evaluation, the officer who oversaw pilot check rides and the procedure for certifying their proficiency in the F-100 and their readiness for combat. In the spring of 1967, Greene had given Maj. Bud Day a check ride to certify that Day was ready for the air refueling that would be required for the Misty missions into North Vietnam. Day hadn't needed much tutoring, and Greene was impressed by his drive and sober determination.

Greene shook off his early jitters and learned to sleep through the nighttime clamor like a veteran. After flying out-and-back missions in the South, he asked if he could transfer into the Misty detachment. This wasn't approved until October 1967, after Bud Day had been shot down, but he was excited nonetheless. Shortly afterward, Greene was riding back to his quarters in the back of a pickup truck when he jumped out, turned his ankle, and ended up in a knee-high cast that was supposed to stay on for six weeks. Eager for action and worried that the war might pass him by, Greene sawed off the cast with a survival knife and reported for duty with his flight boot laced up real tight.

214 ★ BURY US UPSIDE DOWN

Bob Craner, the "master," checked Greene out in Misty. The two pilots had been stationed together in France and Germany as lieutenants flying the F-100. Craner introduced Greene to what "real" gunfire looked like. He took Greene north around Dong Hoi, which was laced with AAA guns of every caliber. The gunners weren't terribly accurate, so Craner used them as training devices. He circled down gradually from 8,000 feet, keeping up a good head of steam—400 knots plus—so they could coast out to sea if they happened to get hit. Greene didn't see any gun sites at first, but once they descended through 3,000 feet or so, the ground lit up like a carnival. Greene turned out to be not quite as grizzled as he thought he was, and he wondered aloud whether busting trees in South Vietnam might not be such a bad deal. Craner just laughed.

By the time of Tet, Greene had spent a lot of time around his pilots. The Ops officer knew even before they did that all the recent turmoil would affect the way they flew. The bad weather alone produced a lot of frustration. Then there was Khe Sanh, and now the Tet attacks. Greene felt sure the Mistys would start to press, partly out of desperation to accomplish something and partly out of revenge—to punish the North Vietnamese. "Look, let's keep our heads on straight," Greene had already started to lecture at preflight briefings. "Pressing and taking risks against dumb targets isn't going to help us win the war."

The news was similar the next day, and the next. The broad assault continued. One of General Giap's bedrock assumptions was that the populace would rise up to join the Viet Cong against the Americans and the "puppet" government of President Nguyen Van Thieu. Every trained eye watched for signs that a popular revolt was brewing. But as the days passed, it became clear that it wasn't happening. The South Vietnamese, with massive U.S. support, had begun driving the enemy forces from many of the cities. Attacks in some of the provincial capitals were quickly repulsed. In Saigon the fighting was pretty much over by February 5, although it was a few weeks longer until the South Vietnamese regained control of Cholon, the Chinese section of the city.[1]

In other provincial capitals, however, such as Dalat, Ban Me Thuot, My Tho, Can Tho, Ben Tre, and Kontum, the fighting was vicious and prolonged. And Hue was being reduced to rubble as the two forces battled block by block. Word began to get out that the Viet Cong and North Vietnamese forces had been executing hundreds of civilians.[2]

For the Mistys, lousy weather compounded the brutality on the ground and made them feel straitjacketed. A break appeared to be on the way, though. On February 7, Don Shepperd and Jim Fiorelli were scheduled to fly together again. They were friends, and Shepperd had decided that he liked to fly with Fio because Fio was in love and didn't take unnecessary chances. For the first time in a long while the weather was forecast to be CAVU—ceiling and visibility unlimited.

Just after midnight the evening before, a mortar attack awakened the two pilots—and everybody else on base. Sirens blew and illumination mortars lit the sky to help find any enemy forces that might be approaching the perimeter. Everybody wondered if this would be the start of a big attack, similar to the one that had shaken Bien Hoa. The pilots hauled ass toward the bunkers. After the first few explosions, however, all was quiet.

Fio and Shep went back to bed, then straggled into the early briefing at 4:00 a.m, dead tired. The briefing covered the usual, with one bit of added emphasis—others were taking care of Khe Sanh and South Vietnam. The Mistys needed to stay focused on the North. They took off in the dark as Misty 11, the afterburner lighting the morning sky. Passing 15,000 feet, they could see artillery shells continuing to explode in Hue. Cricket, the ABCCC, called them with an important request. The Special Forces outpost at Lang Vei, about five miles west of Khe Sanh on the Laotian border, had been attacked overnight and the Marines at Khe Sanh had lost radio contact. Would Misty 11 fly by and take a look?

Shepperd and Fio made certain there were no B-52 strikes scheduled to take place in the area. Just after daybreak they began their letdown south and west of Khe Sanh, ever mindful of the reports of intense AAA lining the hills surrounding the Marine outpost. They could see Lang Vei clearly from twenty miles away—the weather was indeed good. As they got closer to Lang Vei, they dipped to low altitude and began to circle.

The carnage that came into focus was surreal. It looked like a tornado had hit the outpost. "We've got bad news for you, Cricket," reported Shepperd. "The camp looks like it's completely destroyed—like a nuke went off. There are no signs of life and there are three destroyed tanks near the perimeter."

"Tanks?" replied Cricket. "Tanks? Are you sure?" It was the same reaction Ed Risinger had received when he told Cricket there had been tanks north of the DMZ only two weeks before. In fact, there had been another warning of tanks. After Risinger's report, in mid-January, another FAC had reported seeing five tanks in Laos on January 24. An air strike destroyed one of them.[3] Then, early in the morning on February 7, Capt. Frank Willoughby, the camp commander at Lang Vei, made a frantic radio call to Khe Sanh. "We have tanks in our wire!" he shouted, requesting artillery, illumination, and air strikes.

Until then, none of the senior U.S. commanders really believed there were NVA tanks in the South despite the reports from Risinger and others. And yet Willoughby could see them right before him. Ten tanks, in total, had attacked Lang Vei, helping enemy ground troops overrun the compound. Three of the tanks—those spotted by Shepperd and Fiorelli in the wire—had been destroyed, but the rest helped turn the battle into a rout. A few of the U.S. defenders had fought their way out in the middle of the night, and a handful, including Captain Willoughby, were able to get evacuated by helicopter the next morning. But most of the five hundred troops who had manned Lang Vei ended up dead or missing.[4]

The reports of "tanks in the wire" struck fear in the hearts of the defenders at Khe Sanh and at U.S. military headquarters in Saigon. After all, Khe Sanh was still surrounded, cut off, and totally dependent on air for resupply. And the weather often prevented that. The predicament began to seem so dire that in Washington, policymakers desperate to avoid another "Dinbinphoo" started to consider one of the most severe military interventions imaginable.

On January 31, Robert Ginsburg, a National Security Council staffer, queried Gen. Earle Wheeler, chairman of the Joint Chiefs of Staff, about the prospect of doing some "contingency target analysis" for the use of nuclear weapons in the Khe Sanh area.[5] The next day General Wheeler sent a top secret message to Admiral Sharp, the Pacific Command chief, a message so sensitive it was designated Eyes Only—for Sharp alone to read. Wheeler asked whether there were targets in the area of Khe Sanh that "lend themselves to nuclear strikes."[6] A few days later, newspaper stories appeared with vague details of the idea. Shortly after that, outgoing defense secretary Robert McNamara swore to three distinguished visitors that the Joint Chiefs had "not even discussed" the subject, and that it was "inconceivable that the use of nuclear weapons would be considered."[7] Either he was misinformed or intentionally misinforming.

Of course, Shepperd and Fiorelli had no idea of these deliberations as they circled Lang Vei. But the situation they saw was far more complex than what the planners in Washington and Saigon could have imagined. From an overhead perspective it was obvious that it would have taken several small nuclear weapons, or a few big ones, to wipe out all the artillery and troops dug into caves and spread throughout holes in the mountains. Several others would have to be dropped on the so-called Demilitarized Zone—which North Vietnamese troops had been routinely traversing on their way south—and farther north in Laos, on the numerous tendrils of the Trail. Above all, Washington would have had to nuke Hanoi and Haiphong, where most of the stuff heading south originated. And that wasn't going to happen. Drumming their fingers on the ultimate weapon only indicated how feckless American decision-makers had become.

As frustrated as the pilots were, the intel officers, in some ways, had it worse. For the pilots the bad weather provided a break from the everyday routine—which included getting shot at. For the intel officers, John Haltigan and Roger Van Dyken and Cal Kunz, there was no break. They were continually scrutinizing piles of intel that spilled in from 7th Air Force, trying to improvise when bad weather moved in and scotched all the reconnaissance flights. They scrambled around putting target information together and accomplishing practically nothing while the North pushed its war-making apparatus down the Trail under the clouds. "The intel work is at its lowest ebb ever," Roger Van Dyken confided to his diary in late February. "Tankers are canceled for nearly half our missions and the weather is prohibitive whenever we do fly. . . . We have no good new dope to give the pilots. Their missions are boring and uneventful. They just fly in the hope that maybe today it'll open up."

Bad weather did have a few silver linings. For one thing, it slowed the pace at Misty. Once the Tet Offensive started to ebb, there were opportunities for nice-to-do things that often fell by the wayside. The nonpilots at Phu Cat often pleaded for a ride in one of the two-seat jets, something the Air Force allowed under tightly controlled circumstances. For the intel guys, maintenance crews, and others who routinely worked with the pilots, a backseat ride could be an invaluable chance to learn what it really took for the pilots to do their jobs. It was also a motivational "thank you" from the pilots to those who supported them—not to mention one of the most thrilling experiences ordinary troops could get in the war zone. Rides weren't given on combat missions, especially over the North, but there were other opportunities.

So in late February, Jim Fiorelli offered to give Roger Van Dyken a ride as he flight-tested a Hun that had just undergone a major overhaul. Fiorelli, like many of the Mistys, was a hero to Van Dyken, somebody who routinely dodged hot lead and willingly put his life on the line for the mission. Getting a ride in a fighter jet was a privilege, but getting a ride from a Misty was an honor. To Van Dyken it was like the difference between getting a standard tour of the White House, and being shown around the White House by the president himself.

As the Hun thundered down the runway, Van Dyken marveled at how quiet and smooth it was inside the jet. Wow, he thought, this is what it must be like to ride in a Cadillac! Once they reached altitude, Fio became a rather animated tour guide. "Hey Roger," he said over the intercom as he started his tutorial, "see that puffy white cloud at two o'clock? Watch this!"

Then he streaked straight toward the cloud, which instantly changed from a puff on the horizon to a huge cumulus mass that enveloped the jet. Fio did it again, this time flipping off a corner of the cloud with his right wing. They did barrel rolls, loops, cloverleafs, simulated rocket passes, and a variety of other combat maneuvers. Fio even let Van Dyken take the stick for a few minutes and fly the plane himself. Both of them were having a ball.

They headed east toward the coast, where they spotted a fisherman plying his net in a small bay. "I wonder if he's constipated," Fio mused over the intercom as he executed a crisp wingover, then straightened out into a dive. The nose of the jet was aimed directly at the fisherman. Van Dyken watched the airspeed needle climb and the boat grow larger and larger. The sea was rushing toward the cockpit. Finally, when Fio figured he probably had the fisherman's rapt attention, he

pulled back on the stick and darted between a couple of karst cliff is-
lands that encircled the bay.

Fio was ready for more. He asked Van Dyken if there were any
other maneuvers he'd like to make. But the dive had taken its toll on
Van Dyken's equilibrium and he was struggling to keep his breakfast
down. Van Dyken gamely said he'd be up for a bit more flying—but
asked if they could fly upside up instead of upside down, hoping that
would force the contents of his stomach back where they belonged.
The landlubbing intel officer kept his composure, and when they finally landed he felt a bit dizzy but thought he would be okay.

But the jarring transition from normal gravity to airborne acrobatics and back again quickly caught up with him. Van Dyken staggered
to the Misty office and curled up in a prenatal ball on the floor, where
he slept for an hour. He vomited periodically for the next two days.
Once he recovered, however, he told his friends around Misty that the
ride had been "simply fantastic. I'd do it again. I think."

The slower pace also let the maintenance guys catch a breather, since
it meant fewer bullet holes and less battle damage to fix. Misty had also
gotten a couple of additional two-seat F-100Fs, for a total of six. That
meant there would be spares when one of the jets did need some patch-
ing. The Misty operation was in good shape, on high step, waiting for
its opportunities. When the weather did break, Misty usually claimed
impressive BDA—fifteen trucks destroyed, eight damaged, several secondary explosions, and other fires on one unusually clear day.

But this amounted to "a fart in a windstorm," as one of the new
Mistys, Charlie Summers, liked to put it. Truth was, just as Misty
seemed to be hitting its cruising altitude, the air had started to come
out of the mission. The whole month of January had been a bust, beginning with the big New Year's Day attacks that got weathered out.
The Mistys had spent a lot of time checking out "movers" in Laos that
had been identified by the Igloo White sensor program at Nakhon
Phanom. Except for a grand total of one truck the sensors had helped
them find, those targets had all been duds. Igloo White had been much
more effective at locating troops for the B-52s to bomb, especially
around Khe Sanh.[8] But for the Mistys it merely wasted gas and diverted attention from their principal mission, stanching the flow
through Route Pack 1. The Mistys didn't think they needed sensors or

even B-52s. They needed good weather. Without it, life at Phu Cat amounted to little more than day after day of purposeless malaise.

But for many Mistys, flying over the Trail was still better than anything else the war had to offer. Until early 1968, Misty tours had been limited to four months or sixty missions because of the danger. The Air Force wanted to spread the risk around and not force any one group to bear more than its share. But when Jonesy Jones was approaching the end of his fourth month, he asked Don Jones if he could stay longer. Jonesy argued that he would provide good continuity for the next rotation, which was already starting to arrive. He'd be a mentor of sorts. Jonesy didn't mention that he had an enemy waiting for him at Tuy Hoa, where he was scheduled to return—the squadron commander whose plane he had damaged months earlier by getting too close to it on a bombing run. Jonesy was a bit like a member of the French Foreign Legion: He had no home, save Misty.

The Misty boss liked Jonesy and especially enjoyed flying with him. He called Tuy Hoa to ask if it would be okay if Misty kept him. Since Tuy Hoa would have had to come up with another Misty volunteer to replace Jonesy—and there weren't any—they said, sure, he's yours.

There were daily exhortations from 7th Air Force and lots of pep talk, but there wasn't much they could do to open up the skies over the Trail. At one point 7th decided to send a team up to discuss improving the road interdiction program. Van Dyken had been working on some new ideas and was eager for the meeting. But when they came, the discussion wasn't about roads, it was about SAMs. Some had been making it south into the DMZ, and there was fear they might end up all the way down in South Vietnam, where they could disrupt the devastating B-52 attacks around Khe Sanh. The Mistys needed to watch for them and keep them out of Route Pack 1 "at any cost," according to 7th Air Force.

"And just what the hell does 'at any cost' mean?" asked Mick Greene.

"I think it means they are perfectly willing to sacrifice our asses," laughed Fiorelli.

Still, SAMs got everybody's attention, and when bad weather scrubbed all the missions on one day in February, Don Jones and Mick Greene set up an "educational brief" on tactics and SAMs. It was a refresher course for the experienced Mistys and an important indoctrination for several new guys. Five new pilots had joined Misty in January and two more in early February. Dick Rutan and Whispering Smith were among them, as were Brian Williams and Carroll Williams—"B. Willy" and "C. Willy"—two of the three Williams boys from the 416th. Maj. Elmer Slavey, from the 52d Fighter Squadron at Phan Rang had several thousand hours in F-86s and F-100s and was one of the more experienced Hun drivers in Vietnam. Maj. Charlie Summers was scheduled to replace Mick Greene as the new Ops officer, and Lt. Col. Stanley Mamlock would take over from Don Jones as commander. Summers and Mamlock were scheduled to spend a few weeks at the unit flying and learning the ropes before they took over their new jobs.

Jones and Greene reiterated that the Mistys were to be on high alert for any missile sightings. They relentlessly studied pictures of SA-2s, the Soviet-built surface-to-air missiles that could shoot down a plane as high as 60,000 feet—the same missile that had knocked Gary Powers and his U-2 out of the sky over Moscow. They pored over pictures of the Guideline transporter vehicles the SA-2s traveled on. "Now look, guys," Greene lectured. "What we've just been told is, we are fucking with rattlesnakes. The Thuds up in Route Packs 5 and 6 carry jamming pods and they're supported by other aircraft with electronic countermeasures, jammers, and chaff. We don't have shit on our airplanes. Even our radar homing and warning gear doesn't work. So if we get fired at we're naked. Let's make sure we don't ignore the fact that we're sitting ducks." The words seemed to sober up the Mistys. The room was quiet.

Then Fio piped up. "Well, at least if the weather breaks, we're SAMed-up," he joked.

SAMs were risky, serious business, the Mistys knew—but still, nobody had seen one yet. And until they did, it was just another abstract threat that the guys down at 7th felt obligated to mention. On one depressing monsoon day, Shepperd and Fiorelli barely thought about SAMs as they stared at wall-to-wall clouds over the Pack. The weather was virtually unworkable. Strikers would never be able to get below the overcast to drop bombs. The two pilots drilled holes in the sky over the Mu Ghia Pass, bored.

The ABCCC kept sending them to check out "movers" that had

222 ★ BURY US UPSIDE DOWN

been detected by some undisclosed source—undoubtedly "McNamara's Fence." No matter how enthusiastic the intel honchos were, Fio and Shepperd were finding absolutely nothing that correlated with the tips coming from the ABCCC.

A minor standoff developed between the two Mistys and the controllers. Shepperd and Fiorelli imagined some technician who never left his post staring at a computer screen, convinced that a squad of tanks or a fleet of trucks was slinking around right before Misty's eyes. The ABCCC controllers, using the call sign Cricket, seemed to regard the two Mistys as a couple of faux warriors doing a little bit of flying between coffee breaks. No doubt some ranking officer was busting their ass, insisting that they bang on Misty to produce some results that would validate the fancy sensor project. But if there was nothing on the ground, there was nothing for Misty to validate.

Fio and Shepperd reported no finds. Cricket came back on the radio. "Misty, can you check again?" came the request. "Reports indicate SIGNIFICANT movement in that area."

The two Mistys got irritated. "I say again," Shepperd snorted, "there are no movers—ABSOLUTELY NO MOVERS—anywhere in the vicinity."

Cricket asked Misty to check one more time. Shepperd lost his patience. "Look, Cricket," he growled. "We know how and where to look. Your reports are WRONG! I say again, WRONG! There is nothing. I say again NOTHING! I say once again NOTHING moving in that area."

Finally Cricket desisted. "Roger, Misty. We'll report," they conceded. "Cricket out."

"Fio, let's go home," Shepperd suggested, weary and annoyed. "The weather's unworkable. We're wasting our time. We can't put anybody in today."

"Yeah, you're right," Fio agreed. "Let's make one more run from the south, up to the mouth of Mu Ghia, and we'll go home." Shepperd yawned and began to stow the maps and camera, figuring there'd be no action on the last short run up to Mu Ghia.

Fio was a superb pilot, and cautious, too. He knew where the guns were and didn't take foolish chances. As they approached Mu Ghia, the cloud cover broke up a little bit. Fio ducked beneath the deck at about 1,500 feet, skirting the north-south road networks where gun sites would most likely be located. The altitiude was lower than Colonel Schneider allowed—his minimum was 4,500 feet—but otherwise Fio flew by the book. He flew fast, climbing, descending, and turning to provide a tricky, three-dimensional problem for ground gunners.

"We're probably just wasting our time," he said, "but let's just keep looking under these trees for any signs of activity. We'll run up to the cave mouth at the foot of Mu Ghia. If we don't see anything we'll head home."

"Rodge," Shepperd responded. Then he spotted something. "Hey—there's a vehicle on that road, just to the left!" It was the first mover they had seen all day. It was just one truck, but it was a welcome diversion from the boredom.

They tracked the vehicle, which turned off a dirt road and disappeared into the foliage. Fio dipped down for a closer look. After a few moments they figured they lost him. "Well, looks like just a single truck and he's gone," said Fio. "Let's forget it and go up to Mu Ghia."

Just as Fio turned the plane north once again, at about 1,500 feet, both Mistys saw something streak past the front of the airplane, about a thousand feet ahead. It looked like a flaming lance, long, needle-thin, and burning. The two pilots were perplexed. "What the hell is it?" Fio wondered aloud.

"Don't know," Shepperd answered. "Never seen anything like that. A missile?" They flew home with plenty to discuss. It couldn't have been an SA-2—they were much bigger. When they landed and reported for their debriefing, the intel officer said it sounded like an infrared, shoulder-fired missile. "They've been telling us to expect them," the debriefer said. "This is the first report. We need to get this to 7th. We think the Russians have supplied them to the NVA for the big push down south." Later, at the O club, Fio and Shepperd gave an informal tutorial on IR missiles to anybody who was sober enough to listen.

The weather remained bad over North Vietnam through February, but it was beginning to improve along the Trail in Laos. One day Ed Risinger and Don Shepperd, who had become fast friends, were trolling just north of Tchepone, in Laos, a small village northwest of Khe Sanh with an old bombed-out airstrip nearby. Risinger, flying the plane up front, spotted a clump that looked like a camouflaged vehicle along a side road. He circled the site and decided to dip down to about 500 feet for a closer look, flying right over the clump while dipping his wing. "What the hell are we doing this for?" asked Shepperd.

"I just want to see what that is," replied Risinger. "Looks like a truck."

"You're going to get our asses shot off," warned Shepperd.

Risinger whipped the airplane around and started another low pass, this time descending even lower—to barely 200 feet off the ground. Shepperd gritted his teeth. Just as they passed over the "clump," flashes burst out of it. Suddenly the camouflaged truck looked a lot more like a grouping of fast-firing, medium-caliber AAA guns. Shepperd heard and felt several bullets slam into the fuselage as Risinger pulled the airplane into a steep climb. Looking out the right side of the canopy, Shepperd could see fuel coming from under the wing. "We're hit and streaming fuel!" he shouted to Risinger. They jettisoned the rocket pods so they could climb more easily, but retained the external gas tanks just in case they needed the fuel. Shepperd made an emergency call.

"Mayday, Mayday, Mayday!" he bellowed "Misty one-one is hit north of Tchepone, heading west!"

"Crown has you," came the cool reply. "Say status."

"We're losing fuel," Shepperd reported. "Can you send the tanker our way?" It was the first time Shepperd had been hit on a Misty mission and he was scared. His heart was pumping hard and he was pissed at his comrade up front.

Risinger pointed the crippled aircraft toward Ubon, the giant F-4 base west of the Mekong River in Thailand. A flight of two F-4s that was heading back to Ubon after a mission soon caught up with Misty 11, flying off its right wing. "We'll escort you to Ubon," the flight lead announced. Then he slipped underneath the F-100 to inspect the damage. "We're taking a close look," he said, "and don't see anything major. Just a little fuel leaking from your right wing."

Risinger watched the fuel gauges carefully as the tanker appeared about ten miles up ahead. "Tanker," he radioed. "How about staying with us in case we begin to lose fuel quickly? We've been shot up and right now we have a small leak, but things look okay."

As they got close to Ubon, Risinger declared an emergency with the tower and said he was proceeding to "high key," a position 10,000 feet over the runway from which he would fly a wide circling landing approach. It was called an "SFO," or simulated flameout pattern. If the engine quit, Risinger could "dead stick" the Hun onto the runway, with the power off, like a glider. That turned out to be unnecessary. The aircraft touched down without any trouble and Risinger pulled the drag chute to slow the airplane. He brought the aircraft to a stop in the middle of the runway as fire trucks rushed alongside.

Risinger raised the canopy and threw a sloppy hand salute in the direction of a colonel who had pulled up in a staff car. A fireman put a ladder on the canopy bow and shouted, "We need to get you guys out of this airplane. There's fuel leaking from underneath." The two pilots scrambled down the ladder and threw their gear into a waiting truck, then walked back toward the plane to examine the damage. There were a few holes that looked like they had come from ZPU AAA guns, a relatively new rapid-fire antiaircraft weapon—one more example of upgraded new stuff coming south. The Mistys had seen a few two-barrel ZPUs before, but today's holes had come from a four-barrel gun. Risinger made a note to report the development to intel. There were burn marks where the rounds had entered the fuselage and wings, but the ZPU didn't use exploding shells, thank goodness—that's probably why the plane continued to fly. Fuel was trickling out in a slow stream from holes in one of the wings.

A fireman quickly plugged the holes and the fire trucks started to wash the fuel off the runway. A tug was hitched to the nose landing gear and began to tow the aircraft to the parking ramp so the runway could reopen. If not for the fire trucks, no one would know the airplane was damaged—for the most part it appeared unscathed. "Oh well," smiled Risinger, "now you know what it feels like to get hit."

Shepperd felt a little sheepish—all this clamor and a Mayday call for just a few holes and a minor fuel leak. But he was irritated with Risinger. "You asshole," he snapped. "You got us shot for one fucking truck—a truck that turned out to be triple-A!"

Risinger laughed. Shepperd scowled at him, but let it drop.

It was midmorning and they went into Base Ops to see about getting a ride back to Phu Cat. A C-47 wouldn't be in to pick them up until late in the afternoon. A repair crew would fly in on that plane to fix the Hun, and the two pilots would fly back to base for tomorrow's flying schedule. The Base Ops officer, an old major, offered to assign them a just-arrived lieutenant to drive them to lunch and the base exchange, the BX, where they could pick up a few niceties not usually available at Phu Cat. The lieutenant had been in Thailand just one week and looked like he was about sixteen years old—an easy mark for Risinger.

"Lieutenant, we appreciate you taking care of us," he started. "So, what time of day do you come under attack?"

"Uh, sir, we don't come under attack," replied the fuzzy-faced lieutenant.

"You don't come under attack? What the hell kind of war is this?" demanded Risinger. "What do you guys do for fun?"

"Well, sir, we go to town and shop, or go to a good restaurant."

"Town? For Christsakes we can't even step outside the fence at Phu Cat without getting shot."

"And, sir, there are the massage parlors if you want to really relax. They call them 'steam and creams.' "

"Massage parlors? My God! I suppose you have whorehouses, too?"

"Well, sir, I don't know about that." The lieutenant's face got red.

"Well, if it's like Vietnam, whorehouses are useless anyway. Our PCOD is when we leave the States."

"What's PCOD, sir?"

"Pussy cut off date, son. The VD is so bad in Vietnam, if you contract it they can't cure it and they keep you in-country forever. Haven't you heard the legend of Needledick Steely?"

"No, sir."

"Well, there's a song about it." Risinger began waving his hand as if he were strumming a guitar and threw his head back to sing:

> *Needledick Steely the bug fucker*
> *Slept with a Saigon whore*
> *Needledick Steely the bug fucker*
> *Won't visit the U.S. no more.*

Shepperd could hold it in no longer. He burst out laughing. The lieutenant thought he was being joshed but seemed unsure. Maybe, Shepperd thought, the young officer was suddenly worried about VD. The lieutenant pulled into the BX parking lot and the three got out of the vehicle. A colonel was coming out of the building.

"Captain, where's your hat?" the colonel coldly asked Risinger.

"I don't have a hat, sir."

"Why not?"

"I got shot."

"What does that have to do with a hat?"

"Well, sir, I wasn't planning on stopping in here. I don't take a hat on combat missions and we diverted when we got hit."

"Well, Captain, you can buy a hat inside."

"I don't have any money, sir. I don't carry my wallet on combat missions."

"Well, why are you going into the BX without money?" asked the colonel, becoming flustered now.

"Just looking, sir. It's such a treat to get away from the war and come to Thailand." The colonel gave up and stormed off, shaking his head.

Later that afternoon their young escort took Risinger and Shepperd out to board the C-47 for their ride back to the war. As they climbed the ladder to get on board, the lieutenant said good-bye and saluted. "Don't salute me, Lieutenant," Risinger smirked. "I don't have a hat."

SEVENTEEN

RISINGER'S RAID

Tet changed many men, and Howard Williams was one of them.
Until the furious nationwide attacks, Howie had felt his duty was
to fly close air support missions in the South, coming to the aid of the
embattled troops in the bush. That seemed like the best use of his talents. But he started to reevaluate that after Tet. The onslaught had
demonstrated that the communists' combat infrastructure in the South
was far broader than most people had imagined. Many of the attackers had been local Viet Cong, but it was becoming evident there had
been an alarming number of North Vietnamese regulars fighting next
to them. The complex and coordinated nature of the attacks clearly indicated that Hanoi, not the VC, was pulling the strings. And the explosive firepower, the mortars and artillery and the sheer volume of
guns and ammunition, did not come from the Viet Cong's limited
weapons stores. All that weaponry and expertise and manpower was
coming from one place: North Vietnam, via the Trail.

Howie had always quizzed his brother Roger about the goings-on
at U.S. military headquarters in Saigon, which ordinarily was a typical
bureaucratic rear-area command: Busy, but quiet. The dramatic infiltration of Viet Cong had obviously changed that. They had attacked
the headquarters and the adjoining Tan Son Nhut airfield, forcing a

battle that raged for nearly two days. A small suicide squad had seized parts of the U.S. embassy for six hours.[1] For the first time since going to work there Roger had fired his weapon, and he described the frenzy to his brother. He recorded one tape for Howie while huddled behind a mattress, with machine guns firing in the background and mortar shells dropping onto the base intermittently. Roger related how dozens of rockets and other explosives had pummeled the base. Howie's brother definitely sounded like he was in danger.

Roger had other stories to tell. While the monthlong battle for Hue was still raging, he accompanied a major up to the battle zone, about fifty miles south of the DMZ, to deliver payroll. Roger's job was to be the "gun" protecting the major, and the money. The delivery point was outside the city a few miles, but near the artillery that was bombarding the NVA and Viet Cong holding Hue. Roger was amazed at the ceaseless report of the guns and the shells that never stopped flying over his head. The deluge seemed unbearable.

General Westmoreland and other American leaders promptly declared the Tet battles a major U.S. victory, with thousands of enemy soldiers killed and nearly every attack repulsed. But the sudden peril surrounding Roger Williams reflected a new degree of desperation for U.S. ground troops in South Vietnam. During one week in February, 543 Americans were killed in action and more than 2,500 wounded—the highest weekly totals of the entire war.[2] A dramatic, now-or-never mood seemed to replace drift and uncertainty in the political and military centers of the war. In Washington, incoming defense secretary Clark Clifford declared an end to one-sided truces and cease-fires: "We have been suckers and we are going to quit being suckers."[3] In Saigon, General Westmoreland was reviving a plan to send several divisions west into Laos to cut the Ho Chi Minh Trail once and for all.[4]

Howie Williams saw South Vietnam burning beneath him on missions that now became more frequent than ever. He took it all in and made a decision. Ground support missions were important—perhaps never more so—but the lifeline of the North's entire war effort was the Trail. He was concerned about Monalee and Howard Jr., and his responsibilities to them weighed heavily in his thinking. But if he really wanted to do his utmost for the grunts—for guys like his brother, who was now carrying his rifle around and ducking in and out of firefights—he would have to join the pilots working over the Trail. Every troop truck or ammo carrier or fuel transport he could help destroy would reduce the firepower the Americans would face on the ground, in battle. That would be more effective, and more meaningful, than going after the enemy when he was just yards away from the good guys, firing away.

Howie talked to Roger on the phone in late February and told him he had decided to join Misty. He had become a flight lead by then, and was qualified, and would be following the path of several others from his squadron. Dick Rutan was already there, along with Brian Williams and Carroll Williams. They described a unit that had enormous impact, despite the constraints of lousy weather. Misty was an opportunity to do more, he told Roger. It was the best way for him to make a difference.

Plus, there was the spectacular flying he had heard about, several hours per mission—no formations or wingmen or other constraints, the freedom to do whatever was needed to get the job done. Howie found some of his colleagues in the 416th to be big mouths, including a couple of borderline pilots who performed marginally and didn't seem to care. He was frustrated with staff officers and commanders who flew occasionally for the hours and the mission count, but never bothered to sharpen their rusty skills. Misty, he hoped, would be a chance to fly with real warriors.

It was easy to tell his brother this. Not so Monalee and his family back home. They may not understand, Howie told Roger, and they certainly wouldn't like it. In fact, after Tet, the news back in the States was beginning to sound grim. CBS newsman Walter Cronkite had made his highly publicized trip to Vietnam to investigate the situation, and returned with dire conclusions. "It now seems more certain than ever that the bloody experience of Vietnam is to end in a stalemate," he told millions of American viewers on February 27.[5] At the White House, President Johnson watched the program in dismay, feeling that if they had lost Cronkite, they had lost America.[6] Howie decided not to give his family more to worry about by telling them about his new job right away. Maybe he'd explain it to Monalee when he saw her in Hawaii in April.

As Howie prepared to join Misty in early March, his letters and tapes back home were filled with other news—in particular, a side project he had taken on at Phu Cat. In addition to his flying duties, Howie was the "civic action officer" for the 416th, and he had "adopted" two local schools, attended by about fourteen hundred Vietnamese children. He asked Monalee, who taught first grade in Columbus, along with his sister Jean and other family members, to gather up donations of clothing and school supplies for the kids—many of them orphaned by the war. Boxes were set out in several schools in Ohio, and by the end of February there were enough donated goods to fill a sizable truck. Amidst a busy flying schedule, Howie spent a lot of time arranging for a big Air Force shipping container that would carry the supplies overseas to their destination. He had also tried to start an art-exchange program between some of the kids in the two schools, and the first-graders Monalee taught in Columbus. But after the Tet Offensive the pace at Phu Cat had quickened so much there wasn't any time left for the project. Besides, it had become too risky to leave the base.

The weather was getting better, too, which enlivened things at Misty. On March 7, Don Shepperd and Carroll Williams were scheduled to fly as Misty 11 on a "SAM hunt." During the mission briefing the two dutifully studied intel photos of Guideline missile transporters, and the Fansong radars that tracked planes and guided the SAMs to them. "Remember," the intel briefer said, "an SA-2 site will always be well protected by 37- and 57-millimeter!"

"No kidding?" replied the quiet, unassuming C. Willy. "You mean they will really try to kill us?" Everyone chuckled. They all needed a laugh at four in the morning.

Shep and C. Willy were wheels-up at 6:00 a.m., Shepperd flying in the front, C. Willy handling the maps in the back. As they crossed the DMZ they noticed that the Pack was socked in solid, not clear as forecast. After cursing the weathermen, they flew into Laos to see what they could find. They started northeast of Mu Ghia Pass and began to systematically run up and down the roads looking for early-morning traffic. They had about five minutes of fuel left before "tanker bingo" when C. Willy shouted, "Look down there! Up against the karst! There's four of them!"

Shepperd found the spot, and there they were: four Guideline transporters loaded with canvas-covered missiles. The transporters had
been pulled forward into small trails cut into the jungle and set up to
fire south, away from the karst they were nestled up against. The canvas covering—and the lack of camouflage—indicated the site wasn't
ready. Shepperd and C. Willy circled the area taking photos and looking for the Fansong radars that were an essential part of the SAM
package—plus the AAA, the gun sites, that would no doubt be protecting it all. Strangely, they saw neither. C. Willy called the ABCCC to
ask that fighters be ready as soon as they got back from refueling on
the tanker.

While taking on fuel, the two pilots discussed what they had just
seen. With no radar or gun sites, the missiles must have been en route
to someplace else. But if that were the case they'd probably be camouflaged. Since they were sitting out in the open, maybe the NVA was in
the process of setting them up right there next to the karst.

Controllers from the ABCCC came on the radio. Four SAMs was a
big find, and they were diverting three flights of F-105s from a strike
package that was en route to Hanoi. The strikers would meet Misty
north of the site right after Misty tanked. Shepperd asked C. Willy if
he thought they should turn on the RHAW gear, the radar homing and
warning indicator that detected SAM launches. "Nah, leave it off,"
C. Willy advised. "It's a piece of crap and none of us know how to
work it. It will only be distracting."

As Misty 11 came off the tanker, the ABCCC came back on and
said that the fighters wouldn't be available for another twenty to
twenty-five minutes. Misty 21, meanwhile, was just taking off from
Phu Cat and would be going directly to the tanker, so that it would be
gassed up and ready to step in the next time Misty 11 bingoed. Shep
and C. Willy flew straight back to the Valley of the SAMs to look for
the Fansong radar, the heart of the SAM system. "Where is that sonofabitch?" Shepperd wondered. "It's got to be near the missiles."

Unlike the pilots who flew into the gauntlet of air defense up near
Hanoi, Misty 11 was naked. They had no electronic countermeasures
to jam a missile's radar, no chaff to draw a missile off course, no effective RHAW gear to warn them of a launch. If a SAM happened to
come their way, they would have to rely on their own flying skills to get

away—which even the best pilots who flew up north would say was foolhardy.

They dropped down from 8,000 feet, through 6,000, and were both beginning to scan the landscape when there was a huge bright flash on the ground accompanied by smoke. A missile was coming after them. They both saw it immediately. The cockpit filled with one sound: both of them shouting "Oh, shit!" simultaneously.

"Hold on!" Shepperd shouted. He pushed the plane over in a negative-G maneuver and turned so the missile was at the three o'clock position, off the right wing, a move Shepperd vaguely recalled hearing about in an intel brief from a few of the "big boys" who flew against SAMs in Route Pack 5 and 6 every day. Cameras, maps, checklists, and dirt filled the cockpit and flew in their faces. It felt like a desperate gambit—but they got lucky. The missile corkscrewed wildly and passed behind them, to their right.

As they caught their breath, Shepperd brought the plane level. They tried to figure out what had happened. They guessed that it was a bad missile. Or maybe there was no radar yet to guide it. One thing was sure, however: The SAM was huge. To Shepperd it seemed at least a thousand times bigger than the infrared, shoulder-fired missile that had been fired at him and Jim Fiorelli in February, not far from where they were now.

Finally the F-105s arrived. Shepperd warned them of the missile firing. The four transporters were still in their original locations, and still uncamouflaged—a seductive target. As Misty 11 rolled in to mark the location of the SAMs with smoke rockets, a 57mm gun suddenly came alive, firing from the valley floor. "Hold it!" Shepperd directed over the radio. "We're going to have to take out this 57-millimeter site first." Then he clicked off the mike. "Damn it, Willy," Shepperd said to his copilot, "how did we miss that site?"

They aborted the marking run on the missiles and pulled up again to go mark the gun site instead. But their marking rocket spun out of control and hit far from the target.

They were getting lined up for another pass when the lead Thud pilot came over the radio. "You don't need to mark," he said. "I see the guns."

"My hero, you are cleared!" Shepperd answered, thankful that he didn't have to make a second marking pass on the AAA site. The lead

Thud's bombs went right through the middle of the site and blew the six guns over on their sides—an outstanding attack. It was rare for one striker to take out a whole six-gun site on one pass.

There were a few smaller guns to take care of. Then, with the NVA's air defenses shattered, the Thuds made easy work of the four SAMs, knocking them out one after the other and igniting huge explosions on the side of the karst. By the end of the mission Misty 11 and the 105s were credited with killing an entire SAM site—four missiles and their Guideline transporters, a 57mm AAA battery, and other protecting guns—even though they never found the Fansong radar. It also marked the first SA-2 ever fired at a Misty. Like so many of their missions, it was a victory, but one with ominous implications.

Four SAMs was a huge kill for one day's work, but evidently it did little to dent the NVA's growing supply. Warnings from 7th Air Force about SAMs moving south continued to intensify, and unlike some of the intel that came up from 7th, the Mistys took these reports seriously. They had started seeing them with their own eyes, after all. And when Shepperd and C. Willy got chased by a real live SAM, it made believers of even the most skeptical Mistys.

Ed Risinger woke before sunrise one day in early March and was sitting in his trailer studying organic chemistry when his alarm went off. It would still be more than a year before he could leave the Air Force, but Ed had a plan for himself. Since the Air Force had decided not to promote him from captain to major, he'd ride out his remaining time and apply to medical school as soon as he got out. He still had some college credits to complete before he had all the required courses, and he needed to study for the entrance exams, too. So whenever there was free time he'd pull out a book and bone up on science. On missions when Ed was assigned to the backseat, he'd even bring books in the plane with him and study while the guy in front flew the Hun up to the Pack and back.

Ed was still bitter about being passed over for major, but the Air Force was taking care of him in other ways. Col. Hal Shook, the personnel officer who had arranged for Risinger to curtail his tour in Europe and get to Vietnam, had come through Misty and asked each man what follow-on assignment he wanted. Ed explained his plan about medical school, and Shook arranged for him to become a B-52 maintenance officer at Carswell Air Force Base in Texas—a forgiving job that would leave time for Ed to study and take classes at Texas Christian University. And Don Shepperd, who had taken a lot of science and engineering courses at the Air Force Academy and was a top student, would sometimes tutor Ed during off hours, when he wasn't at the O club telling war stories and drinking gin.

Ed snapped off the alarm so that it wouldn't wake up his trailer-mate, Misty commander Don Jones. He ambled over to Misty Ops to prepare for the first Misty mission of the day. He was scheduled to fly with Howard Williams, who'd be completing the last of his five required backseat checkout rides. For Howie, it couldn't happen soon enough—like most fighter pilots, he hated flying in the back. "It's a little bit like masturbating," he had complained during his first days as a Misty. "You're kind of ashamed and you don't want your friends to know about it."

Risinger was eager to get to the Pack to look for SAMs. Of course, there was the weather to deal with. Ed and Howie were scheduled to hit the Pack just after sunrise, and the forecast was not promising. John Haltigan and Cal Kunz were the morning intel briefers. "There's not a lot of good news," Haltigan admitted. "The weather's supposed to be dogshit again, but let's hope for the best. It's likely the Pack will be socked in—at least in the coastal areas—so you might think about starting in Laos. Up to you." Despite the grim forecast, the cursed February monsoons had been starting to break recently, and Risinger hoped they might get lucky.

Since it was a checkout ride for Howie, Risinger went over routine procedures with him. Howie knew most of it, but Risinger was obligated to play tutor. In addition to the maps and the cameras, Howie would be taking the stick when they refueled, and Risinger gave him a primer. "You won't find aerial refueling much different when you're in the front," he said, "except you can't see the basket as well as you can from the backseat. The main thing today is—keep us located on the maps, so you can plot locations quickly if we see something. Considering the lousy weather, I'll call out the Delta points as we pass over them, to help you out."

Then Risinger went over basic emergency procedures. "If we get in any trouble, we'll climb immediately and try to get out of the area. Re-

mind me to punch off the tanks and the rocket pods. If we are in serious trouble I'll use the term 'ejection' to talk about jumping out of the
airplane. I'll remind you to stow your equipment and get ready. Then
when we're ready to go, I'll use the term 'BAILOUT!' You go first, and
when I hear you go, then I'll go. But don't wait too long or I'll blow
your ass out of the airplane—whether you're ready or not."

"Roger," said Howie, nodding his head in understanding.

"Oh, one more thing," Risinger remembered. "Make sure you
know what you are doing with the camera. It's a constant pain in the
ass, but with bad weather we may only get a glimpse of something important, so be ready and keep the thing handy."

The two pilots headed for the PE room to pick up their combat gear
and parachutes. Howie checked out his pistol, loaded it with six .38-
caliber bullets, spun the cylinder, and placed it carefully into the holster on his survival vest, fastening the strap behind the hammer and
making certain one more time that the gun was not cocked. "The first
thing I'm going to do is throw this thing as far as I can when I hit the
ground." He laughed.

"How come?" asked the PE chief.

"Because I won't need it," replied Howie. "I can run faster through
jungle than the gomers through shit," and he laughed again. Howie
checked his survival radio and moved the "on" switch to make sure
the battery was good. Then the two pilots stepped out into the darkness, heading for their airplane and takeoff.

While growing up in Texas and attending a couple of Christian
schools, Ed had become very religious. He sometimes prayed on the
way to the Pack, which he did on this mission. "Christ was thirty-three
when he was crucified and died for me," Ed whispered to himself in the
front seat. "I'm thirty-four. No man has a right to live longer than
Christ, but if you can see fit, Lord, I'd like to go home and see my son."

As they entered the Pack, it was obvious that once again the
weather forecasters had been accurate. Solid overcast smothered the
ground, from the coast all the way to the mountains. Then came more
bad news—there were maintenance problems with their tanker and it
had been canceled. There would be no aerial refueling for the mission.
"Shit," said Risinger. "Oh well, we'll just plan on one cycle and head
home."

Risinger knew the weather patterns and pointed the plane west. "If the weather's going to break," he told Howie over the plane's interphone, "it will break farther inland first." They started their scouting up near the top of Mu Ghia Pass, looking for holes in the clouds.

Since Howie was ready to move into the front seat, Ed gave him little pointers, the kind that often made the difference between no BDA and good BDA. There was an art to knowing where and when to look. Being able to read the weather and predict when and where it was going to break came with experience. When the clouds opened up, the trick was to duck under the overcast, get oriented quickly, find targets, plot their locations, then call for fighters and get the fighters to strike quickly before the targets vanished. If they happened to come across a truck convoy, the Mistys often bought time with the familiar tactic of strafing the front and rear trucks with their 20mm cannons, to bottle up the convoy. The drivers usually bolted for the nearest tree line and kept their heads down. This gave fighters time to get into the area. If the trucks began to move again before the fighters arrived, Misty would toss a few more 20mm "harassing" rounds into the trucks to keep them stationary. The technique often led to multiple truck kills.

As they scoured the cloud cover, looking for openings, Risinger started to get discouraged. "Howie, it doesn't look like the weather's going to break," he said. "You can see the mountaintops above the overcast, but the clouds aren't getting any thinner. Bad news. But if it breaks quickly, we want to be able to pounce. We're near the top of Mu Ghia now."

Howie marveled at Ed's ability to keep track of where they were. "How the hell do you know where we are?" he asked. "All I see is clouds."

"See those two peaks sticking up through the overcast at our twelve o'clock?" Risinger answered. "They form the northern mouth of Mu Ghia Pass. The pass runs south between them."

As Risinger continued his orientation lecture, a couple of small holes appeared in the clouds. "I'm going to let down under the clouds," Risinger said. "The weather's still too bad to call in fighters, but let's see what we can find."

Just as they broke out below the clouds, Risinger couldn't believe what he saw: Right underneath their aircraft was an SA-2 missile on a launcher in plain sight. All the briefings and warnings about SAMs were true. "Howie, look!" he shouted. "A SAM!" The missile wasn't even camouflaged. As surprised as Misty 11 was to have discovered a break in the weather, the North Vietnamese were caught completely unaware. Obviously they thought the weather would provide an un-broken shield, and all of a sudden an American jet had come scream-ing in 500 feet over their heads.

"Howie, get the camera ready!" Risinger instructed. "I'm going to go north and get some speed, then come back south. I'll put the SAM out the left side."

"Rodge," replied Howie, fumbling with the cumbersome camera. He raised his helmet visor so he could put the viewfinder up against his eye. It was still awkward, so he released the catch on his oxygen mask, letting the mask fall to the side. He reached down to the radio panel and switched from the "hot mic" to the "interphone" position so the cockpit noise from the loosened oxygen mask wouldn't prevent him from hearing Risinger.

Howie placed the camera against his eye just as Ed pulled the air-craft into a tight high-G turn. The camera lens slammed against the canopy, putting a deep scratch in the glass, then banged back against Howie's eye. "Fuck," he mumbled as pain shot through his face.

Risinger hit the afterburner and accelerated to 500 knots as he de-scended to treetop level. He knew the SAM would be protected by AAA. It was risky to be around a SAM anytime, and doubly risky at low altitude. "Okay, Howie, get ready," he said. There was no imme-diate answer. "Do you hear me?" Risinger asked. Howie had forgotten that he had switched to "cold mic" on the interphone, and he reached down and switched back to the "hot mic" position. "Rodge," Howie replied as he propped his arm against the canopy bow to steady the camera.

"Okay, get ready out the left," Ed repeated. "Ready . . . Ready . . . Oh damn! I mean the right!" In the excitement, even the "old head" Risinger was confusing important details.

Howie swung the camera to the right side at the last second. A wide-eyed NVA soldier had climbed on to the side of the launcher and was desperately trying to pull a cover over the large missile. Howie snapped the picture and Risinger pulled up steeply into the clouds.

Risinger checked their fuel state. Using the afterburner and flying at low altitude had burned a lot of gas. They were now below "bingo" fuel for Phu Cat, the minimum reserve considered safe for a normal landing. With the tanker canceled, Risinger faced a decision: Should he take his chances and head for Phu Cat to get the pictures developed, so they could get some fighters moving toward the SAM? Or divert to Ubon in Thailand, where they could refuel, but would lose precious time?

Risinger decided to head home. And he was formulating a plan to go after the SAM.

"Sorry about the last-second change," he apologized to Howie. "Do you think you got a good picture?"

"Fuck, I don't know," Howie said, rubbing his sore eye.

Risinger climbed to high altitude and nursed the remaining fuel carefully. They'd be damned low on fuel when they got home; in fact, they'd be at "emergency fuel" state—less than six hundred pounds remaining. They'd be flying on fumes. But it was important to get home if his plan was going to work.

As they approached Phu Cat, Risinger called in and asked that intel meet them at the airplane. John Haltigan and Roger Van Dyken were on the tarmac when they arrived. "We've got SAM pictures, we think," Risinger hollered. "Get them developed as soon as you can." With the stakes rising, Howie began to sweat, hoping his last-second picture would turn out. As a new guy he didn't want to be a goat.

Risinger rushed into Misty Ops looking for Don Jones. But he was up flying. Mick Greene, the Ops officer, wasn't in the Misty shack either, nor was he in his trailer. Risinger called Colonel Schneider, the wing commander, who was also flying. He called the wing's deputy commander for Operations, Col. Frank Haney, who was on R&R in Hawaii. In desperation Risinger called the 7th Air Force Command Post in Saigon. There he reached a midlevel duty officer who was familiar with Misty. Risinger quickly explained the urgent situation. The NVA was setting up a SAM site north of Mu Ghia, he explained, and he needed to get back and strike it before it moved. "Shit hot!" came the reply over the phone. Risinger took that as permission enough and swung into action.

A short while later Haltigan rushed into Misty Ops with Howie's photo. It was a rush job from the photo shop, but Howie had pulled it off. An SA-2 missile was starkly visible on a launcher with an NVA gomer alongside trying to pull on a cover. "Howie, you're a hero!" Risinger exclaimed.

Like General Patton marshaling his troops for a rapid push, Risinger began to issue orders: "Get me some airplanes," he instructed the sergeant behind the Ops desk. "The weather's bad. We need low-level ordnance for a SAM attack under the clouds. See if there are any Misty birds available." The word came back that all of the Misty Huns were either flying or broken. "What's on the alert pad?" Risinger asked.

"Sir, there are three airplanes with combinations of high drags, na-palm, and CBU," the sergeant answered.

"We'll take 'em," Risinger quickly decided. He rushed to the phone to call the duty officer at 7th. "We're taking the alert birds," Risinger informed him. "They have the right ordnance for low-level attacks under the clouds."

"Shit hot!" the duty officer answered again, unaware of what he was setting in motion.

Risinger wanted to take Howie Williams along with him on the impromptu raid, since he had just been there. But that didn't seem like a good idea, since Howie wasn't yet a full-fledged Misty. As Risinger was deliberating, Don Shepperd and Elmer Slavey, who were sched-uled for an afternoon sortie, walked into Misty Ops and saw the hub-bub. "Get over here you two," Risinger shouted. "We're going to go kill us a SAM."

The three swung into action. Normally an attack on a SAM site would be a complex, well-choreographed affair, carried out by a large force of airplanes equipped with electronic jamming pods and chaff—fine aluminum strips dispensed to confuse the SAM radar. But as Risinger pointed out, there was no time for elaborate preparations. The North Vietnamese were almost certainly moving and camouflag-ing the SAM as they stood there, and it was a race against time. If they waited much longer the SAM would vanish just like the hundreds of trucks that came down the Trail every day.

Risinger reminded Slavey and Shepperd that it had been a long time since any of them had been in a single-seat D-model Hun. Switch posi-tions are different, he warned, so plan your attack carefully. "We need to get ALL our ordnance off on one pass," he stressed. Making multiple passes against the site—which would surely be well defended by the time they got back to it—would be sheer suicide.

When Slavey and Shepperd asked where the target was, exactly, Risinger said, "I'm not sure, but I think I can find it. Besides, it will be right in the middle of the guns." Slavey and Shepperd looked at each other blankly.

Two and a half hours after Risinger and Howie Williams had landed from their first mission, the makeshift attack fleet was at the end of the Phu Cat runway, ready for takeoff. Of the three pilots, Slavey was the most experienced by far, and normally he would have been the flight lead. But Risinger knew where the target was, or at least he thought he did, so he led. Slavey lined up behind him as number two. Shepperd was number three.

Risinger's airplane carried four canisters of napalm, jellied gasoline that exploded on impact, burning everything in its wake. Slavey had four 500-pound "high-drag" bombs designed for low-altitude attacks. The bombs had fins that sprung open on release and slowed the descent long enough to allow the fighter jet to escape before the explosion occurred. Shepperd carried a mix of cluster bombs—small submunitions designed to pepper a large area with thousands of steel ball bearings that punctured metal and killed people—and two high drags. All of the ordnance required the three to pass directly over the missile site at low altitude.

Risinger crossed the DMZ heading straight for Mu Ghia, but the weather was a repeat of the morning mission—solid overcast. He turned the flight east over the water, away from the mountains, and let down beneath the clouds. Turning back west, he accelerated to cross the coast at high speed. The cloud bottoms were at about 2,000 feet, plenty high for the planned strike. As they proceeded toward Mu Ghia, the Quang Khe ferry with its nasty 57mm gun site on the south riverbank lay off to the left. Risinger gave it a wide berth. As he flew up the Gianh River valley, he hugged the north side of the river, away from the known gun sites along the road to the south.

The three-ship flight was in a staggered trail formation, one airplane behind the other with about a mile between them. Near the village of Khe Trung railroad tracks paralleled the river and a small diesel engine appeared, pulling a string of ten cars. Shit, Shepperd thought. We must have bombed this railroad a hundred times and they're still able to keep it open. As they passed the train, a gunner opened up on Shepperd's aircraft from the last railcar, which was no caboose—it was a flatcar that had been modified to hold a AAA gun. Shepperd flinched, but the AAA tracers fell harmlessly behind.

Shepperd looked out at his wings and mentally rehearsed the complicated button and switch setting combinations he would have to use to employ his bombs and CBUs. Getting them off simultaneously on one run would be complicated, he thought. He would have to be like a piccolo player, rapidly fingering buttons simultaneously, with both hands. By now the bravado and enthusiasm were fading and the difficulty of the mission—or was it foolishness?—was starting to become evident.

As tail-end Charlie, Shepperd was soaking up lots of AAA. The first two jets, Risinger and Slavey's aircraft, alerted the gunners on the ground, who were ready by the time Shepperd buzzed past, two miles in trail. They were hosing Shepperd good. Thankfully, it was mostly small stuff, .50-caliber and ZPU. Most of it fell well short. Still, Shepperd clenched his teeth as he began to realize what a dumb-assed idea this was. But he said nothing to his colleagues up ahead. Risinger had preached "radio silence"—lest their transmissions warn the NVA— and Shepperd followed Risinger's direction.

As the terrain rose toward Mu Ghia Pass, the three Mistys were coming closer to the bottoms of the clouds. The ceiling had started at about 1,500 feet, then the clearance dropped to 1,000 feet, then 800. They approached the town of Bai Duc Thong and crossed a railroad bridge Ed had highlighted in his rushed premission "briefing." The bridge would be their IP, the initial point, from which they'd begin the attack run. From the bridge the flight would head 185 degrees for sixty seconds to the valley containing the missile site. Risinger began a 270-degree turn to the north, to create adequate spacing for the aircraft; this would ensure that they each avoided the blast from the bombs of the planes up ahead, yet still kept each other in sight. "Arm 'em up, take spacing," Risinger commanded. But as the airplanes turned south in trail, trouble was looming. The ground rose up to meet the clouds and Ed's aircraft disappeared from sight.

Risinger's voice came over the radio. "The weather's too bad," he groaned. "Let's abort." He sounded depressed, until the radio suddenly crackled again. "Whoa!" Risinger shouted. "They're shooting at me! I'm pickling off in the target area, turning off east and climbing on top. Continue your runs and pickle off when they start shooting."

Slavey continued his run as instructed and reported the same thing. As Shepperd lined up for his run, he set up his bomb switches and made one final check that his master arm switch for the munitions was on. Crossing the railroad bridge, he called, "IP inbound" and hacked his clock. Sixty seconds later he'd be over the target. He hoped he would be able to see it.

At thirty seconds, clouds enveloped the ground. He continued straight ahead, blind except for his instruments. At fifty-five seconds the sky—or rather the clouds—turned bright red with gunfire. Shepperd could feel the shock waves as the blasts beat against his fuselage. The gunfire was coming breathlessly close to the aircraft, with bright red tracers whisking past the canopy. It was like a crazy nightmare. He couldn't see them, and they couldn't see him, but they were both trying to kill each other. And the gunners were coming damned close, even if they were just shooting straight up in the air when they heard the jet's engine. If the volume of gunfire was any indication, Risinger's target plotting had been awfully accurate.

As the guns opened up on him, Shepperd hit the "auxiliary jettison" buttons, which sent his two Snake Eye bombs hurtling toward earth. At the same time he hit the "pickle button"—the bomb-release button on the stick—as fast as he could to release the CBU bomblets from their tubes. He had to fly straight and level until the CBU tubes emptied. Shepperd felt the concussions as his bombs exploded. Then he pulled up in a sharp, climbing turn through the clouds.

When he came out on top he looked to the east, where he caught sight of both Risinger and Slavey. They all joined up in formation and headed toward Phu Cat. The radio was silent, but they were all thinking the same thing: Fuck! The mission was almost certainly a failure. The three pilots thought it was a valiant effort, but it was highly unlikely that they hit the SAM—if it was even there.

As they landed and taxied to the parking ramp, the three noticed a large group of Mistys gathered, all waiting to hear news of a dramatic strike, they suspected. Shepperd pulled into his parking spot and noticed that the commander, Don Jones, was not smiling. He shut off the throttle, and as the engine wound down, the aircraft crew chief scrambled up the ladder. "Stand by for incoming," he warned. "The boss is pissed."

As the three pilots stowed their gear in Ops, Don Jones ordered, "All Mistys into the briefing room!" Jones was normally taciturn, but from the tone of voice he was clearly angry. Jones had arranged chairs for Risinger, Slavey, and Shepperd to sit on. They were lined up one next to the other. The rest of the Mistys formed a semicircle in back of them. Jones faced the crowd, addressing the three seated men as if they were criminals undergoing an interrogation.

"What in the hell were you guys thinking?" Jones began. "You are all experienced pilots. Do you realize you violated every regulation, every procedure, every rule in the books? Do you think you can win this war all by yourself? What in the hell were you thinking about, carrying nape, high drags, and CBUs against an SA-2? Do you think you are invincible? Do you have any common sense?" Jones wasn't seeking answers to his questions. The session went on for thirty minutes and ended ominously. "You three are grounded!" Jones pronounced.

The Mistys weren't used to getting their asses chewed, and Jones's performance achieved its objective. As Shepperd thought over the incident, he realized that Jones was right. The Mistys might have had big balls, but sometimes they had no brains. Good thing guys like Don Jones—and even Colonel Schneider, the risk-averse wing boss—were around to pour some water on their fire.

There was one thing Don Jones had not said in his ass-chewing, however. The "Risinger Raid" might have been dumb—the kind of stunt that produces dead people, and little else—but it was also heroic. Most of the troops in Vietnam wouldn't have had the balls to do it. Finding a SAM, jury-rigging a strike, risking your ass—Sierra Hotel, Jones mused. Shit hot. He smiled to himself, but wasn't about to tell the Mistys.

After getting grounded, the three pilots went to their trailers and showered. Shepperd knocked on Risinger's trailer door and they walked toward the O club. Risinger didn't give a shit. He had been passed over for major a second time at Misty and was getting out of the Air Force and going to medical school. Slavey had only a couple of years to go for retirement and he didn't give a shit, either. But Shepperd was a young officer with a promising future—at least until today. "Thank God the weather was bad," he said glumly to Risinger, "or we'd all be dead."

Risinger looked at him and put his hand on Shepperd's shoulder. "Don," he lectured, "you can't take life so seriously. Every now and then you've just gotta say, 'What the fuck.' "

"Risinger, you asshole," Shepperd volleyed. "I'm never going to tutor you in chemistry again." They headed for the bar to continue the discussion over some gin.

Risinger, Slavey, and Shepperd spent the next three days "on the beach," performing menial duties and helping with mission planning in Misty Ops while others flew. Don Jones avoided the three and said nothing to them. "We're awaiting our court-martial," Ed joked, "or perhaps our execution." On the fourth day, miraculously, their names reappeared on the flying schedule. Jones never mentioned the incident again.

Naturally, each of the pilots made a surreptitious return to the "Valley of the SAM," as Risinger had dubbed it, just to make sure the missile was gone. It was nowhere to be seen.

March 17 was Ed Risinger's last flight. He would be Misty 11, the first flight of the day. The weather was clear for once, but little activity was visible down below. Risinger started out searching from east to west, from the coast over to Laos, and then back several times, with two refuelings. He was eager to leave the wretched war, yet as he traversed Route Pack 1 a kind of sentimentality possessed him. He thought of all the bombs he had dropped, the men he had flown with, the friends he had lost. It had been a remarkable experience.

There was a Mayday call from an F-4, call sign Gunfighter 42. The lead jet—Gunfighter 41, with two pilots on board—had been shot down in the A Shau Valley, a narrow, twenty-five-mile strip of terrain that was a strategic focal point of the war for the Trail. The valley straddled the border between South Vietnam and Laos just south of Khe Sanh and was a key arm of the Trail network. A major NVA staging post known as Base Area 611 sat at the north end of the valley, which had made it a major battleground from the earliest days of the war.[7]

Both of the Gunfighter pilots were alive. The back-seater was on top of a hill in rough terrain. The front-seater was in big trouble, at the bottom of the valley, with enemy troops moving quickly to get to him. Risinger caught up with Gunfighter 42, who led him to where the front-seater's parachute was hung up in the jungle trees. Then, Gunfighter 42 had to leave since he was low on fuel. Risinger made contact with the downed pilot, talking on his handheld survival radio, and asked how he was doing. Not so great, the pilot said. He was in a ditch and every time he lifted his head, NVA troops shot at him. And there were lots of them.

Risinger circled the parachute at 200 feet. Cricket, the ABCCC, told him that rescue choppers were on the way. Risinger had only a few rounds of 20mm left in his cannons. He told the pilot he would fire short bursts right over his head and warned him that some of the shell casings might fall on him. "Keep your head down and your helmet on," he advised. Risinger then dipped down as low as 100 feet—practically treetop level—making multiple passes over the pilot. He didn't fire each time, but tried to fool the gomers while conserving his ammo and buying time.

A Jolly Green arrived, but there were no A-1 Sandy suppression aircraft—a second Jolly had encountered engine problems and they were escorting it home. Risinger would have to stand in for the Sandys. He arranged to make a firing pass just as the Jolly approached the pilot. He had only a couple of minutes' worth of fuel left, and there might be just one opportunity. As the chopper swooped in from the east, hovering about fifty feet over the pilot, gunfire started hitting the rotor blades. Smoke started streaming from the engine, and Risinger was afraid the Jolly would crash on top of the pilot. The chopper had no choice but to pull out. It limped over the hill and headed back toward Nakhon Phanom, trailing smoke behind.

The Jolly was gone and Risinger was out of gas. He called down to the pilot in the brush and told him the Jolly was taking fire and had to leave. The pilot knew that—he had watched it peel away. "Gunfighter, how are you doing?"

"I'm scared," he confided, his voice quavering.

As Risinger was leaving, Misty 21 arrived—Jim Fiorelli and a new Misty, Paul "P. K." Robinson. Misty 21 was a truly transitional crew: Fio, like Risinger, was on his last Misty flight, while Robinson, in the backseat, was on his first. Risinger briefed Fio on the situation and headed home to Phu Cat. As he was approaching the runway, he called the tower and asked to speak to the next team of Mistys due to take off. Don Shepperd and Whispering Smith were waiting at the end of the runway when Risinger touched down. He gave them a quick briefing over the radio, and then Misty 31 scrambled at top speed for the A Shau Valley.

When Shepperd and Smith arrived on the scene, it was a mess. Misty 21 and two A-1s were alternating passes over the pilots. Two Jollys were in the area, and a third helicopter, an Army UH-1 "Huey," was maneuvering to pick up the back-seater, up on the hillside. The rescuers were losing the battle. At one point the chopper crew tried to touch down near the pilot and was peppered with gunfire. The helicopter pulled away and managed to stagger about a mile south before it crash landed. One of the Jollys went to pick up the four-man crew.

Then a two-man Army light observation helicopter—an LOH, or "Loach"—arrived, and the pilot announced he was going in to pick up the front-seater in the valley. One of the Sandys warned him that the gunfire was too intense, but the Loach went in anyway. It headed for the pilot's parachute—a big, white bubble in the trees, visible to all— and was promptly punched full of bullet holes. The Loach barely got away from the trees before crashing.

The Jolly that was picking up the Huey crew went to fetch the Loach crew next. Meanwhile, the first Jolly was going into a hover to pick up the back-seater on the hillside, who, the rescuers had learned, had a broken leg. Jesus, Shepperd thought, this is a bad movie. One F-4 and two pilots down, one Jolly shot up, one Huey down and on fire, one Loach down. . . .

Shepperd fell in behind Fio, who was behind the A-1s. They alternated rocket and strafe passes while the A-1s dropped CBUs and bombs. Shepperd's 20mm guns jammed, so he shot his smoke rockets. When he ran out of those, he continued to make low passes, igniting the afterburner just over the trees, hoping that would intimidate the advancing ground troops and slow them down. Then he jettisoned his rocket pods into the trees. It was like throwing anything handy at an assailant. Still, the downed pilot kept asking them to put their ordnance closer. "They're still coming!" he shouted.

Shepperd looked up at the Jolly, now in a hover over the backseater. He couldn't believe his eyes. A PJ was going down the cable hoist to try to pull out the wounded pilot while the helo was being pummeled with gunfire. The rounds flashed against the fuselage and the rotor blades, yet the pilot held the craft steady while the gomers zeroed in on him.

Finally it seemed like a miracle happened: The PJ brought the pilot up on the winch. The pickup had probably taken less than five minutes, but it seemed like an eternity as Shepperd watched the helo take twenty or thirty hits. That guy has the biggest balls I've ever seen, he thought.

Both Misty jets and the A-1s continued to make low passes over the front-seater. But he sounded increasingly desperate. "Put it on me!" he yelled. "They're all around me!" Then: "I'm breaking my radio. See you after the war." It was over. The shooting stopped and the dejected rescue forces departed. Fio and Robinson and Shepperd and Whispering Smith, out of rockets and bullets, headed home to Phu Cat.

When he landed back at the base, Fio got the same "hose down" reception that Risinger had a couple of hours earlier, in honor of his final Misty mission. The fire trucks on hand for runway emergencies pulled alongside the aircraft as it parked and the engine shut down. The Air Force firemen reeled out the hoses and opened the spigots, dousing Fio as he climbed down the cockpit ladder. The force of the blast knocked some pilots over, but Fio had enough ballast to withstand the gushing water. His fellow Mistys were all there, and somebody produced the customary champagne bottle. Fio guzzled as much as he could, leaving little for the rest of the crowd.

There were smiles and handshakes and pats on the back, but the exuberance didn't last. Everybody knew the day had ended badly, with a colleague, a fellow pilot, falling into enemy hands. It felt horrendous. There was peak attendance at the bar that night. Most of the talk centered on the "big balls" of the Jolly pilots. And they weren't the only ones. Some of the gomers had shown a lot of courage, too, marching through the bombs and bullets to capture the front-seater. Those bastards, Shepperd thought, had faced down the best the U.S. Air Force had to offer—and prevailed. P. K. Robinson, who had just finished his first Misty ride, drank silently on a bar stool off to the side, thrilled by the excitement of it all. But he wondered if he'd ever make it to the end of his own Misty tour.

EIGHTEEN

A HOLE IN THE JUNGLE

Like most of the Mistys, Brian Williams had been practically scared silent by his first few missions. "B. Willy," as he was known, to distinguish him from Howard Williams and Carroll Williams, had come from the 416th, grew up in Seattle and was commissioned through ROTC at the University of Washington. He had gone to pilot training in Florida and Oklahoma, then flown F-100s in Nevada, New Mexico, and the United Kingdom. By the time he arrived at Misty he was an old head, an experienced fighter pilot. But on his first flew flights, he shook like an innocent, young "green bean."

His first flying day with Misty had been a breeze—it was January 1, when bumper-to-bumper traffic clogged the Trail, and the New Year's truce prevented any bombing. But on his second day he had flown with Ed Risinger, who gave him a real-life tutorial on the effects of 57mm flak. Risinger saw a gun site on the ground, then said he was going to roll in and shoot to see if he could elicit some AAA fire. He did, and B. Willy was terrified by the tongues of orange flame erupting from the ground. He could barely breathe as the supersonic shock waves from the AAA shells beat against the fuselage, like a demon hammering madly at the metal.

B. Willy had also gulped at the constant frustration of bad weather, which provided the North Vietnamese with better camouflage than anything even they could devise. On one typically overcast day, he and Jonesy Jones had flown farther and farther north over a socked-in Pack until they found a hole in the clouds. They dipped down and immediately spotted five trucks motoring south in broad daylight. They called for fighters but none were available. So Jonesy, flying the plane in the front seat, decided to make a strafing run. "Oh, shit," protested B. Willy in the back. Not to worry, Jonesy assured him. The Hun they were flying happened to have a busted gun sight, so Jonesy improvised by drawing an X on the windscreen with his grease pencil. They made a run for the trucks, Jonesy trying to aim with the aid of the makeshift gun sight. The bullets plowed into the top of a hillside, so far off the mark that the pilots chuckled to themselves. The truck drivers probably thought the Hun drivers were drunk or shooting at something else. The pilots called it a day and headed home.

The two Williamses, Brian and Howard, had first met when they were at the 416th. Howie's guitar was the icebreaker. B. Willy was one of the guys who fancied himself a musician—despite a lack of talent—and he loved to sit outside with Howie and listen to him croon "The Alligator Song" and other favorites. B. Willy noticed the same thing as many others—Howie had an upbeat, infectious personality and a knack for getting a party started.

By mid-March, after more than two months in the unit, B. Willy was one of the more seasoned Mistys. He had learned important tricks from guys like Ed Risinger and Jonesy Jones and Mick Greene. Howie had just finished his five checkout rides and was coming into his own as a Misty. He had been extremely proud of his role in Risinger's Raid, being the only guy anybody knew about to snap a handheld picture of a live SAM. He had called his brother Roger after that, telling him the whole story and filling him in on what it was like to fly up north. Since he was now in a two-seater, he said, maybe he could arrange to give Roger a ride.

In his letters home, however, he never mentioned any of it. He and Monalee were busy making final arrangements for a week of R&R in Hawaii in April, and their letters brimmed with anticipation. After receiving two tapes with some of the details of the trip, Monalee reminded her husband that she needed specific dates so she could arrange for a substitute teacher at school. Then she let her guard down and allowed herself to fantasize about the reunion. "I do love you," she wrote on March 16, "and any date for R&R is wonderful— I am going to get you—many times—it is really getting bad now with the thought of you and I being together so soon. Mmmmm. I love you."

March 18 was scheduled to be Howie's first mission in the front seat, flying the aircraft, with B. Willy in the backseat. As they taxied out to the runway, an Army prop plane was warming its engines at the far end of the runway. Ed Risinger was on board. His four-month tour at Misty had ended, and he was headed for Bien Hoa, his old base, before catching a flight back home to the States. For a relatively short tour, Ed's stint at Misty already seemed like one of the most important chapters in his life. Ed thought of the many missions full of danger and gunfire, the men with whom he had flown, the laughter, frustration, and sadness. He was proud of what he had done—but not wistful about leaving. Ed could have extended his time with Misty, but his seven-year-old son Edsel Jr. was back in Fort Worth, and Ed couldn't wait to see him. It was time to go.

Ed looked out the window and saw the two-seat F-100F. He remembered that Howie Williams was going for his first front-seat Misty flight that day. Ed smiled as he thought of the wonderful photo Howard had taken of the SAM just a few days earlier. He'd be a good Misty. Finally, Ed's Army plane took off and headed south, the first leg on his journey home. Howie and Brian took off and flew north, toward another murky mission in the Pack.

They were the second mission of the day, call sign Misty 21. As usual, the cloudy weather seemed to foretell aggravation. Once they entered Route Pack 1, Brian and Howie flew for about thirty minutes without finding a single opening in the overcast. They headed west to Laos to see if they could find a break in the clouds there. No luck. So they went to the tanker to get gas and decided to make one more pass over the Pack.

Just as they were on the border between Laos and North Vietnam, up by the jagged Ban Karai mountain pass, a glimpse of the ground beckoned. "Look on the left," B. Willy said. "There's something that looks like a bulldozer."

"I got it," Howie replied. "I'm gonna come around." Howie had just started to roll the Hun into a circle when it felt like a sledgehammer slammed into the bottom of the plane. There had been no tracers and they hadn't seen any gun sites. Neither pilot was sure what had hit them. But there was little doubt they were in deep trouble. When B. Willy looked in the mirror he saw big flames trailing from the left side of the jet. He quickly made a Mayday call, then punched off the drop tanks to make the plane lighter and get rid of the volatile fuel. Howie, meanwhile, turned the plane eastward, toward the highest, most remote area he could see, so they'd be easier to spot and rescue if they had to bail out—which was starting to look like the only option.

Within seconds the flames had spread to within five feet of the cockpit. The fuel line had to be busted, B. Willy surmised. That meant two things: The plane could explode at any minute, and the controls were probably about to fail. They were heading east, into the higher mountains, and as they tried to gain altitude the ground rose up with them. Both pilots prepared to eject, pulling down their helmet visors to protect their eyes and checking that their ejection seat safety pins were out.

B. Willy could feel the heat on his back. He made another emergency call. The fire was right behind him. "We better get out now!" he shouted. "Ready?"

"I'll be right behind you," Howie answered.

Then there was noise, sky, and a rush of cold air. Brian Williams looked up at his parachute. There was a big hole in it. The sky looked like somebody had dumped a trash can upside down, with maps and charts and bits of debris floating everywhere. Suddenly it was silent. Brian looked toward where he guessed the plane was headed and saw smoke rising up out of the jungle. He also looked for another parachute. He didn't see one.

There wasn't much time to look around. Because of the hole in his chute, B. Willy descended rapidly and hit the treetops hard less than a minute after ejecting. He tumbled upside down. His holster snagged on a branch and he ended up suspended in the tree like a diver, head first. But he was okay. He reached up to get his knife to cut himself out of the chute. It took about ten minutes to completely extricate himself from the tree and parachute shrouds, turn off his parachute beeper, and clamber down out of the tree—heart pounding.

The moment he hit the ground, B. Willy clawed at the survival radio in his vest and quickly got an F-4 pilot on the line, who said he had heard the emergency beeper and called the rescuers. They were on their way already. Then Brian looked around. The trees weren't as thick as the tropical jungle he had expected to land in. They were more like the woods back home in Washington state. That was hardly reassuring, however—it would make it easier for any North Vietnamese to see him.

Brian picked up his survival kit and ran, to get away from the area where he had come streaming down, in plain view of anybody who happened to be watching. Every movement seemed to create a crashing noise. Then B. Willy discovered he had left his radio on a stump, back where he had first hit firm ground. He had another radio, but realized he was on the verge of panicking. I've only been here a few minutes, he told himself, and already I've made a goddamn mistake.

He calmed down and moved a few more times, more deliberately now. Howie's split-second decision to point the Hun toward remote terrain had paid off—as far as Brian could tell, no enemy forces were on his tail. He tried to make voice contact with Howie over the radio. There was no response.

Don Shepperd and Lanny Lancaster, a new arrival, had been the first Misty flight of the day, Misty 11. They were on the tanker getting gas when they heard B. Willy's emergency call. "Disconnect now!" Shepperd shouted over the radio to the boom operator who was looking out one of the tanker windows. They gingerly backed away from the refueling hose. Shepperd banked the F-100 directly toward "Delta 37," the shorthand geographical phrase pilots used for the Ban Karai Pass area. He pushed the throttle forward to attain maximum speed without engaging the afterburner, which would have gobbled up fuel they might later need for the rescue.

Misty 11 called Cricket, the ABCCC, which had already heard about the ejection from the F-4 call. In a great stroke of luck, Shepperd and Lancaster passed right over B. Willy on their first pass into the area.

"Hey! I'm right under you!" B. Willy shouted into his survival radio. Lancaster saw the chute immediately.

"Gotcha, buddy!" replied Lanny. Shepperd put the aircraft into a tight turn so that Lancaster could firmly fix the location. Then they moved off about four miles to study the location of the crash site, which was still burning. They buzzed low, peering into the smoldering jungle, but there was no sign of Howie. They avoided flying back over B. Willy's location, fearing that might attract the attention of any North Vietnamese lurking nearby. Lancaster checked back with Cricket. Rescue forces were on the way.

Misty 11 made occasional radio checks with B. Willy to assure him that rescue forces were coming and see if he needed any help. When the Jolly and the Sandys came into view, Misty 11 showed them B. Willy's location and went into a high patrol orbit to preserve fuel in case they were needed later. B. Willy helped guide the rescue forces to him. Over the radio he could also hear them looking for Howie's parachute and trying to make contact with him. But there was no answer.

The Sandys began to buzz overhead. They were shooting at some guys on the ground who might pose a problem, but opposition was relatively light. Then the Jolly Green lumbered into place. It was a text book snatch—quick. Brian talked the chopper in, and it absorbed only a couple of small-arms rounds before hauling him to safety at about 1:15, less than two hours after he had ejected.[1]

The crew made sure Brian was okay, then the chopper commander said, "Let's go look for your copilot." It was an agonizing search. At some point after B. Willy had been picked up, the rescue aircraft started picking up a strong parachute beeper signal that they figured could only be coming from Howie's chute, since no other aircraft were down in the area. But they were unable to make voice contact, which was the only way to figure out where he was and get him out. There was some sporadic ground fire, and the chopper Brian was on took a couple more hits. The rescuers scoured the area for another hour, looking fruitlessly for Howie while Misty 11 hovered overhead. Finally, with nothing more than the tantalizing beeper to guide them, the rescuers turned south and left the crash site at about 2:15. Less than three hours after Misty 21 had been shot down, the incident had ended.

Misty 11 was "bingo fuel" and had to go to the tanker or RTB, return to base. Since there had been no contact with Howie, and another

Misty jet would arrive soon to continue the search, Shepperd decided to RTB rather than use up the tanker fuel scheduled for the next Misty.

Dick Rutan had never flown with his buddy Howie. But he happened to be airborne en route to the Pack with Don Jones when word came over the radio that Misty 21, B. Willy and H. Willy, had been shot down near the Laotian border. Rutan, in the backseat, listened closely to the assembled rescue- effort. When it became clear they couldn't find Howie, he and Jones—Misty 41—streaked north toward the crash site, eager to do anything necessary to help.

They got to the area just as B. Willy was being picked up. But Misty 41 had trouble getting into the flow of the rescue. Essentially, they were bystanders. With so much chatter over the radio, it was hard getting information about where the aircraft had crashed, or what direction it had been traveling. Rutan reached B. Willy on the chopper via a radio relay, but couldn't get clear information from him—after all, he had been on the jungle floor for most of the event. Rutan's frustration boiled over as the rescuers, having gotten no word from Howie, prepared to pull out. He and Jones spun circles over the forest for a while longer, but had no better luck raising Howie than anybody else.

The Jolly flew Brian Williams to Da Nang, and he caught a flight to Phu Cat in short order. His colleagues met him on the tarmac. After a quick debriefing, during which B. Willy described everything he knew about the incident, his fellow Mistys led him straight to the bar. It was a bittersweet gathering. Many of the Mistys had barely known Howie. Tight as Misty was, it just didn't hit home the same way when you didn't know the guy. Brian's return was a chance to celebrate a prodigal son, a colleague who had been temporarily lost and was back in the fold. It was also a much-anticipated opportunity to relish the war stories that made them all feel so vulnerable and alive. They faced death every day, and cheated it, and every tale that celebrated that was a validation of their efforts and the choices they had made. Survival stories cast the enemy in pure black and motivated the Mistys to fly and fight harder than ever the next day.

But some of them took Howie's disappearance hard. Brian Williams, needless to say, was one of them. He was exuberant over his own rescue, but manacled with guilt about leaving Howie behind. Even though he was in the backseat and wasn't flying the plane, he faulted himself for allowing Howie to get into trouble. As an experienced Misty he should have known better and insisted that they fly higher or stand off farther from such a potentially hot area. They should have scouted for guns first and not gotten so excited about finding a rare hole in the clouds. There were plenty of things they could have done differently, and it had been his job to make sure they did.

There was endless speculation about what may have happened to Howie. Since B. Willy hadn't seen his chute, it was possible that Howie had never gotten out of the airplane. But why not? The last thing he had said to Brian was, "I'll be right behind you." He was definitely ready to eject. Had Howie made some rookie mistake, like leaving the seat pins in?

Rutan doubted it. He recalled Howie's ejection during training back at Luke Air Force Base and figured that since he had already been blown out of an airplane once—and survived with his sunglasses still on his face—he would have known exactly what to do this time. Maybe the ejection seat malfunctioned, Rutan reasoned, leaving Howie no choice but to fly the flaming bird as effectively as he could. He might have piloted the jet straight into the trees, doing the best he could in a crash landing.

Don Jones had another theory. He guessed that something had come loose in the cockpit when the canopy blew off, perhaps knocking Howie unconscious or incapacitating him in some other way. Or maybe the canopy had hit him in the head.

There were still other possibilities. Brian hadn't had much time to look around, since he was falling so fast. His own chute had blocked part of the view above, so Howie could have been up there, drifting down but unseen. Maybe he got knocked unconscious when he landed. Or he could have come down in nearby Laos, which was notorious for the murderous treatment of prisoners. As most of the pilots knew, the North Vietnamese had standing orders that any American pilots should be captured and transported up to Hanoi for imprisonment. The treatment along the way was usually brutal, but most of the captives survived long enough to enter the punishing prison system in Hanoi. In Laos, however, it was a different story. Prisoners were often slaughtered on the spot—standard procedure for the extremist Pathet

Lao communist rebels, supported by the Soviet Union, who were not fully answerable to Hanoi.

Dick Rutan was probably most shaken by Howie's loss. The tough, bombastic pilot was both furious and heartbroken about his friend's disappearance. It was Rutan who had coaxed Howie to join Misty in the first place—at least that's what he believed, not entirely aware of Howie's introspection after Tet. Rutan felt responsible for what had happened. If there was anything that could be done, it was up to Rutan to do it.

Doc Echenberg, the new flight surgeon, arrived at the bar and interrupted B. Willy's homecoming fete. Brian said he felt fine, but that was most likely bravado, beer, and adrenaline talking. His left eye was ringed with bruises, like he had gone several rounds with a prizefighter. His left arm had gotten banged up during the violent ejection and the tumble through the trees. Echenberg insisted that B. Willy go to the dispensary for an exam. The doc knew what he was talking about. After resting for a while and letting the adrenaline drain away, B. Willy could barely walk. The force of the ejection and the stress of the rescue had crunched his body and left his muscles knotted. He spent the next day in bed.

Dick Rutan flew with Don Jones the next day. Like all the other Mistys who flew immediately after the shootdown, they headed straight toward the area of the crash. They saw a clean gash in the jungle where the plane had gone in. This suggested that the Hun was still flying level when it sliced into the trees. There was no evidence that the jet had spun out of control or upended itself in a way that would have prevented Howie from getting out. Rutan carefully marked the location of the crash site and estimated its latitudinal and longitudinal coordinates. The parachute beeper had stopped squawking, but successive Misty sorties still kept a vigil over the area for the next forty-eight hours, mindful of Lance Sijan, who had come up on the radio after two days of unconsciousness in the jungle. After convalescing for a day and a half, even Brian Williams wrenched his stiff, strained body into one of the Huns and revisited the scene of the crime. He was able to reenact the incident, but that didn't shed any light on what had happened to Howie.

The wheels of bureaucracy, meanwhile, were grinding away as usual, in both the American and the North Vietnamese militaries. The

37th Tactical Fighter Wing filed its first official report on the Misty 21 shootdown at 11:35 a.m. local time in Vietnam—about five minutes after the plane actually crashed. The message, which went to 7th Air Force, Pacific Command, and the National Military Command Center in the basement of the Pentagon, provided only the barest details: the names of the pilots, the aircraft tail number, the ordnance the plane was carrying.

But a mountain of paperwork was in the making. Throughout the day, follow-up cables documented the rescue, B. Willy's debriefing, and what could be presumed of Howie's fate, in the matter-of-fact tone typical of wartime communications that documented combat deaths by the hundreds. The next day a message from the 37th to the Air Force chief of staff's office detailed what was known about Howie's parachute beeper. The signal had been strong throughout the eighteenth, but when Rutan flew over the area shortly after 8:00 a.m. the next day, the signal was gone. "It is possible," the message concluded, "that natives or hostile forces activated and/or deactivated the radio."

The North Vietnamese were filing reports, too. Shooting down a U.S. jet and the "yankee air pirates" aboard was a huge feat, worthy of medals and other honors. It was even more significant if the shootdown produced live prisoners. Every downed jet, if it was accessible, was a magnet for the North Vietnamese, ransacked by locals looking for valuables and souvenirs and scoured by intelligence experts eager to learn everything they could about American tactics. So the North Vietnamese, always attentive to detail, kept careful records of their achievements.

The Ban Karai Pass, where Misty 21 had gone down, was in North Vietnam's Bo Trach Military District. A unit known as Binh Tram 14, which belonged to the 559th Transportation Group—which built the Trail and was responsible for maintaining it—had jurisdiction over that part of the road network, where it rose into the mountains and then dropped into the valley on the other side of the border, in Laos. The AAA guns were operated by the 18th and the 21st Air Defense Battalions, disciplined units well known to Air force intelligence because they had already scored many hits against U.S. jets. The United States knew little, however, about the fate of most of the pilots who had gone down in that area.[2]

Officers of the Bo Trach Military District kept a list of American aircraft that their troops shot down. Under the heading 1968, there was one entry: On February 15, at 7:00 a.m., gunners had downed an F-4 with two pilots aboard. Now, a record-keeper added a second entry. "1020 hours; 18 March 1968," he scrawled in Vietnamese. "Bo Trach District shot it [the plane] down at kilometer 26 and 20; 1 F100; 1 man killed; 1 alive; they took him and he was lost."[3] To the Americans, Brian Williams had been saved. To the North Vietnamese, he had been "lost." And while the Mistys hoped against their better judgment that Howard Williams was alive somewhere and might return someday, the North Vietnamese knew otherwise.

There were others who knew Howard Williams was dead. Among the many secret operatives in the war—Special Forces and CIA irregulars operating behind enemy lines, the Air America characters who flew for the CIA, the "pinball wizards" at Nakhon Phanom—the most effective may have been the intelligence experts who intercepted enemy radio communications. Some flew overhead in aircraft loaded with the world's most sophisticated electronics. Others manned camouflaged listening posts nestled atop strategic—and often dangerous—high ground.

The information they gathered was some of the most valuable intelligence of the war. Since they were often able to tap into the North Vietnamese Army's own communications, they learned details of battle plans, the location of troops, the status of prisoners, and other vital information. Success was spotty and often there were just fragments of data, but electronic eavesdropping also produced some spectacular battlefield results. Many of the B-52 Arc Light strikes that wiped out legions of troops, for instance, were triggered by intercepts that helped pinpoint the location of enemy units. The very value of such electronic intelligence—ELINT—made it highly sensitive "compartmentalized" information, classified even higher than top secret. If word of the eavesdropping ever filtered out to the North Vietnamese or any of the thousands in the South who sympathized with them, it could shut down one of the Americans' most lucrative sources of information.

One of the radio transmissions that the technicians happened to intercept detailed the death of an American pilot. The shootdown of a U.S. plane and the fate of the pilots were matters of the highest interest to Hanoi. North Vietnamese commanders were likely to relay this kind of information as rapidly as possible. So shortly after the crash of Misty 21 on March 18, a field commander eager to announce the accomplishment reported it over a communications radio. The U.S. operatives gathering the intercepts merely swept up the radio transmissions, which were then sent on to translators and other experts to be analyzed. It usually took several days to determine what kind of intelligence the intercepts contained. This one had some precise information. The North Vietnamese officer provided the serial number listed on the pilot's dog tag as verification. It belonged to Howard K. Williams. The intelligence analysts couldn't tell whether the North Vietnamese had discovered Howard's body in the wreckage of the aircraft or someplace else. But the basic fact of his death seemed to be clear.

Telling anybody outside the reclusive intelligence community, however, was out of the question. If they were to report what they knew, questions would inevitably arise about how they knew it. That could lead to speculation about U.S. eavesdropping capabilities, which might somehow get back to the North Vietnamese, who might become a little more circumspect about their radio communications, which might jeopardize the whole effort.

There were inevitably circumstances in which intelligence held in American hands could significantly impact the lives of U.S. citizens. Resolving mysteries about the missing was one of them. From a military perspective, there was little difference between a troop who was killed and one who was missing. Either way he was no longer available to fight. But to family members and friends back home the distinction was enormous. It meant the difference between a life spent waiting and wondering, and the ability to rage, grieve, and move on. No matter: National security was at stake, and that trumped any individual's emotional and psychological needs. News of the pilot's death would have to remain secret.

So on March 20, two days after the shootdown, the Air Force officially declared Howard K. Williams to be MIA, missing in action. Since Dick Rutan had known him best, he became the summary courts officer, responsible for packing up Howie's stuff, paying his bills, taking care of any unfinished business. It was a grim duty, but one that many pilots had undertaken. A couple of other pilots who had done the same thing for their own lost buddies warned him that the reaction of the family, racked with grief and anger, was sure to be negative. The government and the huge military bureaucracy were amorphous, unsatisfying targets for their anguish. The natural instinct was to find human beings to pin the blame on. Rutan would be in the crosshairs—a name and a face they could hold responsible for their pain and loss. It added to his guilt over the fate of his friend.

For the next several days, every time Dick Rutan flew he passed over the crash site, staring into the incongruous hole in the jungle. What he was looking for he wasn't sure. He wanted to be there if a miracle happened and Howie's voice came over the radio, but it was more like a vigil he was keeping. He kept wondering what had happened, enacting various scenarios in his mind. There was no sign of a parachute. His best guess was that the ejection seat had failed to fire and Howie had never gotten out of the airplane, riding it straight into the ground. The hole in the jungle, Rutan reasoned, probably represented his friend's final resting place.

Rutan got to know that patch of terrain well, memorizing various landmarks. The crash site was in deep jungle, right on the border between Laos and North Vietnam. It was agonizing just looking down at it, able to do nothing. By this point he had been around combat enough to know that a serviceman's "missing" status, when there was a high likelihood he had been killed, was a peculiar kind of torment for the families back home. It encouraged false hope and added profound uncertainty to the pain of losing a husband or father. On one Misty mission, Rutan had been tasked to go investigate an area where an F-4 pilot and his back-seater had become disoriented on a night mission and flown straight down into the ground. The plane had exploded. Rutan's job was to monitor the rescue channel for any word from the two pilots, even though there was virtually no way they could have survived. Rutan heard no radio traffic whatsoever, but he couldn't find any evidence that proved they were dead, either. Still, when the mission was over, he reported to the F-4 commander that the crew had died, hoping the commander would pass that news on to the family members so they could begin to deal with the loss.

Howard's family back in Ohio deserved the same sort of closure, Rutan felt. And he was the one obligated to give it to them. He developed a plan. It was an open secret at Misty and elsewhere that the CIA regularly inserted road watch teams into Laos and Cambodia, and sometimes even into North Vietnam. They'd spy on Trail traffic and North Vietnamese encampments and other points of interest and often provide startlingly good intelligence—if they got out alive, which many didn't. Like other sensitive intel, the information they gathered rarely worked its way down to Misty or other units. But the pilots knew they were there anyway. In preflight briefings the intel officers would sometimes highlight "no-strike" areas designated by 7th Air Force, where nobody was supposed to bomb. There was never an explanation for these exclusion zones, but the Mistys assumed there were Americans or other friendly troops operating down there.

Plus, Rutan knew a couple of the helicopter pilots who ferried the special operations teams in and out, from Nakhon Phanom over in Thailand. He called one of his buddies at NKP and asked if they'd drop him off near the crash site during one of their missions, then come back and pick him up a few hours later. That should be enough time for him to hike up to the wreckage, see if Howie's body was inside, remove his dog tags and other personal items, and perhaps bury his friend. It sounded crazy to Rutan's special ops buddy, but then again they dealt with crazy shit all the time. Sure, he told Rutan. Get yourself over here and we'll see about dropping you off in Laos.

Rutan arranged for a couple days of leave and made plans to hop a flight over to NKP, keeping his scheme to himself. Then the evening before he was planning to go, the phone rang at Misty Ops. "Hey Rutan, it's for you!" the duty officer shouted.

"Who is it?" Rutan asked.

"I don't know," came the answer. "He wouldn't identify himself."

Rutan took the handset. "Captain Rutan here," he announced.

The voice on the other end was stern. "I can't tell you who I am," the anonymous caller began, "but I know what you are going to do tomorrow. Don't do it! It's been taken care of. Do you understand?"

Rutan didn't understand at all. He was shocked that anybody knew about his scheme to hike up to the crash site and thrown off balance by the caller's abruptness. He had no idea what had been "taken care of." Rutan asked who it was, wondering if one of his pilot buddies was playing a prank. The caller would say only that he was a major and couldn't identify himself. Then, with an air of impatience, he asked again: "Do you understand? It's been taken care of."

Confused, Rutan stammered, "I think so." Then before he could ask another question, the mystery major hung up.

Rutan was puzzled over the bizarre call. Obviously somebody over at NKP had mentioned what he was up to and word had gotten around. If some commander got wind of the scheme, it would be no surprise at all that he didn't want some dumb-shit Air Force prima donna tagging along and getting himself into trouble, forcing the special ops guys to put everything on hold to bail him out. But how would he have known anything about Howie?

The best Rutan could figure was that somebody up the chain of command had gotten intel that Howie had been captured by the North Vietnamese, and the same people had learned of his plan to go looking for Howie's Hun. They were telling him not to go to the crash site because there wasn't a body there. He would have been taking big risks to accomplish nothing, beyond checking out a wrecked F-100. This was good news, it dawned on Rutan, as he sorted through the implications. It meant that his friend—whom he assumed was dead—was in fact alive. Howie would be headed to prison, but at least he might return home someday.

Rutan canceled his trip to NKP. Still, the whole episode left him feeling uneasy. If somebody in the Air Force knew Howie was a prisoner, why wouldn't they tell Misty? Or, more important, Howie's family? He felt a current of relief at the prospect that Howie might be alive, but he didn't mention any of it to anybody. He started poking around in the POW reports that passed through intel, however, to see if there was any info that could be a reference to his friend.

NINETEEN

THE START OF THE WAIT

Monday, March 18, had begun as a much more promising day in Columbus, Ohio, than it had at Phu Cat. The winter chill had abated and it was sunny and mild. At Asbury Elementary School, Monalee Williams had recess duty, and as she watched the schoolchildren scamper around on the playground in light jackets, her mind was thousands of miles away. She gazed at the deep blue sky and thought, this is just what the sky will be like in Hawaii—where she was due to meet her husband Howard in a mere three weeks.

The kids went home for lunch, then returned. Monalee was teaching her first-graders one of the afternoon classes when somebody came and summoned her to the principal's office. Routine business, she thought—until she arrived there and saw two Air Force officers in their blue uniforms. One was a chaplain, another was a young female lieutenant. It could only mean one thing.

"Your husband's plane has gone down, ma'am," the chaplain informed her calmly. The incident had occurred at about 11:30 in the morning in Vietnam, which was twelve hours ahead of the time in Ohio. The chaplain told Monalee everything he knew, which wasn't much. Howard had been flying over North Vietnam with another pilot, and the plane had crashed. He didn't know if Howard was alive or dead. Rescue forces were out looking for him at that very moment.

"North Vietnam?" Monalee asked. "What was he doing over North Vietnam?" That was the first she had heard of him flying any missions over the North.

The two officers had nothing to tell her. They didn't have any idea what he had been doing over North Vietnam, or whether the plane had been shot down or crashed for some other reason. They didn't even seem to know much about airplanes. They were just messengers sent from Lockbourne Air Force Base, the nearest Air Force installation. Monalee quickly became frustrated with their lack of insight. Why hadn't the Air Force at least sent a pilot, she fumed, who could explain some of the basics of the missions over North Vietnam, of the area where Howard had gone down, of the prospects for a rescue?

The messengers offered to drive her home in her car. All right, she said. Then she told them that her Ford Mustang had a four-speed manual transmission and asked if either of them could drive a stick shift. The young lieutenant said no. The chaplain said yes. But as they started off, Monalee realized he had exaggerated his own skill with the stick shift. Every time they stopped or started, he fumbled with the clutch and the car jerked to and fro. It was so jarring that Monalee almost told him to get out and let her drive. But she was numb and didn't say anything. Mostly she wondered what she was going to tell her son, Howard Jr. He was only six.

When they got to her two-floor apartment, the messengers escorted her inside. They advised her not to tell anybody about her husband. The Air Force had no choice but to acknowledge when it lost a plane— that was big news, too hard to conceal—but it was best to be more circumspect about the names, or any other information, about dead or missing service members. The enemy could use that information against a captive in interrogations. Plus, too much bad news could start to spoil morale among the all-important wives back home. Monalee struggled to comprehend what the Air Force officials were saying. Obviously she was going to tell her son, she insisted, and her parents and her family. Yes, they understood. Still, it was best to be discreet, they emphasized. For her own good, and her husband's.

Normally when Howard Jr. came home from kindergarten, his mom was still at school teaching. So he'd get off the bus and walk down to the babysitter's apartment, about one hundred yards down the road from his own. But when he got to the babysitter's on this day, she told him he could go home, that his mom was there. He walked home. The two Air Force representatives were still inside. His mom looked upset. He knew something bad had happened. The messengers asked if they could do anything more. Did she want them to stay? Monalee said no, and they left. Once they were gone, she cried for the first time. She sat Howard on a couch and told him that his dad's plane had crashed. They thought that daddy had gotten out, but didn't know where he was. They were looking for him.

Mother and son stayed at home the rest of the day. Howard Jr. didn't completely comprehend what was going on, but he knew what it meant that his dad was a pilot. He had been out to the flight line with him and watched him climb into his aircraft. When his dad had left for Vietnam in the fall, his mom had said he'd be gone for a year, but that maybe they'd be able to see him in six months. It hadn't seemed like a big deal, his father going off to war for a year—that's what all their friends in the military did. But now Howard could tell that his mom was shaken up. Her eyes looked scared. That made him scared.

Monalee called her parents. They came the next day and stayed through the weekend. Monalee was frightened and bewildered, but she also figured she'd get a phone call any day saying her husband had been picked up, he was all right, and might even be coming home for a spell. Of all the military wives she knew, she wasn't aware of any whose husbands had gone missing in Vietnam.

The principal at Asbury Elementary, Steve Drummond, offered a peculiar type of reassurance. As a soldier during the Korean War he had been taken prisoner, without any word being sent back home. For all his family knew, he had simply disappeared. After the truce was declared in 1953, he walked across the border from the North to the South with other repatriated prisoners and picked up his life where it had left off. It was like he had returned from the dead. The story offered hope.

Howard Jr. wanted to know about Hawaii. Would they still be going? "I don't think so," Monalee told him. "Unless they find Daddy.

We'll have to wait and see." It was a confounding challenge, trying to persuade a child to accept uncertainty over whether his father was dead or alive. Naturally, Monalee didn't want to alarm her son. But she also knew there was a chance his dad might not be coming home, and she didn't want to give him false hope. She thought about having to tell him they had discovered a body. If she sugarcoated the information now and didn't signal that bad news might be coming, it might be even more difficult down the road.

A brigadier general at Lockbourne sent Monalee a letter outlining the basic facts of her husband's disappearance: The aircraft had been hit by hostile ground fire, the other pilot had ejected safely and was rescued, the plane "was observed to explode on impact with the ground." It was her first official notification. On the same day she got the letter, the school paper at Kae Avenue School, where Howard Jr. was in first grade, ran a "story" by him. "My mother and I are going to Hawaii to see my Dad," it read. "We will go in an airplane. Bye!"

Monalee tried to get more information from the Air Force officials at Lockbourne. They knew little. She quickly realized she'd go crazy sitting around waiting to hear something. It was important, she knew, for her and Howard to get back to their routines, to stay busy. She planned to send Howard back to school after just a couple of days off, and to keep him focused on baseball. She phoned Howard's teacher, Mrs. Lane, to tell her what had happened, in case Howard got upset or acted out. Another odd coincidence surfaced. It turned out that Mrs. Lane, who was about to retire as a teacher, had been married to a man who forty-five years earlier had been on a plane that disappeared over the Rocky Mountains. She never heard from him again. Unlike most people Monalee was reaching out to, Mrs. Lane seemed to know what it meant to wait and wonder.

Monalee went back to work herself at the same time Howard went back to school. It helped to be back among her colleagues, but something had obviously changed. The teachers she knew best, those who taught kindergarten and first grade, were kind and respectful. But some of the others just seemed to be uncomfortable around her. When she'd walk into the teachers' lounge, people would stop talking. They'd avoid making eye contact with her. Mr. Drummond and Mrs. Lane seemed to be the easiest to talk to. They knew something the others didn't, and Monalee realized she didn't have to explain her feelings or her confusion to them. They already knew.

She took Howard out to buy a puppy. Monalee figured it would be something he could get attached to and love on his own terms. They went to a local kennel, where Howard picked out a mutt that was part terrier and part Chihuahua. It was small enough to sit in his lap, and he could pick it up without exertion. Howard named the pooch Tippy, because it was so small that every time it leaned over to eat or drink, it seemed to tip forward into the bowl.

The machinery for notifying other family members proved to be one of the military's few truly efficient systems. Even before the Air Force duo had tracked down Monalee at Asbury Elementary, another team had arrived at the Williams home in Steubenville to break the news to Howard's mom. John Buckmelter, Howard's childhood friend and local flying buddy, raced right over. The family longed for a hopeful sign from the Air Force representatives, some sense of optimism that Howard would end up okay. The messengers were gentle and polite, but they seemed to be almost deliberately opaque, offering virtually no reassurance.

Mrs. Williams promptly called the other family members who weren't in Steubenville. In Cleveland, where Howard's sister Jean lived with her husband, there had been a radio report that morning about a U.S. airplane being shot down over North Vietnam. One pilot had been rescued, the report said, but one hadn't. Jean had felt uneasy. Then shortly after noon her mother called—and asked to speak with Jean's husband, Jerry. At that point Jean knew for sure that something was wrong. Mrs. Williams, fearing Jean wouldn't be able to handle the news, broke it to Jerry instead, who calmly hung up and explained what had happened to his wife. Angry as she was that her mom wouldn't tell her directly, she was distraught about her brother, her closest sibling. She immediately thought of the last letter he had sent, in which Howard, ever the music buff, had urged her to listen to the new Nancy Sinatra song "Bang Bang, My Baby Shot Me Down." "It's about siblings like us," he had written.

There was only one snag in the Air Force's notification system. Brian Williams's wife, Pat, happened to be an Air Force captain and transportation officer stationed at Cannon Air Force Base in New

Mexico. On the evening of the eighteenth she had been watching TV and heard the news that a two-seat F-100F previously assigned to Cannon had crashed over North Vietnam. It had to be Brian, she felt. But no blue car came to visit her, and she settled into a restless sleep. At 2:00 a.m. the phone rang. It was Brian, calling from Phu Cat to explain what had happened. He told her he was banged up but okay, and broke the unhappy news about Howie. Pat listened, relieved, and ended the conversation with a simple admonition: "Don't be a hero."

When Pat arrived at work the next day, long faces greeted her. "We're so sorry," a couple of her colleagues lamented. After a few minutes of confusion, they sorted out the misunderstanding. In one of the innumerable bureaucratic screwups of the war, the two pilots' names had been reversed on the official Air Force message that went out announcing the loss. The terse note stated flatly that Brian was missing, not Howie. "Nope," Pat assured them. "I just talked to him at two o'clock this morning. He's fine."

Unlike most wives who received calls or visits, Pat had a fairly good understanding of what her husband was doing in Vietnam. She had some friends who worked in intel at Cannon, and they had given her some unauthorized briefings about the kind of flying Brian's unit was doing. They didn't tell her everything, but she put the pieces together. "Someone," for instance, was using jets as FACs in North Vietnam; Brian was doing something "he couldn't tell her about." The mission sounded like it was right up Brian's alley. The daredevils FACing over the North had to include him.

After Brian had called, she thought about staying home the next day, but finally decided it would be easier if she went to work as usual. After the morning staff meeting, the wing commander at Cannon drew Pat aside. "Pat," the colonel said, "you know he will have to go back to flying."

It was a distressing thought, but one she had already begun to absorb. "Of course," she answered with practiced nonchalance, as if she were a jet-jock herself. "That's what fighter pilots do."

It took longer for any real information about Howie to reach Roger Williams in Saigon. For several days after the incident, Howard's brother, the records clerk at U.S. Army headquarters, didn't know anything about it. Then he got a call from the Red Cross, saying only that he should call home. At first he didn't think about Howard at all, figuring something had happened back in Ohio. But he quickly got through to his mom and learned the news.

He sought out Roger Wise, Howie's old buddy from pilot training, who was a staff officer at the 7th Air Force command post in Saigon. Wise had seen the initial message saying what had happened and tried to contact Phu Cat to learn more about the shootdown and Howie's fate. They wouldn't say anything—standard procedure for the guys flying up north. All Wise could do was stress that Howard was listed as missing—not killed—and urge Roger not to become despondent.

That was an easy sell. Roger Williams had so much confidence in his brother that he practically expected him to come walking into his little office any minute, cracking a joke about enlisted men being gullible enough to stand in the presence of officers. But Roger Wise had also made him realize that there was probably a lot more to the story than either of them knew. Howie's brother decided to place a call up to Phu Cat and see if any of the Mistys would be able to tell him anything more. They invited him up to the base and offered to explain everything they knew. Roger cleared the trip with his commanders and put in a request for a thirty-day emergency leave so he could fly home to Steubenville afterward.

Besides gathering information, Roger had one other duty in mind. As good a man as Howie was, he was also a fighter pilot in a tropical, live-for-the-moment war zone, lonely, vulnerable, sometimes scared. Even for troops isolated out in the countryside at places like Phu Cat, there were numerous opportunities for trysts in Saigon, on R&R in Sydney or Hong Kong, and on the bogus "training" missions the Mistys sometimes arranged for themselves in the Philippines and other places. Roger didn't know about any mistresses, but he had spent enough time around troops to know that even the most devoted husbands sometimes strayed. He wanted to get to Phu Cat and go through Howard's stuff to make sure there was nothing that might be hurtful to Monalee before everything got shipped out.

This time Roger traveled to Phu Cat on official orders, so he hopped a ride on a C-130 to Cam Ranh Bay, then on a C-7 over to Phu Cat. He spent most of his time there with B. Willy and Dick Rutan. They sat in Howie's trailer and pored over maps. Brian told Roger every detail he could remember, how Brian had said he was ready to bail out and Howie had said he'd be right behind. B. Willy seemed devastated. He kept telling Roger how sorry he was he hadn't brought Howie back. His brother was a great pilot, he stressed, and had done nothing wrong that accounted for the shootdown. It was a golden BB that got them, not pilot error.

Rutan laid out some maps and showed Roger where the crash site was and explained what it looked like from overhead. There was a long, clean slash in the trees, he said, suggesting the plane had gone in straight and level, not out of control. It was impossible to tell if Howie had still been flying it when it hit. On the other hand, they had never seen a parachute, so they had no evidence that he had gotten out, either.

The parachute beeper was a particularly confounding bit of evidence. Usually the emergency beeper came on automatically, once a pilot's parachute opened up. But there had been no beeper other than B. Willy's after the crash. Then a couple of hours after Brian had been picked up, another beeper came on. Several planes working together had homed in on the signal and traced it to a hut in a nearby village. Rutan had drawn an X on a photographic map, in a clearing that was near the mountain where the Hun had crashed. There were eight or ten huts in the clearing, and the X marked one of them. That was where they thought the beeper had been transmitting from.

There were several possible explanations. Somebody may have found Howie or his body, taken his beeper, and turned it on, hoping to draw rescuers toward the ground so they could shoot at them. Howie could have been taken captive in the hut. Or it could have been another beeper somebody in the village had gotten from another shootdown—they all gave out the same signal. What seemed unlikely was that Howie had been in the hut calling for help on his own.

A few of the other Mistys showed up, stressed how sorry they were, and offered to help in any way they could. All of them seemed to Roger to be very reluctant to say anything about Howie's possible fate. Nobody was willing to write him off as dead, since they knew from scraps of intelligence that some pilots shot down and never heard from ended up as prisoners in Hanoi. Yet being a prisoner was a pretty awful fate, too, because of the horrendous mistreatment. There wasn't much anybody wanted to say either way.

Roger spent just one night at Phu Cat. Before he left, he went through his brother's belongings with Dick Rutan to see if there was anything to "sanitize." They didn't come across anything. Roger took Howie's black address book, just in case. And as a memento he also took a copy of the SAM photograph Howie had taken just days earlier, and been so proud of. Roger flew back to Saigon, where his emergency leave papers had come through. He got on a plane the next day for the long trip back to Ohio.

After about twenty-four hours of travel, he touched down in Columbus, where he planned to visit Monalee and tell her what he knew. He gave her the map Rutan had used to show where Howard's plane went down, the one with the X on it, and explained everything he could about the crash. It was the same drill when he got home to Steubenville. Roger turned out to be the only one who seemed to know anything about the shootdown, and he went over every detail. Neighbors and church members came to express their sorrow and offer support—always talking about Howard as if he were dead. Mrs. Williams, Howie's mother, grew agitated with everybody thinking the worst. But Roger suspected that she was thinking the worst herself.

Eventually Monalee received a typewritten letter from Dick Rutan. In stiff, formal language, he expressed his remorse: "I wish to convey to you the sympathy of myself and the other officers in this unit of which Howard was a member prior to the time his aircraft was downed on March 18. His absence in the unit has been keenly felt by all." Rutan then explained that he was the officer responsible for taking care of personal belongings and other matters. On April 18—a month after Howard's disappearance—he would begin his duties, assuming there was no further word on Howard. Monalee wrote back, providing Rutan with an "inventory" of Howard's belongings to make sure nothing got overlooked.

Rutan put aside his usual freewheeling inclinations and did his duty by the book. He paid Howie's bar bills, which were modest. He sorted through Howie's stuff and made sure it was packed carefully and addressed properly. It was grim work but Rutan had asked for it. This was the real war he had sought, and it was much more devastating than he had imagined. While preparing for combat, he had thought mainly about the risks to himself. Those, it turned out, he had been instinctively equipped to handle. But the sudden disappearance of a buddy, and wrapping up his life as if you were closing out a bank account—that was hard. It was gloom, guilt, anger, and sadness rolling over you in waves, one after the other, then rolling over you again. Facing AAA seemed a lot easier.

He got everything packed up and sent it off to Ohio. In addition to clothing, pictures, letters, and other odds and ends, he included a check for $96.35, the amount of cash that had been among Howard's stuff. He promised to sell Howard's Honda motorbike "for a good price" and forward the money. And Rutan apologized for the condition of some of Howard's things. "I checked the laundry and picked up all his underwear," Rutan wrote. "They are in the shipment. They may not look very clean but that is the best the Phu Cat laundry can do."

Like many fighter pilots, Rutan was not an emotive person. But the sorrow and regret were there on the pages all the same, in the reserved language of men trying to push away pain. "Monalee, I think a lot of Howard and I want to do all I can to see that all is taken care of on this end," he finished one letter. "I am sorry but we have no news as to Howard's status. Sincerely, Dick."

Nearly a month after the crash, when it had finally sunk in that Howie was gone and Misty had more thoroughly investigated the crash, Don Shepperd wrote Roger Williams a follow-up letter. "I'm sorry that I can't provide you with some good news about Howie," he began. Then he told Roger what they did know: The map coordinates of the crash site, the "heavily jungled" nature of the terrain, and the fact that it would be too risky to put in a ground team to look for his brother. Shepperd drew a little diagram describing how the plane had struck the top of a mountain, then slid down the backside of the hill until it came to rest near the bottom. "There is very little left of the wreckage," he said plainly. The only hint of optimism he held out was that someday the mystery of what happened to Howie might be resolved. "After the war I would be very interested in going into the area with you if no further news is heard. In the meantime," Shepperd closed out, "I am hoping with you that Howie was captured and we will be seeing him after the war."

TWENTY

THE WISE MEN

Misty was in transition. Ed Risinger and Jim Fiorelli had left. Several new guys had shown up, and one of them, Howard Williams, had already been lost. More were on the way. Don Jones, the commander, and Mick Greene, the Ops officer, were both scheduled to rotate out in April. Their replacements had already joined the unit and were flying missions, getting familiar with the operation before taking on their official duties.

Lt. Col. Stanley Mamlock, slated to take command after Jones left, was fighting his third war. During World War II he had flown with the Flying Tigers, the American volunteers who helped defend China against the Japanese. He was written off as lost at least once, when his plane malfunctioned and he was forced to bail out over China. A week later, on Christmas Day, 1944, he showed up back at his base, having walked home. In the Korean War, Mamlock had flown F-80 fighter jets. In Vietnam he had been doing research at 7th Air Force for a new airplane being developed when he asked his boss about getting a job out in the field where he could do some actual flying. "Get a replacement," the director of operations told him, "and I'll let you go." Mamlock knew Colonel Schneider, who said he had a major on staff who wanted to learn "administration" and would be happy to take the job down in Saigon. So in January 1968, Mamlock came to Phu Cat, where he worked on Schneider's operations staff.

Mamlock had noticed the Mistys were short on pilots, and he arranged to fly in the backseat on a few sorties. It was a good unit with good people. With Jones due to leave before long, Mamlock asked Schneider if he could take over command of the unit. Schneider tried to talk him out of it. "It's not a good mission," he told Mamlock. "You don't want it." Schneider felt he had no control over Misty, which had the patronage—and protection—of the top guys down at 7th Air Force. He didn't want his man, Mamlock, involved with it. Mamlock persisted, however, and Schneider finally agreed. Mamlock had the seniority for the job, and he'd be the next commander when Jones's time was up.

Mick Greene's replacement as Operations officer would be Maj. Charlie Summers, another mature pilot with ample combat experience. On a previous Vietnam tour he had been shot down and recovered. He had broken his back, though, and it took months for him to recuperate and regain flying status. Summers had the appearance of a choirboy, with a cherubic, smiling face, a fair complexion, close-cropped hair, and an enduring sense of humor. Surrounded by men who swore and drank ferociously, Summers was a teetotaler whose strongest exclamation was likely to be a heartfelt "Oh, gosh," or, when truly stressed, "Darn!" One Misty who had ridden with Summers on a harrowing flight realized the choirboy was a master of understatement when they flew threw a dense field of flak and Summers remarked, "Oh golly, that was close."

A couple of Don Shepperd's classmates from the Air Force Academy, P. K. Robinson and Lanny Lancaster, were also among the new guys. Robinson was a "Buckeye" from Galion, Ohio, who flew F-100s in England before getting some troubling news: He had contracted Bell's palsy, the neurological condition that paralyzes the facial nerves. In Robinson's case it interfered with his ability to blink his eyes, which could cause them permanent damage if he had to eject. Even though Robinson promised that he would close his eyes during an ejection, he was grounded and told that his flying career was probably over. Some friendly flight surgeons recognized his strong desire to fly, however, and appealed to the Pentagon, seeking a medical flying waiver. After months of bureaucratic haggling, they managed to get him back on flying status.

After a couple of flights at Misty, it was evident that Robinson had another unusual problem, especially for a pilot: air sickness. Robinson was fine when he was at the controls, flying the aircraft. But when he was in the backseat, trying to react to the unpredictable jinking, he invariably became ill. He quickly became known as the "king of the sick sacks" since he brought home a full one on practically all of his backseat checkout rides.

Robinson was Jim Fiorelli's replacement, and his first Misty ride had been in the back with Fio, trying to rescue the downed F-4 pilot from the A Shau Valley. His second ride, with B. Willy, had been dominated by a rescue effort, too, as they helped pull two downed pilots from a harrowing situation. His fourth flight was on the same day that B. Willy and Howard Williams had been shot down, and he spent the majority of his fifth and final backseat checkout ride searching for Howie. Robinson began to wonder if he'd ever have a "normal" Misty mission, one that didn't involve a rescue. His fellow Mistys told him the unusual string of shootdowns was probably the result of improved weather and a surge in bombing activity. But there was more to it: The NVA defenses were getting thicker, the air-defense gunners were maturing, and the battle for the Trail was getting hotter than ever.

P. K. finally got to work an actual target on his sixth Misty ride, when he was flying the plane for the first time, with Don Jones in the back. They were staring at the usual cloud cover, stretched over the Pack like a huge white tarpaulin, when a sudden opening appeared at the northern edge of the Pack. As they shot north, they quickly realized that the break in the weather had caught the Vietnamese by surprise—there were several hundred trucks sitting out in the open, right beneath them.

There was even more luck. When the Mistys had called for fighters, one of the pilots sitting on alert back at Phu Cat was Hog Piner, the big Louisiana boy who had been at Misty for four months. He had just finished his time with Misty and had rotated back to the 416th to finish his Vietnam tour. As Piner and his wingman approached the area, they could see the trucks Robinson and Jones had already strafed burning from miles away. Piner told Misty that he was familiar with the area and didn't need a mark. He took out some trucks with his bombs on his first bombing pass. But then the usual anomaly threatened to scuttle the whole mission.

Piner's wingman was Fred Thompson. Unlike Piner, whose jet was loaded with bombs, Thompson was carrying wall-to-wall napalm. It was the first time Thompson had seen such an inviting target. He was so eager to take out some of the trucks that instead of following 7th Air Force ground rules and dropping the napalm in a high-altitude dive bomb, he descended for a low-level attack. That would have been a more effective way to deliver napalm—except that Thompson's jet was heavier than he gauged. He misjudged his descent and flew into the tops of the trees. He muscled the jet up out of the limbs, but it was badly damaged. Thompson barely had time to eject before the aircraft crashed in flames. The truck-killing came to an abrupt halt as Robinson and Jones started setting up a rescue.

It was over much more quickly than the other rescue efforts Robinson had participated in. Thompson had come down in the middle of a group of truck drivers who had just fled the bombing. They were in a foul mood and captured him immediately. It was like they had received an unexpected gift. The drivers were sitting ducks, defenseless against the American planes, and out of nowhere one of the pilots who had been bombing them floated out of the sky and landed in their arms. Thompson wasn't free long enough to even come up on the radio. But the planes overhead spent a lot of time looking for him anyway, and while they were doing that many of the trucks escaped.

Misty was exciting flying, no doubt about that, but Robinson was surprised at the continual disappointments. On his final checkout ride, Robinson watched as an F-4, call sign Gunfighter 08, was attacking a large military truck near the Ban Laboy Ford, along the border with Laos. Instead of pulling out of its bombing dive, however, the plane flew into the trees just beyond the truck. The pilot might have been hit, or maybe he had misjudged the dive. Either way there was little chance he survived. In a voice drenched with dejection, Robinson radioed the news to Don Shepperd, flying in another aircraft. Shepperd took over the rescue effort and continued to listen for the pilot's emergency beeper, to no avail.

Lanny Lancaster, another newcomer, was more sanguine. Gregarious and funny, the prematurely balding pilot had a booming voice made to carry across the plains of West Texas, where his grandmother had raised him. He always wore a mischievous smile on his face, as though he knew something others didn't. Lancaster was one of the least likely Mistys. It was a surprise to him that he had even been accepted at the Air Force Academy, where he always joked that he was in the upper echelons of the bottom tier. He had flown C-130s in Japan and switched to his real love—fighters and the F-100—only when it was time to go to Vietnam.

Shepperd had been scheduled to help check out his Academy classmates on their first few rides. He had been flying with Lancaster in the backseat on March 18, when Howie and Brian Williams had gone down. Lancaster had been the first one to see B. Willy's chute on the ground and had been instrumental in his rescue. It had been good work for a novice.

A couple of days later Shepperd was in the backseat for Lancaster's first checkout ride up front. On the first swing through the Pack the weather was bad, but it got better as they came back from refueling over Thailand. The clearest area was up north of Mu Ghia, where Route Pack 1 merged into Route Pack 2, the Navy's area of responsibility. Lanny suggested that they poke around in Route Pack 2, since they could see up there. Technically the Mistys and the Air Force were supposed to stay out of the Navy's turf, but Shepperd didn't see any harm in it. He agreed.

Within a couple of minutes Lancaster saw two trucks heading south, then three. He kept going farther north into Navy country. More trucks appeared. Lancaster stopped counting when he hit fifty. He climbed for altitude as he called the ABCCC to tell them about the trucks and ask for fighters. The weather continued to improve, and the trucks kept coming, moving slower as they began to bunch up on the road. Finally there were about seventy-five trucks backed up bumper-to-bumper. They couldn't have asked for a riper target.

While waiting for the fighters, the two pilots dipped down and strafed the lead truck. The drivers behind started to jump out of their vehicles and head for the trenches. Lancaster and Shepperd continued to make low, threatening passes, lobbing an occasional rocket or making a quick strafe pass to keep the formation lined up while they waited for the bomb-droppers. The first several fighters to show up had all the right bombs, but they dropped from high altitude using Route Pack 5 and 6 tactics. They missed the whole convoy by a wide margin. Then two F-4s showed up with "Bullpup" guided missiles. When the first F-4 let one fly, the missile promptly nose-dived into the ground. "Here we go again," Shepperd grimaced, disgusted by the prospect of more tepid bombing and another blown opportunity.

But the second F-4 launched a missile that scored a direct hit at the front of the convoy, destroying four trucks and damaging several others. When the pilot tried the same trick at the back of the pack, the missile "went dumb" once again. The first F-4 got off a direct hit, though, wrecking several trucks and damaging the road, which bottled up the rest of the vehicles even more.

Some Navy A-7s arrived on the scene and dropped cluster bombs all over the backup. Now the attack was shaping up as a roaring success. The Navy fighters destroyed so many trucks it was hard to get an accurate count. Lancaster and Shepperd stayed until they were sure everything was burning, destroyed, or damaged. After weeks of cloud cover so thick you could eat it with a spoon, the Mistys had finally gotten a big break. As Shepperd looked down on the carnage, he was sure it was the biggest BDA count Misty had registered during the time he had been there, and maybe since it started.

Their tanker had developed engine problems and headed home early, and they didn't have enough gas to make it back to Phu Cat. So Shepperd and Lancaster diverted to Ubon, which was like a resort compared to their home base. Since there was no war in Thailand, troops could go into the towns as they wished. The Americans and their money attracted hordes of merchants, and Ubon was surrounded by several good restaurants. Shep and Lanny went out for a great Kobe beef dinner before heading back to Phu Cat and mess-hall food.

The next day other Misty flights went up to the same area, directing strikes against the cleanup crews sent to repair the damage. The two-day shoot-up quickly became known as The Great Truck Kill, and it was a big morale booster. The prior couple of months had been demoralizing—Tet and Khe Sanh, constant bad weather, the loss of

Howie Williams—and finally it felt like Misty was regaining momentum. The weather had been clearing and targets seemed plentiful every time the Mistys got a glimpse beneath the clouds. Maybe they'd finally start making a dent in the North Vietnamese supply lines and help turn the tide of the war.

Or maybe not. Back in Washington, in deliberations that were off-limits to the Mistys and all the other troops in Vietnam, President Johnson was reevaluating the entire approach to the war, including how it affected his own future. Fellow Democrats Robert Kennedy, whom Johnson despised, and Eugene McCarthy were threatening to tear the Democratic Party apart fighting Johnson for the presidential nomination unless Johnson agreed to withdraw from the war.[1] On March 20, Johnson telephoned Defense Secretary Clark Clifford with an urgent request: "I've got to get me a peace proposal."[2]

A few days later, Clifford asked Johnson to attend a dinner of "the wise men," sixteen prominent thinkers who had been intimately involved with Vietnam policy over two administrations. The group, which gathered at the State Department, included luminaries such as former secretary of state Dean Acheson, McGeorge Bundy, who had been John Kennedy's national security adviser, diplomat Henry Cabot Lodge, and Supreme Court Justice Abe Fortas—all veterans of past Vietnam debates. Newcomers like New York banker Douglas Dillon brought the perspective of businessmen. Retired generals Maxwell Taylor, Omar Bradley, and Matthew Ridgway represented the military. Johnson's own top advisers rounded out the group.[3]

The wise men listened to briefings with the latest updates on Vietnam and held discussions among themselves. Though some had been ardent supporters of the war in earlier years—and Bundy, Lodge, and Taylor had had a direct role in shaping the war strategy—all but four were now opposed to the war. And Clifford, who had brought them together, wanted the president to start moving toward peace and disengagement, not further into war. General Westmoreland in Saigon had made one of his periodic requests for additional troops, which Clifford opposed. The trend should be in the opposite direction, he felt.

Johnson met the wise men the next day for lunch and interrogated them, one by one. He was startled by their views. Johnson believed a lot of what his generals said—that Tet had been a U.S. victory, that the North Vietnamese were on the run. The wise men were far more skeptical. They told him that Tet had been a disaster that probably had tipped public opinion against the war for good. The only sane course, they said, was to back out of Vietnam. Beginning with Walter Cronkite's report a month earlier, Johnson could feel support for the war slipping through his fingers. If the wise men had now soured on the war, Johnson thought, "What must the average citizen be thinking?"[4]

It was a decisive moment for Johnson. Before the meeting, Johnson had been on the fence—he didn't want to enlarge the war, but he didn't want to quit, either. The wise men persuaded him that one way or another, American troops would have to leave Vietnam. And after enlarging the war for five years, there was no credible way for Johnson to reverse course and pull out.[5]

On the evening of March 31, Johnson addressed the American people on television. He announced that he was withdrawing from the 1968 presidential race: "I shall not seek, and I will not accept, the nomination of my party for another term as your president."[6] He also declared a bombing halt over North Vietnam, except for the lower portion of the country, north of the DMZ. That was supposed to entice North Vietnam to negotiate an end to the war, to get LBJ his peace proposal.

Mick Greene heard the news on Armed Forces Radio, nine days before he was scheduled to go home. "Well, I'll just be a sonofabitch," he muttered. He shouldn't have cared. It would end up as somebody else's problem, not his. But the haphazard, trial-and-error war strategy was maddening, and it was getting guys shot down. Bombing was on, bombing was off. Some commanders felt it was worth risking lives for the war, some didn't. Shutting down the flow of supplies into the South was a top priority—and the whole reason Misty existed—yet the United States was once again giving the North Vietnamese war machine a reprieve.

Greene wondered what the bombing halt would mean for Misty. Technically, it didn't affect Route Pack 1, which abutted the DMZ and remained open to the fighters. But now the NVA would have a free ride all the way down to Misty's turf. It was going to get busy, and even more dangerous. There would be more fighters and tankers available, since they'd no longer be flying "downtown." But without a doubt the AAA and the SAMs would get thicker, too. Had Johnson thought about that?

Don Shepperd was supposed to leave Misty shortly after Mick Greene and return to the 90th Tactical Fighter Squadron—"the Dice"— at Bien Hoa. But Shepperd thought he'd like to stay. The policy at Misty was four months and out, but Jonesy Jones had extended, and Shepperd thought he could, too. He called Lt. Col. Ron Berdoy, an old friend who was the Ops officer at the Dice, and made his request.

"Tell me the real reason you want to extend," Berdoy said.

Shepperd explained that the weather was getting good and he felt he had gained the kind of experience that could make a big difference. A lot of new guys were coming to Misty, and they needed a guiding hand.

"Look," Berdoy told him. "Come home. You've done your part. You've been shot at enough. Wells Jackson wants to come to Misty and it's someone else's turn." Then he reminded Shepperd of Jim Brinkman, a friend and Air Force Academy classmate who had been killed a week earlier near Bien Hoa while flying close air support. "I don't want to send you home in a box like your buddy Brinkman," Berdoy said.

Shepperd relented. He'd be going back to monkey bombing after all. Yet as Brinkman's fate indicated, even that had begun to get dangerous as the NVA relentlessly built up its defenses.

Jonesy Jones was on his way out, too, but Jonesy was a special case. Since his Misty tour had already been extended, Jonesy was allowed to stick around until he had logged one hundred missions. That would be his cutoff point—and he was getting close. No. 100 was on the schedule for April 7, with Maj. Tom Tapman in the backseat. Tapman was "attached" to Misty—he didn't belong to the unit per se, but he was one of the top operations officers at the wing, and he flew with Misty from time to time. Tapman was an experienced fighter jock with almost twenty-two hundred hours in the F-100, more time than most of the Mistys had. He was also a favorite of Colonel Schneider. Tapman was athletic-looking and always dressed impeccably—like he had come right off a recruiting poster. He knew his stuff, too, and Schneider liked to use him to brief visiting dignitaries. He always came across as knowledgeable and professional.

Like most experienced pilots, Tapman didn't relish being in the backseat with anybody. He liked to fly his own plane. But the Misty rules held that anybody who hadn't been through the full program of checkout rides had to fly in the back. Tapman usually asked to fly with Hog Piner, whom he regarded as a bold pilot who avoided unnecessary risks. But Piner had left Misty and gone back to the 416th. When Tapman came up on the schedule with Jonesy, he felt almost as comfortable as if it had been Piner. Surely, he figured, Jonesy would be extremely conservative on his one hundredth and last mission.

After takeoff, Jonesy and Tapman, flying as Misty 11, headed for the top of Mu Ghia Pass. Cresting the pass was the only way for the North Vietnamese to get to the Trail network in Laos, on the other side of the mountains, and it had been very busy lately. There had been The Great Truck Kill and several other successful attacks. After one cycle through the region, however, Misty 11 hadn't discovered much. They headed for the tanker.

After refueling, they flew a bit farther north, into the southern portion of Route Pack 2. Jonesy spotted several camouflaged trucks. No fighters were immediately available, so Jonesy began going after them on strafing runs with his 20mm guns. Carroll Williams—"C. Willy"— was en route to the Pack as Misty 21, and Jonesy called him on the radio to ask for his assistance up on the southern edge of Route Pack 2.

Jonesy, meanwhile, made repeated passes over the trucks, getting lower and slower on each pass. Tapman was getting nervous. This was not his idea of a conservative mission. And sure enough, on the fifth pass they took a hit—a loud hit—somewhere in the aircraft belly. As the senior man in the cockpit, Tapman took the controls, hit afterburner, and started to climb to the west. The left main landing gear had become extended, causing heavy drag on the plane, but with the afterburner engaged Tapman was able to reach 20,000 feet. That bought them only a little bit of time, however: C. Willy had arrived on the scene and told Misty 11 they were on fire. It looked like they needed to get out.

As the man in back, Tapman went first. Then it was Jonesy's turn. As he raised his seat ejection handles and pulled the triggers, nothing happened. He looked down to see what the problem was—at which point the seat fired, severely straining his neck. Jonesy had forgotten about the built-in half-second delay in the system.

Since he went out at 20,000 feet, Jonesy had a long way to fall. He went into a free fall, waiting for the chute to open automatically at 14,000 feet. Eventually, however, it seemed like he had fallen too far, and he manually pulled the D ring on his harness to activate the chute. As it opened and caught him, Jonesy looked up. Tapman's chute was far above him. Tapman had forgotten to disconnect his "zero-delay lanyard," and his chute had opened immediately after ejection. That meant a long, chilly ride to the ground—thirty minutes or more. Tapman wouldn't remember most of it, however—he had been knocked unconscious.

Jonesy recalled his parachute training and made his "four-line cut," slicing four of the parachute riser lines with a knife so that he could steer the chute more precisely to a suitable landing area. While looking around, he was momentarily distracted and almost cut through the main parachute strap. He looked at the terrain below. It was uninhabited, with no signs of enemy troops. Better yet: He wasn't being shot at. Things were looking good, he thought. Then he realized he was heading for the tallest tree in the jungle and had forgotten to deploy his survival kit. He thudded into the tree and smashed down through the branches.

It was a rough landing—but he was uninjured. Jonesy still hadn't hit the ground, however. He was hanging about ten feet above the jungle floor, suspended by his parachute. He swung quietly in the tree for a few minutes, listening silently for any noises. Then he remembered Fio's story, about hanging in a tree a few inches off the ground for hours and realizing he still had his helmet on. He removed it. All he heard was the creak and croak of the jungle, so he shinnied down a sapling to the ground. Terra firma felt great, but his neck was killing him.

Tapman woke up, dazed, just as he was about to crash into the trees. There was no time to cut the riser lines or maneuver his parachute. He was lucky to have a second's worth of notice to cross his legs and arms as he sailed into branches that reached seventy or eighty feet into the air. His canopy snagged some of the tree limbs, and instead of smashing into the earth, Tapman came to a stop with his feet about two inches above the ground. His head was pounding. Blood was oozing from somewhere. He felt woozy and delirious.

C. Willy had watched the whole drama from the moment Misty 11 was hit until the two pilots entered the trees. He had already summoned the Nakhon Phanom rescue forces and was trying to raise the two pilots on the radio. Jonesy checked in quickly. The two Jollys, which had just arrived on scene, lumbered into position and picked him up without a fight. Tapman, however, was preoccupied. He heard voices coming near him in the jungle.

Tapman, always the planner, was determined never to be captured. In addition to two radios, spare batteries, and the typical six rounds of ammunition in his .38-caliber pistol, he carried an extra twenty-five rounds of .38-cal ammunition. He had always planned to fight it out and save the last round for himself. He was not going to prison.

The jungle where Tapman had landed was pretty clear under the canopy of the high trees, with just low ground-cover vegetation. Tapman had been talking to Misty 21 when he heard voices, and he started running west as fast as he could. C. Willy wanted to help, but Tapman didn't know where to tell him to strafe. The downed pilot couldn't spot Misty 21 through the thick trees, nor could they spot him. Besides, Tapman didn't know exactly where the bad guys were. He could only hear them.

Tapman needed rest. He was breathing hard. He took a drink of water, lay down behind a tree in a shallow depression, took out his pistol, and waited. Within a minute or two, a young Vietnamese dressed in green fatigues and a pith helmet stepped out from behind a tree. Tapman didn't wait to see how the surprised lad reacted—he shot the poor bastard in the head immediately. Another young soldier, hearing the shot, raced to the scene. Tapman drilled him, too, then took off running west again.

Finally he slowed down. The rescue forces asked him to fire a pengun flare up through the treetops. It bounced off the branches and fell back to the jungle floor. Tapman tried again. The second shot was more successful and the Sandys got a "tallyho," a firm read on his location. The Jolly thundered into place and promptly hauled the rattled pilot up the winch to safety. He was on his way to Nakhon Phanom, along with Jonesy.

Aboard the helo, Tapman mouthed words to the helo pilot, who couldn't tell what he was saying. The chopper captain took off his headset and leaned toward Tapman, to hear above the engine noise. "What did you say?" he shouted.

"I think I'm queer," Tapman yelled back, laughing. "I want to kiss you." They both chortled.

At Nakhon Phanom one of Tapman's old friends, Brig. Gen. Willy P. McBride, met the helicopter and took the two pilots to the base hospital. Jonesy was fine except for a sore neck. Tapman had cuts and lacerations and an extremely tender left testicle. Once they cleared the hospital, the two were soon en route back to Phu Cat. Virtually the whole unit met them on the tarmac and drove them straight to the bar.

Don Jones asked how they felt. Jonesy said he felt like he had been in a bar fight. Tapman said he was okay, but had a left testicle the size of a softball. "That's okay," Jones deadpanned. "It takes big balls to fly with Misty."

The Mistys decided Jonesy hadn't truly completed 100 missions. It was more like 99½. Since that didn't seem right, they scheduled one more ride into the Pack for Jonesy. He'd fly the plane, but Don Jones, the commander, would be in the back, making sure it was a dull, uneventful mission. They didn't perform any heroic stunts that day, or set any records for BDA. But they did make a conventional, full-stop landing back at Phu Cat. Jonesy could finally leave.

TWENTY-ONE

FLY THE DOC

Dean Echenberg, the flight surgeon, was one of the most unlikely men to end up in a military uniform serving a tour in Vietnam. Echenberg had gone to medical school at Wayne State University in Detroit, where he spent many hours working at the Detroit Receiving Emergency Room—the "knife and gun club" as the docs called it. The ER was great training in dealing with trauma, but Echenberg found he was more interested in treating psychic wounds. He had a knack for helping people ease their emotional pains. When he graduated in 1966, he went to San Francisco to do a one-year internship in psychiatry. Fixing people's heads, he figured, would be more interesting than just fixing their plumbing. Besides, something fresh was brewing in San Francisco, and it sure was a lot more stimulating than the Midwest.

San Francisco in the mid-1960s turned out to be just the right place for a young, unfettered intellectual to explore the secrets of the psyche. Echenberg hung out in the Haight-Ashbury district, where everybody was either a hippie or a cop. He went to see Janis Joplin and the Grateful Dead. There were be-ins and protest marches and all sorts of other events to attend. He and his friends experimented with LSD provided by the Department of Psychiatry at the medical school, before *Time* magazine had identified LSD as the counterculture's drug of choice.

Echenberg's crowd thought LSD helped them look at life in a different way. It was like a door to a different room, one that ordinary people couldn't get to.

Problem was, a lot of people got stuck in the doorway. Echenberg watched as heroin and prostitution drifted into the Haight. Legions of troubled kids started showing up, experiencing bad trips and other problems. Echenberg helped start the Haight-Ashbury Free Clinic, which quickly gained acclaim for its open door and gentle, professional care. Meanwhile, Echenberg took courses in existential psychiatry at nearby Stanford University. This was a trendy new discipline that focused on human behavior as an individual's adaptation and response to other people.

He knew he would end up in the service. Echenberg realized he wouldn't be eligible for any more student deferments once he graduated from medical school in 1966, and the odds were good that he'd be drafted. So instead, he signed on with a program that would allow him to complete his internship and residency in exchange for a two-year commitment to serve as an Air Force doctor. Some of his friends were resisting the draft with all their might. One had even shown up for his induction physical wearing a dress, to persuade the military he was either gay or crazy. But Echenberg didn't resist going to Vietnam like the other people he knew. He wasn't sure what he thought about the war, in fact, and was eager to learn more.

A few of his doctor friends told him about a charitable group that sent docs over to Vietnam to find children in dire need of medical care and bring them back to the States for treatment. Echenberg applied when his internship ended in June 1967, since he didn't have to show up at the Air Force until later that year. He'd spend the summer in Vietnam, see what was going on, then come back to the States in time to make the Air Force gig. Echenberg was all set to leave and had only to complete the final interview at the group's New York headquarters. But when he went to New York and mentioned that he'd be joining the Air Force later that year, they said that they didn't need him after all.

He had the summer to kill, and it turned out to be the Summer of Love. Echenberg grew a moustache and an Afro, wore his cowboy boots everywhere he went, and spent the summer hanging out in San Francisco and cruising around the West Coast in his Austin-Healey. Finally the Air Force called. Through the luck of the draw, they were offering him a plum assignment: a laboratory job at the School of Aerospace Medicine, helping to design incubators that would be used to evacuate children to medical facilities.

Echenberg thought it over—and volunteered for Vietnam. He was more interested in experience than engineering, and he had been itching to get to Vietnam anyway and see for himself what was going on. Besides, he had a feeling he could do a lot more good in a war zone than he could locked up in an antiseptic laboratory.

It was a clash of cultures at Brooks Air Force Base in Texas, where the docs got their military training. Most had little interest in weapons and daydreamed while the instructors showed them how to work a rifle or a handgun. Marching was an exercise in disarray. On his fourth day at Brooks, Echenberg waved at a passing car that happened to contain a general. The next day a notice went around to all the classes: "Don't wave at the generals, salute them."

The "hippie doc," as he called himself, was soon on his way to jungle-survival school in the Philippines, and then Vietnam. As his Pan Am charter flight descended toward Da Nang in late February 1968, the flight crew announced some unusual instructions. The plane would stop only long enough for everyone to get off with their gear. The passengers should run down the stairs and across the tarmac into a shelter next to the end of the runway. They quickly understood the reason for the rushed landing. The Viet Cong were shelling the huge air base, and any plane that lingered on the runway was likely to end up as war debris. Echenberg and all the other passengers did as they were told and bolted off the plane into a bunker—a typical welcome to Vietnam.

Echenberg's assignment was to be the flight surgeon for a number of squadrons flying out of Phu Cat. He'd be responsible for looking after the pilots, treating their illnesses or injuries, and making sure they were fit to fly. There were plenty of other duties, too. He and some of the other doctors and medics on base also would do "medcaps," unannounced drop-ins at local villages to offer care to the locals. At first this seemed noble, but Echenberg quickly recognized the medcaps as a publicity stunt that made the Americans look good but didn't really provide consistent medical care for the Vietnamese. There was one benefit though: A local doctor taught him his first Vietnamese phrase: "*Dung bung, toi bacsi.*" "Don't shoot, I am a doctor."

Misty was part of his responsibility, but only a small part. When Echenberg had fished Brian Williams out of the bar on March 18— after Brian had been shot down with Howard Williams, and rescued— it was his first real contact with this unusual group of pilots who tended to keep to themselves. The Mistys drew him in, though. There was something different about the intriguing little unit that appealed to Echenberg. The TOP SECRET sign on the door at Misty Ops was alluring in itself, and Echenberg had to get a TS clearance before he could work with the detachment. He knew that every Misty had volunteered for the unit. They loved to fly. Misty flights were rarely canceled unless the weather was hopeless; at other units some of the pilots looked for reasons *not* to fly. When the pilots came back from a mission, they'd sometimes sit for hours with the intel officers, detailing truck or troop sightings, as if intensity alone might help them win the war. Unlike a lot of other pilots, who would do anything to get out of Vietnam, the Mistys actually wanted to be there. Maybe they were crazy, but they sure as hell were dedicated.

The senior Mistys set the tone with a quiet kind of strength. Don Jones struck Echenberg as acerbic, yet dry and soft-spoken—likable and highly professional. The younger pilots were boisterous, but there was little bombast or self-indulgent braggadocio. It was a part of a flight surgeon's job to linger among the pilots, to get to know them so that he'd be able to sense if anybody needed particular attention or that something wasn't right. Echenberg found himself spending more and more time with the Mistys, hanging out with them at the bar, sitting around the trailers at the end of the day listening to war stories, enjoying a sirloin steak and a baked potato and a cigar at the O club. They had the same swagger as all other fighter pilots—but backed it up with the credentials of real warriors.

In April the wing honchos decided that Misty needed its own flight surgeon. Echenberg leaped at the chance and got the job. He was elated. Echenberg admired Don Jones and became fast friends with him, even though Jones was about to ship out as Misty commander. Dick Rutan and Chuck Shaheen, the "Crazy Arab," could be wild and hilarious one night, but as serious as surgeons in the midst of a tough operation when a mission was on. He could tell from the other Mistys that they were good pilots, too. And he was awed by Stanley Mamlock, Don Jones's replacement, who had flown in World War II and Korea—when it really took balls to fly. Echenberg felt like he was going to work among heroes.

In one sense Echenberg had it easy as a doctor in Vietnam. Occasionally he'd go to the huge Army M.A.S.H. unit at Dong Ha, just south of the DMZ, for training on how to deal with mass casualties. It was horrifying. In addition to the gore and the blood, there were screams and smells that made the knife and gun club back in Detroit seem like a nursery school. There were few scenarios like that at Phu Cat. Part of Echenberg's job was to race out to the flight line as part of a "crash response" team that would be standing by when one of the planes limped back with problems. But usually the pilots climbed out of the cockpit safe and sound, even if they had been scared to death.

As the unofficial base psychiatrist, Echenberg worked with a lot of others besides the Misty pilots he looked after. Phu Cat had high rates of depression and other neuropsychiatric problems, and there was ample opportunity for the doc to indulge his interests in the workings of the brain. Echenberg treated a lot of pimply-faced young enlisted men going through the equivalent of an adolescent crisis, upset over girlfriends leaving them or other matters of the heart. He could have sent them home with a recommendation that they receive care back in the States—and he had no reluctance about doing that—but he figured they might end up with a guilt trip, for leaving their buddies back in Vietnam. So usually he treated the more manageable cases himself. Other times, Army and Marine grunts would be transferring through Phu Cat on different assignments, and sometimes they'd get sick on the flight line and end up under his care. When he encountered guys who had seen a lot of combat, Echenberg frequently sent them to a station away from their units with a recommendation that they be shipped home. They had seen enough, he figured.

One of Echenberg's patients was an enlisted man who worked in an administrative job. He came to see Echenberg, saying he was depressed. The sergeant claimed that his boss, a demanding officer on the base, had been riding him for months, criticizing his work and always demanding more—the kind of hassle that could easily become overwhelming at Phu Cat, where there were no diversions and little to do but work. Echenberg was keeping a close eye on him, but didn't think he needed urgent attention.

Two weeks after first coming to see the doc, the sergeant shot himself. Suicides were one of the unfortunate by-products of life at Phu Cat, and the man was quickly replaced by another face. But Echenberg struggled with the almost casual way in which he had lost a patient. "The sergeant today put a bullet through his head," he wrote in his journal, reflecting on whether summarizing the case in such a matter-of-fact way conveyed the enormous significance of the end of a life. It didn't—but Echenberg didn't know what other words to use instead.

His psychiatric training helped Echenberg realize immediately that the commanders and pilots at Misty were under tremendous stress. For all the bold banter about getting shot at, the risks took a toll. Planes came back every week with bullet holes in them. Sometimes every plane took hits. It was a nameless, private fear that nobody expressed in so many words, but every Misty knew that death might meet him on the next sortie. When Howard Williams had gone missing, it devastated some of the other pilots—Rutan in particular. He and others sat around and talked about it for hours, clearly troubled. A pall fell over Ops, and it extended into the cockpit. Everybody was gloomy.

Misty, however, didn't seem to have some of the problems that other units did. Echenberg had come across one pilot with another squadron at Phu Cat who was drunk as could be and scheduled to fly the next morning. Instead of going to bed, the pilot decided to stay up and keep drinking: Flying drunk, he calculated, would be safer than flying with a hangover. Another time one of the officers who helped run the O club had gone on a rampage, prompting a panicky call to the doc. While six of his buddies wrestled the guy to the floor, Echenberg jabbed him with a syringe of Valium to calm him down.

It was obvious that drinking was a chief coping mechanism for the Mistys, too. There was no sex, after all, and base facilities were a poor representation of the comforts of home. And nobody could leave the base because it was too dangerous. Gunfire and adrenaline were the only real diversions—and those were the causes of the stress. The O club, not surprisingly, absorbed the brunt of the frustration. Sometimes by the end of the night it looked like one of those North Vietnamese targets after a successful strike. The furniture would be dismantled, like in a barroom brawl in an old western. There were MiG sweeps and other stunts that would end up with everybody wrestling or fighting or being kicked out by the security police.

Don Jones's farewell party could have been a med-school seminar on stress-reduction techniques. Jones was scheduled to leave on April 20, right around the time several other Mistys were due to move on. So the party served as a farewell to Don Shepperd, Brian Williams, and Carroll Williams as well. The Mistys drank and reminisced for a while, and then Jones said a few words.

His command had started roughly, he recalled. Two planes went down in his first ten days, and Bob Craner and Guy Gruters had been captured. "For a while," Jones reflected, "it looked like the Misty losses would start to rival those of the Japanese kamikazes in 1945." But he and Mick Greene had preached smart tactics and prudent flying, and it seemed to work. Battle damage was reduced and they didn't lose a plane until Howie and Brian Williams went down in March. The future would see some tough flying coming up, however, and he wished them the best. Jones finished his short speech by saying he felt honored to have commanded such courageous men. They had all made a difference, he felt.

The Mistys cheered their boss. There was one toast to Jones, then another. Somebody tossed a glass against the bar wall, and the rout was on. The barware didn't stand a chance. Soon every glass and bottle in the bar had been smashed against the wall. An inch of glass carpeted the floor. Echenberg had just started getting to know the guys, and he watched the wild antics with amazement. Were these the same men who showed such care and skill when they flew?

When Mamlock took over as Misty commander, he was fully aware that the drinking and roughhousing were just the guys blowing off steam. "Raise all the hell you want," he told them. "But pay the consequences." The Mistys always had to clean up whatever mess they left at the O club and pay for whatever they broke. Sometimes paying the consequences meant getting banished from the club by Colonel Schneider. But as Echenberg got to know the Mistys, he discovered a strange phenomenon: This group of volunteers seemed to have fewer physical and psychological problems than other units. Phu Cat was a tough place to serve, with regular combat for the pilots, daily danger of in-coming fire, and no escape from the drab confines of the base. The rate of psychiatric problems at Phu Cat was nearly the highest of all the U.S. bases in Vietnam. Echenberg saw one pilot who got an uncontrol-lable skin rash and hives on every combat mission—yet desperately fought going home. He saw few problems like this at Misty, however. Their stress-reduction program, no matter how unruly, seemed to be working.

In addition to the young Turks, some seasoned, mature pilots were also coming into the unit. Mike McElhanon had arrived the day after Howard Williams had gone missing. Unlike many of the thrill-seekers who became fighter pilots, McElhanon was thoughtful and serious and bent on self-improvement. He had joined the air cadets shortly after graduating from high school, and as he rotated from base to base in the Air Force he took college courses wherever he could, finally earn-ing a bachelor's degree from the University of Southern California. He had also gone to flying safety officer school and been a flight instruc-tor. For most of his career McElhanon had flown the F-101 air defense interceptor, switching over to the F-100 before going to Vietnam. When McElhanon arrived at Phu Cat his first job was to be the 37th Wing's flying safety officer and maintenance test pilot, checking out birds after maintenance had been performed.

In addition to his experience, McElhanon also had a bearing that made him seem almost fatherly compared to some of the younger Mistys. He was tall, handsome, fit, and sharply dressed, whether in uniform or not. When he had gone off to pilot training, his high school girlfriend, Sandy, had become engaged to another guy. When Mike re-turned and she saw him, she took off her ring and married her high school sweetheart instead. He had that kind of alluring, captivating ef-fect on women.

Maj. John Overlock arrived about a month after McElhanon. The tall, athletic, dark-haired pilot had spent most of his flying time in the F-100, and he and his wife, Bev, had become close friends with P. K. Robinson and his wife, Reta, when both men were young pilots in En-gland, learning the ropes. Then they had both ended up in Vietnam to-gether, working in the command post at Tuy Hoa, farther south. When there was word of an opening at Misty, they both applied. The bosses at Tuy Hoa picked Robinson, because Overlock's job in the CP was more important. But the next time a pilot came from Tuy Hoa, Robinson guessed that Overlock would be the one getting off the plane. He was.

Overlock was an old head when it came to the Hun, but he was also introverted and moody and hard to get to know. During one Misty mission with his old pal from England, Overlock was in the backseat and felt that Robinson wasn't giving him enough stick time. Overlock didn't say anything. But the next time Overlock flew with Robinson in back, he wouldn't let his crewmate touch the stick.

McElhanon and Overlock found they had a lot in common, including a calm, deliberate approach to the Misty work and a desire to stay safe. They both knew it was dangerous—neither had told their wives about it when they volunteered—yet neither was an adrenaline junkie like some of the other fighter jocks. Shortly after Overlock arrived in April, he sat down with McElhanon. They discussed how to stay alive over North Vietnam and how to react if a younger, more aggressive pilot was taking too many risks or doing something stupid. McElhanon counseled diplomacy and lots of informal, cautious guidance to the younger guys—over drinks, if possible, when they'd be more open to advice. "But if you feel endangered," McElhanon urged, "grab the stick, and then beat the hell out of the guy when you get back on the ground." They both laughed. But they flew together whenever they could, more comfortable with each other's style than with some of the other Mistys.

There was one advantage to life on a remote, isolated outpost like Phu Cat: The base had the lowest rate of venereal disease in the theater. It was simply too dangerous to step outside the wire. The Viet Cong were out there, and even the prostitutes were considered dangerous. Some were supposedly VC sympathizers, who would attack their patrons when they were most vulnerable. Echenberg preached sexual caution all the time, warning his men that many of the Asian venereal diseases were almost impossible to cure. The scary rumors about VC prostitutes and Echenberg's lectures kept most of the troops in line.

Naturally there were a few Mistys who thought it'd be safe to break the rules, just once. One day Chuck Shaheen, the consummate bachelor, had a few beers with an American civilian working at Phu Cat.

After a couple of hours at the O club, the man persuaded him to go along on an off-base adventure. The civilian ended up taking Shaheen to what appeared to be a brothel for a couple of beers. Shaheen would never say what happened there, except that he was awfully antsy to get back to Phu Cat. Two weeks later rumors went around about an air policeman who had gone to the same area—and ended up dead. Shaheen never knew if the story was for real, but he decided to limit his adventures to R&R destinations like Sydney and Hong Kong.

Elmer Slavey came to a similar conclusion after his own soiree into a local village. Slavey, a scheming, suntanned jokester, was Misty's riverboat gambler. One day he was playing dice with two civilian contractor friends at the O club when they got severely drunk and decided to take their chances off-base. Since whorehouses were off-limits, they went to an establishment known as a "sensual bar." Slavey woke up aching at 2:00 a.m., with no idea what had happened. All he knew was that his wallet was empty. He stumbled back to the Phu Cat front gate reeking of liquor, with no ID card. The gate guard listened to Slavey's story and thought it was the funniest thing he ever heard. He could have arrested the bedraggled pilot, but let him back in instead. Slavey wasn't scheduled to fly, so he staggered back to his trailer and slept until noon.

When there was time, the doctors at Phu Cat did what they could to help the local civilians. As Echenberg got to know his boss, he began to express his discomfort with the "medcaps," the unannounced visits to surrounding villages. The docs would hand out cough syrup and bandages and ointments and try to create the impression they were doing something meaningful, but there was no follow-up care and tough problems were simply overlooked. From a medical perspective, the visits had dubious value.

Instead, Echenberg and his boss decided to set up the Phu Cat version of the Haight-Ashbury Free Clinic. It was a small facility just outside the front gate where they could operate an X-ray machine and hold regular hours, thanks to volunteers among the base medics. It was the closest thing to continuity of care that most of the Vietnamese had ever seen.

The Vietnamese had horrendous health problems. The military doctors saw more plague, cholera, and malaria in a week than most civilian physicians would see in a lifetime. Tuberculosis was rampant. With manpower and medicine running short, they had to draw cutoff points to decide which cases to accept. The rule for TB was that to treat a case, they had to be able to see the X-ray lesions, indicating lung damage, from across the room. Still, the locals were getting care that was not available in their villages, and Echenberg felt the humble little clinic made a legitimate impact.

Echenberg's contact with the Vietnamese people, outside the fence, let him see the local impact of the war much more closely than the other troops stationed at the base. He became good friends with a few Vietnamese doctors, teachers, and provincial leaders and their families. He visited their houses and had long talks with them about the war. By that time the story of Hue was starting to become clear. The communists who had attacked the town had clubbed or shot to death practically every civic leader, professional, and intellectual they could get their hands on. It was clearly not the work of a few armed renegades: Hanoi ordered its troops to kill civilians as a matter of policy. Echenberg's new Vietnamese friends lived in constant fear, knowing they too would be killed if their towns fell or if the communists won the war.

Sometimes local health problems showed up at Phu Cat. The Air Force hired lots of Vietnamese to clean, dish out food, and do other menial labor on the base. One day a Vietnamese worker who made salads in the mess hall was diagnosed with hepatitis, and Colonel Schneider ordered everyone on base to get a shot of gamma globulin. To demonstrate how serious he was, Schneider volunteered to be first in line for the shot. As he lowered his flight suit and Echenberg pushed the needle into his butt, the wing commander fell to the floor in a dead faint—in front of all his troops.

Echenberg loved to fly, and he caught rides with anybody he could. As a flight surgeon it was important to get some air time, to understand the jobs of the men he was looking after. And Echenberg took full advantage of the privilege. He flew with the C-7 Caribou cargo haulers who went to far-flung Army and Marine outposts, including Khe Sanh. He became friends with Fred Carpenter, who flew the O-1 as a FAC out of nearby Qui Nhon and would take Echenberg along when he could. Echenberg hopped rides with the "Pedros," the local helicopter rescue detachment that flew the twin-rotor HH-43 helicopters on rescue missions in South Vietnam. He even practiced going down the rescue hoist into the jungle and coming back up, in case he ever had to participate in a pilot rescue.

Echenberg wanted to fly with Misty, too. It was part of his job to know what his pilots experienced on their missions. He also yearned to get up there in one of the Huns and feel the thrill of the Gs, experience the jinking he heard everybody talk about and feel what it did to the body, and see the targets and terrain that the Mistys referred to as if they were landmarks in their own neighborhoods. Echenberg asked Charlie Summers whom he should ask for permission to go on one of the Misty flights. "You'll get along much better in the Air Force," Summers told him, "if you don't ask permission. If you want to do something, just do it."

An opportunity arose. After Don Jones's farewell party, the flying had started to get hairy. Many of the Misty planes were getting shot up and galumphing back to Phu Cat with holes in them. It seemed like a stretch of bad luck, and some of the pilots started talking about a jinx. Then somebody had a bright idea: A good way to break the jinx would be to "fly the doc." Mamlock gave approval, and Echenberg's name appeared on the Misty flight board for the first time.

Lanny Lancaster was the pilot, and they flew as Misty 21, the second flight of the day. It felt eerie to cross into North Vietnam from the Gulf of Tonkin, but nothing much happened for the first half hour. Then Lanny spotted a line of trucks headed along a road going up the side of a mountain. He came around for another look and pointed them out to the doc, then said he was going to fly in closer. The pilot seemed excited, and so was Echenberg. Then, as they went into a steep dive and began to roll in toward the trucks, there was enormous pressure on Echenberg's body. The mountain that the trucks were climbing began to fill the windshield as they flew toward it. It got bigger and bigger.

Then without warning, Lanny got very upset. "I can't pick it up!" he began to yell. "I can't pick it up!" On the duplicate set of controls in the back, Echenberg could feel Lanny pulling all the way back on the stick as he tried to pull the plane out of the dive. The nose began to lift, and all Echenberg could see was the green mass of the mountain in front of the plane. Horror gripped the doc. He began to realize they were about to plow into the face of the mountain. He grabbed the ejection seat arms and tucked himself in, sure they were either going to eject or crash.

There had been a few moments like this before, when it seemed more a matter of when the end would come than if. One night Echenberg had been out on the flight line at Tuy Hoa, to the south, when Viet Cong sappers attacked and started throwing grenades and satchel charges. Then mortars started coming his way. While trying to bolt away from the attackers—who he could see darting around in the darkness—he almost ran smack into one of the explosions and was hurled onto his back. Another time he had been returning from an off-base event when automatic weapons fire erupted across the road. There was no choice but to run the gauntlet of bullets.

Those had been panicky moments. For some reason he felt much calmer now, in the sealed cockpit of the Hun. He was sure it was all over, and there was nothing he could do about the mountain, now racing straight at them. Then Lanny coaxed the plane higher—and they skimmed right over the top of the mountain. "Wow!" Echenberg exhaled. "That was close!"

"Yeah," Lanny replied, sounding discouraged. "I had those trucks in sight, but then I lost them and I couldn't pick them up." It had been the trucks Lanny couldn't pick up, Echenberg realized—not the nose of plane. The pilot had had no worry whatsoever about clearing the mountain. It wasn't a near-death experience after all.

Echenberg kept the miscalculation to himself and had just started to relax again when warning lights started flashing on the panels in front of him. "Oh, shit!" came an exclamation from up front. This time, Echenberg knew, even the pilot thought they were in trouble. The doc could hear Lanny starting to breathe heavy. He desperately wanted to know what was going on, but didn't want to distract his pilot and protector. There was nothing for Echenberg to do except sit tight and stare at the flashing lights on the panel in front of him. Then Lanny provided a quick update: "We gotta get out of here fast! We're headed feet wet!"

They started to climb for altitude. Lanny turned the plane toward the coast, although he didn't seem to know exactly what was wrong with the aircraft. The best guess was that they had taken some kind of hit. Maybe he wasn't going to break the jinx after all, Echenberg thought. Then he started thinking about an ejection. It would be better to get fished out of the drink, he realized, than to try to survive on the side of that mountain. That thought brought to mind the one Vietnamese phrase he had been told to remember above all else. Could he remember the words? "*Dung bung, toi bacsi,*" he mouthed to himself. "Don't shoot, I am a doctor."

They made it to the water and called Da Nang, the nearest air base, to explain their situation. Then some of the lights stopped flashing and they didn't have to bail out after all. When they landed at Da Nang they inspected the Hun and didn't find any holes. It had been some kind of electrical problem, not a sneaky ground gunner. The mission was a bust, but at least they brought the plane back in one piece.

About a week later a direct order came down from 7th Air Force. It specifically said that flight surgeons were not to fly over North Vietnam or Laos. It didn't say why, but Echenberg learned through the grapevine that a flight surgeon had been killed on a plane flying out of Thailand. The Air Force was short on docs and couldn't afford to lose any more. Echenberg presented the document to the Mistys at the bar. "See," he boasted, "it's official. Mistys are expendable. Docs are not."

TWENTY-TWO

PRISON LIFE

Dean Echenberg felt at home with Misty. He'd go to Misty Ops when he needed a break from other chores, read the intel reports, follow the briefings and the battles, shoot the shit with whoever happened to be around. One day Echenberg discovered the POW reports, classified top secret, that would come rattling over the secure teletype from 7th Air Force. As he flipped through several pages of one report, bound together like a magazine, his sphincter tightened.

Echenberg had witnessed some rough things in just a couple months in Vietnam. The Army field hospitals were veritable charnel houses. An Army intel officer he knew would occasionally take him off-base to see what was going on in the countryside. It was a harsh scene. Some of the ground troops he encountered had been in brutal hand-to-hand fighting and were disturbed couch cases. He had also been at the big Army hospital at Dong Ha—where there was a facility for treating wounded enemy prisoners—when a flood of injured GIs came gushing in. Seeing their injured comrades enraged some of the soldiers on the base, and it was easy to imagine them brutalizing the Viet Cong prisoners, given the chance.

What Echenberg saw summarized in the POW reports, however, was even more upsetting. First there had been the POW "death march" through downtown Hanoi in the summer of 1966. American POWs had been shackled together, two-by-two, and paraded through a North Vietnamese mob out for unruly justice. Citizens had lined up block after block, and whatever they were angry about, they were encouraged to take it out on the Americans. They beat, kicked, maimed, and spat on the defenseless prisoners, withering brutality that some compared to the Bataan Death March of World War II.

There were other snippets of information: pictures of gaunt, haggard men with glassy, empty eyes, obviously under extreme stress. The settings were usually staged, as if to depict prisoners doing productive work in a humane environment. But Echenberg could look at the pictures and tell that the men were being systematically abused. Intelligence reports hinted at torture. After Echenberg read the reports, he couldn't sleep and would lie awake at night thinking of the ordeal his fellow Americans were going through up in Hanoi. It was yet another worry the Mistys carried around, he realized—they knew a miserable fate awaited pilots who got shot down and captured. It was not the sort of burden most people brought to work every day.

Three Mistys were among the POWs Echenberg was reading about. The doc hadn't known any of them personally, but he had heard plenty about all three. A lot more had happened to them, however, than anybody at Misty was aware of.

Bud Day had been the first missing Misty. He and Kipp Kippenhan had gotten shot down on August 26, 1967, while hunting for SAMs near the Fingers Lake, just north of the DMZ. Kippenhan had been picked up quickly, but nobody heard a word from Day or saw his parachute. Rescue craft patrolled the area for hours—including the helicopter that had Kippenhan on board—but they heard nothing from Day and ultimately they gave up.

While they had been gazing futilely into the jungle below, however, Bud Day had been looking up at them—with heartbreak, since he was already a captive. Just seconds after Day had landed, while he was still attached to his parachute, a shocked North Vietnamese trooper had bashed through the brush and pointed a rusty old rifle at the now helpless and badly injured major. Then he stole Day's watch. More North Vietnamese arrived and tore off his boots and his flight suit. They were marching Day off when the Jolly with Kippenhan roared over low, drawing a barrage of ground fire. The chopper moved slowly while Kippenhan and the crewmen scanned for Day. After a short while, with no sight of Day, the chopper peeled off to escape the withering ground fire. Day's captors celebrated. They had a prize in their possession and would be duly rewarded. Day, however, sank into despair. From the soaring freedom of his cockpit—where he was in total control—he had been plunged into a cruel, oppressive world that he would come to liken to Dante's Inferno.

As the chopper skimmed out of sight, Day's captors led him to a dismal little hut, where they replaced his bloody, rumpled, sweaty, mud-covered flight suit with a set of ragged black pajamas. They tried to march him off barefoot to a nearby camp, but his knee had been smashed during the ejection and he could barely hobble. They prodded him with rifle butts to his back. Day was paraded through a series of villages, where the locals massed as if on command and layered abuse after abuse on the "yankee air pirate." They spit on him, hit him with sticks, punched him, kicked him, and yanked him by his hair to get him back on his feet every time he fell down.

The grim parade finally ended at a North Vietnamese camp that, Day guessed, was twenty or thirty miles north of the DMZ—smack in the middle of Route Pack 1. Day was stuffed into a hole in the ground roughly the size of a casket. His legs were roped together, and his arms were tied above him to a patchwork of logs that formed a makeshift roof. He was in terrible pain.

After a couple of days, his guards began to write him off for dead. Day looked the part. His body was battered and on display for all to see. The sharp end of a shattered bone was sticking out through the skin on his right arm. The right half of his face was mangled, the eye so swollen he couldn't see out of it. Day played the cripple well, barely moving during the day except to drag himself toward the puny bowl of rice and the thin, weedy soup the guards placed in his pen. The guards beat him repeatedly, to punish him for his intransigence, but they began to lose interest. They even stopped tying his arms to the ceiling, figuring he was far too feeble to go anywhere.

One night, two new guards arrived and dragged Day out of the hole, to an interrogator who sat on a chair a few yards in front of him. The interrogator asked questions that Day refused to answer. The guards beat him and battered him with their rifles. Day fell down and they kicked him, then forced him to sit upright. It was dusk. Day pretended to be disoriented—but noticed where the sun was setting. He calculated which direction was west.

The next night they summoned him for interrogations again. This time, after he refused to answer, they tied his feet together, then hung him upside down from the beam of an A-frame-style shelter. He swung like a side of beef. The pain in his broken limbs was agonizing and he could feel and hear the broken bones grating as he hung for hours, the rope slowly stretching, until his head began to rest on the mud floor. At first Day worried that his neck would break as the weight of his body pressed down on it. Then he nearly suffocated as his head became twisted beneath his body. Once the rope stretched enough for his shoulders to bear some of the burden, it seemed like a relief. But as he considered how long the war would likely endure, and contemplated endless hours, days, and weeks, maybe even years of this kind of treatment, Day decided he had to try something audacious and risky.

The next evening, as his guards chatted out on the dirt road several yards from his pen, Day wriggled free of the ropes binding his legs. He slipped quietly out of the hole and clambered over the bank of a nearby rice paddy. He banged his broken arm on the ground as he splashed into the water, but managed to bite back a scream, and the guards appeared oblivious. He had escaped the noose for now, even if the hangman was about to set the hounds on him.

For the next ten days Day navigated south, step by excruciating step. He had no shoes, and his feet quickly became shredded. His damaged leg had stiffened and he practically had to drag it behind him. Bombs rained down—American bombs. They came one after the other in a "stick," about one hundred feet apart in a straight line—a classic B-52 strike. The bombs threw tons of earth into the air and produced a deafening roar that deadened his senses and seemed to go on for hours. Worse, the heat from the explosions fused the clay, sand, and rock in the soil into a kind of glassy obstacle course that threatened to eviscerate his feet further. On another night he was injured by shrapnel from an explosion he guessed was a bomb dropped by a U.S. fighter. There was a kind of poetic justice in it all, Day mused. "Live by the bomb, die by the bomb," he thought.

Water was plentiful, if often contaminated, but nourishment was scarce. He scrounged berries, devoured an occasional raw frog, and licked drops of water from inside the curls of banana leaves. Days passed with no food, and Day worried about his body's ability to function. His skin was so ravaged by sun or wounds or filth that elephantine jungle mosquitoes could scarcely find a landing pad on him. He was so immobile from his broken bones and shredded, shoeless feet that he routinely spent hours in one spot, delirious, unable to move. Day thought about his colleagues back at Misty, and about his wife, Doris—"Dorie," whom he had long ago nicknamed "the Viking" for her Norwegian heritage. Her family had belonged to the Norwegian Underground during World War II, and virtually every member had endured some kind of torment or agony at the hands of the Nazis. The thought of their principled resistance was one of the things that kept Day motivated. And he thought of his four adopted kids, back home in Arizona with Dorie, probably becoming aware, at that moment, that their dad had been shot down and was considered MIA, missing in action.

Somehow he managed to gain strength and continue moving south. Day wanted to get to the Ben Hai River, the one dividing the North from the South. He finally made it. He knew that U.S. forces and freedom were only a few miles away. He fashioned a float from bamboo logs and branches and lowered himself quietly into the water. The current was surprisingly swift as he began to float and paddle toward the south bank. At one point as he was drifting downriver, an NVA soldier near a house overlooking the river caught sight of him. The soldier tilted his rifle toward Day, but either lost him in the afternoon glare or decided that the strange sight was just another pile of debris floating down the river and gave him no more notice.

As he reached the bank, Day dragged himself up into South Vietnam, toward freedom. He still had several miles to go to reach U.S. forces, however. And the place was crawling with NVA and Viet Cong patrols, usually of about a dozen troops, some who looked only fourteen or fifteen years old. They carried huge packs that were brimming with camouflage that reached up over their heads. It was remarkably effective, he thought. One patrol passed by less than a foot from Day's hidey-hole, sending his heart into silent spasms.

There were signs of Americans, too. Day came across a huge pile of abandoned C rations, the food tins that constituted field grub for American GIs. Every one of them had been expertly punctured in accordance with Army procedures, so that any spare food rotted and became useless to the enemy. But the sight was encouraging all the same—maybe it meant the area was also crawling with American or South Vietnamese patrols. Maybe he would come across one of them and be saved.

The haggard, filthy officer vacillated between euphoria and despair. There were moments when he measured his progress and tasted freedom and knew he would make it back into friendly hands. But there were darker spells when Day was crazed with hunger, delirious, and so disoriented he lost faith in his own instincts. His mind swam with strange and distant memories, of Sunday school back in Sioux City, Iowa, of sitting in a boat with Dorie fishing for crappie. And this while he was trying to slither away from a half dozen NVA who were hacking their way through the jungle just feet away. Other times he talked out loud, then recognized the breach of discipline and ordered himself to be quiet.

There were tantalizing signs that freedom was imminent. On what he guessed was the ninth day of his escape, he saw two Marine Corps choppers hovering over a landing zone not more than a couple of hundred yards up ahead. By this time he had traveled twenty or thirty miles, barefoot, through jungles, rice paddies, and mud. He had swum, or at least floated across, a swift river and crossed back into South Vietnam. He was about to be rescued! Day tried to figure out a way to move rapidly toward the LZs, but as he was maneuvering through the bush he came into a clearing where an NVA soldier was washing his clothes in a stream. The enemy trooper had his back to Day, and the American spent five minutes silently circumnavigating him on tiptoe. Day wasn't detected, but he watched dejectedly as the choppers pulled away slowly. He missed them. He'd have to wait till Day 10.

The sky the next morning was overcast, the first glum weather since he had escaped. As Day tried to find the helicopter landing zones, he realized that the choppers were gone and not coming back for a while, since there was no base or troop position in the area. He had hoped the choppers were inserting a patrol, but they were likely just picking one up. As he tried to figure out what to do next, his spirits sank. He became aware of just how feeble he had become. He did his best to judge where American positions might be, but instead wandered into a bombed-out, abandoned village. He poked around until he realized he was out in the open and exposed. He darted back into the jungle.

Then he heard voices. Then shouts. They came from behind him. He turned around to see two young Vietnamese faces staring at him. Not sure whether they were North Vietnamese or South, Day paused. Then he saw the AK-47 rifles in their hands. His mind raced, his stomach trembled. He tried to dart off the path, into the brush, but was so lame an old woman could have tracked him down. The soldiers began to fire. A bullet pierced his left thigh, another his left hand. Still Day dragged himself under the biggest, thickest bush he could find.

It took the soldiers a few minutes, but they found him. They were teenagers, Day estimated, enjoying one of the sweetest moments of their brief military careers. They brought Day to their commander, who treated him more respectfully than the earlier tormenters. A soldier offered him some rice and some ghastly smelling fish sauce, which he greedily accepted. A medic looked at his wounds and did what he could to soothe them.

But Day's luck had run out. He had journeyed to within about two miles of the Marine Corps base at Con Thien, about six miles south of the DMZ, in South Vietnam. Virtually all of his extremities were useless, with bullet holes in one arm and one leg, the other arm broken, and the other leg swollen and shattered. One eye was badly damaged. He was so beat up that when he was transported back north, NVA porters carried him in a sling hung between two bamboo poles. They put a blindfold on him and cracked him on the head every time he tried to sneak a glance outside of it. Day still schemed—he would escape again if he could. But his captors were smarter this time, and when Day was returned to the primitive prison where he had received his first punishments, life got even harder.

In Vinh the "professionals" took over. He was wired to the roof this time with telephone cord, and when it came time for interrogations, the torture was indescribable.[1] A particularly sadistic interrogator called "the Rodent" twisted Day's broken bones until he heard them shatter and snap. The Rodent kept screaming, "You are a creeeminal.

I will creeeple you," and he was true to his word. By the time Day was sent to Hanoi, he was in critical condition. The truck ride north, like the others, was an excruciating experience as he was bound tight and tumbling from side to side amongst barrels of gasoline.

Day's first stop in Hanoi was a fetid little complex the prisoners had nicknamed "New Guy Village," a particularly cruel version of a welcome center. It was part of the bigger prison the Vietnamese called Hoa Lo, which the Americans had dubbed the Hanoi Hilton. The French had constructed Hoa Lo during their occupation, in the 1940s and early 1950s, to house political prisoners. The Vietnamese inherited it after the French defeat at Dien Bien Phu. Complete with guillotine, the NVA now used Hoa Lo to house the "American war criminals," pilots shot down over North Vietnam.

The purpose of New Guy Village was to intimidate new prisoners through torture and let them know what the price would be if they didn't "cooperate fully"—give the interrogators what they wanted. The indoctrination made one thing perfectly clear: Prisoners would be at the mercy of their captors unless they capitulated. Guards put Day through the "rope treatment," one of the most difficult torture methods to endure. His feet were bound tightly together, shutting off circulation. Then his hands were bound together behind his back and his arms were pulled up and over his head and tied back to his feet. It produced excruciating pain and made it almost impossible to breathe, making Day feel like he was suffocating. Then the guards would leave him in this position for hours.

There were other torture sessions, too. In between them, Day would be thrown onto a cell floor that was often covered with water, and left without food. He'd sit in the cold and dark listening to rats scurry about, unless they were drowned out by the screams of fellow prisoners being tortured.

As a major, Day ranked as one of the more senior officers in the Hanoi prison system, which qualified him for special treatment: He was kept isolated in solitary confinement, forbidden to communicate with the other prisoners. He was repeatedly interrogated, beaten, subjected to the rope treatment, and starved. His cell was icy and frigid in the winter and suffocatingly hot in the summer. After interrogations, the guards would place him in a sitting position with his hands and feet in crude metal stocks or irons. The guards and interrogators seemed to take a perverse pride in showing off their favorite forms of torture.

Eventually Day got a roommate, Norris Overly, a B-57 pilot he had met earlier in his career. Like other inmates, they both got shifted periodically between several camps, which had acquired sardonic nicknames like the Plantation, Alcatraz, Briarpatch, Camp Faith, Camp Hope, Dirty Bird, Dogpatch, Farnsworth, the Zoo, Mountain Camp, Skidrow, and Rockpile.[2] And the captives, despite the best efforts of the North Vietnamese, formed the "4th Allied POW Wing" complete with a formal chain of command that issued orders and granted approvals for POW actions such as escape plans. Day became a "building commander" at the Plantation and several other camps where the North Vietnamese dumped him.

Prison officials greatly feared any kind of organization among the POWs, and communication among prisoners was forbidden. Getting caught whispering or leaving notes resulted in severe punishment. So in June 1965, four POWs—Capt. Carlyle "Smitty" Harris, Lt. Phillip Butler, Lt. Robert Peel, and Lt. Cmdr. Robert Shumaker—all imprisoned in the same cell in Hoa Lo—devised a secret way of talking. Harris remembered an Air Force instructor who had shown him a secret code based on a five-by-five alphabet matrix, minus the K. Each letter was communicated by two separate tapping patterns. The first designated the horizontal row in the matrix, and the second the vertical row. The letter H, for example, was represented by two taps, followed by three taps, as indicated in the matrix:

TAPS	1	2	3	4	5
1	A	B	C	D	E
2	F	G	H	I	J
3	L	M	N	O	P
4	Q	R	S	T	U
5	V	W	X	Y	Z

The letter X was used to signal the end of a sentence, and C was used in place of K, as in "Joan Baez Succs"—a transmission that went around the camp frequently once prison officials started playing the antiwar activist's songs over the public address system. When the guards weren't around, the prison halls often sounded like a wood-pecker convention. Tapping out abbreviations got to be a game, such as: GBU for God bless you, often sent after a prisoner was known to have endured a harsh interrogation session. GN stood for good night, ST for sleep tight, DLTBBB for don't let the bedbugs bite. It was pitiful humor, but a form of resistance against the captors. And it became much more than a method of passing rudimentary messages. With long, unbroken hours in the cells, tapping became conversation, a way to convey humor, sadness, elation, sarcasm, and excitement.[3]

Over time, Day got to know who some of his prison-mates were. Air Force colonel John "Jack" Flynn, who had been shot down two months after Day, was the most senior American in prison and there-fore commander of the 4th Allied POW Wing. Air Force lieutenant colonel Robbie Risner, who had gone down in 1965, was second most senior. There were a number of Navy aviators, too, such as Lt. Cmdrs. Jeremiah Denton and James V. Stockdale—both 1965 arrivals—and Lt. Cmdr. Richard Stratton, who had been shot down in 1967. These men rarely saw one another, but the prisoners had been compiling a list of all three hundred or so Americans in Hanoi's various torture camps. And the prisoners had been ordered to memorize all the names as they came through the walls, letter by letter.

The Mistys didn't know anything about Day's story, or even whether he was alive or dead. They had more information about Bob Craner and Guy Gruters. The two pilots, they knew, had been captured alive. Their plane had been shot down just before Christmas, and Craner had managed to get off the quick transmission to Jim Mack, cir-cling overhead, before the North Vietnamese took his radio: "Tell my wife I love her," Craner had instructed, "and I'll see her after the war!"

Craner's final words had had an air of insouciance, but it was a grim situation he and Gruters had found themselves in on the ground. As they had floated down in their parachutes, they could hear bells ringing in the surrounding villages—a signal for the residents to go capture the "yankee air pirates." Gruters managed to hide for only forty-five minutes before NVA soldiers surrounded him. They stripped off his flying gear, gave him black pajamas, and took him to one of the villages, where they put him into a temporary holding prison.

Craner's capture had been just as quick. He came down in the middle of an open field and was promptly surrounded. His captors took him to the smoldering wreckage of his aircraft and paraded him in front of all the gun crews that had shot at him. There were six gun sites, each manned by a crew of eight gunners. They punched him and kicked him. As Craner looked around, he couldn't believe the amount of matériel moving south along the roads.

The next day a guard was assigned to escort him to the holding prison where Gruters was being held, when the guard inadvertently turned on the survival radio. Craner grabbed the radio and blurted out that he and Gruters were captured and provided an approximate location, then offered some intel on all the guns and trucks he saw moving south. That's when Jim Mack and Jim Fiorelli tried to talk the guard into accepting a gold bribe and releasing Craner. The guard had sounded intrigued, but when Mack and Fio appeared overhead in their F-100, he became angry, took the radio back, and threatened Craner. Later the guard offered Craner the opportunity to "run off into the jungle," so the guard could shoot him as an "escaping prisoner."

The two pilots were shackled in leg irons and handcuffs in the temporary holding prison. The torture began right away, as the captors sought basic information. Gruters and Craner offered minimal facts, reciting phrases from the Geneva Convention along with their name, rank, service number, and date of birth. As the beatings became more persuasive, eventually they both gave inane cover stories with fictitious squadron numbers and bases, insisting that their job was "flak suppression." They revealed nothing about the top secret Commando Sabre operation.

On Christmas Day 1967, after five days of mistreatment and interrogation, they were moved to Vinh, sixty miles north of where they were shot down—the same place Bud Day had endured torture by "the Rodent" as he passed through on his way up to Hanoi. En route they were displayed to villagers who were allowed to spit on them, kick and punch them, and hit them with sticks.

In Vinh the two were put into the "Bamboo Prison," a rickety, wooden building with a number of cells inside. It was only a way station, but the prison had been specifically designed for interrogation to extract tactical information from prisoners headed farther north to

Hanoi. The pressure and torture increased greatly. Craner and Gruters were kept manacled, in leg irons that were cinched tight so that they inflicted almost unbearable, constant pain. Interrogations took place in open cells, so prisoners in adjoining rooms could get a taste of what was coming their way through the bamboo walls. Craner and Gruters noted a prisoner in a nearby cell being repeatedly beaten, numbly repeating his name, rank, and service number, and refusing to give any other information. The interrogators were obviously infuriated and beating him to the verge of death. At one point, after listening to the torture for a while, Craner and Gruters began to scream to draw attention to themselves and away from the unfortunate punching bag down the hall. But the beating continued.

After two or three days in Vinh—they were losing count—Gruters persuaded a guard to unshackle him so he could use the toilet. He rubbed his limbs, trying to restore circulation, as he shuffled toward a filthy latrine. As he passed the cell of the hapless prison-mate who had been repeatedly pummeled, Gruters peered through the bamboo. He saw a man who looked small and slight, slumped against the wall. The man appeared to be barely conscious, but Gruters gave him a thumbs-up. The lackluster face behind the bamboo bars grinned—or grimaced—back.

Soon after, Craner and Gruters were removed from their compartments and taken to the cell of the mystery prisoner. The guards made motions for them to gather the man up and take him outside to clean him up. As they entered the cell, both noticed that the lump on the floor was a mass of raging infection. Although he appeared small as he slumped in the corner, they noticed he was rather tall as they began to pick him up and place his arms around their necks. Then his mouth opened. "Guy?" he whispered. "Are you Guy Gruters?"

"Yes!" Gruters answered quickly. "Who are you?"

"Lance," the prisoner mumbled, trailing off. He didn't give his last name, but Gruters and Craner both knew immediately it was Lance Sijan. They were astonished. Gruters and Sijan had been close friends who met when they were both cadets in the same squadron at the Air Force Academy. And Sijan's tale was well known at Misty, since he had been the target of one of the most frustrating and disheartening rescue efforts in North Vietnam. Back in November, when his F-4 had been blown out of the sky, Sijan had spent nearly two days unconscious on the jungle floor. Jim Mack and Jim Fiorelli had been flying overhead two days after the crash when Sijan came up on the radio for the first time. Over the next twenty-four hours, more than 125 aircraft had flown in shifts, trying to find his exact location and pull him off the side of a steep, karst mountain. One helicopter had even hovered right overhead before it was driven off by gunfire. Finally, Sijan stopped transmitting over the radio, and the rescuers were forced to give up.

His ordeal since then had obviously been devastating. Gruters didn't even recognize his old friend. Sijan had lost at least a third of his body weight. Half the time he was delirious. As Craner and Gruters wiped Sijan down with some dirty rags, they realized he was too weak to say much. They encouraged him to come up with a cover story, at least feed the interrogators some bogus info to forestall the beatings. Sijan refused, saying he could still handle it for now. And sure enough, the interrogators kept beating him, concentrating on his open wounds to inflict maximum pain and punishment.

Eventually the three pilots were thrown into the back of a six-by-six military truck, the start of their journey to Hanoi, two hundred miles to the north. They weren't the only cargo: Several fifty-five-gallon barrels of gasoline were stuffed in beside them. Even though they were traveling at barely ten miles per hour, it was a punishing ride. The truck bounced along on pitted, bombed-out roads, navigating through and around bomb craters and taking detours to avoid being attacked by American fighters like those the prisoners in the back had flown. Bob and Guy took turns cradling Sijan, while the other fended off the barrels tumbling about the truck bed, threatening to explode or crush them all. Along the way they passed through settlements where villagers gawked at them and occasionally reached into the truck to take a jab at the prisoners.

Things looked even worse when they got to Hanoi. The three pilots were immediately separated and placed into individual interrogation cells in New Guy Village. They each experienced the rope treatment, along with other brutality. When the torture sessions ended, they were thrown into solitary confinement in bare cells, without food. But in between some of the torture sessions, Craner and Gruters were placed with Sijan and ordered to care for him. That gave them a chance to co-ordinate the information they were giving the interrogators. And Craner and Gruters gradually learned the rest of Sijan's story as he slowly sputtered out the details of his ordeal.

Sijan had been terribly injured when he ejected from his F-4. One leg was badly broken, with two bones protruding through his skin. Using only his arms, he had dragged himself backward through the jungle until he was a mass of cuts and abrasions. Somehow he endured for forty-two days without food—the last ten without water—before a posse of villagers finally apprehended him several miles from where he had been shot down. One of the prison workers back at Vinh, who spoke halting English, had told Gruters that despite his crippled con-dition, Sijan had knocked out a guard in the village where he was being held, then escaped. Supposedly it had taken nearly a day for searchers to hunt him down again in the surrounding jungle.

Even though Sijan was in desperate condition, the interrogators at New Guy Village spared him none of the torture. They continued to beat on his open wounds with their hands and with clubs. He was de-nied basic medical attention. After several days of indoctrination, Craner, Gruters, and Sijan were thrown together into a cell with two inches of standing water on the floor. The filthy blankets were com-pletely soaked through. It was winter and extremely cold.

For food, the guards would slip in a bowl of rice each day, with a few tiny pieces of chicken or pork and some stringy, putrid greens. It was virtually impossible to get enough calories to maintain any sem-blance of health or strength. The three POWs shook continually as their bodies struggled to maintain body heat. Sijan was catching pneu-monia. Craner and Gruters repeatedly asked the prison guards to get him a doctor. They pleaded for antibiotics. But no help came.

When Sijan was lucid, he could be ferocious. Occasionally, when a guard would slide open the tiny window in the cell door to check on the captives, Sijan would growl like a caged animal. The guard would quickly close the door and Sijan would laugh. It was his way of fight-ing back. But to Craner and Gruters, much of the time he resembled a creature from another planet. There was little they could do except take turns holding him in their arms like a baby, trying desperately to keep him warm.

Sijan's pneumonia worsened. He hacked like a four-pack-a-day smoker and his fever soared. He didn't complain, though, and even managed a joke from time to time. One afternoon, after waking up from a nap, Sijan looked over at his cellmates and croaked, "Hey . . . How about going out . . . get me a burger . . . and french fries."[4]

Sijan was sinking fast, however. Craner and Gruters repeatedly begged for medical care for their comrade as he visibly weakened. Sijan tried to eat and wanted to exercise. And of all things, he kept talking about escaping. The spirit was willing, but the body was collapsing. Soon, Sijan could only mouth words, then syllables. The three prayed together: "Our Father . . ." Gruters asked Sijan if he had made his peace with God—one blink for yes, two for no. Sijan blinked once: Yes.

Finally, it seemed like it was about to end. Sijan was having trouble breathing. His eyes were reeling in his head. Craner and Gruters insisted that a doctor come. Three soldiers arrived at the cell and began to move Sijan onto a wooden pallet. In one final burst of strength, he called out for his father. "Dad, help me," he cried. "Dad, I need you!" Then he was gone.[5]

Craner and Gruters didn't see him die, but they knew there could be no other outcome. And it broke their hearts. They had watched his decline with amazement. Sijan's determination had seemed to grow stronger as his body had grown weaker. Having known and cared for Lance made Craner and Gruters even more insistent on resisting their captors and surviving as POWs. Among other things, they had to get home and tell the story of Sijan's remarkable courage.

A couple of days later Craner was transferred from Hoa Lo to the Plantation, a prison in the northeast corner of Hanoi that had also been a residence for French officials during the early 1950s. Gruters, for reasons only the NVA understood, remained in Hoa Lo, counting bugs and staring at the walls. Craner was placed in a cell next to Navy pilot John McCain, whose father, Adm. John S. McCain Jr., had replaced Admiral Sharp as head of Pacific Command. As Craner learned the tap code, he and McCain communicated quietly, making solitary confinement a little less solitary. Craner started to learn about some of the other prisoners in the system. There was good news: rumors that Bud Day was among them. The tappers also explained the habits of the guards and interrogators, and the odd ground rules that dictated who received torture, and what kind. Not surprisingly, the worst treatment was reserved for the most "uncooperative" prisoners.

One day Craner happened to see one of the interrogators who had tormented the three of them at New Guy Village. Craner gestured to get his attention and asked what had happened to the cellmate he had last seen being carried out on a stretcher. "Sijan die," the official murmured. "Spend too long in jungle. Sijan die."[6]

As Bud Day, Bob Craner, and Guy Gruters settled into a forced, uncomfortable routine, their wives back home did the same. They had one thing in common: lots of unanswered questions. The Air Force knew little about the fate of the Misty prisoners—and didn't even know whether Bud Day was alive. And what little they did know they were loath to tell. Many of the details of aircraft losses were classified. Other information might upset the families more than was necessary. It was best for them to keep a low profile—any publicity might get noticed by the interrogators in Hanoi and be used to extract sensitive intelligence from the prisoners.

Audrey Craner was still living with her son, Lorne, eight, and daughter, Charys, five, outside of Langley Air Force Base near Norfolk, Virginia. She had heard virtually nothing from the Air Force since getting a letter from Mick Greene explaining what the Mistys knew about Bob and Guy's shootdown. She was getting angry and bitter and beginning to ask for answers more forcefully. Bud Day's wife, Dorie— "the Viking" had put up with all kinds of strains during Bud's two-decade career. But nothing had prepared her for this, including the official attitude of the Air Force. It had become like an extension of her family, but now they were keeping her at arm's length, telling her not to rock the boat. Sandy Gruters and her two daughters had moved in with Guy's parents in Florida, where the whole family could support one another during Guy's time in prison. They wrote to him nearly every day, in care of the International Red Cross, but Guy never got the letters. Mail was a privilege the North Vietnamese refused to allow.

TWENTY-THREE

"BODIES BABIES MOTHERS FATHERS"

There weren't many morale boosters for the American prisoners in Hanoi, but every now and then something would trigger a spark of hope or send a current of excitement through the camps. Perhaps the most effective stimulant was the sound of U.S. planes roaring over Hanoi, and especially the explosions as bombs fell. The prisoners knew their mates were still up there, sticking it to the communists, fighting for the victory that would free them from their dismal cells. Sometimes they even cheered, risking the wrath of the sadistic guards.

The skies had gone silent, though. President Johnson's decision to suspend all bombing near Hanoi left the prisoners wondering where their fellow air warriors had gone. Was the war over? If it was, why weren't they being released? Was Washington going soft on Hanoi—again? Would the prisoners end up being forgotten?

Johnson hadn't intended to undercut what little hope the POWs could muster, but the bombing halt caused dismay throughout the U.S. military. With North Vietnam free to do as it wished in most of the country, the pace of its war effort was sure to quicken. Factories and other industrial facilities could crank out as much matériel as capacity would allow. Trains steaming in from China and ships arriving from the Soviet Union were able to run unimpeded, bearing thousands of tons of war goods. All of it traveled down an open conduit to Vinh, the coastal city just sixty miles north of the DMZ. Only south of there were U.S. pilots permitted to attack the men and weapons heading into combat against Americans and their allies. It would be like facing a tidal wave of war goods that backed up at Vinh and then came flooding into the South.

It had been a hot spring. The North Vietnamese siege of the Marine outpost at Khe Sanh lasted for seventy-seven days, all the way into April. The Army's 1st Cavalry Division (Airmobile) finally reopened Highway 9, which connected Khe Sanh in the west with Dong Ha on the coast. The 1st Cav found that the NVA had largely abandoned the area. There were crates of AK-47s and ammunition and tons of unopened supplies, but the trenches that had been dug, steadily moving forward toward the Marine base, were empty. It was obvious why. The 1st Cav saw hundreds of enemy corpses, some buried in shallow graves, some simply lying where they had fallen—the carnage produced by repetitive B-52 strikes.[1] No wonder the North Vietnamese were so desperate to get SAMs down south.

On April 11, General Westmoreland declared the battle of Khe Sanh over. He talked about the tremendous beating the North Vietnamese had taken at the hands of U.S. airpower, with the familiar statistics: the number of artillery rounds fired at the enemy, the number of fighter and bomber strikes flown. The B-52, he said, had been THE factor that broke the backs of the North Vietnamese. Like Tet, he said, Khe Sanh had been a great victory.[2]

But then the Marines began to quietly dismantle their base at Khe Sanh, blowing up bunkers, filling in trenches, toting truckloads of unexpended ammunition down Highway 9. It didn't make sense to the uninitiated people back home in the States, watching the war on TV. If it had been so important to fight for Khe Sanh, why give it up now, voluntarily? This lonely outpost far from civilization had been the great anchor to Westmoreland's strategy, the key to shutting down the Ho Chi Minh Trail. Why was it suddenly dispensable?[3]

Nobody in Saigon or Washington would say so, but after months of stalemate—and several opportunities to tip the effort solidly in U.S. favor—the North was beginning to win the Battle for the Trail. And like so many other battles in the war, the most decisive action didn't take place on the ground among fighting men, but in briefing rooms and lavish offices among diplomats and politicians. Bit by bit, Washington was ceding the vital supply lines to the communists. The bombing halt allowed an unfettered buildup of war goods in the North. The abandonment of Khe Sanh signaled the end of Westmoreland's ultimate dream of sending troops into Laos and Cambodia to cut the Trail on the ground where it fed into the South. The whole Trail interdiction effort was being compressed into a tighter and tighter area. At the center of that area was Route Pack 1, and the Mistys.

Despite deep skepticism at Misty about the underlying strategy, on the surface the bombing halt seemed good for business. Suddenly targets were everywhere, and not just because of surprise breaks in the clouds. There was simply more traffic on the roads, and there was no way to camouflage it all or send it all south during darkness. Trucks were so plentiful that sighting two or three was no longer a cause for excitement. It was a routine event.

Accompanying all that traffic, of course, was a multiplying arsenal of air-defense weapons. Since they were no longer needed up north, AAA guns started popping up near intersections and ridgelines that had gotten little attention till then. SAMs were no longer a rare sighting. The additional targets came with a higher price: Misty birds were coming back with more holes than ever.

During one two-week period, every single plane flown by Misty got hit at least once. Yet the Mistys got lucky, like a bunch of cats with nine lives. P. K. Robinson was in the backseat one day with Wells Jackson, a tall, muscular pilot who always seemed to find a way to get things done, when they took a hit straight down the engine intake. When they got back to Phu Cat they found a clean hole that exited just in front of the compressor blades, where it probably would have taken out the engine: a typical near miss.

The bombing halt also freed a lot more fighters for Misty to work with. Before, Hanoi and other targets in Route Packs 5 and 6 were the top priority, except when Misty found a SAM or something else was urgent, like a rescue. That meant Misty often had to wait for bombs, hoping all the while that the target wouldn't escape. Sometimes the Misty pilots used their own 20mm guns to bottle up a truck convoy or tear up a train while awaiting fresh fighters from the alert pad or others returning from weathered-out missions up north. But now there were plenty of fighters available, often on extremely short notice. All of the planes that had been flying "downtown" or attacking targets elsewhere in the North suddenly needed something else to do, and there was no shortage of opportunity in Route Pack 1.

It was a mixed blessing, though. 7th Air Force decided to send many of the freed fighters, usually F-4s or F-105s or Navy A-4s or A-7s, out on "armed reconnaissance" missions, flying up and down along the main roads looking randomly for targets in areas where bombing was still allowed. That overlapped with Misty's work, but there were some big differences. Misty's F-100s carried little external ordnance, just two pods of marking rockets, which meant they used less gas, were more maneuverable, and had more time to spend looking for targets. They also knew the area from months of study. Misty could pinpoint where the AAA was and where the targets were likely to be. They spent less time trolling through the enemy defenses at low altitude, and were less likely to get shot down. When the bomb-droppers showed up, the Mistys usually had targets ready, eliminating the need for multiple passes.

The armed recce flights, as they were known, could be clumsy and dangerous. The fighters often flew into the Pack weighted down with bombs, which limited their maneuverability. They weren't trained for reconnaissance and were liable to fly into risky areas unaware. The Thud and F-4 drivers based in Thailand also had a tendency to underestimate the challenges in Route Pack 1. Compared to Hanoi—considered the most heavily defended city on earth—Route Pack 1 seemed like the bush leagues to them. There were few SAMs, and you could actually see through the AAA. That made them less cautious and created the false impression that they could fly lower with less risk of getting shot down.

The targets in Route Pack 1 required more attention, too. Up north, the planes often went against huge complexes like the Thai-Nguyen Steelworks or Phuc Yen Airfield. In Misty's terrain the quarry was often a single truck, a small storage area, or a camouflaged ferry. The fighters found they had to spend a lot more time orbiting, searching for targets, and maneuvering for attack. The targets in Route Pack 1 also demanded accuracy, which meant dropping from a lower altitude and dealing up close with the AAA. It was like the difference between smacking a home run and sinking a fifty-foot putt, and many of the F-4s and F-105s didn't have such a good finesse game. Even though the defenses were a bit thinner in Route Pack 1, many pilots got shot down there because they didn't exercise the caution they had practiced up north near Hanoi.

P. K. Robinson was flying with Dick Rutan one day when the ABCCC sent them a bunch of Thuds who wanted to get into the Pack for a quick "counter." The rules at the time said that any pilot who flew one hundred missions over North Vietnam got to go home, and each time they crossed the border into North Vietnam it was a counter—one mission. The only pilots the "hundred mission rule" didn't apply to were the Mistys, who crossed into North Vietnam at least three times on every mission, in between refuelings, and spent most of their time at low altitude to boot. But most Mistys didn't mind helping out with a counter, especially for the Thud pilots, who usually did good work.

Robinson marked a target for the Thuds, and the lead pilot rolled in. As he released his bombs, his F-105 took a AAA hit. The plane streaked toward the water but was burning badly. Finally the pilot ejected. Robinson eyeballed the parachute all the way to the ground and watched as the pilot quickly unbuckled his parachute harness on a wide-open coastal plain. There was very little cover for evading capture. The pilot gave a quick wave to the passing Misty and ran into a nearby hedgerow. His parachute beeper was blaring, but he forgot to turn it off, so Robinson and Rutan were unable to talk to him. They could see several dozen people running across the field toward the pilot's position, but there was little the Mistys could do. They strafed to no avail and hung around until dark, with rescuers holding "feet wet" off the coast. But nobody could attempt a rescue if there was no radio contact with the pilot.

That night at the bar, Robinson and Rutan had an impassioned discussion. Robinson prided himself on his flying discipline. He religiously adhered to sound tactics, carefully measuring the risks associated with each target before attacking. And he felt they had made a mistake. They put the Thuds in on a bad target, in a bad area, he said. "It was a poor decision, not worth the loss of an airplane."

"P. K., you can't think that way," Rutan insisted. "This whole war is a blow job. You know it and I know it. There isn't one fucking target in all of North Vietnam worth the loss of an American airplane and pilot, but that isn't the point. Our job is to keep the crap from getting to the gomers who are killing American kids, and that makes it all worth it. It's as simple as that. Everything else is bullshit." Rutan wasn't the most subtle Misty, or the most introspective, but he had quieted P. K. for the night.

It was sometimes hard to say no to Dick Rutan. During one rescue effort, an F-105 pilot went down late in the day, and the rescue forces couldn't get organized in time to get him out before darkness fell. Rutan and Steve Amdor, a stocky, athletic new Misty who had been a running back at the Air Force Academy, were the FACs on the case. Since they knew where the pilot was, they flew the next morning as Misty 11, the first Misty sortie. The downed pilot had an injured back and could barely move. The Sandys and Jollys and other rescue forces had finally been assembled and were moving in when the ABCCC, using the call sign Cricket, came on the radio and announced that Blue Chip, the command post at 7th Air Force in Saigon, had ordered the rescue to be postponed. Rutan, suspicious, asked why. Cricket relayed the question to Saigon and came back on to explain that the rescue package would interfere with a B-52 strike that was scheduled nearby. Rutan became furious.

"Cricket, Misty one-one," Rutan said. "Do you want to fly over here and tell that personally to the pilot on the ground?"

"We'll check and see what the story is," Cricket replied.

Rutan persisted, next calling the rescue coordinators on another frequency who used the call sign Crown. "Hey Crown, Misty one-one," he repeated a moment later. "What is the scoop down there? What am I going to tell this boy on the ground down here? Tell him nobody is interested in him?"

"We're checking it out," Crown answered again, sounding embarrassed.

Rutan came on again. "Crown, Misty. I want to know *exactly* what I'm to tell the guy on the ground."

Crown realized that Rutan was not asking a rhetorical question. "Okay, I'll see if I can find out," the controller said. Then he offered Rutan a little more detail. "We're behind you. There's a general officer at Blue Chip who's been on the line here for the last half hour, and he's the one calling the shots."

Amdor and Rutan debated the situation. "You don't realize what's going on in the general's mind," Amdor argued. "We have a big operation going on, and one guy gets shot down and the pet project gets blown to hell."

Rutan wasn't buying it. "Tell the guy to blow his brains out," he said of the general. "I don't give a shit. The guy down there's hurt and we could get him out. Possibly it's the guy's life. He's not going to make it otherwise. What will I ask him—dig his grave? Lay there and rot?" Rutan put the plane in a couple of rapid, high-G turns that strained both pilots.

"Must you put my ass through all this?" Amdor protested.

"I've got to get my frustrations out on something," Rutan snorted. "Might as well be this beautiful airplane."

While Crown was waiting for Saigon to reply to the captain who refused to call off the rescue, Misty 21 showed up, with Charlie Summers in the front and P. K. Robinson in the back. They looked the scene over and saw only a few guns. Fighters were already on station. All they needed was Saigon's blessing. "It's not that hard a rescue," Charlie Summers said to everybody listening on the radio, "if we can just get them interested down there."

Rutan was still fuming. "Big heroes my ass, these fuckin' people have blown it," he muttered. "This war is being run by amateurs. Rank amateurs, candy-ass rank amateurs."

Crown finally came back on with some news. Blue Chip had reversed its position. The rescue could continue. In less than two hours a Jolly pulled the pilot out. When Rutan returned to Phu Cat, he found he had been invited down to Saigon to explain his effrontery in person to the general at Blue Chip. Some supportive honchos at the wing tipped off General Momyer, the 7th Air Force commander who was Misty's most senior supporter, and he sat in on the meeting. After hearing what had happened, he sided with Rutan.

Lanny Lancaster had some thoughts about what to do with all the fighters bumping into each other flying armed recce in Route Pack 1. He approached the Misty commander, Stan Mamlock, and asked if he could go down to 7th Air Force. He knew the chief of staff down there,

Brig. Gen. Ted Seith. As a cadet at the Air Force Academy, Lanny had been "manager" of the football team, responsible for carrying balls and equipment, filling drinking bottles, fixing broken helmets, and handling other chores. Seith, much older, was a colonel and the deputy commandant of cadets. He had also been a football player, and he hung around the team. The two had become friends. So Lancaster asked Mamlock if he could go to Saigon and appeal directly to his old football buddy. Mamlock agreed and decided not to ask permission from the wing. "Go for it," he said.

In Saigon, Seith listened to Lancaster's proposal and sent him to see Brig. Gen. Dale Sweat, who oversaw all the missions in Route Pack 1 and Laos. Sweat was willing to hear Lancaster out, but was also busy and impatient. The Misty pilot was on the hot seat.

Lancaster explained the problem. "Sir, fragging 'armed recce' into RP-1 is dumber than dirt," he said, arguing that assigning bomb-laden fighters to find their own targets was poor use of the airplanes. Sweat sat up straight in his chair. He wasn't used to hearing such blunt talk from a young captain. Lancaster continued, "The real problem is that the fighters aren't familiar with the terrain and they can't find targets. If they find targets, it's because they are low and slow, and then they get shot down." Lancaster could have stopped there and gotten high marks for moxie, but he kept going. "And another thing, sir. The bomb-droppers can't hit the broad side of a barn, unless they're F-105s or from the Navy. But it isn't their fault. You guys are fragging them wrong. What fighters need in RP-1 is 750-pound bombs and cluster bombs, not rockets, napalm, and gun pods." The general stared at him, red-faced.

Sweat recovered. "What exactly would you have me do?" he asked, humoring the rowdy young pilot.

"Sir, put the right ordnance on the fighters and frag them to Misty," Lancaster answered—let Misty find the targets, in other words, and start loading your airplanes right. "We'll get you some real BDA," he promised boldly. The other Mistys would have agreed with everything Lanny said, even though he had just told the emperor he was wearing no clothes.

Sweat stood up. "I'll do that," he said curtly. Then he tossed Lancaster out. Lanny went back to Phu Cat figuring that the trip had probably been a waste. If he was lucky, nothing would happen. It wouldn't be surprising, however, if Colonel Schneider got word of the exchange and Lanny ended up in hot water.

To everybody's surprise, things changed after Lanny's visit to Saigon. "Armed recce" flights were dramatically reduced in the Pack, and Misty began to get more fighters, including a lot of F-105s, their favorite bombers.

It had become a zero-sum game, however, and for every additional plane sent into Route Pack 1, the North Vietnamese added an additional gun. For every new squadron of fighters, the NVA trucked in a regiment of air defenders. By early June, encountering dense AAA was a daily hazard. And strikes against SAM sites in Route Pack 1 were becoming routine.

One day Shaheen was flying with a new Misty, Dick Durant, when they marked a SAM near the coast, south of Dong Hoi, for a flight of two F-105s flying out of Thailand. The flight lead was Maj. Carl Light, using the call sign Master 01. The Thuds were getting to be damn good bombers, and Master 01 destroyed the SAM on his first pass. Then he asked if Shaheen had any more targets. This was no lightweight out for a quick counter, Shaheen told Durant. This guy was hungry for kills. Shaheen told Master 01 he had a number of trucks to the south, but they would have to be careful because there was lots of AAA in the area. "Let's go get them, Misty," Master replied.

On the way to the target, Shaheen cautioned the strikers again about the AAA. To be safe, he told them, make only one pass. The two planes should come from divergent directions. Shaheen rolled in to mark and, as he predicted, a wall of flak filled the sky. "See what I mean?" he radioed to the Thuds.

Master 01 rolled in and dropped his bombs. The moment he raised the nose to pull up, he got hit. The plane caught fire immediately and the pilot had no choice but to bail out just seconds after the strike. Shaheen promptly went into a rescue orbit at low altitude, threatening to fire on anybody who tried to reach the pilot. When Light came up on his emergency radio, Shaheen directed him to a wooded area and told him to hunker down while Misty organized a rescue effort. Shaheen continued to make low passes into the AAA and strafe gun sites in the area. He buzzed the woods where Light was hiding, along with a nearby village, to keep locals from rushing out to capture the pilot.

Two Jolly Greens arrived and waited offshore for the gun-suppressing Sandys to show up before they would come in for a rescue. Shaheen told them there wasn't much time and begged them to try to pull the pilot out. He was only a few kilometers in from the coast and they could reach him easily. Shaheen even offered to lower his gear so that he could fly slower and lead them to Light's location. But they wouldn't do it. Durant, in the backseat, thought Shaheen was starting to push too hard, and he cautioned the front-seater. "You're really hanging it out," he warned. "There are going to be two aircraft down instead of one if we don't get out of the weeds."

As other fighters arrived to help with the rescue, Shaheen led them in on whatever guns he could find. He was careful not to hit any huts or homes, though, figuring that would enrage the villagers, who might kill Light if he were captured. Lanny Lancaster arrived with John Overlock, P. K. Robinson's buddy from England, in his backseat. Shaheen was getting low on fuel and his aircraft was developing radio problems. Lancaster took over. Shaheen diverted into Da Nang, refueled, got his radio fixed, and returned to Phu Cat to brief his bosses on the rescue activity.

Robinson was the duty officer for the day in Misty Ops. He monitored the rescue effort and at the end of the day went to the bar with the returning Mistys. Shaheen was hot. He insisted that if the Jollys had come in right away, before the gomers got organized, they would have had a chance to get Light out. Most of the Mistys felt they would simply have lost two helicopters. They discussed what to do next and a heated argument developed over whether it would be possible to rescue Light the next day. Shaheen felt that if they sterilized the area by attacking all the gun sites, they could still rescue the downed pilot. But Light was in an area surrounded by AAA—even more than the Mistys were used to dealing with. Most of the Mistys—less emotional about the situation since it hadn't happened on their watch—thought it would be suicide to go in there. Shaheen went to bed drunk and angry.

P. K. Robinson shook him awake the next morning with encouraging news. Light had come up on the radio at daybreak. "We've been killing gun sites all morning," Robinson reported. There was a catch, though. It seemed apparent that the NVA had left Light where he was as bait and brought in many additional guns overnight. They seemed confident that they could take down a few more planes and probably snag Light in the bargain. Shaheen dressed as fast as he could and went to Ops. He was scheduled to fly with Don Kilgus, who had been with Misty since March, longer than Shaheen. But since Shaheen knew exactly where Master had gone down, he flew in the front seat.

They arrived at the battle as it was reaching a climax. Two other Misty flights, piloted by Charlie Summers and Lanny Lancaster, had already directed strikes that had taken out numerous guns. Smoke was rising from at least a dozen holes in the ground. The sky was so full of planes that it seemed like half the Air Force was in on the fight. The NVA had moved in lots of additional firepower, too, but were getting walloped. They had knocked down one F-4, but both pilots got out safely over the water and were picked up. And Light was still at large—if the gomers had been trying to nab him, the rescuers had managed to fend them off.

Out of nowhere, an NVA truck pulled out of the trees and sped over to one of the 37mm gun sites. The driver jumped out, hooked one of the guns to the back of the truck, and peeled off with it in tow. It was an astounding act of daring, and the whole war stopped to watch the show as an A-1 Sandy went after the truck. It clattered down a road at what must have been 60 miles per hour with the gun bouncing along behind. The A-1 made three passes, dropping ordnance all around him. But during every pass the driver seemed to go even faster and he survived each time. Finally the truck disappeared into the trees. It was frustrating to lose the gun, but if anybody deserved a bit of luck it was that gutsy little driver.

Only two guns were left by the time Shaheen and Kilgus arrived. Shaheen controlled strikes that took out both of them, and finally, when there was no more shooting, the Sandys and Jollys came in. They pulled Light out without picking up any more fire—unusual for a rescue, since the NVA typically held a few guns back to use on the vulnerable Jollys. Shaheen was flying low and slow, in the weeds, alongside the Sandys and Jollys until they were feet wet. It was a risky thing to do, but it was a salute to the rescue forces—whom Shaheen considered the real heroes of the war, despite their reluctance the day before. Now that the pilot had been rescued, he reflected that maybe they had been right to wait it out after all.

The Mistys had lost a number of pilots to enemy captors in areas of intense ground fire, but the Master 01 rescue was the first time anybody had rescued a pilot surrounded by so many gun sites. The effort led to new rescue tactics and techniques for methodically eliminating guns in heavily defended areas. And Shaheen was nominated for the Air Force Cross, the valor award just below the Medal of Honor. Shortly afterward, Carl Light paid a visit to Phu Cat to thank the Mistys personally.

Shaheen wasn't there, however. Like a number of pilots who did a lot of intense flying, Shaheen regularly got sent on R&R, to blow off steam and unwind from the stress of combat. Pilots also had regularly scheduled vacations, then there were other excuses to get out of Phu Cat. With so many airplanes coming and going—and commanders willing to look the other way—plenty of opportunities arose for the Mistys to apply their ingenuity.

One of the trappings of fighter outfits were "party suits" from Hong Kong, a fighter pilot fad in Vietnam. The merchants in Hong Kong could make anything in twenty-four hours, so virtually every fighter squadron had its own brightly colored flight suits, which would be fashioned with irreverent patches for squadron parties. It was one of the few diversions in a dreary war. One of the Misty patches read FAC YOU, emblazoned over a map of North Vietnam. Another read AAA ANYONE? And there was the obligatory YANKEE AIR PIRATE, with skull and crossbones.

Mamlock had suggested that Shaheen go to Hong Kong to acquire some new party suits. They'd be good for morale. Lanny Lancaster forged some official-looking orders that got Shaheen, armed with measurements for all the pilots, on a C-47 heading that way. Mamlock expected Shaheen to be back the following day, but apparently he took a detour. After a week Mamlock asked where the hell he was and sent the squadron first sergeant to fetch him. The first sergeant found Shaheen calmly sipping mai tais and Singapore slings on the veranda of a swanky Hong Kong hotel. When he got back to Phu Cat, Shaheen explained the delay. He had told the Hong Kong tailors there was no rush, and it had simply taken them a while to deliver respectable, top-quality goods.

Two days after the huge Master 01 rescue, the docs and medics at

Phu Cat had a special training session planned. Most of them made occasional trips to the big Air Force hospital down at Cam Ranh Bay, where casualties would be sent if they needed more care than was available at the typical base dispensary. Trips to the hospital allowed the medical people to bone up on new techniques and maybe gather some needed supplies.

But the main attraction was nurses. Real, live women. Americans, too. Most of them young and single.

Dean Echenberg and the rest of the Phu Cat medical contingent had invited a planeload of them to travel up-country for an evening, for an "orientation" on field medical-care techniques. The official reason for the trip won the approval of hospital commanders, and the docs and nurses prepared for a big party. The docs sent down a Caribou transport plane and about a dozen nurses got on board. Except for the crew of the plane, nobody else at Phu Cat knew about the visit. There were practically never women on the base, and the last thing the docs wanted to do was turn a bunch of horny, obnoxious fighter pilots loose on their nurses.

The crowd was socializing and drinking in one of the rooms near the dispensary when a call came in. There had been some kind of Viet Cong attack in the village of Phu Cat, about five miles from the base. A lot of civilians were injured and were being brought to the base dispensary. As they began to arrive, the details of the attack became clearer—and the results were horrifying. Several VC terrorists had thrown four hand grenades into a building where there was a community meeting. Dozens of children had been inside, and they were now being hauled into the dispensary, tattered and shredded. The doctors and nurses ended their party and went to work.

It was gruesome, exhausting duty. The dispensary quickly filled with blood and body parts. Parents and family members staggered around in a daze, desperate for their children to be saved. The doctors and nurses had experience with combat injuries and trauma, but this was worse than anything they had ever seen. The sight of so many mauled children was like a vision of hell. Echenberg worked on one girl, six years old, who lay on a bed, not moving. Her father looked on uneasily, and Echenberg communicated to him that his daughter would be okay. The girl opened her eyes once while Echenberg was looking her over. But then she threw out her arms and legs in a spasm and fell back on the bed. The doctor leaned over and blew air into her lungs. He thought she gave a response, a brief moan, but he had been fooled. She was dead. Echenberg had spent less than twenty minutes with her.

Three hours later, when the survivors had been evacuated to bigger hospitals and there were no more mangled patients to treat, the doctors and nurses felt like collapsing. Most of the victims had been children—18 dead, another 70 seriously wounded. The caregivers were covered with blood. The dispensary looked like a slaughterhouse.

Echenberg had worked most of the night with one nurse, a tall, pretty woman with short, dark hair. They had said little to each other as they worked intensely on the victims. After the ordeal ended, they sat chatting, although they didn't really know what to say to each other. Echenberg found her sweet, strong, and comforting. The two decided to go for a walk, to get some fresh air and breathe a little more freely. They wandered around the base in the dark, going nowhere in particular. At one point a base policeman drove by in a jeep. He was so astonished to see a woman on the post that while he was staring at the nurse, he nearly lost control of his vehicle and tumbled into a ditch.

The doctor and nurse ended up near the end of the runway. With exhaustion overtaking them, they lay down on their backs in the warm grass. It was a clear, summer night and the stars above looked magnificent. Before either of them knew what was happening, they were holding each other, comforting each other, needing each other, seeking some respite from the hours of anguish they had just endured. They made love in the grass while artillery boomed in the distance and aircraft took off over their heads. Then they walked back and went to bed, saying little. In the morning, she and the rest of the nurses flew back to Cam Ranh Bay.

Echenberg struggled to understand how anybody could be so savage as to murder children. It was the worst thing he had seen in Vietnam. He was keeping a Jack Kerouac kind of journal and dabbed his laments onto the page. "They are killing their own kind," he wrote. "Bodies babies mothers fathers. Brains falling out of gazing young heads onto green stretchers. The blood turns black. Why. Terrorism has new meaning—children crying children dazed, phased staring asking nothing as yet, except please stop the pain American doctor. Please stop the pain."

Then he composed a poem:

> The return, to the land of Oz
> The return, full as the leaving
> Welcome back with [bouquets of] bodies
> Awakening hate.

Echenberg's buddies back in San Francisco and elsewhere in the States had been sending him letters, razzing him about the war. "What the fuck are you doing there?" they'd ask, sure that their friend the "hippie doc" was appalled by America's behavior in Vietnam. But Echenberg had begun to realize how brutal—barbaric, really—the communists could be. The young doctor had been ambivalent about the war when he first showed up in Vietnam. But he could no longer humor the antiwar protesters he knew. Yes, combat was inhumane, and atrocities happened on both sides, especially during the heat of battle. But he didn't see the communists as "freedom fighters" or "revolutionaries" like the crowd back in San Francisco. To him the communists were savages who terrorized civilians and anybody who disagreed with them. Echenberg had friends who cheered "Uncle Ho," friends whom he had once viewed as sympathetic dreamers. Now they seemed completely deluded.

TWENTY-FOUR

NIGHT MISTY

Lanny Lancaster was feeling emboldened by his success in getting 7th Air Force to cut back on the armed recce flights, and he cooked up another idea at the bar one night, with the help of Dick Rutan. If Misty could ferret out trucks and other targets in the daytime, when they were mostly hiding, why couldn't they do the same thing at night?

One of the biggest limitations of the Misty concept was that it left a nighttime sanctuary for the North Vietnamese, which, everybody knew, was when they moved the majority of their men and supplies south. So much traffic was going south that they were now seeing some of it by day, but that was a trickle compared to the after-hours flow. Lanny and Dick decided that Misty could fly both safely and effectively at night. They'd need some extra gear. The Huns would have to be equipped with air-delivered parachute flares that would illuminate a target area as they drifted down. If the fighters could see the target, great—they could go ahead and attack. If not, Misty could still mark with smoke rockets under the descending flare.

After they had sketched out the scheme, Chuck Shaheen—"the Arab"—joined them at the bar. "You want us to do what?" he chortled. Shaheen was a Californian whose family had come from Lebanon.

Dark-skinned and dark-eyed, he looked like he should be wearing a *dishdasha,* and he had the wry smile of the savviest merchant at the souk. "What the hell is the matter with you guys?" he clucked.

Lancaster and Rutan argued their point. Giving the NVA twelve hours of respite every day, they said, was no way to win a war.

Shaheen looked at his fellow Mistys as if they had suggested flying naked. "I guess in war there are no dumb ideas," he scolded them, "but yours is the closest I've heard in a long time. Look," he insisted, "nights are for sleeping, drinking, and fucking. Fighters can't hit shit in the daylight, so what can they possibly hit at night?"

The discussion trailed off. Lancaster didn't ask any other Mistys their opinion, but using his newfound powers of persuasion, he worked the idea with Mamlock and the wing bosses. Lo and behold, "Night Misty" was born.

With a considerable lack of enthusiasm, the Mistys suited up to see what they might accomplish in the darkness. P. K. Robinson flew on the first flight with Lancaster in the back. The weather was clear, and they launched right after sunset. Right off the bat they had one pleasant surprise: The sights were stunning at night. The stars looked electrifying and beautiful.

Robinson penetrated the Pack at 15,000 feet, above most of the AAA. SAMs could reach much higher, though, so they stayed alert for that telltale burst of flame and smoke. There was another startling sight: They could identify every road in Route Pack 1 because they were thoroughly illuminated by truck headlights. Robinson was excited. That crazy Lancaster might actually be right—night-flying might turn out to be rather productive. They might not even need to drop the illumination flares—the targets, lighting themselves up, were even more visible than in the daytime.

The first set of fighters checked in—Gunfighter F-4s from Da Nang. "Gunfighter, this is Misty," Robinson called out. "I have you in sight. Do you have me?"

"Roger, Misty."

"Okay," he continued, "we have several hundred trucks lined up right below us on Route 137 and Route 1. They're driving with their headlights on. You are cleared to attack. Do you see them?"

"That's a negative, Misty."

That was odd. The line of trucks was so visible, it practically dominated the shadowy landscape. Robinson tried again. "Okay, Gunfighter. I have you in sight. We'll stay clear of you. You're cleared in on the trucks at your one o'clock position on the highway."

"Misty, Gunfighter. I don't see any trucks."

"Okay, do you see the trucks at your three-o'clock, out along the coast?"

"Negative, Misty."

"Okay, do you see the line of lights on Route 1?"

"Negative."

And so it went all night long. As the Mistys began to figure out, lights that looked as bright as floodlamps from 5,000 or even 8,000 feet, where the Mistys flew, could be invisible at 15,000 feet, where the fighters began their roll-ins. Plus, cockpit lights in the fighters created glare that reflected off the canopy and made it even harder to see out at night. The few fighters that did think they saw headlights dropped bombs that missed the roads by miles. It was another agonizing dilemma. The NVA was parading down the Trail in plain sight. The Mistys had all the bombs they needed to break things up. Yet they could do nothing. "You gotta be shitting me," Robinson moaned. "The Arab was right. Let's go home."

On the way back to Phu Cat, Robinson flew over some of the Pack's familiar landmarks: Finger Lakes, the Disappearing River, and Ban Karai Ford. He went "Christmas tree" above each, turning on all the aircraft exterior lights to see if the air-defense gunners on the ground were on alert. They were—as soon as he turned on the lights, the AAA opened up. He and Lancaster actually enjoyed watching the gunfire. During the day they saw only some of the tracer rounds. At night, however, they could see every tracer and follow the trajectory of the glowing rounds against the blackened sky, and watch the warhead explode into flak at the end of its flight. It was better than the Fourth of July. And if they were forcing the gunners to burn up a few thousand rounds of AAA ammo, well, maybe they were accomplishing something.

Robinson argued for dropping the whole idea of Night Misty. But he got scheduled for another mission, this time with Chuck Shaheen. Making things worse, Robinson was assigned to the backseat, where he usually got sick. The two pilots took off and headed for the northwest corner of Route Pack 1, above Mu Ghia Pass. As they were approaching the pass, their trusty F-100 suddenly belched fire from every orifice, accompanied by a startling *bang!* It felt like the plane had blown up. The concussion was so powerful that it knocked Shaheen's feet off the rudder pedals.

As they regained their composure, the pilots analyzed the gauges. Most of the ones that monitored engine performance were pegged in the full hot position. The FIRE WARNING and OVERHEAT lights were also illuminated. Shaheen retarded the throttle, which brought the EGT, exhaust gas temperature, off the peg on the gauge. That might keep the engine from burning up, but it also put the plane into a gradual descent—the reduced power couldn't sustain level flight.

Shaheen headed for the nearest base—Nakhon Phanom, in Thailand—and turned his transponder to EMERGENCY, so the radar sites would know immediately that his plane had a problem. They were gradually losing altitude, though, and it didn't look like they were going to make it. Robinson called the ABCCC from the backseat to tell them he thought they were going to eject. At that moment Robinson saw a karst peak flash by the right wing in the darkness. They were below the mountaintops. Robinson started to feel certain they were going to die. Then he thought of something. "Chuck," he shouted, "have you tried the afterburner?" In the excitement, both of them had forgotten about one of the airplane's most basic and useful functions. Shaheen pushed the throttle outboard into afterburner. It lit with a roar. The aircraft started to climb.

Things were looking better. If they had to eject, they might be able to do it over Thailand, friendly territory. And there was still a chance they might land the bird. As they flew toward NKP with the fire-warning lights still glowing, Robinson called the tower.

The main runway, it turned out, was closed for repairs. They could land on the taxiway, the controller told them, but it was a narrow shot: just 50 feet wide and 5,000 feet long, less space than most jets needed to land. Plus, there was no barrier at the end. If they overshot, they'd end up in the boonies, where the landing gear might snag in the soft ground and send the aircraft cartwheeling.

"Do you think you can land it?" Robinson asked from the backseat.

"I don't know, but I'm going to try," Shaheen answered. "If it looks bad, we can always bail out."

They approached NKP at about 20,000 feet. Shaheen figured the engine would conk out once he came out of afterburner, which meant he'd probably have to land without any power. That would put them in a dangerous no-man's-land. If they overshot the runway, the plane wouldn't be able to climb out for a second pass—but they'd be too low to bail out. They'd have to hit it exactly right. It would be a risky procedure in daylight, under optimal conditions. Doing it at night on a short runway came with odds neither of them wanted to think about. But for the moment it seemed preferable to jumping out.

As they began landing preparations and turned toward the runway, Robinson became concerned. "We're too high! We're too high!" he shouted. Then he backed off, realizing he probably wasn't helping Shaheen concentrate. "Do you want me to shut up?" he asked.

"No, keep talking," Shaheen said. "If it doesn't look good to you, you can bail out anytime you feel we're in deep shit." Shaheen was running different scenarios through his mind. They'd need the drag chute to slow them down. If the chute malfunctioned and didn't deploy, he planned to collapse the landing gear and skid down the taxiway on the belly of the plane—anything to avoid tumbling into the weeds.

They did everything they could to slow the plane as it descended toward the taxiway, but were still going 20 knots too fast as they crossed the threshold where the pavement began. Robinson quickly calculated that at that speed they'd need an extra two thousand feet of runway. He prepared for a crash landing. Shaheen muscled the jet down onto the taxiway, deployed the drag chute, and tapped the brakes, being careful not to blow the tires. It seemed like a miracle: They stopped with room to spare.

Fire trucks raced up to the plane. Both pilots were shaking when they climbed out of the aircraft. A stream of engine parts littered the pavement behind them. They made their way to the officers club, which was open twenty-four hours, and celebrated life. "Fuck this Night Misty shit," Shaheen opined after guzzling a drink. Robinson agreed.

When maintenance crews inspected the bird, they found that the engine had shed a compressor blade, which flew backward and wrecked the rest of the engine. The jolt the pilots felt had been a compressor stall—a disruption in the proper air-fuel mix in the combustion chamber that caused the fuel to ignite in front of the combustion chamber, sending flames out the front and back of the engine. They had literally been riding an explosion. It was remarkable that they had been able to stay airborne. That old Pratt & Whitney J-57 was one tough engine, Shaheen thought. It might buckle and shed parts, but it would usually get you home.

———

Colonel Schneider, the Wing King, whom many Mistys considered Enemy No. 2—right after the communists—had finally headed out the door. His tour at Phu Cat was over. Most of the Mistys bid Schneider good riddance. They thought he had been unsupportive of Misty and in fact viewed him as being an obstructionist. But Stan Mamlock had a different perspective. He liked and respected Schneider. They were old veteran fighter pilots and friends. Mamlock, who was due to rotate out himself as Misty commander, had cut a deal with Schneider when he took over the unit. "Keep your distance," he told the boss, "and let me run Misty. I'll keep them under control. If I screw up, fire me." Schneider said he would—but he had also lived up to his end of the bargain and given Mamlock a long leash.

A lot of bullet holes had made their mark during his tenure, but Mamlock didn't lose any airplanes. Schneider had never been persuaded of Misty's usefulness—he still thought the unit consisted mainly of undisciplined, out-of-control cowboys who took unnecessary chances. But he had kept his hands off the unit. "Schneider was a smart guy," Mamlock told his pilots. "I liked him and he stayed out of my hair. He was a good shit." Chuck Shaheen had some pungent words of disagreement, but Mamlock had old-head status and had earned the respect of all the Mistys as a competent commander who flew the tough missions with them. They gave careful thought to what he had said. During deliberations at the O club, a majority conceded that Schneider, more or less, had been right—he had been walking a fine line between "supporting" the unit and trying to keep the Mistys alive.

Schneider's replacement was Col. Leroy Manor, a no-bullshit fighter pilot who had flown in World War II and Korea. Manor wasn't about to get outflanked by Misty, or any other upstarts, but he also took a serious interest in the mission and vowed to support the unit. The Mistys were his boys, just like the pilots in all the other squadrons. Misty's "special relationship" with 7th Air Force didn't bother him at all—he alone was responsible for their success or failure, he said. After a year of bickering with higher headquarters, it was a welcome change. For the first time, Misty crewmen felt like they had a "daddy" on base and were a respected part of the wing.

Still, Manor had heard plenty of stories about the wild young captains in Misty, uninhibited hotshots like Chuck "the Arab" Shaheen and Dick "Killer" Rutan. Manor wanted to fly with Misty—to take the measure of these precocious pilots himself—but there were informal restrictions. The Air Force didn't want any wing commanders flying over the North. Senior officers had access to highly classified information. If any were shot down, it could give enormous leverage to the North Vietnamese.

But Manor's vice wing commander, Col. Preston Hardy, was eligible to fly with Misty, and Manor sent him out to check on the fabled unit. Hardy wasn't thrilled with the idea, and neither were the Mistys. But the new Misty commander, Lt. Col. Bud Bacon, was eager to keep peace with the wing, and he grudgingly welcomed the opportunity. Another new Misty, Capt. Dave Jenny, drew the short straw and was slated to be Hardy's driver.

Jenny was a broad-shouldered, humorous young captain with dark brown hair and a receding hairline. He grew up in South Carolina and got his Air Force commission from the Citadel. He had flown the F-101 air-defense interceptor before heading for Vietnam and had relatively few hours in the F-100. During the preflight briefing he and Hardy viewed each other suspiciously, despite the patina of civility.

Hardy had little familiarity with the Misty role over North Vietnam, and Jenny concentrated on cockpit procedures. He wanted to make sure there were no basic misunderstandings in the event of an emergency. Jenny reemphasized the ground rules for an ejection: "Now, Colonel, if we take a hit and have to jump out, I'll try to get us to the water, or the mountains, whichever is closer. I'll jettison our tanks and rocket pods and try to hit afterburner and climb. Since you don't go north very often, I'll handle all the radios." Hardy's eyes got wider as the briefing went on. "If it looks like we're going to have to get out of the airplane and we have time to talk, I'll use the words 'eject' or 'ejection.' If I want you to go, I'll use the term 'Bailout! Bailout! Bailout!' Any questions?" Hardy said no. The two headed for the airplane.

As they entered the Pack, Jenny marked some targets on a truck park north of Dong Hoi, along the coast, for several flights of fighters. They flew for four and a half hours and refueled twice. The last flight they worked consisted of two Marine F-4s. They were attracting a good deal of AAA, although most of it was missing well off to the side and above. The gunners started to perfect their range, however, and a few rounds started to come close, one going off right in front of the cockpit. The pilots could smell the cordite from the bursting shell. Jenny was concerned and headed back to his tanker, to have the boomer look over the top and bottom of the aircraft.

The boomer said he didn't see any holes or fluid leaks, so Jenny headed back to the Pack and went back to work. Then he felt an unusual vibration in the rudder pedals. The oil pressure gauge was fluctuating slightly. Jenny knocked off the attack and headed for "feet wet" over the Gulf. He hoped it was just a gauge malfunction, but as a precaution he locked the throttle at 90 percent RPM and went minimum afterburner to climb. Over the water he turned south and headed for Da Nang, the closest base.

Suddenly his gauges showed the exhaust gas temperature climbing to over 1,000 degrees. Then he heard several loud bangs and the engine began to cough. Jenny eased the throttle back. That stopped the banging and coughing, and the exhaust temperature came down a little. But there was a serious problem. Jenny thought he better tell Hardy to stow everything and prepare to eject.

"What did you say, and what is that noise?" Hardy demanded. His voice seemed to have risen an octave. Jenny told him that he thought the engine was failing and repeated that they should "prepare to eject."

In an instant Jenny heard a loud *bam!* It got windy. When Hardy had heard the word "eject," he went, leaving Jenny in a 400-knot convertible.

"Holy shit," Jenny thought. "What am I going to tell Leroy Manor when I land this aircraft without his vice commander?" Misty was under Manor's scrutiny to start with, and now Jenny had just dumped his main man in the Gulf.

Jenny told the ABCCC to mark his position because his back-seater had just jumped out. ABCCC asked his intentions. Jenny said he intended to land and asked for a vector to the nearest base. But about that time, the Hun gave up the ghost—the engine quit and Jenny punched out.

Jenny and Hardy ended up only twelve miles apart in the water. A Jolly Green helicopter picked Hardy up out of the water and the pilot asked him what he was flying. Hardy told him an F-100. The Jolly pilot was a Coast Guard officer on an exchange tour with the Air Force, and he wasn't yet familiar with Misty and their two-seat F-100s. He knew the Hun as a single-seater, so he headed off for Da Nang without looking for another pilot. About twenty minutes later, Hardy asked if they had heard anything from his front-seater. The Jolly pilot, fearing he had left Jenny bobbing in the Gulf, did a rapid about-face and went back to look for him.

Jenny, however, had already been fished out. A helicopter from the USS *Camden* had heard his beeper, picked him up, and taken him back to the ship. The ship's captain was an F-8 Crusader fighter jock doing his boat tour, and after Jenny got a quick medical exam, the two had a great time swapping war stories. The Catholic chaplain suggested they break out the "mission whiskey," reserved for special occasions. A bottle appeared, and Jenny wondered for a moment how he would explain booze in his bloodstream to Doc Echenberg, who would surely give him a thorough checkup when he got back to Phu Cat. The captain got on the horn and called 7th Air Force in Saigon to tell them the *Camden* had just rescued an Air Force pilot from the Gulf. Did they want him back? Jenny hoped they wouldn't ask Leroy Manor.

Jenny was able to call home from the ship. He wanted to let his family know what had happened before they read about it in the paper. His dad told him he sounded a little drunk.

When he got back to Phu Cat, he talked to the maintenance guys about the plane. Jenny assumed they had taken some AAA hits that damaged the engine, but he learned that the mechanics had serviced the bird with an inordinate amount of oil after the previous flight. The best guess was that they had blown a main engine seal and the Hun had just run out of oil and burned up. The J-57 engine in the Hun, unlike many others, would run a long time without oil, but not long enough to get Jenny to Da Nang.

For a couple of days everybody at Misty held their breath, waiting to see if Colonel Manor was going to clamp down on the unit. Jenny heard nothing. The incident was classified as a mechanical failure, not a combat loss, which may have kept the boss calm. Whatever the case, nobody asked, and Manor more or less left Misty alone.

The unit continued to follow its own rules. Bud Bacon, the new Misty commander, was intrigued with the idea of Night Misty. The pilots who had flown at night were ready to give it up and told him it was a waste of time. But Bacon wanted to see for himself. Bacon had known some of the Mistys before he got to Phu Cat. He had been an English professor at the Air Force Academy, where Lanny Lancaster and P. K. Robinson were his students. And Bacon had flown F-100s with Chuck Shaheen in England.

Shaheen was violently opposed to any more Misty night flights. But Bacon insisted, and since Shaheen had flown as many night missions as anybody else, Bacon scheduled a flight with him.

Forcing Shaheen to do something he didn't want to brought Bacon a tinge of satisfaction. He and Shaheen had worked together at RAF Lakenheath in England and didn't particularly like each other. Their personalities were dramatically different. Bacon was a proficient straight arrow likely to become a general. Shaheen loved to fly, but had decided early on that a military career wasn't for him. He had no military future to worry about and was always on the edge of trouble, pushing the envelope. Since he had no points to earn with Bacon, he decided to make the nighttime checkout as uncomfortable as possible.

They took off for the Pack with Shaheen in the front seat and Bacon in back. When they found the inevitable night traffic, Shaheen began to circle above clusters of truck headlights. The ground gunners started firing wildly at the aircraft noise. Shaheen helped them out, craftily reaching down and turning on the aircraft's exterior lights. The AAA quickly zeroed in on the Hun. Then Shaheen turned the lights back off.

"Damn, this is dangerous," said Bacon. "I didn't think the AAA would be able to find us at night."

"Yessir, it is dangerous," replied Shaheen. "I don't know how those sonofabitches do it."

On their way to the tanker, while skirting thunderstorms and lightning, Shaheen took off his oxygen mask and lit up a smoke. "Put out that cigarette!" Bacon demanded. "Do you want to blow us up? Shaheen, I'm going to have your ass!"

"Just trying to calm my nerves," the Arab chuckled. "This night flying is stressful." What the hell is he going to do, Shaheen thought—send me to North Vietnam to get shot at? They landed back at Phu Cat with no further incidents. But that was the end of Night Misty.

The daytime war was mushrooming anyway, and Misty was calling in some strikes that dwarfed the BDA reported by the unit in earlier days. There were so many targets that sometimes it was hard to decide between them—trucks, SAMs, bridges, ammo dumps, boats, artillery pieces firing across the DMZ into the South. On a single day in May, Lanny Lancaster, John Overlock, and several other Mistys were so busy destroying trucks that they didn't even get around to calling in fighters on some fuel storage drums Charlie Summers had found until it was nearly dark. When they did attack the fuel dump, flames burned so bright that they were able to keep bombing the valley well into the night. Lancaster and Overlock went to the tanker five times and were continuously airborne for eight hours, a Misty record.

A week later, in sketchy weather, the same pair directed strikes against two SAMs in one day—missiles were no longer a rarity. On another mission, P. K. Robinson and Charlie Summers came across a SAM that was well camouflaged near Bat Lake and called in fighters that blew it up. Then Summers, who had the best eyes in the unit, saw something that looked like rocks. They called in a few fighters, and the rocks produced explosions that seemed to light up all of Route Pack 1. They figured it was an ammunition dump and kept calling in fighters until nightfall. On July 1, John Overlock discovered another ammo dump that became a two-day project. The inferno was bigger than anything most of the pilots had ever seen. There was a mammoth explosion about every fifteen minutes, and thousands of secondary explosions that seemed to occur almost constantly. On the third day, Charlie Summers flew by bright and early and saw twelve trucks parked right in the middle of a charred bare spot that had been covered by triple-canopy jungle the day before. Charlie strafed them to scatter the drivers and then called for fighters. Misty added another twelve trucks to its tally.

All the successful strikes generated enthusiasm and the impression that they were making a difference in the war. Several of the pilots started asking to extend their tours at Misty. The experienced guys had a good handle on the intricacies of the Trail network, situational awareness that would take weeks for replacements to develop.

That was all true. Misty was a decisive factor that helped win many battles in Route Pack 1. But there were also plenty of indications that the fight for the Trail had become a losing cause—all of the damaged planes, the shootdowns, the huge amount of time and the fleets of aircraft dedicated to rescuing pilots instead of working the Trail. Misty saw all this up close—too close, in fact. The malaise and indecision that surrounded the war in Washington and Saigon hadn't yet engulfed Phu Cat. In fact, for fighter pilots, Misty was spectacular, exhilarating work, the greatest flying most of them had ever experienced. Besides, with AAA getting hotter, SAMs coming online, and aircraft losses mounting, there weren't a lot of new volunteers for the unit. So Dick Rutan, Charlie Summers, Lanny Lancaster, P. K. Robinson, and Wells Jackson were all allowed to stay with the unit beyond the four-month deadline, until they reached one hundred missions.

The seasoned Mistys got to know some of the terrain in Route Pack 1 almost as if they were grunts walking the ground. But there was one target they could never figure out. The Disappearing River, as the Mistys called it, was actually a cave mouth at the end of the Song Troc, at the eastern edge of the mountains that rose toward the Laotian border. The Song Troc "disappeared" because it flowed into the cave, beneath the vertical face of a karst mountain, and nobody could tell where, or if, it emerged.

Several miles north of Mu Ghia Pass, Route 101 split off from the main artery of the Ho Chi Minh Trail and wound down through a valley on the North Vietnamese side of the border. It crossed the Song

Troc about three miles east of the cave. The road had been cleared all the way up to the water's edge, on both sides of the river—but no bridge was visible. The river was too big to be forded on foot, so the Mistys guessed that at night or during bad weather, the North Vietnamese used a pontoon bridge, ferry, or boat to move traffic across the river—and hid it inside the cave.

The river was stoutly defended by 37mm and 57mm AAA guns—more evidence that the cave housed something important. Mistys had put in multiple strikes against the cave, trying to collapse the mouth or get a bomb inside. It seemed impossible. The mountain that loomed over the cave was so high and steep that pilots had to pull up way before they could coax their bombs into the opening. The cliff face was scarred with the pockmarks of bombs flung by pilots who had pickled their ordnance too late, when they were climbing away from the mountain. Other bombs fell short, the pilots eager to get out before they crashed into the mountain.

The AAA made a one-in-a-thousand shot even less likely. Mick Greene had once directed an F-105 with a "Bullpup" optically guided missile against the cave opening, hoping the missile's ability to be steered might help get a hit. The Bullpup was a powered missile with a 250-pound warhead that the pilot guided to its mark by using a joystick inside the cockpit. The missile had flares on the back that helped the pilot keep it in sight. It was the best weapon available for a target that had to be struck horizontally, near ground level. But to steer the missile accurately, the pilot had to fly a straight, steady flight path and keep the flares in sight all the way to impact. This made him predictable and vulnerable to ground gunners.

The game F-105 driver, hoping to tally a target that had eluded every other fighter jock who had tried to go after it, went into a shallow dive and launched the missile several miles away from the cave opening. All went well for about three seconds as the pilot carefully maneuvered the Bullpup straight in toward the cave mouth. Then the AAA gunners caught on to the attack. A few guns opened up at first. "Misty, I'm picking up some ground fire," the pilot reported. Then some more guns started firing. The 105 driver started to sound nervous, and his voice took on a higher pitch. "Hey, they're shooting pretty heavy," he informed Greene. Then it looked as if every gun on the mountain was trained on the 105 and firing as rapidly as possible. Suddenly it looked like a kamikaze mission. A soprano voice came over the radio. "Misty, I'm aborting and getting the hell out of here!" the pilot squealed. "This is suicide!" Greene agreed. As the pilot pulled up, the Bullpup went out of control, crashing into the weeds amidst the detritus of hundreds of other wasted bombs and missiles.

In mid-July, P. K. Robinson was giving a new Misty, Don Harlan, one of his checkout rides when they heard the unmistakable sound of a parachute beacon: *Chirrrrp, chirrrrp, chirrrrp.* They looked down at their RMI, the radio magnetic indicator gauge, which helped pinpoint the direction of an emergency transmitter. The needle was pointing directly at the Disappearing River.

As Robinson and Harlan approached the distinctive landmark, the downed pilot came up on the voice frequency. "Mayday! Mayday!" he barked. "This is Panda 01!" That was good news—the pilot, call sign Panda 01, was alive and conscious. Robinson made contact with his wingman to learn what he could. The wingman was almost out of fuel and had to depart, leaving the rescue effort in Misty's hands. He told Robinson where he thought his buddy had landed: smack on top of the karst wall that towered over the Disappearing River.

On one hand the pilot was lucky. A bit more wind while he was descending would have blown him straight into the valley below, where the river flowed into the cave. He would have been captured immediately. But all those guns down in the valley protecting the contents of the cave made the skies above a shooting gallery. A rescue there would be one tough proposition.

It was late afternoon and the light was fading, but the best chance to get Panda out was to do it quickly, before the gunners got oriented and figured out what was going on. The rescue crews were already on their way. Robinson called the ABCCC and requested all available fighters. He and Harlan started putting in some strikes on the gun sites they knew about—several of which were already firing.

The Misty jet needed gas and had started to head to the tanker when the ABCCC called. They could divert some fully loaded F-105s to the Disappearing River, but the Thuds were low on fuel and couldn't loiter. They'd need to drop quickly. Robinson was getting desperate for gas by then—but the downed pilot was desperate for the bombs from the 105s.

Robinson decided there was no choice but to get back on station and hope his gas held out, since the inbound 105s had no idea where the pilot was and couldn't drop without a mark. They called the tanker and asked them to stay as far north as possible. "Roger, Misty," the pilot responded. "We've been listening on frequency. We'll come to you."

Harlan and Robinson hurriedly rolled in and marked some gun sites with a smoke rocket. They told the 105s to hit the smoke, but to avoid hitting the karst at all costs. The Thuds got the picture. Then Misty pulled off the marking run and headed for the tanker, running on fumes. The tanker was supposed to fly in a racetrack pattern thirty miles offshore to make sure it was out of the range of North Vietnamese antiaircraft defenses. Robinson's gauges showed that he had only 400 pounds of fuel remaining—and the gauges were unreliable under 500 pounds. A flameout could occur at any time. Robinson told Harlan that if they were lucky they might make it "feet wet," but that they probably wouldn't make it to the tanker. Harlan's heart was pounding, but he was a quiet, good-natured guy and kept his worry to himself—it felt like even the tiniest bleep from his mouth might distract his copilot and cost the final drop of fuel that might get them to the tanker. Robinson got on the radio. "Misty is headed out!" he bleated into the microphone. "EMERGENCY FUEL!"

The tanker radioed back with some of the most welcome words Robinson had ever heard. "Roger Misty," the pilot reassured him. "We've been listening. We're at your twelve o'clock position, five miles." This put the tanker over the coastline of North Vietnam, some thirty miles north and west of where it was allowed to be. The tanker was also in SAM country and about as vulnerable as a plane could be—huge and unmaneuverable, with a bellyful of gas. Robinson slid into the refueling position with the needle reading slightly below 200 pounds. He wasn't breathing, but he was praying. With his feet shaking on the rudder pedals, he delicately slid the refueling probe into the tanker basket on the first try—there might not be another. The Hun began to gulp gas. They filled up and headed back to the Disappearing River. "Ain't Misty fun?" Robinson teased Harlan once the tension had lifted.

The scene at the Disappearing River was discouraging, however. The SAR forces, search-and-rescue, had been shot up and were returning to base. It was getting too dark to continue. Robinson talked to Panda on the radio and told him the news. Panda sounded okay. Robinson assured him they'd be back at first light. As Robinson was about to leave the area, ABCCC called to let him know that two F-4s would be dropping some cluster bombs north of the pilot, well clear of his position. No problem, Robinson replied. But when he glanced over his shoulder to check out the strike, he saw antipersonnel bomblets exploding over a wide circle—including the karst on which Panda 01 was bedding down. The CBU canister had malfunctioned and opened early. "CEASE FIRE! CEASE FIRE!" Robinson screamed into the radio. Then he called Panda again to see if he was okay. He was. Agitated and leery, Robinson and Harlan finally returned to Phu Cat.

Nobody had ever envisioned that it would become such a significant part of their job, but by the summer of 1968 the Mistys had become experts at orchestrating rescues. Robinson knew that Panda was in a tough spot, hemmed in by some of the most dense AAA in North Vietnam. Getting him out would take planning, determination, and luck. And one other thing, he decided: the best fliers available. There were guns protecting the roads, the cave, the river crossing, and who knew what else, creating overlapping arcs of fire. Getting down low enough in the valley to drop accurately while working around the karst mountain added another dimension to the difficulty. Robinson personally called the Ops officers at the various bases that would be involved in the effort the next morning, telling them that this was a job for the first team. Bud Bacon finally told him to go to bed. P. K. would be flying the first mission in the morning, with Bud in the backseat.

They took off before sunrise as Misty 11. Lanny Lancaster and Steve Amdor were the next sortie, Misty 21. The plan was for Lancaster to fly directly to the tanker, top off, and be ready to relieve Robinson. Then they'd cycle on and off the tanker, so that one of them would always be controlling the rescue, and stay as long as it took.

It was clear and calm near the Disappearing River, with no ground fog—unusual for the Pack. Robinson checked with Panda. He was up and ready.

Most rescue efforts were convoluted affairs, with a lot of improvisation, rushing, waiting, and unexpected problems. And even though

Robinson had called for the best sticks available, he could see that there was plenty that could go wrong. The gun sites that had been hit the previous day were reconstituted and active. One new AAA battery was visible, and there were probably others. Robinson was pumped, but he also knew the day could end with the same frustration the Disappearing River had dealt out on many other missions.

He called the ABCCC and told them Panda was ready to go. It was time to bring on the fighters and start killing the guns so the helicopter could come in and get Panda out. Usually there was a delay while the controllers lined up the fighters, but the ABCCC told Robinson there were three flights of F-105s, four aircraft each—a total of twelve planes—stacked up and waiting for targets. Robinson checked with the first flight of F-105s, call sign Bull.

"Say position," Robinson squawked over the radio.

"Bull's at 20,000 feet," came the response. "Have you and the target area in sight. We're ready for your mark."

The fighters had already lined themselves up for the strike, without any direction from Misty. "Wow!" Robinson said to Bacon. "This IS the first team!"

Robinson began marking, then stood off and watched the show. One after another the fighters flew in, with the efficiency of a team that had practiced together all season and was ready for the playoffs. There was minimal radio chatter or fussing, and little break between bombing runs. The bombs were accurate, too. The Thuds had silenced most of the gun sites before Robinson and Bacon had to refuel even once.

By the time Misty 11 flew to the tanker and Misty 21 took over, the challenge was no longer the big AAA batteries, but smaller, single guns scattered throughout the valley. The stream of fighters continued unabated for a couple of hours, and a steady flow of bombs rained down around the Disappearing River.

Finally, Robinson couldn't see any gun sites remaining. He made low, trolling passes over the area and failed to draw any fire. It was time to call in the Sandys, who would take over from Misty as the "on-scene" rescue commanders, and the Jollys. The rescue package was supposed to be circling over the border, in Laos, twenty minutes' flying time away. Robinson hoped the wait wouldn't give the NVA enough time to sneak in additional guns.

Robinson called the SAR forces and was about to ask their estimated time of arrival when two A-1 Sandys burst over the top of the karst above the cave, right over the pilot, and dived into the Disappearing River valley. They had obviously been listening and took it upon themselves to get a head start on the border crossing.

The Sandys buzzed through the valley like angry hornets. There was no ground fire, and the Jolly lumbered onto the scene. Immediately it settled into a hover over the downed pilot. To Robinson and Bacon it looked like a blimp floating over the karst. Robinson fully expected to see the Jolly explode in flames at any minute, but there was still no visible ground fire.

Suddenly a stream of tracers erupted from a clump of bushes just across the river from the Jolly. The tracers arced directly at the helicopter. "GUN FIRING! GUN FIRING!" everyone shouted into the radio at once. One of the Sandys, who was just north of the gun, rolled in on it from 1,000 feet. The pilot put himself directly between the gun and the helicopter to distract the shooter. Tracers from the gun bracketed him on both sides. The Sandy dived right down the stream of bullets, firing his 20mm cannons and 2.75-inch rockets straight into the gun. It was a pure, mano a mano dogfight: one gun, one plane, both firing as furiously as they could and hoping not to be the first to die. The Sandy's rockets totally enveloped the site, but the ground fire continued. The Sandy strafed all the way down the chute until he was only a couple of hundred feet above the gun. Then he dropped his cluster bomblets, which smothered the site. When the Sandy pulled up he was just a few feet off the ground—and finally the gun was silent.

Robinson and others watching from above felt like they had stopped breathing for ten seconds while the showdown unfolded. It was one of the most remarkable things any of them had ever seen. The Sandy had made himself the target in order to spare the Jolly. The NVA gunner had stood his ground, too, an astounding show of courage considering that every other gun in the valley had been blown to bits. If it had been sport, both men would have stood up, dusted themselves off, and shaken hands after knocking each other down. But one of them was dead.

A voice broke in over the radio. "Jolly's got the pilot!" the helicopter commander shouted. "We're egressing west!" The Sandys broke off and flew in a protective wheel around the Jolly as they left the area. The rescue was complete.

Robinson was elated. He performed a victory roll over the Disappearing River. As he took one last look at the area before departing, he saw clusters of bomb craters where the gun sites had been. Every structure in the area was charred. Wisps of smoke snaked up out of every clump of foliage. They had knocked out all the defensive forces around the Disappearing River—for a day. The whole effort, involving dozens of airplanes flying for several hours, did nothing to slow the flow of supplies down the Trail. But it felt like success.

TWENTY-FIVE

"YOUR WAR IS OVER"

By the end of July, Charlie Summers had flown his one hundredth mission and added a couple of extras. That had taken just over five months—nearly twice as much flying as some of the earlier Mistys had done. Dick Rutan and P. K. Robinson figured that if all went well, they'd hit 100 sometime in August. Rutan wanted to push a bit further, maybe get 115 or 120 missions and firmly set the Misty record. Lanny Lancaster expected he'd hit the 100 mark in September, and that Wells Jackson would later in the fall.

With increasing regularity, however, the Mistys were seeing signs that their longevity was only theoretical. Dick Rutan was in the backseat one day in late July with Don Harlan, who was still fairly new to Misty. Rutan was giving him some pointers. They had just refueled over the Gulf and were heading back toward the Pack when they heard a Mayday call from Strobe 10, an RF-4C reconnaissance jet.

The RF-4C was an F-4 with cameras instead of guns. It had replaced the RF-101 as the main reconnaissance aircraft in the war. Their missions yielded important photographic intelligence, and the Mistys used their photos regularly for target study. Like the Mistys, the "recce birds," as they were called, carried a two-man crew and flew "solo"—

without a wingman. "Alone, Unarmed and Unafraid" was their motto. Rutan suggested a variation: "Alone, Unarmed and Scared Shitless," just like the Mistys occasionally.

As Rutan and Harlan listened on the radio, Strobe 10 said he was coming out of North Vietnam toward the coast, just above the DMZ. The plane had taken a hit and there was smoke coming into the rear cockpit. It was losing hydraulic pressure and was heading feet wet. Rutan determined that he and Harlan were nearby, and as the senior pilot on board, he took the controls from the backseat and plugged in the afterburner to catch up with Strobe 10. Finally they saw the plane, and the two Mistys slid into close formation on Strobe's wing. They were a few miles out over the water, heading south, parallel to the coast. Strobe said he was going to try to make it to Da Nang.

Don Harlan was the first to notice a tiny flame flickering in a small hole in the aircraft's belly. They pulled in closer and could see smoke seeping out of the seams in the belly. They relayed the news to Strobe. The pilots were silent for a moment. Then Strobe 10 acknowledged the fire and said they were going to bail out.

Rutan and Harlan backed away to give Strobe room. They were flying at 10,000 feet and less than 300 knots, ideal conditions for an ejection. Rutan had never seen an ejection up close and personal and thought it would be fascinating to watch. As the smoke increased, however, nothing happened, and Rutan started to wonder what the hell the crew was waiting for. Finally the rear canopy opened and split away from the aircraft, clearing the tail by twenty feet. Then the backseat started up the rails and the rocket motor ignited, propelling the seat straight up in the air. When the rocket stopped, the seat's drogue chute came out and the seat rotated backward 90 degrees, leaving the pilot facing straight up into the heavens. Looking back over his shoulder, Rutan could see the parachute canopy open as the seat separated and fell toward the water. The crewman swung like a charm on a necklace. Picture-perfect, thought Rutan.

But as he looked back to the RF-4, he couldn't believe what he saw. In just the few seconds it had taken for the back-seater to eject, the front cockpit had become totally engulfed in fire. The front canopy was still attached to the plane, and the only thing they could see through the inferno was the white dot of the pilot's helmet. It looked to Rutan and Harlan like a huge blowtorch was shooting flames up out of the cockpit floor. The flames surrounded the pilot, then vented into the rear cockpit and up into the open air, streaming over the tail of the plane. A plume of dense black smoke trailed behind.

Most horrifying, the pilot was sitting straight up, motionless, as if oblivious to the immolation. Without the flames, it would have looked like he was calmly enjoying a casual ride. Rutan began to scream into the radio: "Strobe 10, bail out!! Bail out!!" The aircraft started a shallow descent. "My God, look at it burn!" Rutan shouted to Harlan. He pulled in close to the burning aircraft and screamed "Bail out!" again, as if being closer and yelling louder would make a difference.

From close up they could see that the intense heat had charred Strobe's canopy. The pilot's helmet was no longer visible. The plane's paint began to blister, and there were a few small explosions that blew some of the panels off the crippled jet. The whole nose became a charcoaled mess and the plane tipped over into a dive.

Even as it became apparent that the RF-4 was about to crash, Rutan flew close by. The plane, unpiloted now, had turned back toward land, and from an altitude of about 500 feet it finally dived into the beach, about one hundred yards in from the water. Suddenly it was Harlan who started yelling. "Goddamn it, Dick, pull up! Pull up!" he shouted. Rutan had been so intent on following Strobe that, without his copilot's warning, he might have hit the beach right beside Strobe.

Rutan pulled up. Then he called in the sad news about Strobe. A moment later a question came back. Was there any chance of survival? "Negative survival," Rutan replied, his voice heavy with dejection. "Negative survival."

They turned around to check on the back-seater in the water. Rutan noticed an unusual amount of radio chatter about securing Strobe's crash area and dispatching a medevac helicopter to it. He had seen a lot of combat crashes, and once it was reported that there were no survivors, rescue efforts normally ceased. It seemed odd that there was so much interest in this particular crash site.

Harlan and Rutan quickly caught sight of the back-seater, who was still in his parachute about 5,000 feet above the Gulf of Tonkin. The sea was rough, with big waves and lots of foam. They saw a motorized sampan heading out from the beach, obviously aiming for the back-seater. They made a low pass. The boat contained three or four people and was flying what looked like a South Vietnamese flag. But they weren't sure. Unable to tell whether the boat was friendly or hostile, they decided they couldn't take any chances.

Harlan was back at the controls and he made another pass, very low this time, right across the craft's bow. That did nothing to dissuade the men in the boat, who continued on their course. The pilot's parachute was getting close to the water, and they had to do something. "Well, should we kill them?" Harlan asked. Rutan suggested that they make a firing pass in front of the boat. Harlan placed a long burst of 20mm in the water right in front of the boat, just as the back-seater was hitting the water. That did the trick. The boat made a sharp turn and headed back to shore. A Jolly Green arrived after a while and plucked the pilot out of the roiling seas.

Harlan and Rutan headed back to work in the Pack. They hit the tanker once more and headed home to Phu Cat. As they were taxiing in after landing, they saw a sea of colonels waiting on the ramp. "I don't know what we've done," Rutan said, perplexed, "but it must have been a doozy."

As the engine was winding down, the first colonel up the ladder yelled over the noise in an angry voice, "What are you doing here? You should have landed at Saigon!" Then he asked about Strobe 10.

Yes, it was awful, Rutan said. And he had a cockpit voice tape of the whole thing. The colonel's eyes widened and he grabbed the tape recorder from Rutan's hand. The two pilots climbed down the aircraft ladder totally bewildered. "What the fuck is going on?" Rutan asked.

"It was General Bob Worley," the colonel said, handing the recorder back to Rutan. "Get in a blue uniform and pack a bag. A T-39 will be here in thirty minutes to take you both to Saigon. They want you to brief the generals."

Worley was the vice commander at 7th Air Force, Momyer's No. 2. Suddenly all the fuss made sense. Generals rarely flew into the North, no matter how badly they may have wanted to. It was risky putting such senior commanders, with their deep knowledge of the whole war effort, over hostile territory. The two Mistys quickly realized they'd be on center stage down in Saigon. On the ride there, Rutan listened to the tape. It was a good thing he did. In his frustration over losing an-

other comrade, he had lambasted the war effort and the generals running it. He decided to do some careful editing. It wouldn't be hard to
believe that the recorder had frittered out under the stress of a Misty
ride.

In Saigon it seemed that every general wanted his own private briefing. Rutan and Harlan played their tape over and over. Unlike some of
the brass, Worley had a reputation as a roll-up-your-sleeves warrior
who on any given day would prefer to fly a combat mission than tend
to the administrative details of command. He would have fit right in at
Misty. Rutan and Harlan learned that after several combat missions in
Vietnam, that reconnaissance flight was scheduled to be Worley's last
ride before transferring out of the theater to another job. He had volunteered to fly and didn't have to be over North Vietnam that day. Just
like a lot of others.

———

During the second week of August there was a farewell party for John
Haltigan, the intel officer who had been with Misty almost since the
beginning. The pilots and commanders came and went every four or
five months, but over his one-year tour Haltigan had seen Misty grow
from a back-of-the-envelope outfit with no resources and experimental
tactics to one of the most sophisticated operations in 7th Air Force. In
the summer of 1967, when he had arrived, Misty was obscure and
poorly understood. A year later it was legendary—or at least notorious. Haltigan had made some wonderful friends, lost one of them—
Bob Craner—to the North Vietnamese, and experienced heartbreak
and elation at Misty. There were so many memorable moments, but he
thought most fondly of the day Jonesy Jones was rescued after being
shot down, and the high that came with welcoming him back.

The Mistys gave him the same kind of send-off reserved for the pilots. Everyone showed up in their Misty party suits for a steak and beer
dinner. Bud Bacon served as the master of ceremonies. There was endless ribbing, and several of the Mistys offered testimonials to how useless Haltigan's briefings had been. P. K. Robinson presented him with
a commemorative briefing wand and a card that read "Use this for
identifying AAA sites, trucks, storage areas, and blow jobs"—fighter
jocks' favorite phrase for a bureaucratic wild-goose chase. Then, in

sincerity, they told him that even though he had never flown with them, he was a Misty at heart. When Haltigan left Phu Cat a couple of days later, he wasn't sure what he had been through during his year there, but he knew it was one of the most remarkable and special experiences he would ever have.

There was another going-away party a few days later, for John Overlock, Chuck Shaheen, and P. K. Robinson, all of whom had their last flights coming up. Parties usually came after the final sortie, since nobody wanted to take the last, safe landing for granted. But this time the party came a few days early. Bud Bacon was scheduled to go away on R&R, and as commander he didn't want to miss the festivities in honor of three of his fliers. And Robinson and Overlock, old friends from earlier flying days in England, had planned a week of vacation in the Philippines right after their final missions, before they headed back to Tuy Hoa together to finish out their Vietnam tours.

There was the usual drinking, laughter, and camaraderie. The pilots told lies, kidded each other mercilessly, and relived the details of exciting missions. With three pilots to toast, there were more profane tributes than usual. Chuck Shaheen had bought some firecrackers during one of his trips to Hong Kong for party suits, and he planned to blow one off during the obligatory speech by his dear friend, Bud Bacon. He lit the fuse with a cigarette and held the tiny bomb behind his back for a few seconds, waiting for the right moment to toss it on the floor up toward the podium. But like so many other things in the war, something went wrong, and a loud *boom!* filled the room as the firecracker blew up prematurely in Shaheen's hand.

Everyone turned around to see what had happened. Shaheen stood there as innocently as he could, desperately trying to conceal the searing pain in his hand. When he thought he could duck out unobtrusively, Shaheen hurried to the restroom. A newcomer, Ted "the Pillow" Powell, came in as Shaheen was jumping up and down, soaking his burned hand under the cold water. Powell's unwanted nickname had come from Shaheen, who rode Powell relentlessly about his paunchy appearance and asked how the hell he had gotten fat on food from the Phu Cat mess hall.

"Sonofabitch that hurts!" Shaheen screamed. Powell smirked. "Hey, how about a little sympathy?" Shaheen pleaded.

"Sympathy? You want sympathy?" Powell sneered. "Okay. I'm sorry you're such a dumb fuck." Then he walked out.

The party went on late into the night. The first mission the next morning, Misty 11, would be flown by John Overlock, with Mike McElhanon in the backseat. It would be Overlock's last Misty flight. McElhanon, who had been the wing's safety officer before coming to Misty, dragged himself away from the party early and went to his trailer to write his wife, Sandy, a letter. He figured that with all the whiskey that had flowed at the party, at least someone in the cockpit should be dead sober. Overlock left the party later, around 1:00 a.m., with Chuck Shaheen, his trailermate. It was an unusually quiet night under a bright moon. The Spooky gunships weren't firing into the countryside as they so often did, and no illumination flares lit up any VC who might be lurking. The two pilots reflected on their Misty tours during the short walk back to their quarters and then tumbled into bed. Overlock would have to get up in just a few hours for the morning brief.

Misty 11 broke ground as scheduled. Four hours later Chuck Shaheen and Ted Powell took off as Misty 21, with Shaheen at the controls. As he entered the Pack, Shaheen called for Overlock in Misty 11. The Mistys habitually briefed each other on the radio to exchange information as they entered and departed the Pack. The incoming Misty would bring the latest intel, and the departing Misty would recommend where to start looking for hot targets or warn of missiles or changes in AAA locations.

But this time Overlock didn't answer. Shaheen called several more times, without raising Misty 11. Finally he called the ABCCC. "Have you heard from Misty 11?" he asked.

There had been no word from the plane for over an hour. Shaheen contacted the airborne rescue control. They had received no emergency calls from the Pack and heard no emergency beepers.

Shaheen went back to the ABCCC. "Hillsborough, what is the last time you heard from Misty 11?" he asked. "What did he say and where was he?" The info was very sparse. The last call from Misty 11 had been garbled, but they believed he had said he was headed for the tanker, which was orbiting over the Gulf. Misty 11 hadn't given a position, though.

Shaheen switched to the tanker frequency. "Have you guys heard from Misty 11 lately?" he asked.

"Negative, Misty."

"Have you heard any beepers in the last hour and a half?"

"Negative, Misty."

This was all certainly strange, but Misty 11 could have had a radio failure. Maybe they had diverted to Ubon or some other base.

Shaheen checked again with the ABCCC: "Have you checked to see if Misty 11 went into Ubon or Nakhon Phanom?"

"Roger, Misty, we've checked. He's not there. Same for Da Nang and Chu Lai. No one has seen or heard from him."

The hair on Shaheen's neck began to stand up. Things were looking grim. He switched to the rescue frequency. "Crown, Misty 21. It looks like we've got a Misty down. No one has heard from or seen him and we can't raise him on the radio."

The rescue controller confirmed that they had had no contact with Misty 11, but they had received no indication that an aircraft had gone down, either—no parachute beepers, no reports of smoke or fire, nothing suspicious. Misty 11 was simply missing.

Crown, the rescue controller, began the procedures for handling a missing aircraft. He reported the loss to the 7th Air Force command post, which then checked with Phu Cat. They called Misty Ops to find out when the aircraft's fuel would expire, how many people were on board, and the "personal authenticator" information—three personal questions to which only the downed pilot would know the answers.

Then the process flowed backward, with 7th reporting all the information to the airborne rescue coordinator. Crown then informed all pilots in the area that an aircraft was down and to be alert for beepers or other indications of a crash, and especially survivors.

Shaheen knew the process, and while he waited he climbed to high altitude to conserve fuel and get the best radio reception. He called regularly for Misty 11 and listened intently for any beeper. One chirped briefly at some point, but it lasted only a few seconds and could have come from anywhere.

P. K. Robinson eventually checked into the Pack. Like Overlock, he was on his last Misty mission. Shaheen told Robinson the gloomy news and headed back to Phu Cat. The Mistys all knew by then, and a bunch of sour faces met Shaheen on the ramp. Misty hadn't lost a plane since Jonesy Jones had been shot down four months earlier. Most of the current Mistys weren't in the unit then. And only Rutan, Lancaster, and Robinson had been at Misty when the unit last lost a pilot, Howie Williams. For all of the battle damage the planes absorbed, few of the Mistys had been around the unit for a shootdown.

The Mistys probed Shaheen for information about Overlock and McElhanon. He knew precisely nothing. P. K. Robinson returned late in the afternoon, with no new information either. It should have been his last mission hose-down, a raucous celebration of his final flight as a Misty, with champagne and lots of backslapping. Instead, he was devastated that his friend John Overlock had disappeared. Robinson's last day as a Misty was shaping up as his worst.

Nobody was in a mood to celebrate anything. They all spent the rest of the day, and much of the night, over beer, trying to figure out what had happened to the two disappearing pilots. Both were careful and mature, unlikely to dip far below allowable minimums or take foolish risks. McElhanon had been the wing safety officer and a stickler for procedure. Overlock was no cowboy, either. Wells Jackson recalled one mission when he had an urge to sneak up to Phuc Yen Airfield, far north of Route Pack 1, and strafe any MiGs that might be on the ramp. Overlock, riding with him, had talked him out of it.

The two pilots might have crashed in the water while heading to the tanker, or been downed by coastal air defenses, a SAM, or even by some kind of overwhelming aircraft failure. But if they had been that close to the tanker, they would have established radio contact—and the tanker had heard nothing from them. Plus, there were no parachute beepers. Obviously they could have gotten tagged by AAA or a SAM at low altitude, but the Hun was a durable old bird that rarely blew up. Even if hit at low altitude they should have been able to get off a Mayday call and probably eject. It was damned unlikely, but it did happen every now and then. Nobody knew. Their buddies had simply vanished into thin air. It was wrenching, but the war went on and there were new missions to plan. Besides, there was always the last-ditch hope that Overlock and McElhanon might end up as POWs and emerge once the war ended.

The following day was scheduled to be Chuck Shaheen's "champagne" flight, his final Misty mission. Dick Rutan asked to fly in his backseat. Rutan and Shaheen had attended rival high schools in California, hung out in the same places, and "chased the same fat girls," according to Rutan. He thought it would make some nice press back home for him to accompany Shaheen on his last flight. He could see the headline: LOCAL BOYS FLY LAST MISSION TOGETHER.

Shaheen was in a foul mood from the previous day's loss. But he was looking forward to his last-mission hose-down and to completing his Misty tour. They'd spend some time looking for Overlock and McElhanon, and other than that, Rutan intended to oversee a calm, easy mission in a safe area—there would be no risky stuff for Shaheen on his last mission. He'd make sure Shaheen got back in one piece. They even asked 7th to send them some single-seat F-100Ds from Phu Cat—guys who usually worked in the South—to use as their bomb-droppers. The F-100 wing at Phu Cat had several "patch-wearers"— fighter weapons school grads, experienced pros who were disciplined on the stick and accurate with their bombs. The Mistys were tired of bad bombing and figured some seasoned F-100 jocks, their buddies, could help them get some good BDA.

On their first two cycles through the Pack they stayed high, searching for any sign of Overlock and McElhanon. No luck. Near the hamlet of Quang Khe, north of Dong Hoi, they had spotted a truck parked on a road, with a small supply area nearby. As far as they knew there were no guns in that part of the valley. It was just the sort of target they were looking for. They wanted to make sure the F-100s, on their first mission up north, didn't get spooked by heavy ground fire. And the target, clearly visible, should be a piece of cake for the Huns, Rutan figured.

The plan was to top off at the tanker out over the Gulf, meet the F-100s at the target, throw in a quick mark, and watch the action as the hotshots from Phu Cat blew away the truck and the supplies. Then Shaheen would fly one last nostalgic loop over the Pack before they returned home to champagne, a hose-down, and maybe a little laughter.

With a full fuel load from the tanker, Shaheen turned back to the west. As they met the coastline, Shaheen banked, pulled, and threaded his way through the curtain of .50-caliber, ZPU, 23mm, and occasional 37mm that always greeted them as they went "feet dry" and headed inland.

Three F-100s arrived on schedule. Misty joined up with them and marked the single truck. Each Hun made three attack runs. Bombs rattled the bushes, but after nine passes, nobody had touched the truck. Shaheen decided he'd show them how to do it. He instructed them to hold high and dry while he made one final strafe pass. Then they'd all go home together. "Watch this," he said.

Rutan wondered aloud whether it was a good idea to strafe so low—especially on Shaheen's last mission. Shaheen dismissed the worry. There weren't any guns around, and despite the prohibition on low-level shooting, most of the Mistys did it anyway.

As they approached the target, Rutan told Shaheen he was flying too low and too slow. Chuck agreed and hit the afterburner to gain airspeed. They rolled in on the target and Shaheen flew down the chute, down, down, down. He wanted to make sure his last pass would not be in vain. Rutan squirmed in the back as they passed through 4,000 feet, then 3,000, then 2,000, and still Shaheen had not opened fire. Rutan would have been even more upset, except that he hadn't seen a single round of gunfire.

Shaheen finally started squeezing the trigger well below the tops of the hills. He emptied the guns. His last pass was going to be epic. He wanted to see the truck blow up before his eyes, a fitting and glorious end to his Misty career. With great satisfaction he watched his 20mm rounds completely cover the truck, then he pulled hard on the stick to avoid the karst cliff looming in front of the aircraft. "Take that, you sonofabitch!" he yelled.

At that moment it sounded like Pete Rose struck the bottom of the airplane under their feet with a baseball bat. The loud *whack!* evoked the usual response: "What the hell was that?" Then there was a whooshing sound, and in Rutan's rearview mirror all he could see was fire. They were so low he could even see the glow of the flames reflecting off the karst wall. There was no question what had happened—they had been hit by an unseen gun. As Shaheen pulled up, Rutan looked around and saw there was no good place to go to eject.

"We're on fire!" Rutan yelled.

"Mayday!" Shaheen shouted over the radio.

The Phu Cat F-100s holding in the target area told Shaheen that his plane was "torching"—fuel was leaking from the aircraft and being set on fire by the afterburner plume. Shaheen came out of afterburner and the fire went out, but he looked at his fuel gauge and it was going down rapidly. There was a big hole somewhere in the airplane. At the rate they were losing fuel, they weren't going to make it to the coast. "Shit!" snorted Shaheen as he reengaged the afterburner. He figured he'd get as much airspeed and altitude as he could out of what fuel they had left. With the afterburner engaged, the fire reappeared and they looked like a giant ball of flame streaking through the sky.

Rutan suddenly heard a "rattlesnake" sound in his headset. He looked at the instrument panel and noticed the RHAW indicator, the radar homing and warning gear that detected SAM launches, was going wild. A strobe warning light was flashing and the SAM LAUNCH light was lit up. There were four F-100s in straight and level flight cruising out to the coast—sitting ducks for a SAM—but the two pilots quickly decided they had bigger problems on their hands. Normally they would have called "SAM break!" and bolted for the deck to out-maneuver the missile. But with practically no fuel for any fancy flying, they just turned off the RHAW gear and flew straight ahead.

They made it feet wet and were preparing to eject just as the engine quit. The Hun was now a glider, and their best hope was for a smooth water landing in their chutes. They were about ten miles offshore, if they were lucky, at about 10,000 feet. Rutan pulled up his ejection handles and the canopy blew off the airplane. Shaheen heard the blast and the whoosh of the backseat departing. Shaheen followed. One of the other F-100 pilots thought about shooting down the pilotless air-plane as it drifted toward the sea, figuring that would make him the only American pilot in Vietnam with an F-100 "kill." But he thought better of it and watched the two parachutes all the way to the water.

For some reason Shaheen began to tumble violently through the air. He spread his arms, which stabilized his fall, but the automatic-opening parachute hadn't opened automatically. So he pulled the D-ring and his canopy blossomed. The rest of his descent was textbook perfect. He searched the water for enemy boats and didn't see any. As he touched the waves, he pulled his parachute quick releases and settled gently into the warm water, not even getting his helmet wet. God, this is easy! he thought. Then he thought about sharks and clambered into the life raft that had popped out of his survival kit.

As he was drifting down in his parachute, Rutan looked around for Shaheen but couldn't spot him. Rutan began to cut the specially marked riser lines to improve his ability to steer the parachute and realized he had sliced 90 percent of the way through the main parachute strap that supported his canopy. My God! he thought. A hundred and five Misty missions and I die by my own hand?!

Rutan was so shaken over the parachute that he almost forgot to inflate his life preserver, another near-death experience—with all the gear he carried, he would have sunk to the bottom of the Gulf like a brick. He remembered just before hitting the water. Then the chute settled right on top of him and he got terribly tangled in all the shroud lines. He finally worked his way free, pulled the raft over, and got in. He looked up and there was the HC-130 airplane that carried the rescue controllers, 500 feet above. It flew right toward him and dropped a smoke marker in the water, then went off to look for Shaheen.

It would be a while before the Jolly Green rescue choppers arrived, and Rutan suddenly felt very alone. He could see the coast in the distance and wondered if the NVA would try to come get him. He thought about his Misty career. He had only a short time left on his Vietnam tour, and he had been planning to spend it all at Misty, ending up with more missions than anybody else. But this wasn't what he had in mind. Damn that Shaheen and his fucking truck, Rutan thought. His zest for the mission felt like it was fading by the minute.

Two of the old reliable Jollys finally showed up. Rutan popped a smoke flare and one of the choppers broke toward him. The other continued on, disappearing from sight. Rutan gathered all his gear, his helmet, gloves, mask, survival goodies, and tossed it all overboard. That's how they had learned to do it in survival school. He'd get out of the raft and the helo would hover, drop the sling, and hoist him up.

But as Rutan rolled out of the raft and swam away, he saw that the Jolly wasn't hovering at all, but landing in the water and taxiing to him. He felt like a fool. He could have stayed in the raft and didn't even need to get wet. A PJ pulled him on board, then jumped into the water and swam around, policing up Rutan's raft and helmet and all his other belongings. Rutan sat on the webbed seat in the chopper, wrapped in a warm blanket, trying to relax.

Shaheen was getting picked up by the second Jolly at about the same time. When the chopper settled onto the water, Shaheen thought, Oh my God, the Jolly's crashed! He had never seen a water rescue and didn't know a Jolly could land on water. Then, as the Jolly taxied toward him across the wave tops, he figured out the helicopter's magic. "Gee, a helicopter that floats," he mused. "Imagine that."

The crew offered Shaheen a cigarette, wrapped him in a blanket, and told him Rutan was in a sister ship. The two helicopters joined up and flew in formation to Da Nang. Rutan exchanged a thumbs-up with Shaheen and tried to sleep during the long ride back to Da Nang. Shaheen started wondering about his next problem—how to tell his superiors about his strafe pass, which violated all the rules and resulted in the loss of an airplane.

When they got to Da Nang, Rutan's helo couldn't get its gear down. The pilot finally reverted to a backup method, using compressed air that forced the gear down with a loud bang. It was the last sharp noise Rutan wanted to hear for the day. Looking out the door of the Jolly, he could see a sea of brass waiting for their arrival. Shaheen sidled up to him on the tarmac and, after a quick hug, whispered, "Dick, what do we tell them?"

"You're the pilot-in-command," Rutan said. "Tell them anything you want and I'll back you up." The entourage wanted to know where they got hit, what hit them, what their altitude was, and other details of the shootdown. Shaheen fudged enough to get off the hook, and a few minutes later they were placed in an open jeep and driven to the hospital. They got a quick checkup, a jigger of the traditional cognac, and were pronounced fit.

They ended up standing alone outside the hospital in a driving rainstorm, lugging all of their gear, which the PJs had thoughtfully returned. As they tried to hitch a ride back to the flight line, they realized they were no longer returning heroes, the center of attention. They were just a couple of soaked, nondescript fighter jocks looking for a ride. A few hours later they climbed aboard an Army Caribou transport that was headed to Phu Cat. It dumped them at an Army cargo ramp, at the opposite end of the base from Misty.

They were still wet, and it was well after sundown. They got a ride back to Misty Ops, but nobody was there. The next logical thing to do was go to the O club. When they arrived they saw a huge banner. WELCOME HOME! it read. The Mistys hadn't bothered to wait for the guests of honor—most of them were already well into the party. After the mystifying loss of John Overlock and Mike McElhanon, the Mistys welcomed Rutan and Shaheen as if they had returned from the dead. And the two prodigal pilots were overjoyed to be home. But something was different. Doc Echenberg noticed that both men, usually assertive and confident, looked sheepish. He had never seen Rutan so subdued. And when things finally settled down and Rutan related his version of events, it was obvious he was shaken. "That's it," he promised. "I'm not doing it anymore."

The next day Shaheen and Rutan debriefed their bosses and told them exactly what they had done, and how low they had been flying. They thought they'd catch hell. But a commander who gets troops back from hostile territory in a war has the same ambivalent joyfulness as a parent who finds his children after they've been lost all afternoon—punishment seems impossible. So Bacon and other wing officials thanked the two pilots for being forthright—and that was all.

Rutan still had about two weeks left in his Vietnam combat tour, but 105 Misty missions and a shootdown suddenly seemed like enough. He asked Bacon for a respite. "Sir," he said, "would it be all right if I don't go up there anymore?"

Bacon smiled. "Rutan," he replied, "your war is over."

Echenberg and Rutan forged some papers, with Bacon's blessing, and went off for a week of R&R in Sydney. They were both more stressed out than either realized. Instead of checking into the "R&R district," where most American troops went, they asked for the most expensive hotel in town, and checked into the Wentworth. The next thing they did was head for the bar. Their Yankee accents quickly drew attention, and before long they couldn't buy a drink. Imagine that, they thought—a country where they LIKE Americans!

It was strange getting reoriented with the civilized world. The first challenge was road traffic. Phu Cat was so isolated that neither of them had seen a stoplight in months, and crossing the street without getting hit by a car required extra concentration. The first time they approached an intersection they stood at the curb, studying the phenomenon and giggling. Before long the old instincts returned, and they managed to cross the street safely, right along with the other pedestrians.

With their American accents they got more attention from women than either could have imagined in his wildest dreams. Echenberg had said they both needed some TLC, and the pilots ended up splitting off for a few days. Echenberg met a smart, shapely schoolteacher with an overbite that reminded him of Gene Tierney's. She had an innate sympathy for the needs of a man at war and wanted to help her newfound American lover escape the ordeal of living in a combat zone, however briefly. The doc, used to taking care of others, was as content as a child to let somebody take care of him. They talked and ate and drank and made love and promised to write, and felt so intensely drawn to each other that the woman, who was engaged, said she was going to end her relationship with her fiancé. Echenberg felt guilty about that, but the pang was overwhelmed by the feeling that he was in love, and he didn't really notice the guilt until he got back to Phu Cat.

When Echenberg met up with Rutan at the end of the week, he asked if Dick had gotten any TLC. Rutan just smiled. He had nearly died thanks to Shaheen and his goddamned truck, but his serious demeanor had vanished. He looked rested. His icy blue eyes now danced with humor. All he would say was, "Australia is a great country."

The news, when they returned, was disheartening. After a summer of close calls, Misty had lost two airplanes in two days, and Bud Bacon was feeling the heat. Misty's chief patron and protector, General Momyer, had been replaced by a new commander at 7th Air Force, Gen. George Scratchley Brown. He had a lot of units to get to know, but the shrinking fleet of planes at Phu Cat put Misty at the top of his in-box.

As General Brown and his staff scrutinized the operation, they noticed that many of the missions routinely lasted more than five hours, and sometimes as long as eight. Misty's planes were soaking up AAA hits practically every day. Bob Worley's death was still fresh, and Rutan had caught the attention of the big shots down in Saigon with his tape recording of the event. And now Rutan, like Worley, had gone down on his last mission. Was this "last-mission phenomenon" just a coincidence? Or was there something in a pilot's psyche that might

lead him to do something dangerous or stupid when he knew his combat tour was ending?

Brown visited Phu Cat for an extensive briefing on Misty. He talked
to the pilots and looked at the collection of handheld photos—trucks,
SAMs, storage and supply dumps, practically anything in Route Pack
1 that could be seen from the air. Brown was not an experienced fighter
pilot, but had flown the B-24 bomber in World War II and had participated in a famous low-level bomber raid against oil refineries in
Ploesti, Romania. Defenses were murderous, and eleven planes were
shot down in the prolonged attack. Brown, then a major, was in a
group whose lead plane crashed, and he took over the lead position
and led the battered group back to its base.[1] He listened intently to the
Mistys and asked relevant questions. For a general, he seemed to know
what he was talking about.

Everyone expected Bud Bacon, the Misty commander, to be fired. It
didn't happen. Instead, Brown directed that future Misty missions be
limited to four hours in duration—no exceptions. The Mistys were
angry. That would limit their effectiveness. They'd be forced to abandon some targets because of an arbitrary time limitation. And what
about rescues? That was something they all thought about, but nobody asked. The Misty philosophy was that it was better to ask for-
giveness after the fact than permission up front, and they assumed that
when a pilot was down, all bets would be off and the new restrictions
wouldn't apply.

After Brown left, the Mistys had a soul-searching session with Bud
Bacon. He wasn't happy with the new restrictions, either, but he also
knew that Brown had a point. The Mistys did hang their asses out
every day, but many of the targets were simply not worth the risk. The
Mistys were going to comply with the new rules and he didn't want
any bullshit from anybody. If the restrictions got in the way, they'd find
new ways to do their job. Anybody who didn't like it could leave.

A rumor surfaced that Phu Cat was going to become an F-4 base
and that the Misty operation would move farther south to Tuy Hoa,
along the coast. Everyone wondered if that would mean the end of the
unit as they knew it. Already the F-4 was becoming the airplane of
choice in Vietnam. In Brown's first days, 7th Air Force had directed
that a new fast FAC operation be set up at Da Nang, using the F-4s al-

ready based there. Misty would train them, with P. K. Robinson and Lanny Lancaster designated as project officers. The Da Nang pilots came to Phu Cat first, and flew in the backseat with the Mistys. Then Robinson and Lancaster went to Da Nang and flew in the back of the F-4. The Da Nang pilots turned out to be good sticks, and Robinson and Lancaster organized the best cram course they could, drawing on all the things Misty had learned from getting shot at and hit.

Like all F-100 drivers, Robinson and Lancaster had long derided the two-engine F-4 as a "weenie's" airplane. "Two engines, two pilots?" they'd razz the F-4 jocks at the bar. "No way that's a fighter." The single-engine F-100, they'd insist, was an airplane for men with hair on their chest. But when they got into the backseat of the F-4 for their first mission, they were pleasantly surprised. The engine power was awesome. The F-100 could barely be coaxed through Mach 1, but the F-4 could make Mach 2—handy for keeping up speed in the Pack.

Flying with the new guys, however, was nerve-racking. After five months at Misty, Robinson knew the ins and outs of Route Pack 1 as well as anybody, and knew all the tricks of the ground gunners. The new FACs didn't, and it was a torment to sit in the back with brand-new pilots, nauseated, while they dragged him through one flak burst after another. Robinson could have grabbed the stick at any moment and steered them clear of danger, but he knew from experience that the only way to teach a pilot to be a FAC was to let him fly. So he chewed holes in his tongue and endured the stress, including one flight with a pilot who got curious about something on the ground and flew as low and slow as Robinson had ever been in his life. He wondered if he'd survive being a tutor.

As they finished their stint with the F-4 drivers at Da Nang, Lancaster joshed that since the F-100 FACs were known as Misty, maybe the F-4s should be called Cloudy. The F-4 guys took the hint, but not the bait. They decided on the more sinister-sounding Stormy.

Misty was scaled back as directed, but attacks on trucks, SAMs, gun sites, supplies, and storage dumps continued. The NVA's air defenses got tougher and tougher, and there was no shortage of daring and amazing rescues. New pilots arrived, and the old heads showed them how to get beneath the cloud cover and find the hot stuff. On one overcast day, Wells Jackson, an aggressive flier who had been with the unit since April, helped a new Misty find some SAMs being trucked beneath a broken cloud deck that settled in as low as 500 feet in some places. They made one pass around the clouds to find the SAMs, and another to guide in some 105s with bombs, with the sound of AAA popping all around them. They felt some explosions but weren't about to risk a third pass to see what it was that they had blown up.

Lanny Lancaster tried another innovation, calling in naval gunfire on nettlesome targets in the Pack from a cruiser stationed twelve miles offshore—a reprise of experimental tactics from the early days of Misty. The 8-inch shells, Lancaster reasoned, might be able to get to the targets when the weather was bad and the cloud cover was too low for fighters. As a test, the ship fired numerous rounds at the gun pits surrounding the Quang Khe ferry, a critical crossing point along Route 1, the main highway that ran down the coast. A few rounds hit their targets, but most missed. Lanny persisted, however, and visited the Navy to refine their targeting procedures. There were a few more tries, and the idea was gaining ground when Lanny hit his one hundredth Misty mission. He left the unit, but the Air Force kept working on the idea, and used it fairly effectively when the battleship *New Jersey* arrived offshore in October 1968.[2]

On October 30, 1968, a Misty named Frank Kimball strafed two trucks on the north bank of the Quang Khe River, along the coast just above Dong Hoi. The trucks were the last two targets destroyed by Misty in North Vietnam. The next day, on the eve of the presidential election back in the States, Lyndon Johnson announced a complete halt to the bombing of North Vietnam.[3] It seemed unbelievable at Phu Cat, since what bombing they were still doing was the last defense against the North Vietnamese men and matériel gushing into the South. But attitudes toward the war in America had shifted in tectonic ways that were not completely perceptible at Phu Cat, and Johnson could no longer run a war that the majority of Americans didn't support.

Misty continued to fly missions in Laos, and on November 15, after Richard Nixon had defeated Hubert Humphrey in the race for president, Wells Jackson flew his 107th Misty mission, eclipsing Dick Rutan's record of 105. There was the ritual hosing-down and the usual ribald toasts at the bar. But the Misty cast was different and things were changing. As with the war itself, the air was going out of the mission.

TWENTY-SIX

CUT OFF

The rumors turned out to be true. After President Johnson halted all bombing in the North, Phu Cat became an F-4 base. The Misty operation and its F-100s were relocated to Tuy Hoa, farther south. The FACs continued to operate in Laos, where the danger remained high. Vast portions of the Trail still ran through Laos, and the North Vietnamese moved many of the air defenses that used to be in Route Pack 1 across the border. Targets were plentiful, and Misty still attracted some of the best, most determined pilots in the Air Force.

Commanders up the chain became less tolerant of Misty's antics, both in the air and off the clock. Just before the move to Tuy Hoa, one Misty commander, Maj. Clyde Seiler, was fired on the spot after a huge party that ended with him and some of the other pilots shooting their pen-gun flares into the air—which was strictly forbidden, since firing flares was a signal to the security police that the base was under attack. There were new restrictions regarding the duration of Misty missions and the way they flew. The special status informally bestowed by General Momyer dried up.

The F-100 was also an aging plane, on the verge of obsolescence. Other FACs, flying the newer F-4, were becoming more effective. That didn't eliminate the danger of flying with Misty, however. On August 9,

372 ★ BURY US UPSIDE DOWN

1969, two Mistys named Lee Gourley and Jefferson "Scottie" Dotson vanished on a mission out of Tuy Hoa, over Laos. As with John Overlock and Mike McElhanon, no one heard anything and no one had any idea where they had gone down. Seven other airplanes were shot down during the Tuy Hoa era. Most of the crew members were rescued, but Larry Whitford, one of the Misty commanders, was killed along with Patrick Carroll when their plane crashed on November 2, 1969. There had been no emergency call, but the Mistys found a smoking hole in the jungle in Laos and could make out some aircraft wreckage.

By then the air war was changing. As the United States disengaged from the war and sought a peace deal with Hanoi, bombing became a tool for forcing the communists to the negotiating table, and little more. A few trucks or oil drums or AAA guns along the Trail—even SAMs—didn't matter very much anymore. The Air Force bombed in the South, to aid its allies, who were now doing most of the ground fighting. But the policy in Washington was to turn the war over to the Vietnamese—"Vietnamization" was the awkward phrase—and bring the troops home.

Misty went out of business in 1970. The end came with a whimper. 7th Air Force shut down the unit with a simple one-line message:

"This confirms the Misty FAC program termination, 12 May 1970."

Over three years, 157 pilots had served with Misty. Thirty-four of them had been shot down while with the unit, a loss rate of 22 percent. Two had been shot down twice. Three had become prisoners, and seven others, including Howard Williams, John Overlock, and Mike McElhanon, were listed as missing. Nobody was sure what had happened to them.

Their disappearances produced a powerful and turbulent gravitational tug on those who were left to deal with their absence. Instead of being drawn to a person, however, the mothers and fathers and wives and sons and daughters back home were pulled toward a black hole that produced a swirl of confusion, and no concrete answers.

Roger Williams had faced a simple choice after his brother Howard was shot down. U.S. government policy stated that no two immediate family members would be required to serve in a war zone. Roger could have avoided Vietnam altogether in the first place, since his brother

CUT OFF ★ 373

was being sent there. But he had volunteered for the war, partly in the hope that if he went, Howard would take advantage of the exemption to request duty someplace else. But Howard didn't.

Roger thought again about the policy after Howard disappeared, and his mother and sisters urged him to serve the rest of his three-year tour someplace else. But he saw no option besides returning to Vietnam. Howard was there, somewhere, and more powerfully than ever, Roger felt the need to be as close to his brother as he could, even if he didn't know exactly where that was. And he wanted to do something for his brother. Anything. That had to be in Vietnam.

Roger returned to Saigon with a mission. He was going to help find Howard, or at least others like him. Roger had had a discussion or two with his commanders about his future in the Army, and one of them had suggested he might make a good warrant officer—an enhanced rank between sergeant and commissioned officer reserved for enlisted soldiers who became valued technical specialists. Roger had risen quickly for an enlisted man and had obvious skills beyond merely carrying a gun or filing papers. And some warrants flew helicopters. So as soon as he got back to Saigon, Roger filed papers to become a helicopter crewman. It was the best way he could think of to get closer to Howard, wherever he was. Roger was upbeat. Maybe there was something he could do after all, besides waiting for the bureaucracy to come to life and figure out what had happened to his brother.

Roger's papers were rejected immediately. His commanders had seen it all before: soldiers driven by anger and frustration over the loss of a buddy or family member, resolving to "do something." There could be little doubt that such troops were motivated. Whether they could be effective was another question. Soldiers trying to bring fallen comrades back from the dead, trying to right unrightable wrongs, were often unreliable and sometimes dangerous. They took too many risks, needlessly endangering others and themselves. They were driven not by dedication to the mission, but by the unshakable desire for answers—and sometimes by a thirst for revenge. There were plenty of others who could do the job courageously and competently without the added burden of having something to prove.

Roger sank into the despair of powerlessness. If his brother was going to return, it was going to be thanks to providence, not him. He started to go on drinking binges, swearing to pals that he'd get even with the bastards who had shot down his brother. But he knew he wouldn't. By the summer of 1968, Roger had grown disillusioned with the Army and with the war and decided to get out. His three-year tour was scheduled to end in September, but he had the option of early separation, leaving ninety days before the official end of his enlistment. So in July he "took a drop" and went home to Steubenville, where he wandered around in a foggy state for a while looking for work. He felt strange, disconnected. The "real world" was nothing like Vietnam, and it was even more surreal without his brother.

Monalee Williams had learned very much, and very little, in the months following her husband's disappearance. The information conveyed by Dick Rutan and Roger Williams and a few others in the F-100 community revealed a world she had known practically nothing about, the world of the pilots flying the dangerous missions over North Vietnam. Yet the more she learned, the more unanswered questions there were. Why hadn't Howard told her about Misty? Why had he joined? Had he thought about her and Howard Jr. when he decided to take the risks? And, of course, there was no news at all about what may have happened to him. Nobody seemed to know anything about that, not even a couple of Misty pilots she had heard from who supposedly were in the middle of it all.

Shock turned to numbness and anger, yet Monalee continued to feel as if she would get a phone call any day saying her husband was fine. Family and friends, including other pilots' wives, were providing strong support. People began to tell her about support groups for the families of troops who were prisoners in North Vietnam or who had been reported as missing in action. But Monalee kept to herself at first, focusing on her teaching and on Howard Jr. She talked to her son every day about his dad and showed him pictures all the time, making sure he stayed familiar with what his dad looked like. Her parents persuaded her to go to Florida for a summer vacation, but the whole time she felt like she should call the Air Force, just to check on whether there was any new information.

Other wives of the missing did little more, even though they too agonized over everything they didn't know. When Sandy McElhanon had heard the news about her husband, she called Lt. Col. Clay

Wilkins, one of Mike's best friends. The two families had been assigned to a number of bases together, including one posting where
Mike and Clay were both instructor pilots. And Clay and his wife,
Marion, were godparents to both the McElhanon kids, Kelly and
Paige. That summer, Wilkins was working at a staff job at Pacific Air
Force headquarters in Hawaii, where he had access to a lot of classified information about Air Force activities in Vietnam. But he could
learn nothing about his friend Mike, except that his plane had disappeared. Sandy also got a briefing on the incident from staff officers at
Carswell Air Force Base, near her rented house in Fort Worth. The
story was the same. Nobody knew anything.

Bev Overlock, whose husband, John, had been in the plane with
Mike McElhanon when it disappeared, had felt even more cut off.
Since she had moved into an apartment near her parents' home, in
Miami Lakes, Florida, instead of staying near one of the Air Force
bases, there was no local Air Force community to fall back on. After
the initial visit, when the officers in the blue car had come to tell her
what had happened, she got practically no information. Beyond pro
forma notifications and apologies, there were no letters from any of
John's fellow Misty pilots. One of Bev's friends got shards of information from her husband, who was friends with P. K. Robinson. But by
the time it got back to Bev and she pieced it together, one thing was obvious: Nobody knew what happened. It was not long before Bev had
strong doubts about whether her husband was even alive.

She and John had come from different backgrounds and lived
somewhat independent lives, which turned out to be fortunate. Bev realized quickly that she needed to do something besides wait on the unresponsive Air Force. She was used to getting by on her own, and it
took very little gumption for her to go out and get a job in the clothing
department at Burdines Department Store. She also volunteered at a
children's home next to her apartment. Instead of fellow pilots' wives,
her closest counsel was her roommate, Barbara Bartlett, her friend
from modeling school.

There was one unambiguous message the Air Force gave to all three
wives: Don't say anything about your husbands being missing. They
had each greeted that warning with indignation, but generally abided
by it as the initial shock sank in. All of them supported the war and the

work their husbands were doing, even if they didn't know much about it. They had not yet found reason to question the government or its war policies. Besides, they knew the Air Force had a point. At Monalee's home she got occasional phone calls from people irate about the war who would tell her, "Your husband is killing babies" or make other disturbing statements. Howard Jr. was old enough to pick up the phone—and fascinated by the contraption—but forbidden to answer it.

After the shock of their husbands' disappearances, it became maddeningly quiet. They got no news, and there was nothing they could do. In Texas, Sandy McElhanon, who had always been outgoing and social, seldom went out. Tommy and Rachelle Manly, longtime friends, called her constantly, but Sandy would make excuses to get off the phone or wouldn't answer at all. She was confused, afraid of saying anything. It was strange. She was desperate for information, yet at the same time she wanted to wash the military out of her mind. Merely glimpsing an Air Force flight suit made her break down in tears. Every night she and her two girls prayed that their daddy would come home safe, and soon.

As the first Christmas without her husband had neared, Monalee thought about what she should say in her Christmas cards when she updated friends about her family's life in Columbus. She decided to say nothing about Howard to those who didn't already know. At the bottom she signed all three of their names. They were still a family, after all, and Howard might still come home someday, and everything would return to normal.

Time did not ease the burden. Instead it made the weight heavier. Knowing nothing, and stifling the anger, was tolerable for a while. But as the weeks and months marched by, it became impossible to contain the explosive frustration fermenting inside the wives of the missing.

Those who had disappeared, it seemed, dropped to the bottom of the food chain. The war itself had sparked protests that had been going on since President Johnson began his bombing campaign against North Vietnam in 1965. The antiwar movement had rooted and grown. The United States at the end of the 1960s seemed like a funhouse-mirror image of what it had been just ten years earlier. Not only were young people experimenting with drugs, dressing as if they were color-blind,

and causing their parents cardiac arrest with free love and countercul-
turalism, but they were shaking their fist at the government like never
before. Television coverage of the war had become bold, and a bloody
and confusing guerrilla war was being played out in millions of American homes. It became glaringly obvious that there was a great discrepancy between the glowing reviews of the war effort coming from the
government and the large number of body bags coming home.[1] Richard
Nixon had won the presidency in 1968 largely because he promised to
end the war and bring U.S. troops home. Peace talks with the North
Vietnamese had begun in Paris shortly afterward, although it was more
like bickering than negotiating: The two sides started by arguing over
what shape the negotiating table should be. Still, the United States had
staked out its opening bid, and a nonnegotiable U.S. demand was the
return of American prisoners being held in North Vietnam. There was
some talk about accounting for the missing, but in the speeches and
headlines, the MIAs tended to get lopped off.

In January 1969 the Air Force asked a number of family members
to come to Carswell. There was some film of several POWs that the
United States had gathered from a variety of international journalists,
both TV and print, who had been allowed to see the prisoners and film
or photograph them. Since the North Vietnamese hadn't supplied any
names or other identifying information, the Air Force wanted help
identifying the prisoners. Some of the wives and other family members
had become suspicious by this point and wondered if this was some
sort of ploy by the Air Force to quiet dissension and keep them in the
closet. But when they saw the film, they were appalled and infuriated.
The prisoners were emaciated and reminded many in the room of inmates in German concentration camps. Their brittle movements suggested crippling injuries. None of the people viewing the film
recognized any of the prisoners, but they all knew how to spot human
beings in torment, and that's what they saw on the screen—and their
government didn't seem to be doing anything about it.

Sandy McElhanon had attended the gathering and met Paula Hartness, whose husband, Gregg, was Don Shepperd's best friend. He had
been shot down while flying a slow FAC mission in an O-2 over the
Trail shortly after the U.S. elections in 1968. Flak from a 37mm AAA
battery had blown the back end off the plane, and Hartness had

pushed his copilot out the door while the plane spun toward the ground upside down. But nobody knew if Hartness had had time to get out himself, and he and the plane had disappeared into the jungle. Sandy and Paula became fast friends and vowed to press every button they could to get information. And unlike the government, they'd share whatever they learned with anybody who was interested.

The horrendous sight of the emaciated POWs seen by the families at Carswell stirred many in attendance to break their silence. Bonnie Singleton, wife of Jerry Singleton, an Air Force Academy classmate of Don Shepperd, Jim Mack, P. K. Robinson, and Lanny Lancaster, had already been pestering the Air Force to send her and other wives of the missing to Vietnam, to draw attention to the troops whose fate nobody knew. There was a growing feeling among the family members that the Air Force viewed them as a pain in the ass, an embarrassment to be swept under the rug. Bonnie wanted to kick up a fuss, to get some articles written. She wanted Americans to know that hundreds of their countrymen were somewhere in North Vietnam, with no acknowledgment by the North Vietnamese—who wouldn't even say, as required by the Geneva Conventions, whether these men were dead or alive. And from her perspective, the U.S. government wasn't showing a great deal of concern, either. The Air Force's biggest worry seemed to be keeping the wives quiet—even if that meant getting nasty. There were even rumors that the Air Force might cut the salary payments to their missing men, which would leave their families in a severe bind. In a desperate effort to keep the women quiet, some of the Air Force liaison officers even suggested that wives who spoke out would be cut out of the information flow regarding their husbands if they didn't follow the service's rules. Mistrust was growing, and in addition to anger and pain, some of the wives were beginning to feel considerable hostility toward the Air Force.

The wives weren't getting any answers anyway, and threats to cut them out of the loop only enraged the women further. Bonnie knew Felix McKnight, publisher of *The Dallas Morning News*. He agreed to run an article about four Dallas-area wives—Bonnie Singleton, Sandy McElhanon, Joy Jeffrey, and Paula Hartness—whose lives were on hold while they agonized over the unknown fate of their husbands. It ran in April with the headline ARE WE WIVES OR WIDows? Finally, the women felt, their husbands' cases were getting some attention.

It mounted. Murphy Martin, a newscaster for a local TV station, WFAA, called and said he'd like to do a segment on the women's plight. He cautioned them that he didn't know whether he'd be able to fill the thirty-minute slot he had in mind, and he couldn't guarantee any coverage. But after he met with all of them, he said he could fill several hours with their stories.

The program was scheduled to air at 10:30 a.m. on a Sunday morning, weekend prime time for newsmaking stories. Before it aired, Texas congressman Olin "Tiger" Teague got wind of the program. Teague was a combat veteran himself who had participated in the 1944 D-Day landing as an Army second lieutenant. By the end of the war he had become the second-most-decorated soldier after Audie Murphy, with three Purple Hearts, three Silver Stars, three Bronze Stars, two French medals, and a chestful of other honors. He retired from the Army as a colonel, and once in Congress he had become the powerful chairman of the House Committee on Veterans Affairs. His position, and reputation, gave him considerable clout.

Teague had just been with the navy on the *"Bonnie Dick"*—the aircraft carrier *Bonhomme Richard*. The Navy pilots drew many of the highly dangerous bombing missions over the North, in Route Pack 6B—which included parts of Hanoi and the country's main port, Haiphong. The sea service had lost dozens of pilots, many of whom were either known to be prisoners or listed as missing. The pilots on board the *Bonnie Dick* had bombarded Teague with their concerns about the treatment of POWs in Hanoi and the sluggish search for the missing. They begged him to do something.

Teague asked if he could be on the WFAA program, face-to-face with the women. The station agreed. Instead of trying to stifle their concerns, he welcomed them and promised to become an advocate for them. Meanwhile, H. Ross Perot had been watching, and he got interested in the cause. The animated, energetic Perot was a Naval Academy graduate who had founded Electronic Data Systems and become a billionaire after the company won several lucrative government contracts, and went public in 1968.[2] Perot aggressively recruited Vietnam veterans, putting them into important jobs right off the battlefield. They might be only twenty-seven years in age, Perot liked to say, but they were forty in maturity—and they knew how to work twenty hours a day without complaining.[3]

The public response to the Sunday morning program turned out to be so strong that WFAA offered to sponsor the four wives on a trip to Paris in April, when another session of the peace talks was scheduled. Ross Perot also promised to assist with future funding. Murphy Martin, the TV·newscaster, would go with the wives and produce yet another piece for the station to air. The goal was to arrange a meeting between the wives of the missing and Le Duc Tho, chief negotiator for North Vietnam. The footage would be irresistible: four abandoned wives—widows, for all intents and purposes, at least as far as the viewing audience was concerned—confronting one of the communist masterminds of the war in Vietnam. It would be one hell of a scoop.

Despite good intentions, the trip had taken on the melodramatic air of theater. The Air Force learned of the trip—not hard, since it was being promoted on WFAA—and asked that the entourage stop in Washington first, for "briefings." But the meeting began with an ultimatum: "You can't go," the Air Force "briefers" insisted. When that failed to dissuade the wives, the Air Force officials tried to make sure they would stick to MIA issues while in Paris and not criticize U.S. war policy. North Vietnam viewed their husbands as war criminals, not as POWs, the officials warned. If their trip became a political crusade, they could adversely affect the peace talks. "You are going for information," the Air Force officials sternly warned them, "not for policy!"

The entourage flew on to Paris, where it enjoyed good hotels courtesy of WFAA. P. K. Robinson happened to be attending school at the University of Paris. After Misty, he had been awarded an Olmsted Foundation Fellowship, a highly competitive and prestigious scholarship for promising young officers and their wives. These up-and-comers would take immersion programs in foreign languages and study local politics and culture in preparation for the multinational demands to be placed on globe-trotting senior officers.[4] Robinson had been unaware of the wives' trip, but he read about it in *Le Monde,* the Parisian daily.

The TV station had provided a driver and an interpreter. The group wasted little time and went straight to the North Vietnamese embassy, on a quiet side street away from the bustle of central Paris. Martin went into the guard shack at the entrance to the compound, and the runaround began. The guard said they'd have to leave because they didn't have an appointment, even though they had sent letters and telegrams saying when they'd be coming. Martin was not about to slink away and give up his story, however, and he bullied his way up to the front door of the embassy and knocked. The boldness worked, and the group was invited in and led to a room, where they waited to see what would happen next. They were seated in a reception area with comfortable chairs and a couch and served "red" tea.

After a few minutes a low-level functionary came in and said the North Vietnamese did not know who any of these American strangers were, and, at any rate, they did not have an appointment. They'd have to leave. Martin and the wives were not going to be dismissed, however, and the two sides arranged a meeting for the next day. At least they had pulled off a faster start than the official peace-talk negotiators who in 1968 had bickered for days before even sitting down at a table with one another.

The next day they met with a North Vietnamese official, who sat across a table from them with several folders spread out in front of him. The man reverted to the increasingly familiar refrain—he didn't know who they were, or why they were there—even though the folders in front of him contained pictures of their husbands and even their children, and the wives themselves. The women explained that they were simply looking for information on their husbands. A servant brought red tea and cookies. Then the official told them their husbands were war criminals and went on to explain why. He slid a series of photographs in front of them, and the wives recoiled at what they saw: the tattered bodies of children, torn to shreds, supposedly by bombs dropped by Americans. Sandy McElhanon struggled to remain composed while looking at the pictures. The other wives squirmed, visibly unnerved. Finally the macabre viewing ended. The cold-eyed North Vietnamese official wrote down the names of the wives and their husbands on a yellow legal pad—even though he obviously had all of that information in the files in front of him. He flipped perfunctorily through one of the folders, then looked up at the group. "We have no information on your husbands," he declared. That adjourned the meeting, and he left the room.

They went back to Texas, and WFAA aired a program called "Red Tea and Promises" that detailed the inattention toward the missing and their families. Ross Perot had been closely following POW and MIA activities as well as the situation of the four Dallas wives. He was particularly moved by Ricky Singleton, the young son of Jerry Singleton, who had never seen his dad.[5] Perot decided it was time to get more deeply and personally involved. He suggested forming "United We Stand," a Texas-based organization for the families of men who were missing or imprisoned in Vietnam.

The new group, with start-up money from Perot, rented a building on Henderson Street in Fort Worth that became a gathering place for Sandy McElhanon and other Air Force wives and family members. It was no mere social club, however. Perot was a man with vast ambition, and he had in mind a huge advertising campaign that would encourage Americans to write letters in support of the POWs and the MIAs and their families. Perot even said he would personally deliver the letters to the Paris peace talks.[6]

So the group began to generate thousands of letters—to officials in Washington, to the North Vietnamese, to the media, to the United Nations, and to politicians in other countries. They insisted on better treatment for the prisoners in Vietnam and protested the callous treatment of their families by the U.S. and North Vietnamese governments. And they called for more information on the missing. At times the United We Stand office was filled to the ceiling with letters. Strangers called to ask if they could help. TV segments and newspaper stories covered their efforts, and the women running the campaign got more and more motivated as it gathered steam. None of it provided any answers about their husbands. But at least they were doing something.

TWENTY-SEVEN

"IF ONLY I KNEW"

Waiting for the missing to return was an awkward vigil. Bev Overlock went to a couple of events in Washington, D.C., for the wives of POWs. But she got no comfort from their company. Many of the wives seemed too emotional, even irrational. Yes, their losses were grievous—just as hers was—but their anger seemed to border on hysteria. And there was strange talk that maybe the U.S. government was keeping news of the prisoners or the missing secret, and other potential conspiracies. Bev found it disturbing rather than soothing. She decided not to go to any more such gatherings.

She found support in other places. The Bible was one of them. Her grandmother had introduced her to the Bible and to faith, and she redirected Bev to those influences now. Bev read the stories of Job and Jesus and others and thought to herself, "Faith changed their lives. They faced tough things and dealt with it. I can do the same thing." She went through ups and downs, but tried hard to avoid self-pity. Meanwhile, she was working her way up at Burdines Department Store and was supporting herself. Most of her husband, John's, pay went into a savings account.

Sandy McElhanon, after about a year in the house that she and Mike had rented in Fort Worth, bought another house nearby and started making plans to move back to the country, with horses and animals. She started looking around for some land.

Time passed slowly, but the changes under way were profound. Howard Williams Jr. was only nine in 1970, but unlike most kids his age, he had a keen awareness of events relating to the war. The huge antiwar protest at Kent State University—just 140 miles northeast of the Williams home in Columbus—was so vivid to him that it was as if it had taken place in his own backyard. When National Guardsmen opened fire on the crowd and killed four demonstrators, Howard began working through the kinds of complexities that even adults struggle with.

He would watch the evening news and memorize the latest tallies of Americans killed and wounded in Vietnam. The antiwar arguments—which were seemingly everywhere by then—seemed to make sense to him. Why would his country be sending men like his dad to Vietnam, to kill people who had nothing to do with America? What was the point? And yet his dad had chosen to be part of the military machine that was over there fighting the war. Everything he heard about his dad was positive, and it was hard to understand why such a man would be over there doing the things people were saying. He decided that his dad had joined the Air Force and gone to war not because he wanted to fight, but because he loved to fly.

Kelly McElhanon, Mike's seven-year-old daughter, was thinking some hard thoughts, too. She was old enough to remember her dad and some of the places they had lived. A posting in Taiwan had been one of her favorite times. She had taken ballet lessons there, and people knew her all over the base. There was a men's and women's softball league and she became a team mascot. Kelly desperately missed her dad and paid close attention to news about the prisoners. It all seemed so surreal that it was hard to believe. Nothing made sense to a seven-year-old. No explanation offered a reason why her dad was gone, beyond the blank assurances that he had just disappeared.

The families were tugged in two directions: On one side was a life they had known and cherished—but it was a life that was probably gone. On the other side was a different life, one they didn't want but would probably be forced to accept. For the time being they were hovering in the middle, not willing to discard the old and not yet ready to embrace the new.

There were no epiphanies—just difficult everyday decisions—but Monalee was dragging herself into the future. She realized it was important to refocus on Howard and on herself instead of waiting for the phone to ring. She quit teaching and enrolled in a master's program in psychology at Ohio State. Monalee knew a woman who was a school psychologist and enjoyed listening to her describe what she did. A psychology degree would allow her to move up a step or two on the academic ladder and earn a little more money. Since she was drawing her husband's pay, she could afford to quit work for a while, so she became a full-time student.

She still wrote regular letters to Howard on the lined, one-page sheets the North Vietnamese provided for correspondence with American prisoners. There were two points of instruction at the bottom, in Vietnamese, with English translation: "1. Write legibly and only on the lines. 2. Notes from families should also conform to this proforma." The wives never got letters back, and they wondered whether their brief messages went to the prisoners or to the incinerator. But what else could family members do? The prisoners were under the total control of the North Vietnamese, and whatever the ground rules were, the family members had to play by them.

Monalee's frequent but brief missives had the chatty, detached tone of an annual form letter to casual acquaintances. The rules allowed just one page of writing, and everyone presumed the letters were censored by North Vietnamese apparatchiks on the lookout for diabolical hidden messages—if they were delivered at all. So the wives and mothers had learned to stick to basic facts, avoiding anything that could be considered controversial, and to keep emotions to a minimum. "Dear Keith," Monalee wrote on February 2, 1971, "I am in my second quarter at college. I am enjoying it. . . . Howard is busy working on a science project for school. We may go skiing if we get some snow—right now it is raining. All are fine—car has been good, too. We both love you so much—love is very strong. God be with you. Love, Monalee." And then, she cried.

On April 3, 1971, Monalee wrote to tell her husband she had decided to move to a bigger apartment. "It has a big basement and I've sent for all our things," she assured him. She also relayed the news that she had gotten a 3.5 grade-point average at Ohio State in the second quarter. A couple of weeks later the news was that Howard Jr. had started playing baseball. He played first base. In June, she added that Howard was hitting well, and that she had ordered a new Dodge, which would arrive in a month. "Didn't have any trouble with the other but would need to put money into it before winter," she explained. Then she ended, "Love you so much, our love is stronger than all. Good night. God bless. Monalee."

There was much more going on, needless to say, than the cursory updates scrawled on North Vietnam's one-page note cards ever revealed. Monalee had gotten involved with a couple of groups formed for the families of those missing or captive in Vietnam, such as the National League of Families of American Prisoners and Missing in Southeast Asia. She got to know a few other wives in the area who were in the same predicament she was. Monalee was no rabble-rouser, but occasionally she would speak before the Jaycees, business organizations, school audiences, and other local groups, part of the overall effort to keep the plight of the POWs and the MIAs in the public spotlight. Often she'd speak along with Chris Moe, whose husband, Tommy, was a pilot who had been shot down and was a prisoner in Hanoi. Chris would describe the awful treatment the prisoners were getting, in flagrant violation of the Geneva Conventions. Monalee would talk about the need to get more information about the missing, and to pressure the North Vietnamese government to reveal what it knew about such men. Monalee and her friends collected signatures at the Ohio State Fair and helped distribute bumper stickers and urged people to write thousands of letters, constantly agitating for a cause the Air Force, the Department of Defense, and the White House seemed to have forgotten.

In an appeal she wrote on behalf of Project Freedom, an Ohio-based POW/MIA support group, Monalee explained in calm, thoughtful terms the difficulties of waiting and wondering: "Recently I found a card that says a great deal of what is meant by missing in action. On the front of this card is a picture of two people together—and it means to me all the wonderful, good and precious memories that I have of the years we spent together. Memories have a great deal of meaning now—but they are not enough. And as I read the words [on the card] the reality of everything came into focus. It says very simply, 'Somewhere—somehow—some way—someday.' And although life continues on and I try to lead as normal a life as possible doing the things that I have always done as a wife and mother, these words are always there and have their effect on what I do. It is not always the big decisions like buying a house or not, and thinking that someday soon I may know something and then I can make that decision, but it is the little everyday things, too. . . . I think all of us have had the experience in our lives and not knowing about something that was important to our lives, whether it has been to know about a new job, a transfer, or if a loan would go through for a new home. How many of you have said to yourself 'if only I knew.' I think for an MIA wife this is the first step, to know whether my husband is dead or alive."

By the time Monalee was writing this letter, the fate of the prisoners and the missing in Vietnam had evolved from an obscure subtext of the war to a wrenching national issue. Peace negotiations in Paris had been dragging on for more than two years, and Henry Kissinger and other U.S. delegates had met with North Vietnamese officials dozens of times. The return of American prisoners and an accounting of the missing had become a top U.S. demand. Several independent groups had tried to negotiate the release of prisoners with Hanoi. Even Bob Hope had come up with a plan to pay several million dollars to North Vietnamese charities for children in exchange for the release of POWs.[1]

Through the course of the war the North Vietnamese had released fewer than a dozen prisoners—and each time it had been staged for some kind of propaganda or political gain. Several prisoners had been turned over to U.S. antiwar activists, an obvious effort to promote even greater opposition to the war in America. Three downed pilots released by Hanoi in 1968 reported that they had been treated well, testimony starkly at odds with other information about how U.S. prisoners in Hanoi were being brutalized. The pilots had all been captives for only a short time and were intentionally separated from other POWs and given special treatment. And the occasional photographs and video footage of prisoners released by Hanoi seemed designed to disturb rather than reassure the American public and the family members specifically. The families could see their men shambling hazily in the foggy footage, yet their own government wouldn't do what it took to bring them home.

Seaman Douglas Hegdahl had been released in 1969. The young sailor, an ammunition handler on the USS *Canberra,* had climbed high

388 ★ BURY US UPSIDE DOWN

on the edge of the ship one evening to watch a night bombardment in the Gulf of Tonkin. Suddenly the shock of the guided-missile cruiser's 5-inch guns knocked him overboard. He floated for five hours before being picked up by Vietnamese fishermen and turned over to the North Vietnamese Army, who nearly clubbed him to death before sending him to the Hanoi Hilton.[2]

The NVA selected Hegdahl for early release because he was an enlisted person. He didn't want to go, since the chief rule among the POWs was that all would be released or none. Hegdahl began to misbehave badly, taunting the prison guards. At one point, when peace activist Tom Hayden was touring the prison camp, Hegdahl gave him the finger.

But Hegdahl had a unique talent: a near-photographic memory. The senior officer in his cell block, Navy commander Richard Stratton, ordered him to accept early release and to memorize the names of every known POW. When the North Vietnamese decided to offer early release to some prisoners, it came with a threat: If any of them spoke out about their torture, the remaining prisoners would be battered even more brutally. But Stratton told Hegdahl to blow the whistle once he was back under U.S. control and provide an uncensored account of how the North Vietnamese were treating their American captives. Using the song "Old MacDonald Had a Farm" as a mnemonic device, Hegdahl memorized the names of more than three hundred fellow POWs, along with their Social Security numbers and an identifying trait such as a pet's name for confirmation.[3]

Hegdahl and two other prisoners were turned over to a group of American antiwar activists in August 1969.[4] Once back in the United States, he immediately told the Pentagon everything he knew. The military kept many of the details quiet, but published the names of nearly fifty prisoners who had previously been considered missing. Nixon's defense secretary, Melvin Laird, complained that the U.S. "cannot be content with propaganda-planned releases of a few prisoners at infrequent intervals."[5]

To those who could keep the flame low on their emotions, the North Vietnamese tactics were bald-faced psychological warfare. "Hanoi has been very effective," Monalee continued in her Project Freedom letter, "if one of their objectives has been to wage a battle of nerves. When they have released prisoners . . . it has been 30 days or more from the time they have announced the release of the men and the time they have released their names. You can listen to a lot of news broadcasts and read many newspapers searching for a name. . . . Or they have released very poor quality films so a family can watch and try to identify their husbands and sons. None of this needs to be. . . .

"Although knowing whether my husband is dead or alive is the first step it isn't the last. . . . Can they survive, under the conditions that we know exist? Can they survive with inadequate medical care, when prisoners tell of having wounds that oozed for over a year, of poor diets, when we see films of men who we think look pretty good but don't realize that they have lost 60 or 70 pounds?

"As wives we have been called brave, dedicated, and courageous and if we are any of these it is because we have the best examples in the world—our men. They are the truly brave, dedicated and courageous ones but they are only human and time is not on their side."

As badly as Monalee and thousands of other family members wanted their men back, they also began to understand the implications of that: Those who were still alive were living in abject misery. It was unspeakable, but it might almost be better if they were dead. In fact, that became a more and more likely prospect for those listed as missing, especially as more information began to seep out about who the prisoners were. In October 1971 a U.S. government spokesman said that of more than sixteen hundred troops who were missing in South east Asia, at least two-thirds of them were probably dead.

The wives of the missing were making decisions—whether they realized it or not. Sandy McElhanon was involved with many of the wives, and she quipped that "some decided to be loyal to their husbands, some to prostitute themselves, and some to be alcoholics. And there were some of each." For young women with a lot of life ahead of them, the obligations to the past got in the way of the pull of the future. A few made prompt arrangements with the military to have their husbands declared killed in action so they could move on. Others continued to wait for their husbands, but found the loneliness unbearable and took up with other men. A few cracked. One missing pilot's wife whom Monalee had gotten to know through the League of Families set the table for her husband every night and bought Christmas presents for him and put them under the tree. And in some inevitable cases the pain and confusion became overwhelming, leading to bad decisions and self-destructive behavior.

Ross Perot organized a trip to Asia in late 1971 for Sandy McElhanon and about a dozen other wives. About eighty newsmen tagged along. The plan was to tour some of the Allied prison camps in South Vietnam, then travel to Vientiane, Laos, and meet with North Vietnamese officials there, and demand access to the prisoners in Hanoi. It was a strange and disjointed experience. The tour of the prison camps in the South went smoothly. The wives saw North Vietnamese and Viet Cong POWs, many who looked like they were teenagers, being well treated, getting good medical attention and even prostheses. In some cases family members were allowed to visit them on weekends.

Next, they flew to Vientiane, hoping to meet with North Vietnamese officials who would grant them permission to go to Hanoi. To Sandy, Vientiane seemed like a lawless Mexican border town, except that instead of banditos it was full of communist Pathet Lao soldiers, heavily armed and hateful-looking. Perot supposedly had set up a meeting with officials at the North Vietnamese embassy, but when the group arrived, they were taken to an outbuilding and escorted into a room that was as hot as a tin shack in the desert, even though the shades were drawn. Guards stood outside the door. Nobody arrived to greet them.

They waited and sweated for a couple of hours, and finally Perot and some others demanded to be let out to go relieve themselves. While on this bathroom break, Perot snuck up to the front door of the embassy and started pounding. Nearly a dozen Pathet Lao soldiers immediately surrounded him, their bayonets fixed. Sandy, watching from nearby, thought they'd kill him on the spot, even while the news cameras rolled. But they merely forced him away from the door, and the group was told to come back the next day. When they did, they got exactly the same treatment. They shouted questions at the guards, asking why they couldn't see their husbands if they were merely criminals and not POWs. But nobody would answer and no officials ever met with them. They left the embassy more frustrated than ever.

The strain of the ordeal flared in unexpected ways. At the hotel in Vientiane, one of the wives decided to lay out by the pool in a bikini. That did not fit the "grieving widow" image that had helped Perot's efforts gain publicity and support. With all the newsmen around, he asked a couple of the other wives "go get some clothes on her." An ugly argument developed as some of the wives blew off steam. Sandy realized that the bikini widow was caught between a smothering burden she wanted to put behind her and a defiant need to rediscover herself and enjoy basic simplicities once again. To outsiders it might have seemed inappropriate, but virtually all of the wives went through the same struggle in one way or another.

Bev Overlock made her own efforts to hector the North Vietnamese into providing information on her husband, John. She went to Paris on her own with letters addressed to Le Duc Tho, the communists' chief negotiator, asking for information about her husband. It seemed futile, but Bev wasn't getting any information from the Air Force, so she figured she had nothing to lose. She visited P. K. Robinson and his wife, Reta, whom she had known when both families had been stationed together in England. P. K. offered sympathy and understanding—but like everybody else, he knew nothing about John's whereabouts. Bev went to the North Vietnamese embassy. Walking up toward the door produced a sickening sensation. The guards all seemed to have sly, Cheshire cat smiles painted on their faces, like they knew the answer to the riddle that had been tormenting her. They told her coldly that they had no information, almost as if they enjoyed sending her away crestfallen. She went home expecting to hear nothing.

In 1972 her roommate, Barbara, got married and moved out. Bev looked around for her own place. She bought a townhouse in Miami Lakes, an upscale town twenty miles northwest of Miami.

Sandy McElhanon bought a horse farm in Weatherford, Texas, west of Fort Worth, a place where the girls would be able to ride and enjoy the country. She had worked for a vet when she was younger, and Sandy started learning how to breed, train, and maintain horses. She started playing golf to relax. Congressman Tiger Teague, who had promised to look after the Texas wives in Congress, remained a close associate and good friend. He helped keep the cause of the MIAs alive, for which Sandy was grateful. But there were times when she just needed to withdraw and escape from the heaviness.

It was a heartbreaking struggle between remembering and forgetting. In April 1972, Howard Williams's niece Susan, his sister Jean's girl, wrote a letter to President Nixon. The seven-year-old had not seen her uncle since she was two and didn't really remember him. But she heard about him constantly from family members. "Dir Mr. Nixon," she wrote on lined paper, in letters that regularly broke formation. "Will you hlpe get Unkl Keith back for us. I started to forget what he looks like. We all need him. Love Susan Jean Kahoon."

TWENTY-EIGHT

THE LIST

By the summer of 1972 the war had become so unpopular that Congress was threatening a vote to force the withdrawal of U.S. forces from Vietnam, with only one condition: the return of U.S. prisoners. President Nixon had ordered Kissinger to negotiate more favorable terms that would keep South Vietnam as stable as possible and allow continued U.S. air support, even after American ground troops were gone. But the noose was tightening around Kissinger and his team of negotiators. There had already been nearly two hundred meetings in Paris between the Americans and the communists, and if Kissinger's people didn't come through with some kind of agreement soon, Congress was likely to yank the rug out from underneath them and end the U.S. role in the war on their terms.[1]

For most of the war, the prisoners in Hanoi and those who had gone missing had been considered as a single group: They had all disappeared and were not with their units or their families. The United States had intelligence that identified some of those who were shackled in the Hanoi prisons, and the North Vietnamese had even identified some of them in the media, but there was still a lot of uncertainty about who was a POW and who was MIA.

The distinction became much more important as the peace talks progressed. The return of American prisoners was a bedrock condition of any deal. But an explanation for the missing was more complicated. Some of these men surely *had* disappeared, killed in furious land battles and never recovered or shot down over inaccessible jungle or mountainous terrain that even local North Vietnamese couldn't get to. The communists would not have had any information about them. Troops lost in Laos were typically in the hands of the ruthless Pathet Lao guerrillas, who had their own agenda and were influenced—but not completely controlled—by Hanoi. Yet there was plenty of reason to be suspicious about Americans deemed to be missing and to demand an accounting from Hanoi. The United States knew from voice communications and from information published by the communists in their own newspapers that there were dozens of servicemen who had been captured alive but never acknowledged by the North. What had happened to them? Were they dead? Sick? Had they been killed? By whom? It was a tough subject, among many tough subjects, and the North Vietnamese continually ducked it.[2]

In the spring of 1972, President Nixon ordered the start of Operation Linebacker—the first bombing of North Vietnam in five months. It was a furious and prolonged assault—more aggressive, even, than attacks on the North during the glory days of Misty. The target list was deliberately broad, meant to signal that this time nothing was off-limits. In contrast to Rolling Thunder, bombers flew around the clock, even in bad weather. The Navy began sowing mines in Haiphong Harbor, a risky move that up till then had been sidestepped on account of the Soviet ship traffic going in and out of North Vietnam. The goal was to tighten the noose until Hanoi made meaningful concessions back at the negotiating table.

In early May, F-4s destroyed the Paul Doumer Bridge in downtown Hanoi, a critical choke point on North Vietnam's most important railroad line. A dense concentration of AAA, SAMs, and even MiG fighter jets made the bridge one of the most fiercely defended targets in the world, and it had never been completely dropped before.[3] F-4s also used laser-guided bombs, a new weapon in aerial warfare, to destroy the Thanh Hoa Bridge, another key rail link south of Hanoi. That closed rail traffic to the South.[4] By the end of June, Air Force and Navy jets had damaged or destroyed more than 400 bridges in North

Vietnam and blown craters in over eight hundred roads on the North's supply network.[5]

P. K. Robinson had volunteered to return to Vietnam after his fellowship in Paris, figuring that after spending a year fighting the war, he ought to do what he could to see it through to a positive conclusion. He was flying F-4s out of Korat Royal Thai Air Base in Thailand and had been appointed a flight commander, responsible for a third of his squadron's pilots. When Linebacker kicked off, P. K. led several raids over North Vietnam, including several that went "downtown," over Hanoi. On one bombing run, after pickling his ordnance, he delayed his pullout just long enough to overfly the Hanoi Hilton and ignite his afterburners—a reminder to the guys inside that nobody had forgotten them.

On July 1, P. K. and his flight were scheduled to attack a railroad near Hanoi. Then the mission got changed: It would be a "MiG sweep" instead, an effort to shoot down some of the North Vietnamese fighter jets that threatened the American strike packages flying north every day. As P. K. and his backseat weapons officer, Kevin Chaney, were cruising over North Vietnam trolling for MiGs, the OH SHIT! light on the instrument panel flashed on—a warning that a SAM had been launched. They looked in every direction but couldn't see anything. Then, just as they were about to conclude that it was a false alert, one of the pilots in another plane shouted over the radio, "Pull it up!" P. K. yanked back on the stick, but before the plane could respond, it blew up. A SAM had solidly nailed the F-4, which was now tumbling toward the ground. Both pilots ejected.

P. K. came down in an open field next to a schoolyard. A teacher whisked all the children inside as Vietnamese farmers menacingly surrounded the field. The militia arrived shortly afterward and cut off P. K.'s flight suit with a machete, then marched him in his underwear, blindfolded, in bare feet, off to a truck. His crewmate, Kevin, was waiting there. Both had been beaten along the way, but were okay. They promptly landed in the same prison that P. K. had buzzed just weeks before.

Operation Linebacker intensified through the summer and into the fall of 1972. Nixon stripped away virtually all of the restrictions that had limited the target list during Rolling Thunder, which brought mounting criticism that the bombing was inhumane and harming civilians. The attacks on supply lines and military infrastructure were having the intended effect, however, and constricting the North's ability to wage war in the South. That was forcing the grudging North Vietnamese to be more responsive at the peace talks.

By October 1972 the pressure valve on those waiting for word of the missing seemed like it might soon loosen. After languishing for months, the peace talks seemed to lurch forward in fits and starts: Both sides sensed an opportunity to extract something from the other. There were leaks in the papers about potential breakthroughs. With a deal seemingly near, Nixon called off Operation Linebacker on October 23. Then on October 26, Henry Kissinger held his first-ever televised press conference, announcing that, "It is obvious that a war that has been raging for ten years is drawing to a conclusion. . . . We believe that peace is at hand."

The hand couldn't quite grab the prize, however, and a final settlement remained elusive. Through the rest of the year the deal was off, then on, then off again, as Washington and Hanoi and Saigon in particular each raised fresh objections. It was a fitting, final measure of torment for those desperate for some kind of resolution. As whipsawed as the family members were, however, many had started living for more than the fragile hope that happy news would come out of somewhere. Monalee Williams still told her son about his dad every day, for instance. But she had finally started signing her Christmas cards using just her name and Howard Jr.'s.

A week before Christmas, Nixon ordered the start of Operation Linebacker II, designed once more to pressure the North Vietnamese to sign a peace settlement. For eleven days, waves of B-52s bombarded Hanoi and Haiphong, while the POWs who could hear the assault cheered from their cells.[6] It reminded some of the POWs of the "Sound and Light at the Roman Forum" show in Italy, the tourist extravaganza with booming sound that encapsulated the violent history of the Roman Empire. It was a devastating series of attacks—but the B-52 crews got a rude awakening, too. Improved air defenses—along with poor tactics by a fleet accustomed to uneventful "jungle-bashing" missions in the South—led to ten of the huge bombers being shot down. Seven others crashed on their way back to base, victims of battle damage. The downings killed 28 crewmen, while 33 others went straight to the prison cells not far from the areas where many of their bombs had fallen.

The campaign worked, though. After eleven days and 498 B-52 sorties, the North Vietnamese finally acknowledged that they were out of SAMs and all but defenseless against the B-52s they agreed to negotiate a final treaty. Nixon called off Linebacker II on December 29. In early January 1973, Paris was buzzing with diplomatic activity. This time it looked like it might be for real. On January 9, Kissinger and his North Vietnamese counterpart Le Duc Tho agreed on the outlines of a deal. On the eighteenth they issued a joint statement saying that in five days they would meet to finalize the text of a peace agreement.

In Texas, Sandy McElhanon and some of her friends were paying close attention to the developments in Paris. Tiger Teague had lived up to his word and been a vocal advocate on Capitol Hill for POWs and MIAs and their families. His prominent position in the House also gave him a line in to the negotiating team in Paris, and he often had advance notice of developments in the talks. Some of the negotiators, in turn, used Teague as a sounding board to get a feel for how well various components of a peace plan might play in Washington.

One evening in January, Teague called Sandy McElhanon and Paula Hartness and asked them, in a somber voice, to meet him at his room in the Marriott Hotel in Dallas. They arrived hoping that Teague had finally learned something about their husbands and had some news to impart. Teague stalled for a moment and poured himself a drink. Then he excused himself to go to the bathroom. He was in there for ten minutes, then twenty. Sandy finally knocked on the door and asked if he was all right. He said yes, he'd be out in a minute.

When he finally emerged, tears were streaming down his face. "Tiger, what's wrong?" Sandy exclaimed. He looked at her sadly. "The sonofabitch Kissinger sold you out," he grimaced. Then he explained that in the final rounds of the peace talks, Kissinger had negotiated for the POWs, but not for an accounting of the MIAs. The two women were devastated. Everything they had worked for over the last four years had just been rendered irrelevant by their own government. Apparently their husbands were worthless as far as Washington was concerned. All the speeches and the letters and the pleas to government officials had amounted to nothing.

On January 23, President Nixon announced that Kissinger and Tho had initialed an agreement "to end the war and bring peace with honor in Vietnam and Southeast Asia." On the twenty-seventh the agreement was finalized and signed by all parties. A cease-fire would begin the next day, all U.S. troops would leave Vietnam within sixty days, and all U.S. prisoners would be returned, also within sixty days. As for the missing, there were no provisions.[7]

Public attention promptly turned to what promised to be one of the most dramatic episodes of the war: The return of some five hundred American prisoners who had been enduring brutal conditions in Hanoi hellholes for the last several years. Some of the names were known, but some weren't, and everybody who knew a missing service member hoped that their man would somehow turn up among the anonymous prisoners about to return to civilization.

There were thousands of others, however, who recognized that a great tragedy was unfolding: The five-hundred-plus prisoners would provide answers to a lot of questions. But almost overnight, thousands of other mysteries would be thrown into the permanently unsolvable pile, the sufferers destined to live with endless uncertainty. Sandy McElhanon knew it, Bev Overlock knew it, Monalee Williams knew it, and they all could have explained the dilemma in excruciating detail.

Before releasing the prisoners, the North Vietnamese were due to turn over a complete list of all the Americans being held. Then the prisoners would be flown out of Hanoi in several waves, over the course of about a month. The list became the focal point for everyone who had been waiting and agonizing over the unknown. For nearly five years Monalee Williams had talked to her son about his dad, describing what Howard was like, how he loved to fly and strum the guitar and play with his son. She reminded Howard Jr. of the things the two of them had done together. Any fragment of a memory Howard Jr. had of his dad, she tried to enshrine in permanence.

Monalee had grown accustomed to the idea that her husband was not going to come home. She was one of the wives who had chosen not to go to Paris or to Vietnam, figuring it would accomplish little. She had been busy completing her master's degree and the one-year internship that was required, and she had started working as a counselor in the county school district. She had to work and take care of her son. But she never completely gave up hope that Howard might come home, and she told her son that if he did he would probably be a different man than either of them remembered. Counselors at the League of Families had offered some guidance, and Monalee worked on lowering her son's expectations. "If your Dad does come back," she told him, "there will be a period of adjustment. Don't expect to be going to the amusement park right away." He had probably been eating nothing but rice for five years and enduring numerous other privations. He might be injured or sick or frighteningly gaunt, like those men in the gauzy video clips released by the North Vietnamese. He might even be hard to recognize.

The Air Force told Monalee that once the list was in U.S. hands and the names had been verified as legitimate, they'd notify family members immediately—whether their man was on the list or not. As the day neared, Monalee's mother came to stay with her. One night they were both lying awake in their beds, unable to sleep, when the phone rang. It was about 3:00 a.m. Monalee's mother came into her room. An Air Force official calmly told Monalee that Howard K. Williams's name was not on the list. "I'm sorry, ma'am," he ended. Monalee and her mother stared at each other, not sure what to say. There had been so much grief and sadness up to that point that tears didn't come right away. They talked for a while about routine things, about the weather, about relatives, about other things that required little concentration. It was a new kind of numbness they felt, but for the moment they were emotionally anesthetized. Monalee decided to take a day or two before she told Howard Jr.

Howard's reaction was similar when his mom told him the news. He had hoped desperately that his dad would be on the list. But at the same time, the years, the uncertainty, living in limbo, and the simple reality of growing up without his father had helped armor Howard, now eleven, against any further bad news. He and his mom wept together, and many friends offered continued condolences and support. But at some level he had expected all of it.

Sandy McElhanon and Bev Overlock got similar calls from the Air Force: Their husbands' names were not on the list. It was crushing news, but all the bitterness had helped prepare them, too. They had hoped for the best but prepared for the worst. And now they had something of an answer, unsatisfying as it was.

There was a lot of talk of continuing to search for the missing, of keeping the pressure on the politicians, of making a deal with the North Vietnamese and going in there to look for American remains. But there was also exhaustion over the whole issue, and a growing national need to move beyond the war. And now the families of the missing had been thinned out and fenced off by the very peace deal that brought the POWs home.

Even Kissinger knew it. After the peace deal had finally been sealed, Kissinger traveled to Hanoi, partly as a bit of ceremony to mark the peace, and partly as an opportunity to press for a few additional demands. Kissinger stayed in one of the few elegant buildings left standing in Hanoi, a two-story guesthouse that had been the quarters for French dignitaries during their colonial rule more than twenty years earlier. At one point Kissinger and a few aides, while waiting to meet North Vietnamese prime minister Pham Van Dong, went on an impromptu stroll through the streets of Hanoi. They didn't know it, but they walked within a few hundred yards of many American prisoners still caged in Hanoi's holding pens.[8]

When Kissinger finally met with Dong, he pressed the issue of the missing. The U.S. government now counted about 1,340 men as MIA, more than twice the number being held prisoner.[9] The Americans knew that at least 80 of those had been taken captive by the North Vietnamese, never to be heard from again. It stood to reason that dozens of others, maybe hundreds, had undergone the same fate. In a tense exchange, Kissinger drilled Dong for a commitment to investigate these mysteries and eventually provide some answers. Dong calmly answered that they had no information beyond the names of the prisoners. Conducting such investigations in the harsh, rugged terrain of North Vietnam, he said, could take a year or longer, and he made no offer to begin such proceedings. Kissinger knew full well that the North Vietnamese kept thorough records and must have documented the deaths or other fates of untold numbers of Americans. Retrieving those records would take hours, not months and certainly not years. But Kissinger no longer had any leverage to make such demands, and the discussion turned back to other matters.[10]

TWENTY-NINE

FINAL DISPOSITION

The first wave of prisoners came home in early February. They spent about a week undergoing medical exams and military debriefings at Clark Air Base in the Philippines before flying back to the United States. Despite stringent efforts by the military to downplay the drama and quickly whisk the returnees off to hospitals and homes, the return was a televised spectacle that rivaled the 1969 moon landing. Howard and Monalee watched the TV by themselves, in their apartment in Columbus, as the POWs walked off the plane and were greeted by wives and children they hadn't seen in years. It was very hard to watch. Some of their friends from the League of Families were out at Travis, rejoicing as lost husbands and fathers emerged from the plane. Monalee and Howard cried a lot, without saying very much.

The prisoners were released in the order of capture, and Bud Day, Bob Craner, and Guy Gruters all left North Vietnam on March 14, 1973. Bud required significant medical attention at Clark. His arms were crippled from five years and seven months of repeated "hangings" during torture sessions. Other parts of his body were atrophied or damaged. Air Force officials told him that his half sister, Verna Collins, with whom he was very close, had died while he was in captivity. So had his half brother, Orval Dowell. And there was a letter waiting from his wife, Doris, with pictures of the family and even a sketch of their new home. Bud yearned to hear her voice more than anything he had ever wanted in his life.

Finally, he boarded a C-141 Starlifter bound for March Air Force Base in California. When he stepped off the plane, with misty eyes and a quivering throat, he scanned a thick crowd for Doris. After about four years in captivity, he had begun having trouble recalling her face. He didn't see her, and before he knew it he was at the bottom of the stairs, shaking hands with Air Force generals and other dignitaries. As a newly pinned colonel and a senior officer, Bud was expected to address the crowd. He stepped up to a microphone and expressed his thanks to God, his country, his people, and his president.

Then he heard a pair of high heels clacking on the pavement as a woman ran toward him. He turned to the left and there she was. Doris looked like an angel, as young and beautiful as when he had last seen her more than six years earlier. They embraced and he held her as tight as he could. "Welcome home!" she sobbed. "It has been soooooo long!"

Then Bud saw his four children racing up right behind her. One of them thrust a hand-scribbled note at him. It read: "Welcome home, Dad. We love you very much. We have been waiting."[1]

Bob Craner was in better shape than Bud. After three days at Clark, he flew back to the States with plans to meet his wife, Audrey, and his children, Lorne and Charys, at Andrews Air Force Base on St. Patrick's Day. He landed first at Scott Air Force Base in Illinois and learned that rough storms were impeding flights to the East Coast. After more than five years in prison, Bob had to wait one more day to see his family. On the eighteenth he finally got to Andrews, where his family was frazzled with impatience but overjoyed to see him.

Guy Gruters made a brief stop at Clark before flying to Maxwell Air Force Base in Alabama. A line of cars met the airplane. In one sat Charlie Neel—Guy's crewmate on his first shootdown, nearly six years earlier—and his wife, Linda. Charlie was Guy's driver and "escort officer." In the backseat was his wife, Sandy. Charlie would drive Guy and Sandy back to the officers quarters where they would join Guy's family—his mother and father, two brothers, and three sisters. Then there were his daughters, Dawn, eight, and Sheri, seven. The girls barely remembered their dad, but they were all determined to make up quickly for his absence.

P. K. Robinson had been the Misty "short timer" in prison. It had been unpleasant as hell, but he was in good shape when he was released on March 28 after nine months of captivity. There was a debriefing at Clark, then a military counselor met with him and told him his father-in-law had died while he was in Hanoi. P. K. flew to Sheppard Air Force Base in Texas, where his wife, Reta, was waiting for him. They caught up while P. K. took a month of leave, and went to Aurora, Colorado, where Reta had bought a home while her husband was in prison.

The ordeal finally began to subside for the families of those who returned. For the rest, however, it entered an awkward new phase. Howard and Monalee didn't know whether or not to call some of the other POW families, but ultimately they did. They felt happy for those who had returned, but they also felt cheated. The families whose men had returned, on the other hand, were ecstatic. But they also felt guilty for having gotten good news when others got bad, or none. For several years the families of the missing and the families of the prisoners had faced a common ordeal. Now they didn't.

When her husband didn't come home with the POWs, Bev Overlock decided to change her life once and for all. She had been living in a state of hiatus for five years and felt like she was going nowhere. There seemed to be no choice but to put the past aside and move forward. She petitioned the Air Force to change John's status from missing in action to killed in action, a change that only required the agreement of the next of kin—her.

That was more than a mere paperwork change, however. Service members classified as MIA continued to receive full pay and benefits, as if they were still doing their assigned jobs. They earned promotions at the appointed times and the raises that came with them. Once the person was declared KIA, it was a big financial hit to the spouses. The survivors' pension was only about 55 percent of base pay, and other benefits, such as participation in the military savings plan, stopped. It was never a formal policy, but one thing the military was generous about was extending MIA status as long as possible for the financial benefit of the spouses.

Money was not a problem for Bev, however. She had done so well at Burdines that she had become manager of the entire store. She was living completely on her own pay and had put most of John's salary into savings. The emotional and psychological benefits of putting John to rest, of ending the battle with the Air Force, of distancing herself from those coldhearted communists, outweighed her financial need.

She thought she might get resistance from John's family in New York. But they were just as worn out as she was and felt that standing in the way would just be prolonging the inevitable. Besides, Bev and John had had no children, and she only had to worry about herself— she did not face the additional burden of trying to fashion and preserve a child's image of his or her father. So she filled out some forms, and with the flurry of a pen she opened the door to the rest of her life.

In 1973 she moved to Denver, where her friends Cookie and K. B. Clark, whom she had met during an earlier posting in the UK, were living. Another set of mutual friends, Jim Wallace and his wife, Marta, were leaving for a year and asked if Bev wanted to house-sit and take care of their dog. The change of scenery sounded great to her, so she found renters for her townhouse and headed west. She worked in retail and started making plans to open her own shop in a nearby mall. Although Bev had plenty of money, all of the loans and assets during her marriage had been in John's name, and she had no credit. So she went to the credit union at nearby Lowry Air Force Base, took out a loan, and immediately paid it back. That gave her a credit record she could use to start a business. Meanwhile, she played tennis in the summer and skied in the winter, and felt like she was getting her own life back.

When the Wallaces decided to stay away for another year, she jumped at the chance to extend the house-sitting deal. Bev had a friend who was a developer and was building a shopping complex. He encouraged her to open a doll store in the mall with another mutual friend. The two partners went on a scouting trip to Los Angeles, where they researched the latest retail trends. Dolls were out, they decided. Instead, they opened a lingerie boutique. It was successful from the beginning.

When the Wallaces returned, Bev moved into an apartment complex with a pool and tennis courts and a view of the mountains. While playing tennis one day in 1976 a friend introduced her to Jim Day, a doctor who lived in the same complex. They started dating. Bev's years with John and with the Air Force seemed more and more distant, almost unreal, like a fleeting image glimpsed in the reflections on the surface of a pond. They had been important years. But Bev also knew that you couldn't hold on to life in a negative way, you had to let go of anger and resentment and frustration. She had done that, and Jim felt positive. They got married in 1978.

Monalee Williams and Sandy McElhanon believed, just like Bev Overlock, that their husbands were most likely dead. About two weeks after the last of the POWs had been released, P. K. Robinson paid Sandy a visit. He told her that among the network of POWs, nobody had ever seen or heard of Mike, or of John Overlock. And the prisoners had made a point of keeping a mental roster of all the Americans who passed through the prison system, whether they survived or not. If Mike was still being held somewhere, it was not in the central prison system up in Hanoi, he assured her.

But Sandy and Monalee could not as easily zip up their husband's lives and start over. For one thing, there were the children, who had to sort out what had happened to their fathers. Howard Jr. turned out to be especially curious about anything that called into question the credibility of the government. In 1974, when most of his fellow thirteen-year-olds were becoming sports fanatics and girl chasers, Howard was developing an additional interest: He was fascinated by the Watergate hearings and the undoing of President Nixon. He couldn't believe that the president, of all people, had lied. If you couldn't trust the president, he asked himself, who could you trust? The list, in his mind, was getting pretty small.

Monalee stayed involved with the League of Families and other support groups for families of the missing. Dozens of strangers had started wearing Howard Williams's MIA bracelet, a phenomenon that started as a way for friends and families of the missing to signal their remembrance, and for ordinary civilians to show solidarity with them. People wrote asking about Howard, what had happened to him in Vietnam, and what kind of person he was. It was a surprising degree of support and comfort from people they didn't even know. All of the attention made Howard's dad seem extraordinary to him. He was a war hero. Howard Jr. never heard a negative word about his father.

The Williamses had become close with three other families whose men did not return with the POWs. None of the families retreated into a cocoon—it was practically impossible, after all, with kids growing up, involved in all manner of school activities—but none of them had family close by, and they found it a comfort to spend time with one another. To the wives and the children alike, it was a relief that they didn't have to account for their emotions or explain how they felt when they were around one another. It was simply understood.

The families took several trips together, to Washington, D.C., for national meetings, to New York to attend the theater and see the sights, and to Colorado for a vacation retreat. The retreat offered organized play for the kids and coping sessions for the adults. Grief counseling and other sorts of therapy were largely left to the families, but occasionally psychologists would come in and conduct discussion groups, tossing questions to the kids. "What would you think if your mother remarried?" they asked. Then they told the adults what kinds of answers they got back. The younger kids wanted a daddy, any daddy, and they thought it would be great if there was a man around the house. The older kids were more wary, however, and didn't think their mothers should even date.

Parents of the missing attended the groups, too, and Monalee began to notice that the parents often hung on longer than the wives did. Their children, after all, were irreplaceable; there was no way to "start over" with other children. As for the wives, women without kids, like Bev Overlock, were often eager for a fresh start, and there was little holding them back. The wives with children wanted to get on with their lives, too, and events often propelled them that way no matter what. They had to get the kids through school and pay the bills, and many had to work to pull it off, and many of them were young enough to envision a new life as well.

The children grew bright and bold, like other kids around them—except that they spent a lot more time looking back, trying to learn who their fathers had been. Kelly McElhanon, Sandy and Mike's eldest daughter, thrived in the country. She became good with horses and started to compete in local riding competitions. But she also began paying attention to some of the controversial people saying there were still prisoners in Vietnam, and she developed some strident ideas herself. She seemed to believe her father was still alive, and in captivity. Her younger sister, Paige, had been too young to remember her dad, and seemed less traumatized.

Howard Williams Jr. did well in school and played baseball, and he remained extremely proud of his dad. But his dad also seemed so lofty, so perfect, that it was hard knowing how he would have gotten along with him. Would my dad be proud of me? Howard often wondered. As he grew older, he also became more certain than ever that he was against the war in Vietnam, and against all war everywhere.

As time passed, attention to the debris of the war waned. The war itself ended in 1975, a complete disaster. On April 23, President Ford declared the war finished. "As far as America is concerned," he said, "Americans can regain the sense of pride that existed before Vietnam."[2] A week later the communists stormed into Saigon, facing only light resistance from the collapsing forces of the government of South Vietnam. It had taken fifteen years of fighting, but the communists had achieved a total rout. After so much anguish, there was little desire in the United States to look back on the debacle, and Americans were eager to think of something else.

By 1976 the bracelet campaign had begun to peter out. Those who had been close to the missing continued to wear the bands, but the comforting letters from unknown supporters generally stopped arriving. The only contacts from the broader outside world tended to come from the desperate, the disturbed, and the lonely. Sandy McElhanon got one memorable letter from a prisoner in solitary confinement, which began with a warm expression of sympathy and compassion for her plight. Then the inmate asked if he could meet her when he got out. Yeah, right, Sandy thought.

One day in their apartment, Howard Williams told his mom they should consider buying a house. Apartments are kind of transient, he said. People come and go. A house would seem more stable. Monalee thought about it. She was out bicycling with a friend one day and saw a lot advertised for sale in a nice neighborhood. She asked around about the builder, who had a good reputation. She had never had a house built, and there were a few complications in getting a loan with a husband whom nobody could say for sure was dead or alive. But Monalee worked it out and moved into a new three-bedroom home in the fall of 1976.

They were moving into the future, but there were still some sharp curves along the way. One of the most difficult to manage was the "final disposition" process for drawing the cases of the missing to a conclusion. The question of what to do about more than two thousand MIAs was one of the most contentious issues to emerge from the war. There wasn't much action the United States could take in practical terms, but the treatment of the families and the delicacy with which the government handled many unresolved questions could either ease a difficult process or inflame wounds that were still very raw. Most of the family members had once been loyal, unquestioning members of the military community. But now, many felt cheated and abused by the establishment they had put their trust in. Quite a few were openly hostile toward the government. The Air Force didn't really have any answers to give most of them, but that didn't make the situation any more tolerable for those who felt they had a right to demand answers.

The Air Force allowed many of the MIA cases to remain open indefinitely, prolonging full pay for the spouses and putting off the painful moment when a service member was officially declared dead. But there had to be a cutoff point, and the service decided that if the next of kin hadn't already taken such action, there would be a hearing and an examination of the facts. If there was no evidence suggesting that the man might still be living, his status would be changed from MIA to KIA.

Monalee Williams had repeatedly asked the Air Force to provide her all the information it had on her husband. She got the same response every time: They told her the same basic facts she already knew and said the rest of the matter was classified. So toward the end of 1977 she filed a Freedom of Information request officially asking the Air Force to declassify Howard's file and release it to her. It took four months to get an answer, and what she received was thin stuff: Copies of several messages sent from the wing at Phu Cat in the initial hours and days after the shootdown, a few supplementary reports, and a memo one year after the shootdown, when an investigation into the crash had been completed. All the memo said was that the Air Force had "unofficially" decided to continue Howard Williams's status as MIA. And he had been promoted from captain to major. Virtually nothing else had been added to his file over the next eight years. Then in 1978, the Defense

Intelligence Agency—which had inherited responsibility for gathering intel on MIAs—added another memo to Howard's file. It said simply, "DIA maintains no intelligence information or casualty resolution data pertinent to this case." This non-news had important implications: It cleared the way for Howard Williams's final disposition status to be changed from missing to killed in action.

Some key information *was* missing from Howard's file, however. At no point in ten years had the original radio intercept picked up by the electronic intelligence experts back in 1968—the one indicating that the North Vietnamese had found Howard Williams's body after the crash—ever crossed the threshold separating supersecret intelligence from accessible facts. For a decade this vital bit of detail had stayed in its highly classified hidey-hole—and it wasn't about to come out now. This scrap of information could have changed Monalee's life, and that of many others. Had they known there was persuasive evidence suggesting Howard had died in the crash—even if it wasn't watertight evidence—they might have let go sooner, stepped into the future on a firmer surface than the shifting sand of uncertainty. But even the government's own investigators—who had plenty of security clearances themselves—didn't know what the ELINT eavesdroppers had learned. It was a secret they were determined to keep secret.

On May 15, 1978, Monalee attended an Air Force "status review hearing" at Randolph Air Force Base in Texas. A board of three Air Force colonels—all of whom had flown numerous combat missions in Southeast Asia—would review the case file of Howard K. Williams and decide whether he should be declared killed in action. In Howard's case, the outcome was relatively certain—Monalee wasn't contesting the hearing or asking the Air Force to extend her husband's MIA status—and the hearing was largely a formality. But it was important to Monalee nonetheless. Even after ten years, she had learned so little about what may have happened to Howard—even the basic circumstances of the crash—that she intended to take advantage of any forum where she might learn a few additional facts.

Just after 10:00 a.m., Col. William E. Cordingly, an Air Force lawyer, called the meeting to order. Monalee had waived her right to bring a civilian lawyer, but did have a friend with her, Francis McGouldrick. She had left Howard Jr. at home with her parents. The only other people at the hearing were four Air Force officials responsible for helping process the case. The two women sat with their hands folded on the table while the three board members sat across a conference table from them in their blue class-A uniforms. Cordingly began with a list of formalities, verifying that Monalee had chosen to proceed without a lawyer, making sure nobody objected to the nature of the proceeding, and inviting the board members to introduce themselves. Then he declared, "This board is convened for the sole purpose of making findings and recommendations as to whether a status change is warranted in the case of Lt. Col. Howard K. Williams, who is now being carried in a missing-in-action status."

After some further preliminaries, Cordingly briefly recounted the events of March 18, 1968, when Howard and Brian Williams had been shot down. There were pro forma recitations of matters it was important to "let the record reflect." Then Monalee was given "an opportunity to make an opening statement and to present evidence for consideration by the board." Monalee had no statement or evidence, but she did have some questions. She addressed the first one to Col. Bernard Boshoven, who just like Howard had flown the F-100 in Vietnam. She referred to a statement in the Summary of Facts and Circumstances in Howard's case file, which said that Misty 21A, Howard's call sign for the mission, probably would have had to eject no higher than 2,500 feet off the ground. That may have been too low an altitude to survive. "What altitude is too low in the F-100?" she asked.

"As with any aircraft," he answered, "it's going to depend on the angle the aircraft is on in relation to the ground." Had Howard's plane been flying straight and level, he said, the altitude would have been "well sufficient" for a safe bailout. But if the plane was descending at a 30-degree angle to the ground or thereabouts, "it might not be anywhere near enough." He himself had ejected once at about 1,000 feet and survived without any problem—but that had been from a plane flying fairly slow and level.

Monalee wanted to know if there was any other information not in the file that may have come from POWs or other sources and might shed light on Howard's case. As far as we know, no, was the answer. Then she asked about the area where Howard had gone down, terrain she still knew little about ten years later. Had the Air Force ever done an analysis of how likely pilots were to get rescued or survive, based on where they went down? Don't think so, said one of the panel members. The last thing Monalee asked is whether Howard's file would remain active, in case any new information surfaced that might help explain what happened. We can't say for sure, came the answer, although the Department of Defense and the Air Force were highly committed to continuing to seek information. "I really just would like it on the record that I would want this to continue to be presented for information," Monalee said. "I have a feeling it will be many years, but I do wish to have it, the information, still forwarded. I have no other questions."

Cordingly then explained that the board members would meet in a closed session to determine whether Howard's status should be changed, and the hearing ended. At about 10:45 a.m. he closed the session. The panel members moved to another room to deliberate. They returned fifteen minutes later. Cordingly called the board to order. "Has the board reached its findings and recommendations?" he asked.

"Yes sir, we have," Col. Gene Taft, one of the board members, replied. "After evaluating all of the evidence placed before it by both the United States Air Force and next of kin, the panel finds that on the weight of credible evidence, Lt. Col. Howard K. Williams can reasonably be presumed to be dead. The panel recommends that the status of Lt. Col. Howard K. Williams . . . be changed . . . from missing in action to killed in action." Cordingly shuffled some papers and told Monalee that a transcript of the hearing would be mailed to her. She nodded her head but said nothing further. By 11:07 the hearing was over.

Six weeks later the formal notification arrived. "Dear Mrs. Williams," it began. "It is with deep regret that I must officially notify you of the termination of the missing status of your husband, Lieutenant Colonel Howard K. Williams, since he can no longer reasonably be presumed to be alive." The letter went on for four paragraphs, with an explanation of how the panel had come to its findings and assurances that the U.S. government would do anything it could to gather additional information. It was signed by Maj. Gen. L. W. Svendsen Jr., an Air Force assistant deputy chief of staff.

Finally, the Williams family could go through the motions of putting Howard to rest. His mom wanted to have a burial ceremony at the cemetery in Steubenville where other family members had been interred. The Air Force would provide one headstone, which Monalee wanted to reserve for a formal military burial if her husband's remains were ever returned, so she bought another headstone for the Williams plot. On November 26 an Air Force chaplain came to Two Ridge Church in Steubenville and presided over a music and prayer service. Air Force officials formally presented Howard's medals to his son. There was another brief ceremony sometime later when the headstone was put in place at the cemetery and dedicated.

Then came a memorial service at Fort Steuben, the veterans cemetery in Steubenville. That was supposed to convey an added measure of dignity upon Howard. But to his sister Jean the ceremony seemed shabby, a perfectly fitting ending to the whole ordeal of the last ten years. When she and her brother were kids, one of Howard's jobs was to play taps on his trumpet at Fort Steuben when a veteran was buried. It was a thoughtful setup. One trumpeter would be down in a gully, out of sight, while another would be up on the hillside where the ceremonies took place. The invisible second trumpeter sent the doleful tune echoing throughout the surrounding countryside, a kind of mystifying, eternal effect. But at Keith's ceremony there was no trumpeter. And the cemetery looked unkempt, like they hadn't even cleaned up the loose dirt scattered around. Her brother deserved much better, she thought.

Finally there was a memorial service out at the Steubenville airfield, where Howard and his best friend, John Buckmelter, had washed planes in exchange for free rides and where they had first learned to fly. This was a private service sponsored by Buckmelter and other friends of Howard's in Steubenville's small flying community. Howard had clearly touched a lot of people, and everyone who had known him, it seemed, felt moved to honor him in some formal way. But for the family, the stream of services was beginning to border on overload. All we do is go to funerals, Howard's sister Jean thought.

Tragic as the facts were, closing Howard's case was more relief than sadness. Monalee had received her master's degree in psychology by then and charted out a career as a school psychologist. She enjoyed her work and felt motivated by it. Howard Jr. was seventeen, busy applying to colleges and planning out his future. When the POWs had come home in 1973 and his father wasn't among them, he had figured that was the end—his dad was gone for good. But it hadn't been so easy letting go. Now, he thought, it is really over. We have laid him to rest. And in small ways that became true. All through school, every time a form or document had asked for his father's information, he'd write his dad's full name followed by USAF. But after the status change, he asked his mom what he should write. She said he could either leave it blank or write "deceased." He didn't like writing "deceased," so usually he wrote nothing.

The status review hearing for Mike McElhanon was more dramatic. Sandy McElhanon brought an attorney whose brother had been an Army helicopter pilot who was shot down and missing. Kelly, her daughter, was sixteen and attended as well, along with a couple of friends. Sandy felt she had gotten little more than a runaround from the Air Force over the last ten years. The Air Force had offered no support and seemed to regard the wives of the missing as little more than a nuisance. Kelly was suspicious, and angry, too. She was sure the Air Force just wanted to sweep her dad's whole history right under the rug. The hearing, to them, seemed like a hollow exercise that would simply allow the Air Force to unburden itself of Mike's case.

An Air Force lawyer went through all the formalities and explained what was known about Mike's disappearance. Then he closed the hearing while the board convened to evaluate the facts contained in the 500-page report on the matter. Thirty minutes later they returned. That didn't seem right. Thirty minutes to review 500 pages? Sandy thought. Thirty minutes for a decision that will affect the rest of my life? Then one of the panel members read the same statement that had changed Howard Williams's status from missing to killed. Sandy fumed. Mike was gone, they didn't know where, but they knew enough to declare him dead and reduce her income by 45 percent. It felt humiliating.

Then one of the panel members walked over to her, looked her in the eye, took her hand, and in an authoritative voice said, "Pleasure." Sandy knew this was officer-and-gentleman-style shorthand for, "It has been a pleasure dealing with you." But it sounded callous and unctuous, as if it had been a pleasure getting rid of the McElhanons. The final humiliation, Sandy thought, just like the government's entire approach to the MIAs—no information, just dismissal. Kelly was downright insulted. She was a tinderbox of teenage rage, and the colonel's faux-formal attitude was all the spark she needed. She began screaming, "You took my dad! You took my dad!" as Sandy and the others shuffled her out of the room.

Unlike Monalee, Sandy did not agree with the change in her husband's status. But there was no way to appeal the decision. The government had the final say, and whether the family members were ready to move on or not, to let go of the old life and put it behind them, didn't really matter. When the government decided that your husband was dead, he was dead. The time for waiting and wondering was officially over.

THIRTY

A NEW CURRENCY

Sandy and Kelly McElhanon went back to their ranch and tried to get on with their lives. The past would not stay in its place, however. Sandy met a man through the horse and farm business whom she started dating. He was kind and comforting, and after so much turmoil she could see herself settling down with him. But he tripped over the uncertainty of Sandy having a husband who was officially dead but not necessarily gone. "What if he comes back?" he asked Sandy repeatedly. It seemed like an increasingly remote possibility, but the truth was, Sandy didn't know what would happen if Mike came back. They stopped seeing each other.

Sandy met another man she ultimately married. He was good to Sandy's kids. Kelly liked him and got very attached. But the marriage didn't work out, and Sandy divorced him after seven years. She and Kelly argued frequently over what happened. Kelly insisted that her mom never let go of her first husband and was haunted by his memory. She couldn't commit to the new guy because she had never ended her commitment to the old one, Kelly lectured her mom. But Sandy knew otherwise. She remained angry and bitter about what happened to Mike, about the total lack of information, and the government's eagerness to wrap everything up whether there were answers or not.

But she wasn't haunted by her past. She simply had not married the right man.

Monalee had let go of her husband at least twice—when he didn't return with the POWs in 1973, five years after getting shot down, and when he was officially declared killed in action in 1978. But letting go was not an event, she discovered—it was a process. And the process was still going on. She still wore her wedding rings, and while she had decided she'd be able to live a pleasant, perhaps even happy life without ever being married again, she was certainly not living as if she were single, either.

A friend at the school district, Diane Eversole, decided she was going to make a project out of Monalee. "You're young and pretty," she told her. "I'm going to find you a man."

Monalee said she wasn't interested—but she did begin to realize she was still emotionally married to Howard. She decided once and for all that she had to break that. Howard Jr. had gone off to school at Boston University. So Monalee took off her wedding rings and went out on a few dates. She enjoyed being out with men, dinner and a show typically, but she began to realize how compatible she and Howard had been on values and lifestyle and other important issues. It was something she never even thought of back then, but she thought about it a lot now, as she met men who didn't seem to stand for anything important or just didn't seem serious.

One day Diane mentioned that a friend of hers named Peggy knew a nice man who lived in Toledo, but commuted to Columbus on weekends to visit his mother, who was sick. Diane arranged a get-together for the three women, and over a glass of wine Peggy told Monalee about Fritz Meyers. She had dated him briefly but ended up marrying somebody else she had known for a while. Yet she regarded Fritz as quite a catch. He was separated from his wife en route to a divorce, with one grown daughter. He was an engineer who worked for Owens-Corning, and thoroughly a gentleman. Peggy strongly recommended that Monalee give him a try.

The matchmaker pulled a few strings, and in February 1981, Fritz called Monalee to ask if she'd have lunch with him one Sunday afternoon while he was in Columbus. She agreed. At the last minute he realized he ought to show up with some flowers, and he found a Kroger supermarket with a florist shop. It was a blind date—the two had never seen each other—but when Monalee opened the door to her house, Fritz was overjoyed at what he saw. Lunch went well and he asked her out again. She said yes.

They dated throughout 1981, and by the next summer it was a serious relationship. Fritz was completely aware of her first husband, and Monalee gradually shared the whole story with him. Fritz gave a little thought to whether he should get involved with someone whose husband, theoretically, might still be out there somewhere. But the fact that Howard had been declared deceased—and his impression that Monalee accepted that—seemed to put the matter to rest. "There's a chapter one, and a chapter two," he told himself. Fritz hoped he would be chapter two.

One evening in the summer of 1982, over dinner with Monalee—and her mother—Fritz proposed. Monalee accepted. There was just one formality. Monalee called Howard's sister Jean, up near Cleveland. "Would it bother you if I remarried?" she asked, not asking for Jean's approval exactly, but wanting to know if Howard's closest sibling was as comfortable with chapter two as she was.

As far as Jean was concerned, Monalee had waited splendidly for her husband and shown more loyalty to Howard than any woman could ever be expected to. "I wonder why you haven't done it already," Jean answered.

Fritz resigned from Owens-Corning. With the help of a former employee who worked at Ohio State University, his alma mater, he got hired as a professor. That allowed him to move to Columbus, where he and Monalee got married on December 18, 1982.

Howard Jr. was unable to make the wedding—he was stationed in England and unable to get leave to fly home. He had spent just a semester at school in Boston before deciding he didn't like college. So in 1980 he enlisted in the Air Force for a four-year tour. Military service had been good enough for his father and his Uncle Roger, he reasoned, so it ought to be good enough for him. If he was following in his father's footsteps, however, he was making only part of the trip. He had no desire to become a pilot and was satisfied when the Air Force made him a driver responsible for transporting VIPs and running official errands.

Howard had also begun to refer to himself as Keith, the middle name that he shared with his father. Many people, including Monalee, had called his dad by that name. It felt more grown-up than Howard. Besides, his dad had been generous and brave—perhaps even a war hero—and it made him feel proud to share his name.

One of Keith's first postings was at Lowry Air Force Base in Denver, where he met Jacque Tumey. She was an Air Force brat who had been born in France and gone to school in Germany while her father fulfilled tours as a senior enlisted airman. Jacque was happy to move with Howard to his next posting, in Albuquerque, New Mexico, and eventually to Chicksands, a quiet base about sixty miles north of London. Instead of runways and a control tower, the dominant feature at Chicksands was a huge antenna complex, the hallmark of a sophisticated signals intelligence operation—a gigantic eavesdropping station. The base's secret significance kept a steady stream of VIPs flowing through, which meant Keith had plenty of work driving dignitaries around the base and the countryside in a bulletproof Mercedes.

He and Jacque had gotten married earlier that year. When he learned that his mom was engaged, Keith was delighted. She had taken a long time just to start dating, and even then there had been a couple of losers in the batch. Since he couldn't make it home for the wedding, Monalee and Fritz went to England shortly after they were married to visit and see the sights.

They never completely put Monalee's first husband away. The Air Force still sent Monalee a lot of letters—mostly with cursory information—and she shared all of these with Fritz. Occasionally when there was some matter that needed tending to, he would help. But most of the time Monalee would just add the letters to the stacks of paperwork she kept in a file cabinet in the basement. The ongoing saga of her first husband did not interfere with the budding new life she had with her second. Howard was not forgotten, but she was finally putting him to rest.

Back in Vietnam, however, people were trying to resurrect Howard K. Williams. Or at least parts of him. In 1977 a delegation of U.S. officials had traveled to Vietnam and returned with the remains of twelve U.S. pilots who had been shot down and killed during the war. It was minor news, one of thousands of footnotes in a saga that most Americans simply wanted to forget. But that had opened the door for other opportunities to investigate the cases of missing service members and, if possible, bring home remains.

A working relationship between the United States and the communist government in Vietnam developed very slowly, with lots of suspicion on both sides. But over time, the Vietnamese began to allow U.S. search missions into the country, under strict supervision. The communists wanted to make sure the Americans weren't gathering intelligence, and they also plied their wealthy antagonists for favors in exchange for access to the country. First they asked for help in gaining official recognition by the United Nations. Then came repeated requests for international and U.S. monetary aid. Vietnam had been a poor region to start with, and the aftermath of a debilitating war coupled with stultifying communist economic policies left Vietnam struggling just to feed its people.

The United States was willing to pay a high price to learn as much as it could about missing servicemen. Prodded by the National League of Families, the Pentagon had established an office exclusively focused on searching for missing Americans in Indochina and bringing home remains. The 1982 dedication of the Vietnam Veterans Memorial in Washington, D.C.—"the Wall"—generated a fresh round of attention to the subject. And the Wall became a rallying point for protesters agitating for more action from the government. In 1983, President Reagan met with the National League of Families and said U.S. intelligence agencies were "fully focused" on tracking down missing service men, and that it was a matter of the "highest national priority."[1] Some of the family members, unconvinced by anything the government had to say, were completely skeptical. But others felt that maybe, for the first time, the White House would insist on getting answers from the North Vietnamese and do whatever it took—whether by pressure, or payment—to obtain them.

The presidential-level attention coupled with behind-the-scenes efforts to track down American remains had an unforeseen consequence, however: The United States was essentially creating a black market for information and artifacts relating to its missing servicemen. Nearly all Vietnamese were desperate for money. Hundreds of thousands were seeking asylum in the United States. By the mid-1980s the Reagan administration had decided to offer entry to as many as twenty thousand Vietnamese—if the communists would release them—who were either children of American servicemen or were being persecuted in Vietnam because they had been associated with Americans or carried some other black mark. But that was a pittance compared to all of the people who were trying to escape the communists. At least half a million Vietnamese refugees who had fled their homeland at the end of the war in 1975 were still languishing in camps in Thailand, Laos, and Cambodia. Thousands of others began fleeing Vietnam on rickety boats, to escape political persecution or crushing poverty. A few made it to the United States or Great Britain or other developed countries, but most of the lowly "boat people"—those who didn't drown or get abducted by pirates—became virtual inmates at grim settlement camps in Hong Kong or other Asian countries.

Suddenly it was like a new currency had been created. Even if you had money, you couldn't buy your way into the United States. But if you could provide information about an American GI. . . . To the Vietnamese, it seemed astonishing that anybody would go to such trouble to track down their people—they were *dead,* after all. The North Vietnamese government had pushed nearly a million of its own troops off the cliff of mortal combat, and it wasn't going around looking for their bodies. Yet it was the same American fanaticism they had seen when infantrymen rushed onto a battlefield, under fire, to pull back the bodies of fallen comrades, and when aviators would risk the lives of dozens of pilots, not to mention their multimillion-dollar jets, to pull a single man out of the jungle. As strange as it seemed, the Vietnamese had learned how to profit by giving the Americans what they wanted. This seemed like another chance to do so.

Word got around that the United States was willing to talk to anybody who might know something about the location of Americans who were killed during the war and never retrieved. There might be . . . rewards. And so, like every other sort of unofficial commerce, the black market for information on the missing was rapidly filled with merchandise of dubious quality, and quite a few outright knockoffs. Thousands of reports began to filter in about people who had acquired the dog tags of American servicemen, or whose relatives had. These could have come from a corpse—but the odds were great that they didn't. Dog tags had been loosely regulated during the war and churned out by the thousands. Duplicates and rejects often ended up in trash dumps. If a soldier lost a set, he'd simply ask for a new one. Nobody tracked them. When the Americans left, their dog tags literally littered the country.

Most of the "dog tag" reports turned out to come from areas far from where the troops in question had disappeared. Some were total fabrications. But there was always a chance that a local citizen had found a body and removed the actual dog tags, so the MIA investigators tracked every report and looked into those that had some potential merit.

The first dog tag report on Howard K. Williams surfaced in 1983. It was a typical report, vague and improbable. A woman who lived in Vietnam claimed that a friend of her daughter's, who supposedly had been a former officer in the South Vietnamese Army, had the remains of three Americans, including Howard Williams. But there was no explanation for how a South Vietnamese Army officer would have acquired the remains of an American pilot who had crashed in dense jungle in North Vietnam, close to Laos. It was unlikely that he had been anywhere near the crash site.[2]

Vietnamese scam artists didn't just offer bogus information: Sometimes they trafficked in actual human remains. U.S. intelligence forwarded another report the same year, based on interviews with two Vietnamese refugees. They said that a man named either Nguyen Ngoc Khanh or Xuan Khanh, who had been a major in the South Vietnamese Army, had the dog tags of four Americans whose remains were hidden in Hue. One of these men supposedly was Howard Williams, which suggested that his remains had traveled at least 150 miles from where his plane had crashed. To prove it, one of the refugees produced eight small bags of body fragments, including a tooth and a small piece of somebody's left femur. Forensics tests revealed that the bone pieces had Mongoloid characteristics—they had come from an Asian, not an American.

Sad to say, body parts were easy to come across in Vietnam. It was not well understood that forensic techniques could provide a lot of information about small sets of remains, and even confirm the identity of individuals if there were teeth. Common belief was that if you had a set of dog tags and just a few bits of bone—no matter where they came from—you might just be able to persuade the Americans that you had one of their cherished missing servicemen in your hands. That wasn't the case, but like all bad rumors it took on a life of its own.

A lot of the reports were easy to disprove. Sometimes there was a name and a serial number, but they didn't match. Refugees and other sources occasionally claimed to have in their possession, or to have seen, the remains of people who had served in Vietnam but were alive and well in the United States. The Pentagon knew that since at least 1965, North Vietnamese troops in the field had been under strict orders from Hanoi to strip and bury any U.S. dead they came across and to send the personal effects to higher headquarters immediately. While possible, it was highly implausible that the remains of U.S. servicemen had been carted around Vietnam for years and were just now being offered back to the Americans.

There were more sinister possibilities than a handful of miserable refugees trying to win favor with the United States, for money or asylum. A 1984 Defense Intelligence Agency memo pointed out that in the prior two years, "over 240 reports have been received which pertain to the purported recovery of dog tags and/or remains of U.S. servicemen." DIA analysis showed that 58 percent of the people named in the reports had returned home alive. Another 28 percent had been killed in the war, but their remains were recovered. Only 14 percent of the reports actually related to men who were in fact unaccounted for. The DIA experts puzzled over the implications, but concluded that there probably was a deliberate effort to spread misinformation, most likely traceable to the Vietnamese government and their communist allies in the region: "The governments of Vietnam and Laos should have knowledge of many of the missing men whose names have appeared in the dog tag reports. . . . It is unlikely that private citizens could have recently discovered remains and would be holding them in their personal possession. In conclusion, we suspect that the dog tag reports are part of a managed effort to influence the POW/MIA issue. The information provided is usually precise and some of it could have come only from the U.S. Government files left behind in Vietnam. The Vietnamese Government's motive in flooding the U.S. with this misinformation is unknown; however, by providing such obvious false data they may be attempting to discredit all refugee sources of POW/MIA information."

There were episodes that could have come from a macabre spy novel. Nguyen Van Cung, who had been an economist in South Vietnam, was living in a Malaysian refugee camp. In May 1984 he told American investigators that a cousin of his still living in Vietnam had written him an intriguing letter. The cousin claimed he had purchased the remains of two missing Americans, and he asked Cung to help smuggle the remains out of Vietnam—in export products such as raw cakes of incense being shipped to Singapore or Hong Kong. Then the cousin wanted Cung to contact some people in Texas and arrange for the resale of the remains, for a reward. Cung, a bit wiser than his cousin, wrote back to his cousin warning that such a scheme could get him in grave trouble with his own government, and probably wouldn't impress the Americans very much, either.

It began to appear that small syndicates were getting in on the act. An agent working for the Americans in Ho Chi Minh City—previously called Saigon—was approached by yet another former South Viet namese officer who claimed to represent a group of ten individuals who had been gathering U.S. remains since 1982. As a kind of down payment, the former officer turned over eight small plastic-wrapped packets, each containing some tiny bone fragments. One of them was labeled HOWARD K. WILLIAMS. There was also a list of eighteen missing Americans, which included the eight whose remains had supposedly been sampled in the packets. He asked the agent to smuggle the remains out of the country and turn them over to the U.S. government, "for checking"—which the agent did. Not surprisingly, the remains failed the test and turned out to have Mongoloid characteristics. The material labeled as Howard K. Williams, a laboratory report concluded, could not be associated with him due to "racial contradiction."

Howard K. Williams, it seemed, had been all over Vietnam. From 1984 to 1986, several other people claimed to have Howard's dog tags, or his identification card, along with access to his remains. A letter sent to U.S. officials in Thailand stated that the writer had obtained Captain Williams's remains and presented personal data from his ID card as proof. Then he asked for permission for twenty-nine Vietnamese refugees to be admitted to the United States. To respond, he provided cryptic instructions for contacting a Vietnamese individual living in Australia, explaining that this was necessary "because of being afraid of the government of Vietnam." Whoever contacted this man was to use the following coded message: "I'm 10,000 dong short, and will pay enough to C. Th before leaving Vietnam."

Another refugee, who had already made it to the United States, walked into an FBI office in Salem, Oregon, and said that a friend of his wife's, who happened to live in the village of Phu Cat, was maintaining the ashes and identification tags of U.S. Air Force captain Howard K. Williams. That was an interesting coincidence, since Howard had lived at the air base that had been next to the village and was even named for it. His plane, however, had crashed hundreds of miles away, and it was mighty unlikely that his body had made it back to base while his airplane burned in the jungle.

The Air Force periodically sent updates to Monalee while cautioning her that the dog tag reports were notoriously unreliable. The warning was unnecessary. Unlike some surviving family members, who clung to the flimsiest fragment of information, Monalee and Keith had developed an innate skepticism toward anything the government told them about Howard. Besides, they were busy with their lives, and common sense told them that after more than fifteen years, there was no way Howard was coming back. Monalee was developing her new career as a school psychologist and enjoying life with Fritz. They developed a community of friends associated with Ohio State, where Fritz was teaching, and traveled when they could.

Keith was even busier. The Air Force had taught him a lot and exposed him to many interesting places, but he needed to do something else. During his one semester of college in Boston, Keith had participated in several antinuclear demonstrations. He had developed strong antiwar views and was becoming a pacifist. Then, one day when he was driving an armored truck in England, delivering mail, a mob of antinuclear protesters surrounded his truck. Security police drove them off with tear gas. That was weird. He was used to being on the other side of the cordon and didn't like being aligned with the authorities. Besides, as his pacifist philosophy developed, he was increasingly out of step with the whole purpose of the Air Force. So when his four-year tour ended, he and Jacque moved to Florida, where Keith began attending art school.

They had a son, Ian, in 1986. The marriage wasn't working out, however, and they decided to split up. Jacque took Ian back home to Denver, and Keith followed once his term at art school in Florida was over. He enrolled in an art school in Colorado and began studying photography, working at hotels to pay his way. With a son, a full-time job, and school, Keith had little time to follow developments in Vietnam. Besides, he had decided back in 1978, when his father was finally declared killed in action, that that was the end of it. He wasn't coming home.

The dog tag reports eventually began to dry up as the U.S. government dismissed one claim after another and Vietnamese speculators began to realize that a tooth or a bone fragment found in a farm field probably wasn't worth anything. Besides, more realistic and productive ways to search for the missing began to develop. Since the end of the war, the United States had been pressing Vietnam to help locate and identify the remains of Americans who had died in Vietnam. The most basic request was for the Vietnamese to turn over whatever information they had in their own files regarding Americans who had never been accounted for—the same issue Kissinger had raised when he went to Hanoi in 1973.

Every now and then a set of U.S. remains would materialize in Hanoi and be returned to the Americans. But that was almost always connected to some kind of political event, like an American peace activist's visit to Hanoi, and meant to capture a bit of world approval. Broader cooperation on locating the missing was a bridge too far. For one thing, if the Vietnamese suddenly coughed up information they had been sitting on for years, it would reveal that they *had* been lying when they said they didn't know anything about the people in question. And as long as the Vietnamese had information the Americans wanted—whether they admitted that they had it or not—they had a bit of leverage over the mighty United States. That could come in handy if Vietnam needed something at the United Nations or in some other international forum.

Pressure mounted, however. In June 1985, President Reagan had clearly stated that the United States would not normalize relations

with Vietnam—or end a suffocating trade embargo—until all MIA issues were resolved. That got the attention of the communist leadership,
and the Vietnamese position on MIAs softened. Later that summer,
Hanoi handed over the remains of twenty-six U.S. servicemen—and
this time, they really were Americans. Among them was Navy lieutenant Richard J. Sather, one of the first Americans shot down over
Vietnam.[3]

The Vietnamese gradually warmed to another idea, too: joint exca-
vations, by officials of both countries, of sites where Americans were
believed to have died or been buried, an idea Hanoi had flatly rejected
up till then. In December 1985, the first U.S. excavation team to enter
Vietnam since the end of the war went to a site about six miles northeast of central Hanoi, where a B-52 had crashed in 1972. Under the
watchful eyes of a Vietnamese escort team, the U.S. experts extracted
the remains of several American crew members.[4]

A month later, senior Pentagon officials traveled to Hanoi and
worked out an agreement to speed up efforts to account for missing
Americans. Vietnam also turned over more sets of remains. But the
deep mistrust of the war years persisted, and the two countries feuded
like a bitter divorced couple. In the spring of 1986, Vietnam threatened
to stop cooperating on MIA issues on account of statements from
Washington "that vilify or discredit Vietnam." In April, Hanoi did suspend MIA negotiations, in protest over the U.S. bombing of Libya.[5]

There were other disturbing developments. In the fall of 1985, two
former Army Special Forces soldiers filed an explosive class-action
lawsuit against the U.S. government. In 1981 they had been given a
classified and very sensitive mission: investigate rumors that despite
the POW return in 1973, some Americans were still being held in Vietnamese prisons. They had concluded that about one hundred Americans were still captive in Indochina. Four years later they claimed that
the Defense Intelligence Agency (DIA) was stonewalling on the issue
and concealing intelligence reports regarding possible U.S. prisoners.

They weren't the only ones who thought so. President Reagan's national security adviser, Robert McFarlane, told a group of business ex-
ecutives that he too believed there were still U.S. prisoners being held
in Southeast Asia, even though he didn't have specific evidence. His remarks were supposed to have been private and off the record, but

somebody leaked them to the press.[6] Controversy flared once again. For the families whose wounds were long in healing, the possibility— no matter how remote—that their husbands or fathers were still in cages back in Vietnam was one more searing blow. And if a top White House official believed there were still prisoners, but was sitting on the information—what more evidence could there be of some kind of conspiracy? The issue of the live prisoners began to dominate the agenda of some of the support groups. It gripped the media, too. The prospect of forgotten Americans rotting in steamy jungle holding pens was horrific and enthralling, and it made a much better story line than the diplomatic fretting that constituted the MIA negotiations.

It took more than a year for the freeze to crack, and it was a slow thaw at that. In the summer of 1987 the United States sent retired general John Vessey, a former chairman of the Joint Chiefs of Staff, to Vietnam. Hanoi repledged its cooperation and turned over more than two dozen new sets of remains as a show of good faith. Over the following months the two countries discussed ground rules for investigating possible burial sites. There was talk of opening a U.S. "technical" office in Hanoi, a headquarters for the MIA effort, but that was counterbalanced by concerns over whether such an office would imply diplomatic recognition of the communist government there.[7]

The intelligence experts working the MIA issue began to gain hope that there might be regular opportunities to gather real evidence directly from the scene, instead of sorting through thousands of fifth-hand reports that usually turned out to be bogus. In September 1988 the Vietnamese once again allowed U.S. investigators into the country. They had ten days to look into three cases. That was an impossibly compressed schedule, and the Vietnamese were less than forthcoming. But it was a start. More teams followed. They carefully skirted Vietnamese sensitivities and avoided pointing fingers when it was obvious that the communists had been lying or stonewalling about missing Americans.

In July 1989, Robert Destatte, a senior DIA official responsible for the MIA effort, drafted a memo for Hanoi. He asked for assistance with an especially problematic region of North Vietnam, a narrow corridor along Route 20 near the Ban Karai Pass, close to the border with Laos. "This area contains a disproportionately large number of unresolved cases," he wrote. Of twenty-six Americans who had disappeared in this area—virtually all of them pilots—only one had returned as a POW. And Vietnam had returned only one set of remains from this area. In at least four cases, Destatte pointed out, the United States had intelligence indicating that servicemen lost in this area had been captured, alive, by the North Vietnamese Army. What had happened to them? Were they dead? How did they die? Where were their bodies?

Then there was a brief but revealing reference to Howard Williams. In his case and at least two others, the DIA official wrote, "our information indicates that [North Vietnamese] forces were quickly on the scene of crash sites and recovered equipment, identification media, and remains from U.S. personnel." The Vietnamese may have been stonewalling for the past fifteen years, but the MIA investigators had been doing some important research all the same—in America's own vast archives from the war. As far as Misty, the 37th Fighter Wing, and 7th Air Force officials ever knew, Howard Williams had simply disappeared. Except for the fact that he had never come up on the radio, there was no evidence indicating whether he was dead or alive. And they had no idea whether the North Vietnamese had gotten to the crash site, and if so, what they had found there.

But somebody did know: the electronic intelligence experts who had been monitoring North Vietnamese radio communications at the time. These were the people who, in the mysterious phone call back in 1968, had warned Dick Rutan not to trek up to Howie's crash site because "it's been taken care of." Rutan didn't understand what they had meant, and nobody ever came forward to explain. In the messages that went back and forth between Phu Cat and higher headquarters in the days following the shootdown, there had been lots of speculation about what might have happened to Howie, possible explanations for the emergency beeper that was off, then on, then off again. But there was never any reference to actual intelligence that could have settled the question. And, Lord knows, nobody ever gave Monalee any meaningful information about what had happened to her husband. But the supersecret ELINT had finally been shared with other intelligence officials. In the manner of spies and diplomats, Destatte was using that intelligence to tell the Vietnamese, we know that you know more than you've told us.

Destatte played another card, too. "Information in U.S. files," he wrote, "also indicates that since the war years, [Vietnamese] military and public security personnel investigated at least seven crash sites in this area and recovered remains associated with those sites." Those remains were not among those that had already been handed over to the Americans—further evidence that the communists were not coming clean. Having put Hanoi on the spot, Destatte then made several specific requests. He wanted a U.S. team to be able to interview some of the political officers from Military Region IV, the area around the Ban Karai Pass, who had been responsible for handling American prisoners and forwarding information to Hanoi. He wanted access to one or more of the officers from North Vietnam's air defense command for the region, who would have been responsible for collecting data on aircraft downings and for transmitting that data up the chain to air defense command headquarters.

There was more: Destatte sought interviews with some of the officers in charge of Binh Tram 14, the logistics unit whose area of operation would have covered the area where Howard Williams's plane, and several others, had gone down.

Also, the United States wished to review the unit histories of the 18th and the 21st AAA Battalions, the crack air defense units that had shot down several U.S. jets. "We believe that these records are stored at air defense headquarters in Ha Dong," Destatte volunteered, nudging the Vietnamese along. Finally he asked for access to military and public security personnel who may have investigated the crash sites after the war. If anybody would know what had happened to the remains of pilots, it would be the people who had dug into the actual crash sites.

It took time, but with Vietnam plunging into an economic abyss and becoming increasingly desperate to improve relations with the United States, the MIA investigators began to get what they were asking for. The duration of the "joint field activities" inside Vietnam began to increase, and the Vietnamese began providing more information. There were still more than seventeen hundred Americans listed as missing in Vietnam, but it started to seem plausible that the investigators might be able to bring many of them back to the United States. Even though it had been twenty years or more since many of them had disappeared, the jungle still held clues that could answer what had happened. The bones of Americans had been overgrown with vegetation and become virtually part of the earth itself, but still they waited to be discovered.

THIRTY-ONE

A FISHY STORY

By January 1991 there had been twelve joint field activities in Vietnam. About three hundred sets of remains had been recovered from Vietnam since the end of the war.[1] Procedures had been refined, and both sides were gaining comfort with the process. The Pentagon and the Vietnamese government would work out in advance which servicemen they'd be looking for on each trip, and the Vietnamese, with varying degrees of zeal, would hunt down military officials and local citizens who might have had some knowledge of each American's fate. Whenever possible the U.S. investigators would try to find a burial site or some evidence of remains, the only way to verify that the man in question was in fact dead. The jungle did not readily yield its secrets, but when Hanoi provided the right information, it helped narrow the area of the hunt dramatically.

The thirteenth series of joint investigations began on January 21, 1991, when fourteen U.S. investigators arrived in Da Nang. From there they split up. A seven-man team headed by James Coyle, a civilian specialist, traveled to Dong Hoi, the port city that had been decimated by American bombs during the war. Coyle's team would be looking for the remains of several pilots, including two who had crashed in the Bo Trach Military District, which included the area near the Ban Karai Pass where Howard Williams had disappeared. Howie, however, was not on the list of cases to be researched on this trip.

On January 22, at the Bo Trach District offices, Coyle and his team got their first briefing from the local official in charge of the Vietnamese half of the joint effort. The news was discouraging. Under general procedures that the two countries had agreed upon, the Vietnamese were supposed to do a considerable amount of research before the Americans showed up, to make the fieldwork go more quickly and minimize the amount of time the Americans needed to spend in Vietnam. If all went well, the Vietnamese would have researched all available records, identified witnesses, and even uncovered airplane crash sites by the time the Americans arrived. But as happened often, the Vietnamese were unprepared. None of the preliminary legwork had been done. The investigation was supposed to take place in a municipality called Thuong Trach, a large area that encompassed the suspected crash sites. But the Vietnamese officials had been there only a week—not nearly long enough to track down artifacts and witnesses relating to events that had taken place more than twenty years earlier.

The news got worse. The main road into Thuong Trach, known as Route 20, turned out to be little more than an overgrown footpath that was virtually impassible by truck. The last official vehicle dispatched to the village had slipped off the road and tumbled down a mountainside, killing all the passengers. The U.S. team members asked if they could get there by helicopter. The Vietnamese team leader answered that it would be impossible to commandeer a helicopter on such short notice. If the Americans were insistent on getting to Thuong Trach, he said, the only way in would probably be a thirty-mile hike.

Coyle huddled with his team. They were all experienced soldiers and investigators, some of whom had fought in Vietnam many years ago. All of them had made a career of finding inventive solutions to unconventional problems. Over time they had developed expertise in search-and-recovery tactics, forensics, the handling of remains, and the unique challenges of doing such work under harsh, unpredictable field conditions. Plus, they were stout troopers not easily intimidated by bureaucratic gamesmanship. Complications such as a thirty-mile foot march were inconvenient, but certainly not serious enough to derail their mission.

The unforeseen transportation problems would cause a delay, however. So Coyle and his men decided that in order to tend to all the cases on their agenda, they'd have to split up. Four of them would go to Thuong Trach: SFC (Sergeant 1st Class) Jim Ross, a linguist, would be the detachment leader. The rest of the team included Sgt. Willie Kates, an analyst, Sgt. Jim Lee, a search-and-recovery specialist, and the medic, Navy corpsman Harold Morley. They'd drive as far as they could down Route 20 in the jeeps they traveled in and then hike any remaining distance if absolutely necessary. The other team members would move on to two other military districts where there were cases waiting to be investigated.

While the Americans were devising their plan, a Vietnamese official arrived with some documents they had asked for. They examined the papers carefully and photographed them for future reference. One section was especially interesting. It listed all the U.S. servicemen captured in Bo Trach District. Under the heading 1968, there was an entry that indicated an F-100 had been shot down on March 18 and one pilot had been rescued. The other pilot, according to the log, was deceased. The team members quickly realized this was a likely reference to Howard K. Williams, one of the pilots lost in terrain under Bo Trach jurisdiction. Even though they weren't looking for him specifically on this mission, it was standard practice to deviate from the script whenever there was an opportunity to cross one more American off the list of those unaccounted for.

On January 24, Ross, Kates, Lee, and Morley—the "Thuong Trach element"—left Dong Hoi with their Vietnamese escorts. They headed north to Hoan Lao, the Bo Trach District capital, then turned west, away from the coast. The entourage was traveling on the easternmost branch of what used to be the Ho Chi Minh Trail—but it was in far worse shape than it had been during the war. About twenty miles west of Hoan Lao, the team's jeeps could no longer manage the narrow, pitted logging roads that hugged the sides of the mountains. The Vietnamese members of the team talked nervously about the truck that had lost its grip and plunged off the road. The group decided to go back to Dong Hoi and see if they could rent a logging truck or some other vehicle designed to navigate such rough terrain.

It took another two days, but they managed to get their hands on a

Soviet-made GAZ-66 logging truck, which wound its way along the treacherous mountain road like a water buffalo walking a tightrope. The Vietnamese fretted the whole way, but it turned out the road was passable after all. They reached Route 20 and turned southwest toward Thuong Trach, about thirty-five miles away. They were in truly remote terrain, a backwater that in other undeveloped countries would have been completely ignored by anybody more than a few miles' walking distance away. But Thuong Trach had lain along the Ho Chi Minh Trail, which had made it a vital logistics and air defense hub during the war. Finally, near dusk, the team arrived at the central hamlet in the area. Like many obscure places that acquire strategic significance during wartime, it had become a center of activity far beyond anything the local peasants could ever have imagined. An official military presence still dominated the place. The four Americans built a base camp and settled in for the night.

The next morning they met the chairman of the Thuong Trach Village People's Committee and several other officials with elaborate titles. The interviews were curious from the start. One of the officials, a longtime resident of the village, appeared to have been designated as spokesman for the group. He told the Americans that most of the villagers had no knowledge of any shootdowns or other incidents from the war, because they had been evacuated during the fighting—even though their new homes had been just a few miles away. And as far as he knew, there were only five crash sites in the area. As he ticked them off, a funny coincidence emerged. Three of the sites he referred to had already been investigated, one was on the list to be checked out, and the fifth was one the Americans had been asking about the day before. U.S. records indicated that there had been at least eighteen "loss incidents" handled through the remote village, yet the only ones the appointed spokesman seemed to know anything about were the ones that the Vietnamese had already acknowledged. Another dozen or so—the ones still not officially recognized by Hanoi—well, he had no information on those. Ross, the team leader, and Kates, his analyst, were both thinking the same thing: The man was either simply reciting information that had been supplied by one of the communist minders, or he knew a lot more than he was letting on.

Another villager brought in for the occasion then volunteered an odd story. He recalled being out in the woods one day in 1968 and coming across a pair of U.S. military boots. They were leather from top to bottom with a flat sole affixed with nails—quite different from the green canvas jungle boots the two U.S. soldiers were wearing. The description fit: Those were the kinds of boots pilots wore as part of their flying equipment. The man said he picked up the boots and eventually gave them to one of the local military commanders in exchange for some rice. The skeptical Americans glanced at each other. This was another implausible tale. Had the boots fallen off one of the pilots as he was drifting down in his parachute? Had he taken them off to air out his feet and then forgotten where they were? The Americans listening to the story kept their disdain to themselves, however. Complaining about the duplicity of witnesses was verboten. It would ruffle Vietnamese "sensitivities." They had to make do with the information they got, no matter how specious.

The next day one of the Vietnamese team members approached the Americans and clarified the man's story. Supposedly the man had later explained that he didn't find the boots sitting by themselves in the jungle; he had actually taken them from the dead pilot, just before burying his body on the outskirts of a nearby hamlet. The man also said he'd be able to identify the burial site. By this point it had become apparent that the Vietnamese were poorly prepared for the investigators' visit to Thuong Trach. They had known little about the current conditions of the roads. The official welcome failed to disguise the fact that they hadn't lined up any witnesses relating to the two cases on the agenda. Nor had they reconnoitered the terrain near the crash sites that were supposed to be investigated. Making any progress on those cases was beginning to look hopeless. But now it sounded as if they had lucked into some real information. Even though it related to a case that wasn't officially on the agenda, Ross quickly decided to rearrange other activities so they could go to this putative burial site.

They began hiking to the site the next morning, January 28, with the flip-flopping boot-finder as their guide. Along the way he elaborated on the incident. He had been one of several villagers who helped bury the pilot, he said, shortly after the plane was shot down. The plane and the pilot had come down separately, with the plane crashing a couple of miles farther to the west. His story still sounded fishy, but it felt like he was getting closer to the truth. The U.S. team members wanted to investigate both the burial site and the crash site, but nobody was sure whether the plane had ended up in Vietnamese or Laotian territory, since it was very close to the border. So the Americans decided to postpone that visit until they knew for sure, to make sure they wouldn't be making an unauthorized trip into Laos.

The trail had been relatively flat when they started out. In fact, the team had walked past three large, open fields that could easily have served as helicopter landing zones and saved everybody a lot of trouble—further evidence of poor planning by the Vietnamese. Then the hike became increasingly arduous as they climbed into the rugged karst that dominated the higher terrain. Along the way they encountered Vietnamese villagers traveling to and fro, going about their business. Then they met several young men walking down the trail, carrying bits of aircraft wreckage suspended from bamboo poles. Another striking coincidence: A decade and a half after the war, and locals still happened to be picking through the debris from wrecked American planes? The team stopped the men and the Americans examined the parts. They wrote down serial numbers and took pictures that would help identify the wreckage later. The local men then went on their way and the team continued its upward trek.

Another group of locals passed by. The boot-finder recognized one of them: another man who had helped bury the pilot. The team asked if he would accompany the team to the burial site. The man, who appeared to be in his seventies, was reluctant at first. Obviously he preferred not to get involved in something that went all the way back to the war and was important enough to involve ranking district officials—not to mention two Americans. But when the team pressed and explained how valuable his help might be, he warmed to the idea. Finally he agreed to come along.

The team reached the site at about 3:30 in the afternoon. The two Vietnamese who had helped in the burial directed the Americans to a slight depression in a hillside. The old man in particular had very precise recollections of the burial and the dimensions of the hole he had helped dig. He outlined an area that was about three feet wide and six feet long. Compared to all the vague and bogus information the MIA researchers usually had to sort through, this was pay dirt. The team decided to begin an excavation on the spot. Lee, the expert in the handling of remains, got out his equipment and began to prepare for the dig.

Ross and some of the Vietnamese team members, meanwhile, sat down with the two witnesses to see if they could reconstruct the full story. Ross had little faith in the first witness, the villager who had claimed to find the boots waiting to be discovered in the jungle. He appeared to have been heavily coached in advance, and even now the details of his account kept changing. The old man they had met on the trail seemed much more reliable. It was only by chance they had run into him, and it seemed unlikely that anybody had told him what to say. His memory seemed good. The only problem was that he had been roped into a situation he didn't want to be in, and he knew that there might be consequences if he said the wrong thing or embarrassed one of the local officials. He was reluctant to speak and seemed to keep looking to the first witness for guidance about what to say. Still, the old man represented the best opportunity they were likely to get to reconstruct the fate of whatever American was lying in the hillside grave.

Ross guided the interview along, asking pointed questions and trying to keep the first witness from corrupting the second. Gradually the old man got the story out. He couldn't remember what year it had been, but he had vivid memories of an American aircraft being shot down. Two pilots ejected, he said through a translator. One of them landed on a rise known as Ma Lan Hill. Shortly after the airplane crashed, two other planes and a helicopter arrived overhead. The helicopter quickly rescued the U.S. pilot from the hilltop.

Three days later, the old man said, he had been walking through the area when he saw a parachute snagged in a grove of tall bamboo trees. Then he saw a body lying on the ground, at the foot of the bamboo. It was a white man with blondish hair, about as tall, he said, as Sergeant Lee—who was six-foot-two. He wore a helmet and other gear that fit the description of a pilot's flight suit. The man examined the body and could tell that the left leg had been broken, but there were no other obvious injuries. Then he found the local military commander to tell him about the discovery.

The next day, a lower-ranking military official showed up. It was the witness from the village, the man who kept changing his story about how he happened to acquire the boots. As the old man told it, the official collected all of the dead pilot's personal effects, including his boots, helmet, and parachute. Then the official directed about a half dozen men, some military and some civilian, to bury the body. They dug a hole about three feet deep and placed the body inside, with the head pointing north. He hadn't been to the burial site since, and in fact few local people ever went into that area. There had been rumors that a tiger had dug up the remains and eaten them, and fear of running into one of the vicious animals kept just about everybody away. The Americans asked the first witness some more questions, trying to get him to corroborate the old man's story. After more variations in his version of events, they decided he was completely untrustworthy. There was no point interviewing him any further.

As the investigators pieced the story together, it became evident that it was a close match to what they knew about Howard K. Williams. The approximate date of the incident fit, as did the fact that one of the pilots had been rescued. If the pilot had indeed been found unconscious or dead at the bottom of a tree, that would explain why he had never come up on the rescue radio. The vegetation was thick enough that if he had plunged deep enough into the jungle canopy, it could easily have hidden the parachute and made it impossible to see from overhead. And they knew they were in the area where the F-100 had crashed on March 18, 1968.

There was only one discrepancy. The precise location of the burial site was about three miles west of the coordinates that represented Howard Williams's "last known location." But no Americans had ever seen Howard Williams on the ground in Vietnam, and his last known location was deduced based on Misty reports, the spot where the airplane had crashed into the jungle, and other vague bits of intelligence. The investigators knew from experience that this kind of information was usually accurate enough to get them to the general location of an incident, but was rarely precise enough to guide them all the way to a crash site. It was entirely probable for a pilot to end up three miles away from initial estimates. Still, it would take laboratory work back in the States to determine if any remains they found actually belonged to Howard Williams.

The excavation was delicate, time-consuming work that required special tools, so that any remains or other evidence wouldn't be damaged. All the dirt had to be sifted so that no object, no matter how tiny, would be overlooked. By late in the day the team had removed about eight inches of dirt when they unearthed the first bit of evidence: part of a zipper, which could have come from one of the many pockets on a typical flight suit. It was getting dark, however, and the team needed to finish up its work for the day. They put their tools away and walked back down the hill to the nearby hamlet, Ban Con Roang, where the Vietnamese team members procured a house. The group spent the night there.

They returned the next day to finish their work. It was raining, so the team hung a poncho and some other strips of plastic over the burial site before continuing the excavation. At a depth of about twelve inches they found a three-inch piece of bone and several smaller fragments. A couple of inches deeper they found a piece of a comb and a shard from a broken mirror. At a depth of about sixteen inches they uncovered a tooth—critical evidence, since dental records could help identify the remains—along with another zipper and some snaps from a piece of clothing. They dug a few inches deeper yet, but there was nothing else. The tiny amount of remains indicated that the site had already been exhumed at least once. Maybe there had been a tiger. Maybe locals had pillaged the site or Vietnamese officials had removed the body for some reason. Whatever the case, at about 2:30 in the afternoon on January 29, the Americans decided they had found all they were going to find. They wrapped up the dig and prepared for the hike back to Thuong Trach.

It was much easier going than the uphill climb, until they came to a stream that had been swollen by the rain. With the help of some villagers they made it across and returned to their base camp. The team was back in Dong Hoi on the thirtieth, with one week left to look into other cases on their schedule.

The thirteenth joint investigation ended on February 7, 1991. Three weeks of work by fourteen Americans and their Vietnamese counterparts had led to the recovery of seven sets of U.S. remains, including the handful of material believed to belong to Howard Williams. The teams had hit a number of roadblocks and other frustrations as well. In one case investigators found the aircraft wreckage they were looking for, along with witnesses who told them that a dead American pilot had been found on the ground shortly after the plane had crashed. But they were unable to find a grave site or any remains. In another case investigators interviewed a witness who said he had come across a wounded pilot crawling on the ground, shooting his handgun at anybody who approached. The witness said he had killed the pilot. He directed the investigators to the general area where he said the pilot had been buried, but couldn't pinpoint the exact location, and no remains were found. In another case, a pilot had been wounded while resisting capture by troops of North Vietnam's 4th Regiment. He was finally apprehended by ground troops and supposedly "died due to his injuries" while being evacuated to a different military region. A witness said the pilot had been buried by the side of a trail in the mountains south of Hue, but the team researching the case was unable to find any sign of him.

On March 6, 1991, in accordance with usual procedures, the government of Vietnam formally turned over the seven sets of remains, including those of Howard Williams, to the United States. In a letter acknowledging the exchange, the senior U.S. official in charge of the effort stated that he "highly appreciated the humane policy and goodwill of the Government of the Socialist Republic of Vietnam."

Once in U.S. hands, Howie's remains were promptly sent to the Army's "central identification" laboratory in Hawaii, the premier military facility for conducting the detailed forensic work required to identify body parts. On June 17 the laboratory formally recommended that the tooth and bone fragments dug up near the village of Thuong Trach be identified as those of Howard K. Williams. After twenty-three years the case was coming to a close—but Howie was still in the military system after all, and the bureaucracy took its time. Finally, on February 26, 1992, the Armed Forces Identification Review Board approved the lab's recommendation. Howie had been accounted for.

THIRTY-TWO

LUCKY

It came as a surprise that anybody was looking for Howard's remains. Monalee knew that U.S. investigators were over in Vietnam
researching the cases of the missing. Occasionally there would be a
news report about remains being repatriated. She still opened all the
mail the Air Force sent and dutifully filed it in the basement. But she
had stopped following the details of the never-ending cleanup of the
war. Monalee was busy living another life—chapter two—and it never
occurred to her that she'd have to turn back the pages and revisit chapter one. It was a jolt to Keith, too. He had long ago given up the idea
that his father would come home—in any form—and had thought less
and less about Vietnam.

On February 12, 1992, the Air Force sent Monalee a letter informing her of the activities in Thuong Trach. They had found some remains that might be those of her husband. Suddenly all the old
questions came racing back. What had happened? How had he ended
up there? Why did it take so long to find him? What had he died from?
Had he suffered much? It was a relief when she read the report from
the villager who said he had found Howard dead at the bottom of a
tree, apparently killed shortly after he ejected. At least he wasn't imprisoned and tortured to death. But it was a time of remarkable sad-

ness all the same. When the Air Force finally sent word that the tooth and bone fragments had been confirmed as those of her husband, it felt as if he had died all over again.

The service at Arlington on July 24, 1992, produced a kind of emotional whiplash. It was like the heavy hand of the past had grabbed Monalee and Keith and the other people in their lives by the shoulder and said, "Not so fast." When Monalee had gotten word about the remains and started planning the Arlington ceremony, she envisioned a poignant but low-key event attended by a small contingent of family members. She notified all the people she could think of who had known Howard in some meaningful way, but after all those years she expected few to show up.

But show up they did. There were old friends Monalee hadn't seen for years, and many people she didn't know—including Brian Williams, Howard's crewmate on that fateful day in 1968. Some of the people who came had never even known Howard. Fritz was there, along with his daughter and granddaughter. Keith's ex-wife, Jacque, came, too, and of course their son, Ian. Many of the Air Force people who had known Howard brought their spouses, including some Monalee had never met.

All of these people seemed to have something in common: There was a connection to Howard, to those who had served in the war, and even to the war itself that time had not frayed. Instead of the brief break from the routine that Monalee had anticipated, Howard's burial became the dominant event of the summer. Memories came flooding back—many good ones, but also the awful, nauseating sensations of those first days after the news came that Howard had been shot down and was missing. It was like taking a bite out of something and realizing you had sampled it before—and it had been the worst thing you ever tasted. Keith's mind went whirling back to the terribly difficult years between 1968 and 1973, when he had tried to imagine what his dad would be like when he returned, even as his hope of ever knowing his dad gradually slipped away.

The ceremony was draining. There was a lot of unexpected emotion. Monalee and Keith and a lot of other people there struggled to comprehend how a handful of remains that wouldn't fill a coffee cup could represent a man who had once been so vivacious and warm and funny and decisive. On top of that came the strains of looking after seventy-five people.

Fritz was a big help. He had pitched in with all the arrangements, and once they traveled to Washington, he was on hand to take care of anything that came up. Fritz was also keenly aware of the emotional roller coaster his wife and stepson were on. Over the last ten years he had learned enough about Howard's story to grasp the peculiar torment that came with the uncertainty Monalee and Keith had faced. He even had a role in the story himself, escorting Monalee into a new phase of her life. Fritz was familiar enough with the saga to have a good feel for when to sit back and let events run their course and when to step up and offer support.

Yet even Fritz was starting to feel the strain of so much emotion, memory, and tragedy. And it intensified once the ceremony was over. There were plans for a lot of the guests to become tourists for a few days, to visit the Wall, go to some of the museums, catch up over dinner. Monalee and Fritz were the unofficial hosts. Weeks earlier, when they had been planning the event, that had seemed like a natural thing to do. Since they would all be together in Washington, it made sense to spend a few days visiting and taking in the sights. But that wasn't so appealing all of a sudden. The service had left Monalee and Keith and Fritz and many others in a solemn mood. It felt forced to be out with a group. Everybody went through the motions and acted as if they were enjoying themselves, but it was stressful.

As the week wound down and people started to head home, Monalee and Fritz decided that instead of returning to Columbus right away, they'd go someplace alone for a couple of days. Annapolis, Maryland, was only a ninety-minute drive, and the quaint old sailing town on the Chesapeake Bay seemed like an ideal place to escape and rejuvenate. They checked into a bed-and-breakfast near the waterfront and toured the U.S. Naval Academy. As they walked the cobblestone streets in the center of town, they were thankful to be able to blend seamlessly into the crowds, anonymous faces among hundreds of tourists.

But mostly they sat, thought, and absorbed the quiet. They looked at the water and didn't speak that much. Monalee was in the past and present all at once. In her mind, she replayed the last thirty-five years of her life. She had loved Howard, and she cherished the friends they had made and the experiences they had had. Every time she saw or talked to her handsome son, it reminded her of that. She loved Fritz, too. The engineer from Toledo had opened his life and his mind to her, and helped her become something more than she might have been on her own. In between there had been tears and confusion and fury and regret. And yet, she was happy. Something had gone right. Monalee caught her breath, ironed out the emotions, and silently took Fritz's arm in her own as tiny waves rippled before them. She didn't say it out loud, but she felt one thing as powerfully as if she had stood up and announced it to the whole world. "I'm lucky," she told herself, "to have married two wonderful men."

EPILOGUE

Six Mistys returned to Vietnam in the spring of 2000. It was Dick Rutan's idea.

Misty had been just a pit stop for the pilots who served in the unit during the three years that it existed, a short tour in the middle of a longer one. Most Misty pilots came from other fighter squadrons and returned to them after their Misty tours ended. A lot of the Mistys flew more combat missions with other units than they did with Misty. Virtually all of the Misty pilots had other Air Force assignments after they left Vietnam. Some made a career of the Air Force. Others left the service and became airline pilots, businessmen, lawyers, doctors, farmers, engineers, or ski bums.

But as they got older, the few weeks or months they spent at Misty began to emerge as the most vivid experience of their lives. Even some of the Mistys who went on to great success began to look back on their fast FAC days as the most formative, eventful, and memorable time they had ever spent anywhere. In many ways those had been terrible days—watching friends die and families suffer, and being there as a land of largely innocent peasants blew itself apart. But there had been vitality and meaning at Misty, and the friendships made there were unassailable. And then, when a calendar day dawned or a magic number clicked, it was time to get hosed down and move on to something else.

Rutan decided he had some unfinished business in Vietnam. In his mind he knew the exact location of the AAA gun that had shot him down, and he wanted to stand on the ground at that spot and look up at the sky and imagine what the gunner who got him must have seen that day. He had also left his best friend, Howie Williams, on the ground in North Vietnam, dead at the base of a bamboo tree, according to investigators who had found his remains. Then there was the allure of walking the ground in what used to be Route Pack 1, getting a close-up perspective on the things he used to bomb. There were many, many reasons to go back, and Rutan invited other Mistys to go with him.

Five others took him up on it: Ed Risinger, the high school dropout, who had gone to medical school and become a successful doctor; Don Shepperd, who had retired from the Air Force as a two-star general; Mick Greene, the Naval Academy graduate, who had become an engineer after leaving the Air Force; P. K. Robinson, who had completed an Air Force career and become a bank president; and Wells Jackson, who had retired from the Air Force and started growing coffee on a plantation in Panama. Rutan himself became one of the "famous" Mistys when he was the first man to fly nonstop, unrefueled, around the world in a plane called the Voyager—which hung in the Smithsonian. Most of the six had overlapped at Misty, and those who hadn't kept in touch had gotten reacquainted in recent years at a couple of Misty reunions.

They traveled as tourists, without any government backing. The State Department, in fact, advised against Americans traveling to Vietnam at the time. The twenty-fifth anniversary of the fall of Saigon was approaching, and emotions might run high. There could be anti-American demonstrations.

The Mistys went anyway. The first stop was Ho Chi Minh City, formerly known as Saigon. After a good night's sleep they flew to Hue, the old imperial city that was leveled during the 1968 Tet Offensive. There they met up with a guide and interpreter they had hired. They asked if they could visit Khe Sanh and the Lang Vei Special Forces Camp on the Laotian border, which Shepperd and Jim Fiorelli had seen from the air right after it had been wiped out by a North Vietnamese attack in early 1968. But the guide told them there was nothing to see there anymore, just green, rolling hills that bore no signs of the epic air and ground combat that had once shaken the earth.

Instead, they drove to the old Marine outpost at Con Thien, where Bud Day, the first Misty commander, had almost made it to freedom during his escape. They "formed up" and marched shoulder to shoulder in a ceremonial crossing of the Ben Hai River, which used to form the border between North and South Vietnam. "Misty is back in the Pack," they shouted, "back in North Vietnam!"

They toured some of the villages where Bud Day—who had been presented the Medal of Honor by President Nixon, for his determination to avoid capture and his resistance while a POW—had been imprisoned, tortured, beaten by villagers, and marched barefoot as he began his trek north to Hanoi. They stopped on the shores of "Butterfly Lake," which had a double-wing shape and had been an ideal aerial checkpoint that every Misty recognized. Lots of AAA had come their way from that area, but as they gazed out at the countryside now, verdant rice paddies were all they saw, stretching horizon to horizon, studded with water-filled bomb craters that held shrimp and fish.

Near dark on the first day they reached Dong Hoi, thirty miles north of the old DMZ. The last time any of them had seen Dong Hoi, it was a massive pile of rubble, completely ringed with AAA that protected the river crossings and ferries in the area. It now looked like a poor Mexican border outpost. Their hotel—"the best in town" according to tourist guidebooks they had brought with them—cost ten dollars per day, including meals, occasional hot water, sporadic air conditioning, and mosquito nets. But the accommodations were beside the point. All of them crawled into their musty beds with visions of inviting targets, exciting missions, and old comrades dancing in their heads.

The next morning they finally unraveled the mystery of the "Disappearing River," one of the most agonizing targets of the war. From overhead it looked as if the Song Troc wound into a cave beneath a cliff near the intersection of Routes 101 and 137, an area that had always been heavily defended during the war. But their assumption about the river, they discovered, had been wrong. The river didn't disappear into the cave. It flowed out of it, toward the coast. And although the cave had a small opening, inside it was as big as Carlsbad Cavern—and full of grandeur, a true natural wonder.

The cave had become a tourist attraction, like a Civil War battlefield back home, and the Mistys learned that a lot more had gone on in there during the war than they imagined. The NVA had indeed hidden a ferry in the cave, which they brought out at night so that traffic could cross the river. In addition, the cave had housed the equivalent of an entire community: many other boats, supplies, a hospital, and people taking refuge from the war.

The bomb scars on the cliff face above the cave were still there. The Air Force had lost many airplanes attacking the cave mouth, and it was now evident how futile that had been. The cave was so sturdy and so well protected that the Mistys agreed it would have taken a nuclear weapon to close it—maybe several. As the Mistys drifted out of the cave mouth in a sampan, P. K. Robinson looked up at the top of the cliff and thought of the Panda rescue, when a frightened pilot had smacked down right on top of the cave. Even from his ringside seat, the Panda pilot hadn't been able to tell where the North Vietnamese kept the ferry—probably because he had his head down and his eyes closed, praying.

Farther down the Song Troc, they passed the karst mountaintop where Dick Rutan had once spotted the parachute of an F-105 pilot. But the pilot wouldn't come up on the radio. Dick had gone to the tanker for fuel, and when he returned there was no sign of the pilot. He hadn't shown up after the war, leading to suspicion that the North Vietnamese had found and killed him. Near the end of the river they reached Quang Khe, where there had been another ferry for getting vehicles across the water. Using Rutan's handheld GPS device, the Mistys tried to find the location of the six-position 57mm site that had taunted them regularly from the north bank of the river. There was no sign of it.

The second day out of Dong Hoi was rainy and dismal, just like the monsoon days of January and February 1968. The Mistys stopped at a school fair in a field covered with tents. The kids were celebrating

National Unification Day. When word got around that some Americans were there, the Mistys were mobbed with attention. The school principal invited them to his office for tea, and he turned out to be the local coordinator of the "American War" Veterans Association. More than that—he was an old AAA gunner, and the Mistys suspected he had shot at them, and they at him. The principal wore a Vladimir Lenin pin on his lapel. Yet despite his endorsement of the very system the Mistys had supposedly gone to Vietnam to fight against, there were tangible ties of respect between those who had shot at one another. The Mistys departed with handshakes.

On the way back to Dong Hoi the group encountered a Vietnamese military crew clearing unexploded bombs from a farmer's backyard. They stopped and asked the supervising NVA major if Ed Risinger and Dick Rutan could help. The other Mistys held their hands over their ears as Dick used a probe to delicately seek for war debris beneath the dirt's surface. Sure enough, he hit metal—a bomb fragment? Maybe he had put it there.

The next day the group tried to follow Route 137, one of the principal roads that fed the Ho Chi Minh Trail, all the way up and across the Ban Karai Pass into Laos. But the weather made the roads impassable and dangerous. Frustrated, they headed back to the Disappearing River ferry, the one they had repeatedly tried to find and sink. It didn't look like it had been repaired since the war.

After crossing from the south side of the river to the north on the antique ferry, they drove northwest on Route 101 toward the top of the old Route Pack 1. They were now on another key thoroughfare in the Trail network, traveling the opposite direction of the southbound traffic they had tried to stop day after day. The road was rough and muddy, but they pressed on through the constant drizzle. Bomb craters were everywhere along the road. They wondered how many still contained unexploded bombs. They passed through a number of villages and appeared to be the first Americans many of the local people had ever seen. The villagers wanted to look at them, talk to them, and touch them, especially their hairy arms. Another unavoidable sight was the metal from old 500- and 750-pound bombs, stacked by the sides of the road—scrap metal, being sold for profit.

As they crested a hill in the middle of one of the gigantic karst formations, the Mistys asked their driver to stop. Mary Fiorelli, the Army nurse Jim Fiorelli had married after they both left Vietnam, had given them a nickel to use in an old fighter pilot ritual. Fio had died of a heart attack in 1994, and he had been one of the most beloved Mistys. The six aging men looked around and made sure they were alone on the hilltop. Then they buried the nickel and sang:

> *Hallelujah! Hallelujah!*
> *Throw a nickel on the grass,*
> *Save a fighter pilot's ass.*
> *Hallelujah! Hallelujah!*
> *Throw a nickel on the grass*
> *And you'll be saved!*

Their eyes watered as they looked out on the exotic panorama. If Fio were still alive he would have been there with them, and for a moment he was.

They drove up the valley toward Mu Ghia Pass, where Dick Rutan's gunner had gotten lucky. But like so many days at Misty, the weather was too bad to continue. The roads were washed out, and finally they came upon an impassable ford. They weren't going to make it to Mu Ghia. They got out of their vehicles and trekked over a hill, to an unbelievable sight: a military airfield! When President Johnson had declared a bombing halt over North Vietnam in November 1968, the North Vietnamese built a MiG base among the karst peaks and flew fighter jets out of the old Misty area. "Damn it!" they lamented. "Just think, we could have had a shot at MiGs!"

The clock became a factor, and the group hustled back toward the Disappearing River to catch the ferry before it closed and trapped them in the jungle without food or lodging. Over the next couple of days the group toured other areas, then went back to Hue for one more night before heading south again. Shepperd looked out his hotel window on the old Citadel, recalling how the town had burned during Tet and how he could see artillery shells exploding inside the walled compound. The next day in Hue the Mistys visited the war museums, gritting their teeth at the virulent anti-American propaganda. In the museum courtyard they sat on 37- and 57mm antiaircraft guns—which may very well have fired on 'them—and took one another's picture.

Had the Mistys known about him, they certainly would have sought out Troung Minh Phoung, a seventy-year-old resident of Hue whose job during the war had been to record the details of U.S. airplane crashes in Quang Binh Province northwest of Dong Hoi. On August 16, 1968, he and some members of the local militia had trekked along narrow jungle trails—safer than some of the bigger roads, which were being heavily bombed that very day—to reach the scattered wreckage of an F-100F that had just been shot down. It was the jet that had been flown by Mike McElhanon and John Overlock.

Phoung found parts of the wreckage and removed a data plate that contained serial numbers and would help identify the aircraft. He jotted down detailed notes in the journal he kept. The jet had crashed near a waterfall, in the red dirt characteristic of that part of the country. He didn't see any bodies, but he guessed that the pilots had been unable to eject, because none of the local militia members had seen a parachute or taken any prisoners. The pilots probably rode the airplane into the ground, he surmised, or bailed out too low to survive. Then, after a final glance around, he and his escorts bugged out, eager to reach safer terrain.

Phoung investigated dozens of airplane crashes before the war ended in 1975. Then he became a local education and propaganda official for the Communist Party. He settled in Hue and kept a collection of war memorabilia that included data plates from at least thirty-five wrecked aircraft he had investigated, along with several journals filled with details of the crashes. Nearly the whole trove of information vanished, however, when heavy floods swept through Hue in 1999. The data plate from the Misty jet, and Phoung's fading memory, were among the few artifacts that survived. When American investigators finally tracked him down and asked if he could lead them to the F-100F crash site, however, he couldn't remember where it had been.

When the Mistys returned to Saigon—there was no way any of them were going to call it Ho Chi Minh City—the group visited more war museums. They were fascinating, if infuriating. The "Peace Museum" was filled with pictures of "atrocities" perpetrated against the

Vietnamese people by the "Yankee imperialists." But somehow there was no mention of the systematic murder of intellectuals in Hue, the prolonged torture of POWs in Hanoi, the savage attack in Phu Cat village that had left dead children in Dean Echenberg's dispensary, or hundreds of other communist outrages. But hey, it was their museum.

The Mistys took some day trips and drove past Long Binh, where Mary Fiorelli had pulled bloody, wounded Army grunts from helicopters and rushed them to surgery. They also saw the old Bien Hoa Air Base, where many Mistys had spent time. It was now a Vietnamese MiG base. The group made the obligatory trip to the "Cu Chi Tunnels" to see how the Viet Cong had hidden underground to attack the cities. P. K. Robinson—who had been shot down during his second Vietnam tour, after Misty, and imprisoned for nine months—found the tunnels far too reminiscent of solitary confinement. Unlike the other Mistys, he refused to climb down for a look.

They returned to Saigon for a final dinner on the roof of the Rex Hotel, Saigon's last reminder of the Western decadence that had once gilded the city. French diplomats had dined at the Rex in colonial times, and U.S. correspondents stayed there during the war. Its glory had faded under the communists, and for thirty dollars apiece the Mistys got the most lavish dinner in town, with passable service and surprisingly good wine.

They toasted everybody they knew. The wine and liquor made them melancholy as they recalled the names and faces of lost friends and comrades from more than three decades earlier. The war, they all believed, was poorly planned and badly managed, and they were still angry. Not at the communists, but at their own leaders, especially Robert McNamara and Lyndon Johnson and the Congress that cut off an ally in the middle of a war. Yes, they had been naïve young warriors, but even at twice the age the six Mistys still thought they had gone to war for noble purposes—to assist an ally against the communists. That ally may have turned out to be incapable and corrupt, but they would all have done the same thing if given the choice again.

As the night grew old and the waiters started to turn out the lights and clear the last of the tables, Dick Rutan wanted a final salute. He raised his glass and proposed:

When our flying days are over
When our flying days are past
We hope they'll bury us upside down
So the world can kiss our ass.

The Mistys left Vietnam the next morning. As they took off for home, they looked out the airplane windows and saw a six-position 57mm AAA site guarding the airport. This time, it wasn't pointed at them.

ACKNOWLEDGMENTS

Most of the official Commando Sabre records were destroyed at the end of the Vietnam War—whether deliberately or inadvertently, we don't know. Where possible we have reconstructed the Misty story from formal documentation, but in many cases we have relied on journals, photos, and other personal records of people involved with the unit, and on the vibrant, if fading, memories of the Misty pilots themselves. Virtually every member of the unit we contacted for this book generously shared his time and stories. The same is true of their families. Their contributions are evident in the previous pages.

A few people deserve special thanks: Dr. Ed Risinger, a Misty from November 1967 to March 1968, has become the unofficial Misty "historian." The names, records, phone numbers, e-mail addresses, and family information he has tracked down made all of our research possible. Don Jones, Misty commander from December 1967 to April 1968, has assembled hundreds of pictures and maps that preserved a visual historical record of the unit. Whenever we needed to place a landmark on the map or attach a name to a face, Don hurried in from his yard in Vermont and sent the information over his "wood-burning" modem. We are indebted to Don and John Haltigan for providing the photographs reproduced in this book. Both dug tirelessly through old files and responded promptly to every reequest for help. Their contributions were invaluable.

Monalee Williams—now Monalee Meyers—revisited a painful time in her life at our request and diligently and patiently answered every question we asked. She also opened the file cabinet in her basement and produced relics that many people would have preferred to keep sealed. Sandy McElhanon shared files, letters, newspaper clippings, pictures, and stories that brought tears to the eyes of the interviewer. Bev Overlock, now Bev Day, did much the same, taking us back to difficult times she did not need to revisit.

John Haltigan offered the same kind of gentle, focused support he did as an intelligence officer at Misty. His suggestions for improving the manuscript were invaluable. Dr. Dean Echenberg also reviewed portions of the manuscript and improved it greatly. Jacque Williams provided photographs, letters, and other family memorabilia that were quite helpful.

Rick wishes to express his personal appreciation to his children, Robert and Jessica, who provide unending inspiration, oblivious to all. Deep thanks also to his mom, Carol Newman, for her emotional support and timely babysitting. And Jeanine Jakelich was often on hand with a drink, a joke, and other distractions precisely when they were needed.

Don is indebted to his wife, Rose, whose patience he tested repeatedly during prolonged, moody searches for evasive facts and elusive words. Rose made numerous commonsense suggestions that helped make our writing more readable.

We are also grateful to our editor, Ron Doering, and our agent, Jane Dystel, who guided two first-time authors through the intricacies of developing and writing a book. They were gentle and professional at every turn and largely kept their frustrations with our naïveté to themselves. Mike Newman, who built our Website www.buryusupside down.com, gave our story a classy presence on the Web that entices visitors to learn more about the Mistys. Stephen Rountree, a superb graphic artist, drew our maps with meticulous attention to landmarks and boundaries that helped improve the precision of the whole book.

Turning a bunch of exaggerated war stories into a meaningful narrative can be tricky business. Memories don't always align with facts. Stubborn people, each certain that things happened the way they remember, directly contradict each other. Perspective changes over time. Some gaps in the story cannot be filled at all. We have tried not to state facts or make claims we are unsure about, but it is probably inevitable that mistakes have crept into this work. For that, we blame fighter pilots who have left too many brain cells on barroom floors. And, of course, ourselves.

NOTES

Chapter 2

1. Robert S. McNamara with Brian VanDeMark, *In Retrospect: The Tragedy and Lessons of Vietnam* (New York: First Vintage Books, 1995), 265, 267, 275, 285, 287.

Chapter 3

1. George "Bud" Day, *Duty, Honor, Country* (Fort Walton Beach, FL: American Hero Press, 1989), 69, 74.
2. John Prados, *The Blood Road: The Ho Chi Minh Trail and the Vietnam War* (New York: John Wiley & Sons, 1999), 195.
3. Don Shepperd, ed., *Misty: First-Person Stories of the F-100 Misty FACs in the Vietnam War* (1st Books, 2000), 19

Chapter 6

1. http://www.vietnam-war.info/timeline
2. Ibid, p. 1.
3. http://members.aol.com/warlibrary/vwfbm,vwb52.htm
4. Robert A. Pape, *Bombing to Win: Air Power and Coercion in War* (Ithaca, NY: Cornell University Press, 1996), 175.
5. George C. Herring, ed., *The Pentagon Papers: Abridged Edition* (New York: McGraw-Hill, 1993), 170.
6. Earl H. Tilford Jr., *Setup: What the Air Force Did in Vietnam and Why* (Maxwell Air Base, AL: Air University Press, 1991), 133.
7. Ibid., 138.

8. Ibid., 135.
9. Ibid.
10. Herring, *Pentagon Papers*, 195–96.
11. Pape, *Bombing to Win*, 184.
12. Tilford, *Setup*, 138.
13. Ibid., 138–39.
14. Herring, *Pentagon Papers*, 211–12.
15. McNamara, *In Retrospect*, 285.
16. Pape, *Bombing to Win*, 181.
17. McNamara, *In Retrospect*, 287.
18. Prados, *Blood Road*, 10.
19. Ibid., 44.
20. Ibid., 84.
21. Ibid., 46.
22. Ibid., 92.
23. Ibid., 46.
24. Ibid., 188.
25. Peter MacDonald, *Giap: The Victor in Vietnam* (New York: W. W. Norton, 1993), 262–63.
26. Prados, *Blood Road*, 191.
27. McNamara, *In Retrospect*, 293–94.
28. Prados, *Blood Road*, 217.
29. David Halberstam, *The Best and the Brightest* (New York: Random House, 1969), 647.

Chapter 8
1. Malcolm McConnell, *Into the Mouth of the Cat: The Story of Lance Sijan, Hero of Vietnam* (New York: W. W. Norton, 1985), 41.
2. Ibid., 53–62.
3. There are varying accounts of how Sijan was first discovered. Mack's recollections differ from those recounted in *Into the Mouth of the Cat,* pp. 62–66. McConnell writes that two F-4D Phantoms belonging to the 8th Tactical Fighter Wing, based at Ubon, Thailand, were the first to raise Sijan on the radio. He does acknowledge Misty's role in the rescue effort.
4. Ibid., 70–71.
5. Ibid., 88–89.
6. Ibid., 91.

Chapter 11
1. McNamara, *In Retrospect*, 308.
2. John S. Bowman, ed., *The Vietnam War Almanac* (New York: World Almanac Publications, 1985), 190.
3. Roger Van Dyken diary.
4. Bowman, *Vietnam War Almanac*, 192.

Chapter 12
1. http://www.vietnamwall.org/casualty.html
2. Don Oberdorfer, *Tet!* (Garden City, NY: Doubleday, 1971), 83.
3. McNamara, *In Retrospect,* 308.
4. Herring, *Pentagon Papers,* 212.

Chapter 13
1. Roger Van Dyken diary.
2. Ibid.
3. http://home.att.net/~c.jeppeson/invert_5.html
4. Prados, *Blood Road,* 214.
5. Ibid., 218–19.
6. Ibid., 220, 269.

Chapter 14
1. Jeana Yeager and Dick Rutan, with Phil Patton, *Voyager* (New York: Alfred A. Knopf, 1987), 19.

Chapter 15
1. http://www.cru.uea.ac.uk/cru/tiempo/issue10/mangrove.htm, Professor Phan Nguyen Hong.
2. Oberdorfer, *Tet!,* 110.
3. Robert Cowley and Geoffrey Parker, eds., *Reader's Companion to Military History* (Boston: Houghton Mifflin, 1996), http://college.hmco.com/history/readerscomp/mil/html/mh_020400 giapvonguyen.htm
4. http://www.vwam.com/vets/tet/tet.html
5. http://www.army.mil/cmh-pg/books/vietnam/northern/nprovinces-ch3.htm
6. Stanley Karnow, *Vietnam: A History* (New York: Viking Press, 1983), 540.
7. Ibid., 541.
8. http://www.vwam.com/vets/tet/tet.html
9. Ibid.
10. Oberdorfer, *Tet!,* 131–32.

Chapter 16
1. http://www.vwamcom/vets/tet/tet.html
2. Ibid.
3. David B. Stockwell, *Tanks in the Wire* (Canton, OH: Daring Books, 1989), 5–6.
4. Clark Dougan and Stephen Weiss, *The Vietnam Experience: Nineteen Sixty-Eight* (Boston: Boston Publishing, 1983), 47.
5. Robert Ginsburg, top secret memo to Gen. Earle Wheeler, January 31, 1968, declassified February 14, 1994.
6. Gen. Earle Wheeler, chairman of the Joint Chiefs of Staff, top secret eyes only

message to Adm. U. S. Grant Sharp, February 1, 1968, declassified February 1, 1994.
7. Robert S. McNamara, confidential memo to President Johnson, February 19, 1968, declassified July 2, 1993.
8. Garrett Moritz, "Arc Lights and Super Gaggles: Examining the Air Battle for Khe Sanh," http://www.gtexts.com/college/papers/fl.html

Chapter 17
1. Bowman, Vietnam War Almanac, 195.
2. Oberdorfer, Tet!, 346.
3. Ibid., 173.
4. Ibid., 288.
5. Ibid., 251.
6. Karnow, Vietnam: A History, 547–48.
7. http://www.cc.gatech.edu/fac/Thomas.Pilsch/AirOps/Ashau.html

Chapter 18
1. In addition to the recollections of Brian Williams and others, this incident has been re-created using information from the Defense POW/MIA Office "Intelligence/Administrative Casualty File" for Howard K. Williams, reference number 1095-0-01, declassified at the authors' request.
2. DPMO file no. 1095.
3. Ibid.

Chapter 20
1. Karnow, Vietnam: A History, 559.
2. Ibid.
3. Ibid., 561.
4. Ibid., 562.
5. Ibid., 560.
6. Ibid., 565.

Chapter 22
1. Entire account taken from Day, Duty, Honor, Country.
2. http://www.ojc.org/powforum/powcamps.htm
3. http://www.pbs.org/wgbh/amex/honor/sfeature/sf_tap.html
4. McConnell, Into the Mouth of the Cat, 207.
5. Ibid., 208.
6. Ibid., 210.

Chapter 23
1. Dougan and Weiss, The Vietnam Experience: Nineteen Sixty-Eight, 51.
2. Ibid.
3. Ibid., 54.

Chapter 25

1. http://www.af.mil/bios/bio.asp?bioID=4813
2. http://www.fatherryan.org/navyvietnam/battleship.html
3. Ibid., 581.

Chapter 26

1. http://ohoh.essortment.com/vietnamwarprot_rlcz.htm
2. http://en.wikipedia.org/wiki/ross_perot
3. http://origin.businessweek.com/chapter/posner05.htm
4. www.olmstedfoundation.org
5. http://origin.businessweek.com/chapter/posner05.htm
6. Ibid.

Chapter 27

1. Bowman, *Vietnam War Almanac*, 294.
2. http://www.military.com/Content/MoreContent1?file=nrr_hegdahl
3. Ibid.
4. Facts on File: http://www.2facts.com/Archive/temp/48331temp1969108050.asp
5. Facts on File: http://www.2facts.com/Archive/temp/48563temp1969109740.asp

Chapter 28

1. Henry Kissinger, *Ending the Vietnam War: A History of America's Involvement in and Extrication from the Vietnam War* (New York: Simon & Schuster, 2003), 298.
2. Tilford, *Setup*, 233.
3. Gen. William W. Momyer, *Airpower in Three Wars: World War II, Korea, and Vietnam* (Honolulu: University Press of the Pacific, 2002), 183–85.
4. John T. Correll, *The Vietnam War Almanac* (*Air Force* magazine, September 2004), 63–64.
5. Tilford, *Setup*, 235.
6. Ibid., 64.
7. Bowman, *Vietnam War Almanac*, 338.
8. Kissinger, *Ending the Vietnam War*, 437–38.
9. Bowman, *Vietnam War Almanac*, 358.
10. Kissinger, *Ending the Vietnam War*, 443.

Chapter 29

1. Day, *Duty, Honor, Country*, 233, 270–72.
2. Bowman, *Vietnam War Almanac*, 344.

Chapter 30

1. Bowman, *Vietnam War Almanac*, 354.
2. This and all subsequent information relating to the search for the remains of Howard K. Williams comes from the Defense POW/MIA Office "Intelli-

gence/Administrative Casualty File" for Howard K. Williams, reference number 1095-0-01.
3. Facts on File, December 20, 1985.
4. Ibid.
5. Facts on File, May 2, 1986.
6. Facts on File, December 20, 1985.
7. Facts on File, August 14, 1987.

Chapter 31
1. Facts on File, various reports.

BIBLIOGRAPHY

Bowman, John S., ed. *The Vietnam War Almanac.* New York: World Almanac Publications, 1985.

Cowley, Robert, and Geoffrey Parker, eds. *Reader's Companion To Military History.* Boston: Houghton Mifflin, 1996.

Day, George "Bud." *Duty, Honor, Country.* Fort Walton Beach, FL: American Hero Press, 1989.

Dougan, Clark, and Stephen Weiss. *The Vietnam Experience: Nineteen Sixty-Eight.* Boston: Boston Publishing, 1983.

Halberstam, David. *The Best and the Brightest.* New York: Random House, 1969.

Herring, George C., ed. *The Pentagon Papers: Abridged Edition.* New York: McGraw Hill, 1993.

Karnow, Stanley. *Vietnam: A History.* New York: Viking Press, 1983.

Kissinger, Henry. *Ending the Vietnam War: A History of America's Involvement in and Extrication from the Vietnam War.* New York: Simon & Schuster, 2003.

McConnell, Malcolm. *Into the Mouth of the Cat: The Story of Lance Sijan, Hero of Vietnam.* New York: W. W. Norton, 1985.

MacDonald, Peter. *Giap: The Victor in Vietnam.* New York: W. W. Norton, 1993.

McNamara, Robert S., with Brian VanDeMark. *In Retrospect: The Tragedy and Lessons of Vietnam.* New York: First Vintage Books, 1995.

Momyer, Gen. William W. *Airpower in Three Wars: World War II, Korea, and Vietnam.* Honolulu: University Press of the Pacific, 2002.

Oberdorfer, Don. *Tet!* Garden City, NY: Doubleday, 1971.

Pape, Robert A. *Bombing to Win: Air Power and Coercion in War.* Ithaca, NY: Cornell University Press, 1996.

Prados, John. *The Blood Road: The Ho Chi Minh Trail and the Vietnam War.* New York: John Wiley & Sons, 1999.

Stockwell, David B. *Tanks in the Wire.* Canton, OH: Daring Books, 1989.

Tilford, Earl H. Jr. *Setup: What the Air Force Did in Vietnam and Why.* Maxwell Air Force Base, AL: Air University Press, 1991.

Yeager, Jeana, and Dick Rutan, with Phil Patton. *Voyager.* New York: Alfred A. Knopf, 1987.

INDEX

ABOUT THE AUTHORS

RICK NEWMAN is a writer and editor at *U.S. News & World Report* who covered the Pentagon for seven years, including U.S. missions in Bosnia, Kosovo, and the Persian Gulf. He has written hundreds of stories on the military, including dozens of exclusives, and more than twenty cover stories.

DON SHEPPERD (Misty 34) reported for duty at Phu Cat Air Base on December 19, 1967, and flew fifty-eight missions as a Misty during his four-month tour. With a total of 247 combat missions in Vietnam, he retired from the Air Force in 1998 as a two-star general and head of the Air National Guard. In 2001 he joined CNN as one of their principal military analysts.

ABOUT THE TYPE

This book was set in Sabon, a typeface designed by the well-known German typographer Jan Tschichold (1902–74). Sabon's design is based upon the original letter forms of Claude Garamond and was created specifically to be used for three sources: foundry type for hand composition, Linotype, and Monotype. Tschichold named his typeface for the famous Frankfurt typefounder Jacques Sabon, who died in 1580.